Once I Too Had Wings

OHIO UNIVERSITY PRESS
Series in Race, Ethnicity, and Gender in Appalachia

Series editors: Marie Tedesco and Chris Green

Memphis Tennessee Garrison: The Remarkable Story of a Black Appalachian Woman,
edited by Ancella R. Bickley and Lynda Ann Ewen

The Tangled Roots of Feminism, Environmentalism, and Appalachian Literature,
by Elizabeth S. D. Engelhardt

Red, White, Black, and Blue: A Dual Memoir of Race and Class in Appalachia,
by William R. Drennen Jr. and Kojo (William T.) Jones Jr.,
edited by Dolores M. Johnson

Beyond Hill and Hollow: Original Readings in Appalachian Women's Studies,
edited by Elizabeth S. D. Engelhardt

Loving Mountains, Loving Men,
by Jeff Mann

Power in the Blood: A Family Narrative,
by Linda Tate

Out of the Mountains: Appalachian Stories,
by Meredith Sue Willis

Negotiating a Perilous Empowerment: Appalachian Women's Literacies,
by Erica Abrams Locklear

Standing Our Ground:
Women, Environmental Justice, and the Fight to End Mountaintop Removal,
by Joyce M. Barry

Shake Terribly the Earth: Stories from an Appalachian Family,
by Sarah Beth Childers

Thinking Outside the Girl Box: Teaming up with Resilient Youth in Appalachia,
by Linda Spatig and Layne Amerikaner

Once I Too Had Wings: The Journals of Emma Bell Miles, 1908–1918,
edited by Steven Cox

Once I Too Had Wings

The Journals of Emma Bell Miles, 1908–1918

EDITED BY STEVEN COX

FOREWORD BY ELIZABETH S. D. ENGELHARDT

Ohio University Press Athens

ohioswallow.com

Cover art: (*front top*) Small watercolor by Miles of Lookout Mountain (Jean Miles Catino Collection, Special Collections, University of Tennessee at Chattanooga); (*front bottom*) Emma Bell Miles sketching at the home of a friend, circa 1912 (photo by E. A. Wheatley; Jean Miles Catino Collection, Special Collections, University of Tennessee at Chattanooga); (*back*) art from the cover of Miles's pamphlet of poems, *Chords from a Dulcimore*

Cover design by Beth Pratt

Printed in the United States of America

Ohio University Press books are printed on acid-free paper ∞ ™

24 23 22 21 20 19 18 17 16 15 14   5 4 3 2 1

Library of Congress Cataloging-in-Publication Data

Miles, Emma Bell, 1879–1919.
  Once I Too Had Wings : the Journals of Emma Bell Miles, 1908–1918 / edited by Steven Cox ; foreword by Elizabeth S. D. Engelhardt.
    pages cm. — (Race, Ethnicity, and Gender in Appalachia)
  Includes bibliographical references and index.
  Summary: "Emma Bell Miles (1879–1919) was a gifted writer, poet, naturalist, and artist with a keen perspective on Appalachian life and culture. She and her husband Frank lived on Walden's Ridge in southeast Tennessee, where they struggled to raise a family in the difficult mountain environment. Between 1908 and 1918, Miles kept a series of journals in which she recorded in beautiful and haunting prose the natural wonders and local customs of Walden's Ridge. Jobs were scarce, however, and as the family's financial situation deteriorated, Miles began to sell literary works and paintings to make ends meet. Her short stories appeared in national magazines such as Harper's Monthly and Lippincott's, and in 1905 she published The Spirit of the Mountains, a nonfiction book about southern Appalachia. After the death of her three-year-old son from scarlet fever in 1913, the journals took a more somber turn as Miles documented the difficulties of mountain life, the plight of women in rural communities, the effect of disparities of class and wealth, and her own struggle with tuberculosis. Previously examined only by a handful of scholars, the journals contain both poignant and incisive accounts of nature and a woman's perspective on love and marriage, death customs, child-raising, medical care, and subsistence on the land in southern Appalachia in the early twentieth century. With a foreword by Elizabeth S. D. Engelhardt, this edited selection of Emma Bell Miles's journals is illustrated with examples of her art"— Provided by publisher.
  ISBN 978-0-8214-2086-7 (hardback) — ISBN 978-0-8214-2087-4 (pb) — ISBN 978-0-8214-4485-6 (pdf)
  1. Miles, Emma Bell, 1879–1919—Diaries. 2. Women authors, American—Biography. I. Cox, Steven. II. Title.
  PS3525.I482Z46 2014
  818'.5203—dc23
  [B]

2014000858

Dedicated to the Memory of Frank Mirick Miles (1909–1913)

Contents

List of Illustrations   ix

Foreword by Elizabeth S. D. Engelhardt   xi

Preface   xvii

Acknowledgments   xxiii

Introduction   xxv

CHAPTER 1
Walden's Ridge   5

CHAPTER 2
Return to Walden's Ridge   45

CHAPTER 3
Tragedy and Heartbreak   98

CHAPTER 4
"I Must Be Free!"   150

CHAPTER 5
Pine Breeze Sanitarium   204

CHAPTER 6
A Brief Separation   244

CHAPTER 7
The Good Gray Mother   293

Epilogue   333

Notes   335

Index   347

Illustrations

Following page 133

Emma sketching at the home of a friend, circa 1912

Emma at the age of twenty

Frank in Miami, 1909

Emma with Mark in Miami, 1909

Preface to the journal, 1916

Cover of Miles's 1905 book, *The Spirit of the Mountains*

Cover of Miles's 1919 book, *Our Southern Birds*

Cover of Miles's pamphlet of poems, *Chords from a Dulcimore*

Poem and illustration from *Chords from a Dulcimore*

Small watercolor by Miles of a cabin on Walden's Ridge

Small watercolor by Miles of Lookout Mountain

Watercolor by Miles of her first four children, Jean, Judith, Joe, and Katharine

Small watercolor by Miles of a waterfall

Watercolor by Miles of a fox sparrow, from *Our Southern Birds*

Ink drawing by Miles of a sparrow hawk, from *Our Southern Birds*

Ink drawing by Miles of a cabin on Walden's Ridge

Emma Bell Miles's grave in Red Bank, Tennessee

foreword

Carving Spirit into Rock

The Journals of Emma Bell Miles

ELIZABETH S. D. ENGELHARDT

I have talked with many people about their experience of reading Emma Bell Miles's *Spirit of the Mountains* for the first time.

No matter how many other Appalachian authors we have read, no matter how much women's literature, no matter how many philosophers from the early twentieth century, Miles and her best-known text stick with us. At first we turn the pages at a fevered pace, thinking, Finally! Someone in the early twentieth century is trying to capture how complex Appalachia was. The book portrays men and women, people of different ages, newcomers and longtime residents and even that rarest of creatures, the middle-term settler, neither fully belonging nor fully new. Music, art, teaching, nature, architecture, and philosophy are equals in the discussion. We lose ourselves in the range of people and their concerns. Then, we notice how quickly the end of the book is arriving. We slow down, savoring every page, hoping to delay its end.

Next, we try to describe it to others. We begin straightforwardly—its plot, its characters, and its structure. But we soon find ourselves talking about its slippery nature, its odd turns of phrase, its author who is not its narrator but who may be its voice. We call it a manifesto, creative nonfiction, scholarship, and memoir—none of which is precisely correct. We acknowledge it is not free of its time—some chapters hold up better to twenty-first-century eyes. But we find other parts anticipate today in surprising ways—its calls against unthinking development, its insistence on eating and purchasing locally. Our descriptions dwindle away as we find ourselves failing to capture its many twists and turns.

So, finally, we try to convince others to read it. We become proselytizers, as if the Spirit of Miles's title can be conferred and shared. Have you? Here, let me get you a copy. Tell me what you make of this. Remember what she says about? Did you know she did all the illustrations too? Maybe we should read it together? We feel the book is still a relative secret but we wish that were less true.

The Spirit of the Mountains has been back in print almost continuously since the 1970s, and scholars have worked to piece together its publication history and its author's other works in relation to her era. We know it is a terse book in a time of massive tomes. It blends genres in ways authors struggle to innovate still today. It faces simultaneously forward and backward, prescient and yet rooted to its past. Each time you think you have its meanings corralled, they skitter away from you. Most crucial, however, is what we do not know. Its author is both intimately present and frustratingly absent between the pages. Miles has been difficult to find in the archives, and her tracks in eastern Tennessee have seemed confusing at best, leading to disagreements between biographers, errors in the historical record, and unsettled speculations by scholars and fans alike.

Questions circle her, hounding her legacy like so many unsettled ghosts. Did she think of herself as an educator even if she did not teach secondary school like her parents and her most famous narrator? Did Grace MacGowan Cooke, another Chattanooga writer, steal Miles's intellectual property or did Miles agree to and in fact benefit from their collaborations? Could her husband Frank earn a living for the family and did he? Most important, how did Miles feel about her achievements and setbacks? Really, who was Emma Bell Miles?

With this volume, we finally have some answers. Thanks to the hard work of Steven Cox—first in acquiring and preserving the journals, and then in transcribing the massive number of words therein—we now have an extraordinary document of Appalachian women's writing. Miles in her own words proves just as creative and determined as her fictional and philosophical writings have suggested her fellow mountain residents to be. The family tragedies her biographers have unearthed stand in vivid detail when viewed through the eyes of this hard-working mother writing to cope in the midst of crisis. A community of women writers, who were in and out of each other's homes, finances, and emotional trust, comes into focus.

Across the journals, Miles emerges as a fully realized artist—with both the strengths and the challenges that implies. She is difficult at times. Her responses to friends and family sound prickly and even occasionally downright dreary. She maintains focus on survival—but in some months that means survival of her artistic vision; in others it is the logistics of simply feeding a very hungry, economically insecure family; and in still other months it is the survival of her own broken-down body. Through it all she is a devoted mother whose love for her children motivates her to write with as much unflinching honesty as she can muster. Miles is caught in cycles of pain and joy, faith and despair, making her deeply human. Yet, she is an inspiring observer, with a knack for finding moments of breathtaking beauty; her ability to describe those moments lifts her above the common.

Miles stands at a transitional moment as the language of psychoanalysis enters people's everyday language. Her journals look back to nineteenth-century nature writing and forward to twentieth-century self-reflection. Readers looking for a sweet friend who likes birds will find instead a complex friend who is brutally honest about her own and her acquaintances' failings and strengths. We see her realize that at barely thirty years old she is dying—and that her artistic goals and vision will remain only partially fulfilled. We see her decide that partially is better than not at all, and even as the journals wind down, she begins ambitious projects and dreams of reaching new audiences.

The journals and Miles herself are at turns heartbreaking, frustrating, and revealing.

Miles still poses some mysteries (and I cannot help but imagine she would find pleasure in at least some of that). The journals give us tantalizing glimpses of lost works by Miles. She describes short stories, poems, and even novels. Some were likely just ideas tried out and roughly imagined. Others, she describes mailing off in finished form in submission packets. With this volume now available, scholars and lay readers will be able to search the magazines, journals, newspapers, and publishing houses' archives with more concrete leads. I am certain that what has been a frustratingly slim bibliography of written output by Miles will soon be much more robust. At the least, we will no longer be forced to consider *The Spirit of the Mountains* in isolation from the rest of Miles's creative work.

Similarly, we know that Chattanooga's private art collections and living rooms hold the artistic output of Miles, but with the publication of these journals, we can trace where more of those canvasses were sent. From her narration of her days spent sketching, drawing, and illustrating, we may find new leads to date or collect her oeuvre. Miles did not separate her artistic and written projects; the journals allow us to bring them more closely together and in better view. Our understanding of both will be richer for reintegrating her creative vision.

For as much as *Once I Too Had Wings* gives us a fuller picture of Emma Bell Miles and allows us to revisit our scholarly and passionate engagements with her and her work, that is only half the potential here. As with *The Spirit of the Mountains*, Miles again tells us as much about others as herself. We can read her journals, as Cox's thoughtful introduction suggests, as windows into Appalachian culture, women's activism, and literary communities. Nor is the impact of the volume confined to Appalachian studies, art history, women's studies, and women's literature. The journals have much to offer scholars of early twentieth-century racial and class structures, historians of medicine, naturalists, people fascinated by the struggles of an artistic life, and readers interested in the southern United States' transition out of the nineteenth century and into twentieth-century modernity.

Take, for instance, a story that unfolds between 1914 and 1918 in the journals. Soon after moving into Chattanooga to write for the local newspaper, Miles was mugged by an African American named Houston Green, "on the corner of Vine & Lindsay." An incident that begins on the neighborhood level moves up through city structures (as Miles and Green have to navigate the police and news) and connects with the nation as Miles reads black literature by black writers like Paul Laurence Dunbar and ponders what she finds to be an overly harsh sentence given to Green.

Four years later, the story circles back down to a conversation between two mothers, Miles and Green's mother. Miles wrestles with the social politics not just of Chattanooga or Appalachia, but of the larger United States, from social Darwinism, to racial equality, to suffrage and women's rights, to socialism, to agnosticism and New Thought. At times she sounds in coalition with anyone marginalized by structures of power, be they class-, race-, gender-, or place-based. As she investigates the resources available to her should she try to divorce Frank, Miles fiercely decries the inequalities faced by women and extends that reaction to the rest of the nation's disempowered. At times she seems conservatively protective of whiteness or Appalachian superiority. We cannot dismiss her as simply one thing or another—a racial essentialist, a progressive liberal, a spiritual questioner, or a radical traditionalist. We will have to enter into her world of complicated struggles with big ideas, not seeking simple answers or easy judgments. That may prove the most important change these journals provoke. In the all-too-brief life of Emma Bell Miles, we see reflected our own tangled communities, filled with complexity, peril, and promise.

So what do we do now?

Miles warns us to slow down and get it right. Early in the journals, she strongly criticizes the kind of local color writer who rides through on a train and then makes money off mountain stories. Miles dismissively sneers at their inaccurate descriptions of the fall color (and foreshadows our own era of some mountain tourism), the kind that forsakes actual observation for romantic reveries: "[W]riters of fiction ought to know that each species of hard wood tree has its own peculiar individual color in autumn." She sniffs, "If a little real attention were given to this subject we should read less of 'scarlet beeches' and 'crimson hickories' in the October woods." She lists the actual colors individual species of trees turn. She knows what trees grow in her part of the mountains. She knows which ones may be simultaneously in full display and which follow in discrete progression. With her list, Miles rightly argues that such details matter. If a story wants to claim that place affects people, that culture is inseparable from nature, then those stories had better get the places and nature right. Conversely, if people want to affect the places where they reside in ways other than the merely destructive, then they had best learn to see, learn to wait, learn to listen. I do not know what our consensus about Miles will be after we have seen, sat patiently with, and listened carefully to these journals. But I do know that we now have a fair chance at coming to a deeper understanding of this person, her communities, and their era.

Finally, Miles reminds us to resist the saccharine in our assessment of her and her Appalachia. We would do well to extend that warning to her life, giving us another directive in how to read her biography. Miles occasionally feels sentimental and writes in that register. Some of her short stories and character sketches indulge in sentimental outbursts; occasional entries in the journals do as well. For instance, describing an old spring to which she has hiked, where generations have carved graffiti into the surrounding rock, Miles begins with such sentiment, noting, "Names twenty years gone and more; names of the dead, names of those who have risen out of humble ken." But she just as quickly turns away, rejecting the temptation to freeze romance into stereotypical happy endings. Instead, Miles imagines the tragic and the realistic beyond the moment of carving graffiti. She reminds us that some of the long-past names belong to people "now lodged out of sight in dens of infamy, girls now staid mothers, boys grown to bearded men." Romance does not preclude tragedy—and romance mixed with realism deepens her brief moment at the spring. Some people start out with love stories and end up with economic hardship, bitter struggles between personalities, and death from age or disease. People fall in love, create curiously haunting works of art, fight and make up, live ahead of their time, and are alternately embraced and punished for aiming higher than the community around them. Love and heartbreak exist simultaneously in this wellspring of an Appalachian life.

preface

Shortly before her death in 2000, Emma Bell Miles's daughter Jean Miles Catino (1902–2000) deposited some personal papers, which included letters, family documents, photographs, and small pieces of art, in the Special Collections at the University of Tennessee at Chattanooga. With this donation were four separate handwritten volumes of her mother's journal, spanning the years 1908 to 1918. Miles's journal, seen by very few researchers, covers a variety of topics such as her family life, the nature and culture of Walden's Ridge, and Miles's struggle with sickness, poverty, and heartbreak, particularly the death of her youngest son in 1913. A fifth volume, placed chronologically in the middle of this period, had been donated to the public library in Chattanooga, Tennessee, in the 1940s, by a friend of Emma Bell Miles, Margaret Severance. How Severance came into possession of this volume is not definitively known, although Catino wrote to Miles's biographer, Kay Baker Gaston, that just after her mother's death in 1919, a friend, Abbie Crawford Milton (wife of *Chattanooga News* publisher George Fort Milton), had access to a chest belonging to Miles, which held some unpublished writings. Severance, Catino added, was a neighbor of Milton. Upon the discovery in 1965 that the library had one of the volumes, Miles's twin daughters, Judith Miles Ford and Jean Miles Catino, tried unsuccessfully to get it back. In copies of letters found in Catino's papers, she and her sister Judith declared the journal to have been stolen, but the library administrators, for whatever reason, denied that they had it. The other volumes remained in the hands of Miles's twin daughters until Catino donated them to the University of Tennessee at Chattanooga. (The public library still has the volume today, and fortunately has taken good care of it.) The Catino donation was a nice complement to the papers, correspondence, and research material on Emma Bell Miles deposited earlier at the University of Tennessee at Chattanooga by Kay Baker Gaston, after she published her 1985 biography of Miles.

The journal volumes are fragile after being in private hands for more than eighty years. Miles's handwriting is still legible, despite the brittle paper and fraying covers of the volumes. In 2007, as special collections librarian at the University of Tennessee at Chattanooga, I made plans to preserve the contents of the journal for researchers to consult instead of handling the deteriorating volumes or the fading photocopies someone had made earlier. Word was getting out that the journal was in the Special Collections at the University of Tennessee at Chattanooga, and I had been receiving requests from researchers for access to the volumes. Unfortunately, such handling would certainly degrade them further. Rather than sending the pages out for microfilming, I decided to scan them carefully. Scanning the journal was a time-consuming task; the four volumes in the possession of the University of Tennessee at Chattanooga produced 740 scanned pages. I did not scan the volume held in the public library, although I had a transcription of it, made by someone unknown. (I was able to compare the public library's volume against the transcription to verify that the transcription was accurate and complete.)

Once I had the scans, I began transcribing the journal. Fortunately, Miles's handwriting was neat and fairly easy to read. For words I could not make out from the scans, I examined the original volumes and was able to identify many. There were some, unfortunately, that I could not decipher, and these are marked as [illegible].

At this point I had the intention of publishing the journal, with the support and encouragement of Kay Baker Gaston and scholars Grace Toney Edwards and Katarina Prajznerova. The transcription project took nearly two years. I added in the transcription from the public library volume. When I reached the end (too soon, as I was intrigued by Miles's story), I had a Word document of 540 single-spaced pages, and nearly a quarter of a million words.

The structure, grammar, and writing of the journal show that Miles was an intelligent, articulate, and eloquent writer, something that readers of her 1905 book, *The Spirit of the Mountains*, undoubtedly already knew. Her vocabulary was strong, and words such as *annular, diapason, stertorous, gamboge, batrachian, corymbs*, and *ignesfatui* are sprinkled throughout. I kept Miles's grammar, capitalization, punctuation, and spelling unaltered, leaving words like *any thing* or *some thing* (normally treated as closed compounds) separated, and retaining a few archaic spellings (e.g., staid for stayed). There are very few outright misspellings, and for those I added [*sic*] to show the error was hers.

Entries vary in length from brief statements to several pages of detailed accounts and observances. Miles did not, as a rule, make entries every day, although there are periods in which she did. At other times, days and weeks would go by without an entry. There are many references to individuals who are obviously related to the family but are not clearly identified. It is probable that Miles did not write the journals for publication, or ever think they would be published. Probably she wrote them for her children. However, by 1913 she was using the journal to document the family's plight and hardships, and included some things it seems odd she would want to share with her children.

I knew a 240,000-word manuscript would be too large for a single published volume and that some editing of the journal would be necessary. Furthermore, I felt that editing could be done without degrading the intellectual integrity of the journal. Upon expression of interest by Ohio University Press, I worked toward editing the journal down to 130,000 words, a more suitable length for a single-volume work. Deciding what to omit was my first task. Two of the first things I removed were Miles's entries during the family's trip to Miami, Florida, in late 1909 and the subsequent visit to Lincoln Memorial University in Harrogate, Tennessee, in early 1910, where Miles served several months as a writer in residence. These entries are definitely interesting but depart from her descriptions of nature and mountain culture on Walden's Ridge found in the other entries in her journal. However, there was one passage I regretted omitting from this section, entered on June 28, 1910, as the family was leaving Harrogate, Tennessee, for their return to Walden's Ridge. In the passage, Miles reflects on the people of Appalachia:

The typical Tennessee mountaineers [*sic*] face, what is it? The eyes are blue, as the distant hills are blue; the cheeks are rosy from the tonic air of the altitude; the ancestry of Scotch-Irish, and also the early association with the Cherokee, have given an indwelling look, a mystical brooding, dreaming; yet the face is far from stern—has all the wistful friendliness of the cabins. No matter how depressed by dyspepsia or malaria, no matter how drugged with idleness the man may be, there is ever a fineness, a pathos about him. These faded, shapeless, uncared for clothes are powerless to degrade him altogether; in him is focused the dreamy beauty of the land. There is a wholesomeness, a child like readiness to meet and make friends—he "never saw a stranger," (yet ever a reserve of things is whispered, an inscrutable veil in the blue eyes, a mystery of the hills' buried secrets.) The face is purely native; it blossoms as naturally from the wayside as any other rose of the soil, with the rough innocence of all indigenous growth in which the sap of the earth flows freely. One divines here a love of beauty and of music and of the hearth-fire; deep narrow loves of home and country; purity of descent reinforced by family ties; strong tendency to ideals that cannot fail while evolution holds its course: but on the other hand here is total lack of social consciousness. Good husband and father that he be, the man is utterly lonely—has no public spirit. To go to church and visit his kin from time to time—this is as far as he can reach toward his fellow men.

The deleted entries from these two trips made but a little dent in editing the journal down to 130,000 words. My next step was to identify and edit out entries that provided little or no information on Walden's Ridge, the local culture, nature, Miles's personal thoughts, or important events in Miles's life. I also deleted entries that were repetitive of other entries. I believe I have preserved the integrity of the journals while reducing them to a manageable size.

I separated the remaining entries into seven chapters, providing a brief introduction to each. I inserted in square brackets brief explanations or identifications of the many people Miles referred to, and for longer explanations added numbered endnotes. Miles mentioned many local Chattanooga and Walden's Ridge citizens, some from the more prominent families of the area who had summer homes on Walden's Ridge. Others are part of the extended Miles family on the mountain, often referred to by nicknames. The Miles family is a large one, and the names of Freudenberg, Vandergriff, Nixon, Hatfield, and Hullett found in numerous places throughout the journal are just some of the several families allied to the Mileses. I found Kay Baker Gaston's 1985 biography of Miles, *Emma Bell Miles*, particularly helpful in identifying people, places, and events. The Jean Miles Catino letters to Gaston, part of the Kay Baker Gaston Collection in the Special Collections and University Archives at the University of Tennessee at Chattanooga, also provided information. For others, I resorted (with caution) to books on Chattanooga history, obituaries, and certain family trees available online. In cases of names not identified in an editorial insertion or note and not otherwise obvious from Miles's comments, I was unable to find information on that individual or determined that it was only an insignificant passing reference.

There is quite a bit to digest in Miles's journal. It starts out in 1908 pleasantly enough, as Miles goes into detail on the local nature and customs of Walden's Ridge, her family, and the people of the area. Miles was a keen observer of birds, flowers, and wildlife, as well as local customs. However, the reader must be prepared for the dark turn the journal takes in late 1911, and especially in her description of the death of their youngest son, Mirick, in early 1913. After that, Miles used the journal to describe her family's struggle with poverty and sickness, her deteriorating marriage and home life, women's rights (or lack thereof during that period), her miscarriages (possibly self-administered abortions), her thoughts of suicide, and her battle with tuberculosis. Perhaps unintentionally, she reveals the plight of early twentieth-century women, particularly those of rural Appalachia, before women had the right to vote. In 1916, as she was suffering from tuberculosis, Miles wrote a preface for her children, probably the intended audience for the journal.

I was disappointed to discover that Miles did not use the journal to formally document her creative output, although there are references, many vague, to works of art, stories, poems, and book-length manuscripts, some of which were never published and are now presumed lost. If she ever did keep a list, it has long since disappeared.

The journal ends almost abruptly in 1918, as she reached the end of the volume she was writing in. If she continued in another volume, it did not survive. She was then living in Chattanooga, about ten miles from Walden's Ridge. The last entry in this edited volume is the last entry in the complete version. There is no farewell, no closure in her final entry, which is mostly about birds. Instead, it is a return to the original theme of her journal: nature on Walden's Ridge.

On Walden's Ridge is a small cemetery, still maintained but hidden and unknown to many. There, a small boy was buried one hundred years ago. His grave to this day remains unmarked and unidentified, probably one of several dozen graves marked only by a simple football-sized rock. The youngest son of Emma Bell Miles, who did not see his fourth birthday, is at rest somewhere there, denied the chance at adulthood his four siblings received. His dear mother never got over his death, or the guilt of having to watch him suffer and die. Perhaps her premature death started the day he died, in 1913. It is to the memory of little Frank Mirick Miles that I dedicate this book, on the hundredth anniversary of his death, as a belated memorial to his short tragic life.

Steven Cox
Chattanooga, Tennessee
January 28, 2013

acknowledgments

I was fortunate to have the encouragement, help, and interest of many individuals in the preparation of this manuscript and would like to acknowledge their help in this project. Several Miles scholars before me have been particularly encouraging: Kay Baker Gaston, Grace Toney Edwards, and Katerina Prajznerova. Others to whom I am indebted for their encouragement, help, and support are Valarie Adams, Mark Banker, Noelle Boggs, George Brosi, Jim Douthat, Elizabeth Engelhardt, Michelle Ganz, Mary Helms, Charles Hubbard, Theresa Liedtka, Marcia Noe, Verbie Prevost, Aaron Purcell, Suzette Raney, Viki Rouse, Kit Rushing, and Priscilla Seaman. I am particularly grateful to my editors, Gillian Berchowitz and Nancy Basmajian, for helping me through the editorial process. I also owe a great deal of appreciation to my wife, Dianne, for her constant encouragement and support throughout this project.

introduction

Emma Bell Miles (1879–1919) lived most of her adult life on the southern end of Walden's Ridge, a seventy-five-mile-long mountain ridge in the Cumberland Plateau of the southern Appalachian region of Tennessee. She lived among the scattering of mountain people in the area where the towns of Signal Mountain and Walden would be established. She was one of the earliest naturalists to live and work in the southern Appalachian region. She is also somewhat difficult to define, as she was an artist, poet, writer, mother, and wife. Her short life was filled with hardship, but she still managed to create art, whether in visual form or with words. Miles loved the nature that surrounded her and had a keen artist's eye in describing, drawing, and painting Walden's Ridge.

She was born Emma Bell in 1879 in Evansville, Indiana. Her parents, Benjamin Franklin Bell and Martha Ann Mirick Bell, were both schoolteachers. Emma's early years were spent in Rabbit Hash, Kentucky, a small town on the Ohio River near Cincinnati. Her father had a teaching position just across the river, in Rising Sun, Indiana, and ferried across daily. Also born with Emma was a twin brother, who died shortly after his birth. Because of Emma's delicate health, the family moved to the gentler climate of Tennessee in 1890. They first lived in Red Bank, just north of Chattanooga, but a year later relocated to Walden's Ridge, near today's town of Signal Mountain, an area that overlooks Chattanooga. The Bells secured teaching jobs on Walden's Ridge in a school that served the children of the mountain people.

Despite this, Miles rarely attended the schools herself.[1] Books, *Harper's Monthly* magazines, and nature were her classroom. She reportedly had learned to read at the age of three and at a young age read books such as Lew Wallace's *Ben-Hur*, Nathaniel Hawthorne's *The Marble Faun*, and John Bunyan's *The Pilgrim's Progress*. As a teenager she discovered the works of Henry David Thoreau. Intelligent and curious, Emma showed a talent for art. In 1899, she began taking lessons from the Chattanooga artist Zerelda Rains, and later that year enrolled at the St. Louis School of Art with the help of Rains, who was on the faculty. After two years of study in St. Louis—two unhappy years, as Emma noted in letters to a benefactor and friend, Anna Ricketson—Emma planned to further her art education by studying in Europe.[2] But her plans changed because of Frank Miles.[3]

Frank Miles had roots on Walden's Ridge and was a product of the mountain culture. His ancestors were among the earliest white settlers on Walden's Ridge. The courtship between Emma and Frank began when Frank, a driver of a mule-drawn wagon that shuttled travelers up and down the mountain, provided Emma with transportation to Chattanooga.[4] He shared with Emma a love of nature. Emma shared her love of literature with Frank, and they would read to each other passages from the works of Thoreau. After her second year in St. Louis, while she was spending the summer back on Walden's Ridge, they decided to marry. Although her parents did not approve of the union, the couple married in October of 1901, just a month after the unexpected death of Emma's mother. In late 1902 their first children were born, twin daughters Jean and Judith. After that, a son, Joe; then a daughter, Katharine; and lastly, a son they named Frank Mirick, the maiden name of Emma's mother. They would call him Mark.

The relationship between Miles and her parents was strained by the time Miles was in her late teens. In addition to objecting to her relationship with Frank Miles, her father refused to honor his late wife's will, in which she left the house to her daughter.[5] Perhaps the property had been hers, and hers alone, to bequeath to Emma. However, in the early twentieth century Benjamin Bell would have had no legal obligation to honor the will. This deepened an already existing rift between Emma and her father that lasted the rest of her life.

After their 1901 marriage, Frank and Emma settled on Walden's Ridge, first living in the house in which her parents had lived. Her father, by then a widower, was living and teaching north of Chattanooga in the small town of Soddy. With little means and money, she and Frank provided the best home they could for their children, but their first homes were little more than shacks and once even a tent. Frank found odd jobs, most paying very little, while Emma used her artistic talents, selling paintings and giving art and sewing lessons. They were all happy, and Miles was in her element, immersed in the nature and culture of the mountains. During this period she began writing poems and stories about mountain life and culture, while raising their children. Miles was a devoted mother, and family was important to her. Her writing revolved around her life and experiences as a mountain woman. In 1904, she established herself as a published writer by selling her first poems to *Harper's Monthly*. The first, an eleven-verse poem titled "The Difference," appeared in the March issue.[6] She followed that up the next month with another poem, "Homesick."[7] In June, an essay titled "Some Real American Music" appeared in *Harper's Monthly*.[8]

The Spirit of the Mountains *and Early Writings*

In just a few years Miles compiled enough material for a nonfiction book that focused on the triumphs and hardships of life in southern Appalachia. In 1905 she published this book, *The Spirit of the Mountains*, through a New York publisher, James Pott and Company. How she connected to this publisher is not known, but the link may have been through Alice MacGowan and Grace MacGowan Cooke, two sisters from Chattanooga who were published authors friendly with Miles.[9] MacGowan and Cooke were the daughters of the *Chattanooga Times* editor, John Encill MacGowan. They began publishing books in 1901, and in 1904 Miles provided some illustrations (credited to Miles and E. Lynn Mudge) for Cooke's novel, *A Gourd Fiddle*.[10] In letters to her friend Anna Ricketson, Miles mentions helping MacGowan with two novels, *Judith of the Cumberlands* (1908) and *The Wiving of Lance Cleaverage* (1909), which was dedicated to Miles. In a 1907 letter to Ricketson, Miles described the sisters as "warm friends" who wrote for *Harper's Monthly* frequently, and in 1909 mentioned in a letter that Alice MacGowan had given her a typewriter in return for her help on a novel.[11] The MacGowan sisters moved away from Chattanooga in 1906, first to New Jersey and then to Carmel, California. There they participated in a writers' circle that included Upton Sinclair and Sinclair Lewis.[12] Despite their distance, Miles and the MacGowan sisters remained in touch.

Certainly, Miles's publications in *Harper's Monthly* made her an author a publisher could take a chance on. James Pott and Company, although not a major publishing house, had been publishing books for several decades and leaned toward religious and spiritual subjects. *The Spirit of the Mountains* has ten chapters describing mountain life and culture of southern Appalachia written from the perspective of a female schoolteacher on Walden's Ridge.[13] Scholar Elizabeth S. D. Engelhardt states that "Miles picked up her pen to write a manifesto on mountain society because outside influences were exploiting the region she loved."[14] Indeed, Miles was already aware that the wealthier citizens of Chattanooga were encroaching on the mountain natives as they built summer homes up on Walden's Ridge to escape the heat in Chattanooga. She was ambivalent toward this development, resenting the city natives' close presence but still profiting from it by selling them her artwork. It could be argued that *The Spirit of the Mountains* was semiautobiographical, as she relied on her experiences and observations to create the scenes of mountain culture, though changing the names of those she featured. This book began her work as an interpreter of mountain culture. Even though Miles was not born there, Walden's Ridge was her home and, in painting as well as writing, her landscape. She was immersed in the mountains, the wildflowers, the birds, the people, and their customs.

Although Miles had received formal training in art, writing apparently came naturally to her. For *The Spirit of the Mountains*, Miles used her talents in both literature and art. She included six original paintings of landscapes and individuals, some from photographs as models. Her mother-in-law, Jane Winchester Miles, is the model for a mountain grandmother in one illustration; her husband, Frank Miles, is the model for a typical mountaineer in another. She did several paintings and drawings of people, mostly children, but her main focus was the land around her—the mountains, bluffs, rivers, waterfalls, and forests. There is a direct relationship between her writing and painting—a chronicle of Walden's Ridge as God made it: natural, beautiful, and wild.

The Spirit of the Mountains, with only five hundred copies printed, did not get much notice at the time it was published.[15] However, it may well have been one of the earliest books by a native writer that described the southern Appalachians,[16] although there had been previous recent shorter works. In 1899, William G. Frost published an article in the *Atlantic Monthly* titled "Our Contemporary Ancestors in the Southern Mountains."[17] In 1896, New England ornithologist Bradford Torrey visited the area and wrote *Spring Notes from Tennessee,* which included a chapter titled "A Week on Walden's Ridge."[18]

A search of the main literary magazines at the time the book was published revealed no reviews or mention of *The Spirit of the Mountains.* But it *was* read at the time, and two slightly later books today considered important monographs on southern Appalachia quote passages from *Spirit:* Horace Kephart's *Our Southern Highlanders* (1913) and John C. Campbell's *The Southern Highlander and His Homeland* (1921).[19] Dr. William Stooksbury, the president of Lincoln Memorial University in Harrogate, Tennessee, was so impressed by the book that he hired Emma as author in residence for the spring 1910 term.

If Miles received an advance or royalties for *The Spirit of the Mountains,* she never mentioned this in her personal writings. When it was published, American writers such as Theodore Dreiser, Upton Sinclair, Thomas Dixon, Edith Wharton, and Kate Douglas Wiggin were the authors filling shelves in bookstores across the country. A search today in a national library database shows only thirty-nine extant copies of the 1905 edition of *The Spirit of the Mountains* in libraries in the United States and Canada, none being further west than Illinois.

Over time, however, the book became a well-known source on mountain culture. In the 1960s it was "rediscovered" by Appalachian scholars. *The Spirit of the Mountains* described mountain life and traditions, with particular insight into the experience of women living on Walden's Ridge in southern Appalachia at the turn of the twentieth century. According to scholar Mark Banker, "*The Spirit of the Mountains* reflected positive notions about cultural diversity and concerns about modernity, which emerged in the minds of at least a few American intellectuals from the trauma of the 1890s."[20] David Whisnant, in his introduction to the 1975 facsimile edition published by the University of Tennessee Press, notes, "One is struck by her profound bi-culturism and her only subtly implicit politics. She was a keen observer of the complex interplay between mountain people's lives and life elsewhere, and the book's politics arise quite naturally and organically from her close attention to that interaction."[21] Whisnant adds that "the central fact of Emma Bell Miles's life and the predominant theme of her book is ambivalence and bi-culturism."[22]

Even though the financial success of *The Spirit of the Mountains* was limited, Emma Bell Miles continued to write stories and poems. Prior to 1908, most of what Miles had published besides *The Spirit of the Mountains* had been poems in magazines such as *Harper's Monthly, Lippincott's,* and *Century.* Starting in 1908 and for the next six years, she published more than a dozen short stories, her main output in fiction writing. Mostly set in the mountains, these stories appeared in national magazines such as *Harper's Monthly, Red Book, Putnam's,* and *Craftsman.*[23]

Shannon Brooks observes that Miles's short stories "tend to be short on plot and character development and long (too long) on romance, cliché, and melodrama. In her defense, Miles is less interested in her characters for their own sake than she is in their lives as metaphors for the larger life struggles of mountain folk."[24] Grace Toney Edwards points out that in Miles's short stories, "her whole body of fiction is a crusade for the liberation of women, coupled in her mind with the oppression of poverty."[25] Indeed, Miles knew poverty only too well, and in the early twentieth century, before women had the vote and were still bound by nineteenth-century laws, beliefs, and customs, wives had little legal standing in their marriages, and in the eye of the law were basically servants with few rights.[26] In essays Miles would later write, the topics of feminism and the suffrage movement did emerge, and Miles was well aware of the limitations put on women in early twentieth-century America.[27]

Miles earned a little money through her writing; however, this irregular income could not help the family permanently overcome constant want and a hand-to-mouth existence.

Emma Bell Miles's love of nature, keen observation, and contented family life were reflected in her early writings. She began keeping a journal in 1908. Miles wrote the journal in five separate volumes, in longhand. For many years they were in the possession of Emma's twin daughters, except for one volume that had been donated to the Chattanooga Public Library in the 1940s.

Infrequently consulted by scholars, Miles's journal reveals the nature of the land around her but would also document a difficult period in her life, marked by financial strain, personal tragedies, and deteriorating health. As to why she began the journal, she stated in a preface written to her children in 1916:

> Dear Children, if you keep nothing else of my writing I want you to keep this book, for in it I have told how happy we were. At the time I began it my stories were beginning to sell, and we were for the first and only time free of painful want. I was full of love and delight in your babyhood; and made the book of gathered hours of happiness; as people sometimes store rose leaves in a jar, to sweeten your lives."[28]

As a child, Miles had kept a journal, but this has not survived. Journal writing, as well as reading, were popular activities for girls in the Victorian era, the period of Miles's adolescence. Girls were known, and even encouraged, to spend significant time throughout the day in reading and journal writing. It enabled them to confide parts of their lives and desires they could not reveal to any living person, especially their parents. It also provided a means to express privately any rebellious thoughts or attitudes.[29]

In the first years of her journal, Miles wrote of Walden's Ridge customs of life and death, of the natural world around her, and of her young family. These observations of daily life were similar to her writing in *The Spirit of the Mountains*. In the early years of her married life, she seemed content to live the life of the traditional mountain wife and mother. But she saw mountain life from an educated, cultured perspective, having been to larger cities such as Cincinnati as a child and St. Louis as a student in her teens. As a result, she was able to describe in eloquent terms the local color and customs. Walden's Ridge in the early twentieth century was a natural Eden, as described in her early journal entries. Birds of many species were abundant, as were wildflowers, and Miles made note of them. After several years, Miles would use the journal to document her and her family's struggle, and the theme shifts from nature to women's issues, while still documenting life in southern Appalachia.

Miles's adult journal, which she began at the age of twenty-nine, documents the harsh reality not only for mountain women but for many women in the early twentieth century. At times heartbreaking or cynical, but hauntingly beautiful, the journal takes the reader back to a time and place that have been romanticized in the historical literature on the Appalachian South.

By the time that Miles began writing her reflections on nature, the genre of nature writing was not new. Writers like Thoreau, John Muir, and John Burroughs had already established their reputations as major American naturalists. The nineteenth century had also seen nature writing by women in America. Like Miles, Susan Fenimore Cooper (1813–1894), daughter of writer James Fenimore Cooper, also kept a journal of her nature observations, written in the 1840s and published in 1850 as *Rural Hours.*[30] Cooper made a name for herself as a woman naturalist. Other women naturalists emerged later in the century. Most were from the East Coast or Midwest. Miles was certainly the first from the southern Appalachian region.

Miles's journal also gives us a glimpse of historical events between 1908 and 1918. There are references to the sinking of the *Titanic,* the inauguration of President Woodrow Wilson, the outbreak of World War I, the lynching of Leo Frank in Atlanta (which made national news), and the local appearance of Buffalo Bill Cody's Wild West Show. The references are made in passing, but provide anchors to the outside world that may have seemed a bit foreign to Miles and the people around her.

Family Life

During Miles's journal-writing years, Frank tried to support the family, but paid employment was scarce on Walden's Ridge. He worked mostly as a farmer, but did not earn enough to buy food, clothes, and medicine for his family. They lived in constant debt, relying on credit with local stores. Because Frank had trouble finding good paying jobs, Emma was often the main breadwinner, even if the money came in a handful of coins or a few dollars. She sold paintings to the wealthier citizens of Chattanooga, and the money she earned from this factored heavily into the household income. She was not afraid to work, and was willing to do so. However, the demands of her family made it difficult. She had to cook, shop, clean house, wash clothes, and look after the children. Traditionally, women in Appalachia during this period did not work outside the home for wages. Financial instability would eventually strain the Miles's marriage. Frank's traditional "mountain" way of supporting their family differed from Emma's more modern way of earning money. In a 1914 journal entry, Miles wrote that Frank had told her during an argument over the issue "that he can make a living if I will be satisfied with the living he can make."[31] Changing gender roles for mountain women and a growing reliance on the regional market economy in mountain life were underlying themes in their frequent disagreements over finances. If only, she would write several times in her journal, her family would give her the time and space to write and paint, then she could earn more money. But, in that society, she was expected first to be at, and tend to, the home. Women, during her lifetime, were dependent on husbands for financial support. Courts typically viewed women as employees of their husbands, which made it difficult for women to work for wages outside the home.[32]

Readers might find Miles's many journal entries on their financial plight tiresome, as it emerges as a recurring theme. However, at no time does she acknowledge that her parents warned her against marrying Frank Miles. There is no trace of a "too proud to accept charity" attitude in her journal or letters. Miles seemed only too willing to accept whatever support friends and admirers offered, from taking in and providing for the children, to sending boxes of food and old clothes. Miles's letters to her friend Anna Ricketson, who occasionally sent gifts, convey her plight in sly references that can be interpreted as cries for help, if not outright requests. At times Miles seems to project a sense of entitlement, and perhaps others saw this too, as some friends tend to disappear from her journal for periods, or altogether, possibly from frustration and weariness at being subjected to her desperation.

Frank's inability to support his family in comfort, combined with Miles's willingness and ability to make money through her creative work, made him an easy target for the first biographers of Emma Bell Miles, who portrayed Frank in a completely negative light.[33] However, there is no real evidence to suggest he was a shiftless or lazy mountain man. Nor was he a drunk.[34] To be fair, he *was* frequently working, helping his father or a neighbor, usually in farming, but such work yielded very little income for the family. When he was not working, he was usually looking for work, as Emma notes frequently in the journal. But, as jobs were difficult to come by, she added that he was often frustrated and "out of heart."

Despite his shortcomings as a provider, Frank had good qualities. He was wonderful with animals, and his children always maintained that he was a good and kind father. Miles's writing about Frank's good qualities seems to indicate a deeper fondness and love, despite other journal entries in which she seemed to have lost all respect and perhaps love for her husband. In 1913, Miles wrote in her journal, "I have sworn by the death-stains on the white slips which I keep, that I will free myself and the children from this man's dead weight."[35]

In the winter of 1909, the Miles family, along with a family friend, spent several months in Miami, Florida. Both Miles and her young son Frank Mirick (Mark) were sickly, and she wanted to escape the cold winter on Walden's Ridge. South Tennessee winters are not extremely cold, but at the higher altitude of Walden's Ridge, in poorly insulated cabins, a normal winter can be uncomfortable. So, with the financial help of her friend, Miles and her family spent the winter months in south Florida. Miles seemed to enjoy their stay there, and wrote two essays on Christmas in Florida.[36] They stayed until the spring of 1910. From Miami they went north to the Cumberland plateau, where Emma had been offered an opportunity to work at Lincoln Memorial University in Harrogate, Tennessee, close to the Tennessee-Kentucky border. The invitation came from Dr. William Stooksbury, the school's president, who had enjoyed *The Spirit of the Mountains*, and he offered Emma a term position as author in residence. Frank was hired to do physical labor on the grounds of the university.

In June 1910, Emma and Frank completed their work at Lincoln Memorial University and returned with their family to Walden's Ridge. Up until then, their living arrangements on Walden's Ridge and in Chattanooga had been mostly in rented cabins, rooms, apartments, and a tent. Once, they even moved in with Frank's parents in an area of Walden's Ridge that Emma called "Smoky Row." In her journal, she made no effort to hide her disdain of the neighborhood, noting the children born to unmarried parents and the disreputable characters who lived in the area. She often fretted over her children growing up in such an environment. Likewise, Frank's family did not approve of, or trust, Emma, in part because she worked outside the home and was educated, and also because her writing about the area conflicted with the oral tradition of storytelling in mountain culture. As Edwards points out, "A written literature was so foreign to their orally based culture that scarcely could they be expected to conceive what 'Emmer' was doing; they realized that it sometimes brought in money, but beyond that its significance was lost."[37] In 1912, after a brief escape to work in Chattanooga, Emma wrote in her journal: "Had an indignation meeting on my hands. Grandma exhausted her eloquence trying to persuade me to stay at home. Oh how they all pity my children—not to the extent of doing something for them in my absence however. And what tales are being circulated! Grandma can't read but she knows that literary folks will do to watch—"these here writers and typewriters" is her phrase."[38]

Miles's art and writing allowed her to move among a class of people in Chattanooga more educated than the mountain folk on Walden's Ridge. This association no doubt intimidated and frustrated Frank. When he happened to be in their company he seemed out of place, and Miles certainly was aware of this, noting in her journal in 1914, "Frank went with me, and I think his enjoyment was scarcely marred by the fact that he was the only man in the room who did not wear a collar. I have never been able to make up my mind whether this attitude is to be accounted unto him for common-sense or mere carelessness. I could gladly give him the benefit of the doubt if he would learn daintier ways with handkerchiefs, tooth-brushes, and under-clothing."[39]

Despite his inability to make enough money to support his family, Frank clung to traditional notions of the gendered division of labor. He believed that Emma's main role in the family was to care for their children, clean their home, and work their garden, while he found work outside the home. One of her daughters would remark, years later, that the children knew she wrote and painted, and that this occasionally brought in money, but "she was just Mamma to us." However, as Miles built a reputation as an artist and writer, she could no longer fill the traditional role of a mountain woman that Frank imagined. She had rich friends in town; her poems appeared in the newspapers, as well as reviews of her public lectures.

Miles's reputation outside of Walden's Ridge resulted in occasional relief from poverty. She had friends who helped her and her family. Occasionally a box of old clothes or reading material would come up the mountain or someone in Chattanooga would buy one of her paintings. She was grateful for the desperately needed money, but knew that her work was worth more than she was forced to sell it for. In August 1916, she noted despairingly in her journal that they could hardly be friends to her when they bargained their way to ridiculous prices for her art.[40] However, some of her friends and supporters were much more genuine. An older wealthy couple, the Wheatleys, who lived in the nearby community of St. Elmo, were particularly kind to Miles. At one point they welcomed her into their home for a week's rest and recovery from the toils of keeping house for her family. Her admirer and benefactor Anna Ricketson was also helpful, occasionally sending money and supplies, and always encouragement. Ricketson was a writer and literary critic who lived in New Bedford, Massachusetts, and had known Thoreau, whose work Miles highly valued.[41]

Emma constantly marketed her writings in an effort to increase the demand for her work. In 1912, she assembled a small volume of her poems, which she titled "Chords from a Dulcimore."[42] Her goal was to make a profit of $500, a sum she thought would provide for her family for quite some time. She hand-painted the cover of each book so that each volume was unique. To help sales, she would individually illustrate the inside pages on request, something she also did for *The Spirit of the Mountains*. It is not known how many copies of *Chords from a Dulcimore* were printed or how many she sold, but the price people were willing to pay did not make the project as profitable as she had hoped.[43]

Tragedy

In early 1913 tragedy struck the Miles family. In late January Miles's youngest child, Mirick, died of scarlet fever. For days Emma and Frank had known he was sick, but could not afford a doctor. When a doctor finally did see the young boy, it was too late. Miles filled several pages of her journal with the heartrending details of his final moments.

She must have found it cathartic to write about it in her journal. In one of her longest entries, Miles filled several pages describing her young son's final hours and minutes. She seemed somehow inspired in writing about her tragedies, and did not shy from the cold, brutal truth. Young Mirick, not even four years old, was buried in a small cemetery on Walden's Ridge. His site was unmarked, as were many graves in the cemetery, except for simple stones and rocks indicating a gravesite.[44] After Mirick's death, Miles vowed in her journal never again to bring into the world a child she could not support and protect. Despite several more pregnancies (Frank obviously being unwilling to help in that regard), she kept her pledge. How she managed to end those pregnancies is not clear, but it is possible if not probable that she found a way to abort them. She later referred in her journal to her actions as murder, perhaps flippantly, but honestly. Abortion, of course, was illegal during this period, but not uncommon in America, the Appalachian region, or around the world. Women wanting to end an unwanted pregnancy tried various "folk methods" for self-inducing a miscarriage; these included ingesting abortifacients such as herbs like pennyroyal and tansy, drinking toxic potions such as gin mixed with gunpowder,[45] and taking medicines or draughts pregnant women were strongly advised against taking. Indications that she may have resorted to these measures occur in several entries in her journal, particularly in 1915, a time when she was considering divorcing Frank; she wrote that Frank had consulted with an attorney and "that he can divorce me for the death of those unborn children."[46] Several places in the journal reveal evidence of missing pages, at least twelve, having been torn out, perhaps to hide the drastic measures she had taken. Later in the journal, she would allude to this self-editing.

The death of Mirick proved to Miles that changes were needed in their living situation. Perhaps it was the long account of his suffering and their helplessness that she entered in her journal that caused her to realize just how bad their situation was. It may have helped her temporarily deal with the heartbreak and tragedy. The ordeal could also be regarded as the start of the decline in her health and emotional strength. They desperately needed money; they could not get by on the few things they could grow or trade. Facing this grim situation, she also realized that supporting the family would be up to her.

Temporary Separation

On several occasions during the 1910s, Miles temporarily left her family and Walden's Ridge, against Frank's wishes, to work in Chattanooga. In the summer of 1913, she had taken up residence in Chattanooga, staying in the Frances Willard Home for Women, a lodging for working single women established in the mid-1880s and named for the founder of the Women's Christian Temperance Union. This provided a respite from familial duties. At the Willard Home she was free to earn some money by teaching art lessons, working at the newspaper, and marketing her artwork. In 1914 she secured work at the *Chattanooga News* with a column titled "The Fountain Square Conversations." In this column, which ran for three months, and over thirty installments, she recorded imaginary philosophical conversations between a fireman statue in a fountain square and some animals, mostly birds, on topics such as nature, women's rights, and current events.

By 1914, Miles had shifted in her journal from detailed descriptions of nature and the mountain culture on Walden's Ridge to accounts of her family's struggles. She also recorded her desire for a better living situation, as well as her attempts to make that dream a reality. The journal may have provided some relief to Miles, as it was her only means to unburden her soul. It may also have served as an outlet for Miles to reflect on or analyze her situation, if she did indeed go back over and read what she had written. Psychoanalysts in the early twentieth century, following Freud's practice, were beginning to use journals and diaries as tools in treating patients.[47] Such personal writings and reflections can serve several roles for the writer: confidant, friend, and surrogate therapist; they can also provide relief, self-reflection, self-analysis, and perhaps narcissistic enhancement.[48] Personal journals can be a vehicle for the writer to reflect on his or her past, and can provide a record of self-development and a means for prescriptive living. Miles's journals, written at a time when the importance of journals as windows into the minds and psyches of the writers was just being realized, are early examples of this phenomenon, as they show the progression from nineteenth-century journal writing to more introspective twentieth-century writing.

Miles longed for a divorce, but she found that obtaining one was not easy or practical for a woman, at least in Tennessee. In 1913 she consulted a lawyer about obtaining a divorce and freeing herself from Frank, but was dismissively told that there was little she could do. "But after inquiring thoroughly into it, he [the lawyer] told me I am pretty near helpless—have no legal case unless I could prove Frank to be of unsound mind."[49] Still eight years before women could vote, Miles found herself a victim to a male-oriented society where women had little say in their rights. At that time divorces, which had seen a rise in the United States in the early twentieth century, were generally given only for "marital crimes" such as adultery, desertion, nonsupport, and cruelty.[50] Miles might have made a case for nonsupport, but the fact that Frank was still living at home and attempting to support the family (and, in his mind, actually was doing so) might have made her case hard to prove. There are no indications in the journal that Frank had been unfaithful, or absent for long periods of time, or violently abusive. Nonetheless, several times Miles started the motions for a legal separation or divorce, but never followed through, either because she changed her mind or because she let Frank talk her out of it.

Frank may have considered her occasional moves to Chattanooga a betrayal of her family and him. Given that Frank had a large extended family of parents, siblings, cousins, nieces, and nephews living all around them, her moving out and finding work had to have been humiliating for him, and perhaps gave the appearance that he "couldn't control her" or provide for his family.

While living in Chattanooga, Miles also gave public lectures on nature themes such as the local birds, for which she received some money, though this income was usually low and infrequent. During this period, she continued to write in her journal. She described happiness and relief while living in Chattanooga and writing for the *News*. Things were looking up. She was often received by the Chattanooga elite and attended parties and other social events. On weekends she returned to her family on Walden's Ridge, and occasionally some of them, including Frank, came down during the week to visit.[51] However, Frank's visits were not always happy reunions. They often argued. Frank pleaded with her to come home and, at times, threatened her. Then he would tearfully apologize. Most of the information we have about Frank's actions and reactions come from Miles's written accounts, which of course represent only half of the story.

On July 24, 1914, after a break in the journal of several weeks, she wrote despairingly of her situation. Her words indicated that she was once again pregnant: "All is lost now; my hope, my health, all sacrificed to a man's pleasure. This is the destiny of women, under the laws and customs of our mad and cruel civilization. God deliver my daughters from such love as has ruined me."[52] This apparently was a reference to Frank's insistence on his husbandly rights which, before the days of effective birth control, often resulted in children wanted or not. Her pregnancy ended her job at the newspaper, although the pregnancy did not last. She wrote in her journal a few weeks later that she had miscarried.[53] Her attitude toward Frank's behavior is evident when, in 1915, while convalescing at the sanitarium, a fellow patient remarked to Miles on how much her husband surely loved her. Miles wrote in her journal, "I might have answered that there is a love that kills."[54]

Tuberculosis

After a gap of several months in the journal entries, Miles noted on February 6, 1915, that she was in the Pine Breeze Sanitarium, which was a tuberculosis sanitarium in Chattanooga.[55] She had not previously mentioned in her journal that she had tuberculosis. She had been sickly as a child, and as an adult was often frail, weighing less than one hundred pounds at a height of five feet four inches. However, she took some solace in being at the sanitarium. She wrote, "To be free of the power of sin! Ever since Mark died—and before that, since I first realized the same and the cruelty of bringing children into life unprepared for—I have longed to be free. Of late I have torn out of these records the pages which told the worst of my situation, for I wished to remember them no more forever, and the children must never know. But even through this last peaceful, pleasant, almost happy winter I have wished it were possible to free myself."[56] In this entry she admits to having torn out the pages in her journal, perhaps since they revealed the desperate measures she resorted to in avoiding bearing more children. If this is, indeed, what she is referring to, we may never know for sure, since she undoubtedly destroyed those pages.

Without the money to afford treatment in the sanitarium, Miles depended on the generosity of friends and admirers who arranged for her to stay at the facility. The Pine Breeze Sanitarium had opened in 1913, and was situated on top of Stringer's Ridge, which ran alongside the Tennessee River. The high elevation seemed suitable for tuberculosis treatment of that era, and the location also appeared to be safe from the smoke and smog of the city. There was plenty of air circulation in the buildings where the patients were housed, and they slept on the porches when the weather was suitable. This was the common approach to treating tuberculosis in that period, when approximately 50 percent of sufferers survived this infectious disease.[57] Miles suffered through tuberculosis during the World War I years, a period that saw a rise in mortality rates for tuberculosis sufferers, perhaps due to the attention given the war.[58] Prior to 1950 it was estimated that it was fatal in 80 percent of cases within a five- to fifteen-year range.[59] Pulmonary tuberculosis, which Miles had, was a common form of the infectious disease, known for remissions and severe relapses. Over the next four years Miles would experience this course as the disease slowly ate away at her health.

Those without the funds to afford proper medical treatment and care were at a disadvantage, as the Miles family knew all too well. They had lost their young son in 1913 for lack of money to pay a doctor to see him in time. In rural Appalachia, the poor often had to resort to home remedies or whatever folk remedies had been passed down over the years.[60] In Appalachian culture, women were frequently deferred to in health matters in the family. Woe betide, then, the mother and wife who became sick and needed the support and health of her family in receiving treatment and care. She often found that she did not have time to be sick.[61]

During her convalescence, Miles continued to write, paint, and draw, and being away from her family made it easier. She also butted heads with the sanitarium's superintendent, Mrs. Natalie Plewes, as she reported in the journal. She worked on a manuscript about her reflections on nature, titled "The Good Gray Mother." She also began working on a book on southern birds, and sold at least one short story, to *Mother's Magazine*.[62] However, her melancholy and depression turned to hopelessness, as she realized that even if she recovered, she had nothing to look forward to. By this time, her children had been taken in by families and friends better able to take care of them. The twin girls, Jean and Judith, were sent off to schools. Frank and the other children were living with his parents. The reality weighed heavily on Miles. When one of her twins got homesick and wished to come home, Miles lamented, "I don't know how to get her to understand, that there is no home to come home to."[63] Such longings for family life often caused her to reconsider her feelings for Frank. While she wanted to be free of him, she still occasionally referred to him as "my dear man." In a 1916 journal entry, Miles even wrote of considering a painless suicide by taking a narcotic plant, but she did not follow through with this plan.[64]

Christian Science and New Thought

It was during 1916, while convalescing at Pine Breeze, that Miles turned to Christian Science. She had been visited by a Mrs. Labar, whom she described as a Christian Science healer. She wrote in her journal, "To save time I told her at once that I believe the teaching that Spirit is all and nothing else is real, but I don't seem to know how to live my beliefs. I told her plainly that I am not afraid of death, that my trouble is I don't want to live."[65] Nevertheless, Miles began studying and practicing Christian Science up to a point. There are references to Christian Science throughout the remainder of her journal. But after a year of studying and practicing Christian Science, she wrote in her journal, "Certain aspects of this teaching I can't accept . . . But at present C.S. flouts and condemns all natural sciences, sweepingly,—and then turns round and borrows its most convincing illustrations and parallells [*sic*] from astronomy and biology! I have myself learned too much spiritual law in the study of the natural world, considering the lilies and beholding the fowls of the air, to call my belief Christian Science."[66]

Miles had dabbled in the New Thought Movement several years earlier, and Christian Science had its origins in that movement. Miles had published an account of the family's Miami trip in the *Nautilus*, a New Thought magazine, in 1910.[67] In 1914 she began making several references, mostly in passing, to the movement. The New Thought Movement was founded in the early 1800s by Phineas Quimby, a philosopher, mesmerist, and healer. The movement attracted a number of philosophers and spiritual thinkers. Mary Baker Eddy, a patient of Quimby's, took his teachings further, disavowing some, and further developing the belief that God was the ultimate healing force in the universe. Eddy formed the Christian Scientist Association in 1876 and in 1879, the Church of Christ, Scientist. That Miles would turn to these movements is not surprising. Not particularly religious but more spiritual in character, it would have appealed to someone like Miles, who was closely attuned to nature. Not being able to afford proper medical care, Miles would no doubt have welcomed the idea of healing herself through the Christian Science beliefs, given the family's financial struggles. This alternative approach to healing also would appeal to her freethinking attitudes.

Death

In 1918, Frank found steady work in Chattanooga, and rented a house in an area called Hill City (today North Chattanooga) not far from the Pine Breeze Sanitarium. Miles made her last entry in the journal on August 19, 1918, ten years after she began keeping it. The last entry is mostly about her work on the bird book, which would be published as *Our Southern Birds*. The entry suggests, perhaps, a desire to return to the simple life she led when she began the journal, and to escape her failing health and desperate family situation of her later years.[68] This last entry does not appear to be a farewell; it was merely recorded on the last available page of the journal she was using. If she continued the journal in a new volume, it did not survive.

Miles left the Pine Breeze Sanitarium in October 1918, and moved into the rented house in Hill City. Weak and worn out, she died there on March 19, 1919, several months short of her fortieth birthday. That year, 3,938 people would die in Tennessee from tuberculosis.[69] Miles's final book, *Our Southern Birds*, in which she provided the text and illustrations, was published just weeks before her death.[70]

Miles was buried in a cemetery a few miles from her last residence, in the town of Red Bank, now a Chattanooga suburb. Tall trees block the view today, but at the time of her burial the grave site offered a clear view of Walden's Ridge nearby.[71] About ten years later, Frank moved to California, where their son Joe was then living. Frank died and was buried there in 1947.

In the years following Miles's death several short biographies appeared. A friend, Abbey Crawford Milton, included a brief biography of Emma when she published some of Miles's poems posthumously in 1930 under the title *Strains from a Dulcimore*.[72] In a history of Signal Mountain and Walden's Ridge, self-published in 1962 by Cartter Patten, whom Miles had painted twice when he was a child, Patten wrote several pages about Miles.[73] A longer biography, written by Chattanooga librarian Adelaide Rowell, appeared in a 1966 issue of the *Tennessee Historical Quarterly*.[74] Rowell drew from the journal that had been deposited in the Chattanooga Public Library in the 1940s, but made other claims, including a poor characterization of their father that particularly enraged Jean Miles Catino and Judith Miles Ford, Miles's twin daughters. Two book-length works followed. The first, a PhD dissertation in 1981 by scholar Grace Toney Edwards, is described by Edwards as a "literary biography." In 1985, journalist and historian Kay Baker Gaston published a book-length biography on Miles. Gaston had access to the journal, personal writings, and correspondence of Miles, as well as cooperation and input from several of Miles's children, particularly Jean Miles Catino. Other articles and book chapters about Miles and her writings have appeared in the last forty years.[75]

There is still much about the life and work of Emma Bell Miles that merits further critical evaluation. Her fiction writing and poetry, which appeared in national magazines in the early twentieth century, have received some critical reviews or studies (mostly mentioned in this introduction) but to this day remain mostly overlooked. Her nature writing, including *The Spirit of the Mountains;* her "Fountain Square Conversations," which appeared in the *Chattanooga News* in 1914; and her correspondence have also seen some scholarship in the past few decades, but beg for more today. The recovery, if it were ever to happen, of her lost manuscripts, particularly "The Good Gray Mother," certainly would add to her legacy, and to the field of conservation and nature writing of the early twentieth century.

The artwork of Emma Bell Miles has also been understudied and largely ignored. Her paintings have never been cataloged, or accurately listed, as she sold many of them as fast as she could produce them. Unfortunately, Miles kept no known record of the art she produced, so there is no way to determine the amount or breadth of her output. There are still some paintings and drawings in the private collections of the families who had summer homes on Walden's Ridge in the early 1900s, but others have managed to travel farther in the past century. There have been at least two exhibits in the past thirty years in the Chattanooga area, one at the Hunter Art Museum in Chattanooga in the 1980s, and one at the Signal Mountain Public Library in 2012. Mostly watercolors, oils, and drawings, many of Miles's illustrations are of landscape and mountain scenes of Walden's Ridge, and display a remarkable artistic talent.

Lost Works

From references in her journal and correspondence, it appears that Miles wrote quite a few stories and book-length works that apparently were never published and have since disappeared. No record or register has been found in which Miles noted her publications or writings. According to Jean Miles Catino, in a 1979 letter to Miles biographer Kay Baker Gaston, Abbie Crawford Milton, a friend of Emma's, took a chest that had belonged to Miles shortly after her death.[76] The manuscript of "The Good Gray Mother" is believed to have been in this chest, as well as other unpublished works. The National Book Company, which had published *Our Southern Birds,* and had an office in Chattanooga, had been given the rights to Miles's unpublished literary works by Miles shortly before her death. The National Book Company soon folded and the Globe Publishing Company of Morristown, Tennessee, acquired the rights to her works, including a manuscript on wildflowers, with illustrations by Miles, in the same vein as *Our Southern Birds*. The Globe Publishing Company did release an edition of *Our Southern Birds* in 1922 but never the wildflower book. Shortly after its reissue of *Our Southern Birds*, it too folded.[77]

In 1952, Zerelda Rains, who had given Miles her first art lessons more than fifty years earlier, wrote to Jean Miles Catino, and mentioned she had recently found a copy of "The Good Gray Mother" manuscript, which Miles had sent her before her death. Rains, then living in New York City, also wrote that she had arranged for someone in a "major publishing company" in New York City to look at the manuscript.[78] It apparently did not meet with approval, as it was not published. "The Good Gray Mother" manuscript surfaced several times over the next few decades before disappearing and has yet to be recovered, despite several attempts by others to locate it.

There are other works Miles apparently wrote that have not survived. In a 1909 letter to Ricketson, Miles mentioned having collaborated on a novelette with another local writer, Caroline Wood Morrison.[79] It is not known what this work was. In 1912, Miles wrote in her journal that she had sent seven stories to a friend, referred to only as a "Miss Holly."[80] Five of these stories, "Clay's Marget," "Cometh Not in by the Door," "The Healers," "Cost What It May," and "The Great World," have not been discovered in published form, nor have the manuscripts survived. A few weeks later, Miles referred in her journal to another story, "Mystic Words," which also has never been found in manuscript or print.[81] In May 1912 Miles makes reference to a novel (unnamed), and is disappointed that her friend Grace McGowan Cooke would not be in New York to help her place it with a publisher.[82] This may be "The Flower of the Sun," a novel Miles refers to a few weeks later in the journal, but indicates it had not yet been written.[83] Another story, "Dan Riley," is mentioned in her journal in September of that year.[84]

In early 1913, Miles refers to a "storiette" titled "Fortune's Wheel," sent to a "Mr. Stoner." In September of 1913, Miles mentions in her journal a one-act play she has written with Margaret Severance, a local writer and actress, titled "A Timber Redbird."[85] In 1915, Miles refers to having received $25 for "a Madonna story" but doesn't mention from whom.[86] In 1916, there is a reference to a story titled "A Mess of Greens" that had been accepted by *Mother's Magazine.*"[87] For several months later that year there are references to a manuscript of a novel, titled "Bitter Herbs." Miles writes that she even received some money for this work from the MacGowan sisters.[88] She also references a short story, "The White Cow," that had been accepted by *The Youth's Companion* magazine in 1916.[89] In 1917, a story titled "A Destroying Angel" is mentioned in her journal.[90] These are just some references to stories and book-length manuscripts that apparently were never published and have since been lost. There were other references, less detailed, in her journal to stories and drafts, as well as countless poems.

Emma Bell Miles remains a significant female Appalachian writer and artist who has received only limited scholarly attention. Her most notable work, *The Spirit of the Mountains*, remains a useful source for students and scholars of Appalachian culture and literature. However, her personal journal provides readers with a much more realistic and less romantic depiction of life for a woman in the male-driven Southern Appalachian region during the early twentieth century. The journal takes us to a complicated environment, where the modern world conflicted with the traditions of the mountains. Emma Bell Miles was very much a modern-thinking woman by today's standards, but one who had the misfortune to be born in the nineteenth century and live at a time when women had very little say in how their lives were led. As she struggled with the conflicting roles of artist, poet, writer, naturalist, daughter, mother, and wife, she wrote her journal for her children to read, remember, and contemplate. She left her children little else, but she did leave them a lesson. In the preface to her 1916 journal, perhaps sensing her premature death, she reminded them: "Love one another as I have loved you, and try to be patient as I have never been. Above all things, be kind."[91]

The Journals of
Emma Bell Miles,
1908–1918

Preface

Hollywood, Signal Mt., May 11, 1916

To Judith and Jean and Joe and Katharine—

Dear children, if you keep nothing else of my writing I want you to keep this book, for in it I have told how happy we were. At the time I began it my stories were beginning to sell, and we were for the first and only time free of painful want. I was full of love and delight in your babyhood; and made the book of gathered hours of happiness, as people sometimes store rose leaves in a jar, to sweeten your lives.

Later, as you remember, things changed. I had resolved to live above disease and all unhappiness and shameful things; and until the terrible breaking sorrow and shame that was put on me, I think I kept my resolution as well as any one could. Often I have been too harsh with you; when you remember this try to understand that I was at the time struggling for a chance to live, and forgive me.

And O my darlings, if you learn nothing else from my notebooks, let them teach you that the happiest times may be changed and darkened by unkindness in the home, and that the best opportunities are wasted by neglect. Love one another as I have loved you, and try to be patient as I have never been. Above all things, be kind.

With everlasting love, from Mother.

one

Walden's Ridge

By 1908 Emma Bell Miles had published the work many feel defined her creative output. *The Spirit of the Mountains* was published in 1905, and in this book she detailed much about life in southern Appalachia. These were good times for her. She had a young family—two twin daughters, a son, and a younger daughter. A fifth child would be born in 1909. The family was getting by, meagerly but happily.

In 1908 Miles began writing her journal, describing all that nature afforded her on Walden's Ridge, in southeastern Tennessee. She named and described the flowers, the birds, and the local customs. Emma was twenty-nine years old. Names of relatives—mostly those related to her husband, Frank—are mentioned.

In 1916 she added the opening preface, when things were looking bleak and she was suffering from tuberculosis. By this time she was extremely bitter toward Frank, who proved unable to adequately support the family.

May 24, 1908

Summertown.[1]

To the old Wash Vandergriff place. Sunday on old farm: deserted log house standing in its orchard. This hill top sees the whole sky, and far over the woods. Deep under those domed treetops that drowse and droop in the sunshine, is the "gulf" with the creek hid at the bottom, sliding under the laurel.

Now are the most vivid greens of the year. Little haze, no dust, no blurs of heat; a still bright day, on the crazy rye-fields and on the woods and pastured wastes. Star-root: scurvy-root: pink-root: late honey suckle like a red flame in the thicket, its color ranging thro' pale buff and clear yellow to orange & crimson. Sleepy butterflies: emerald beetles.

Church-bell rings far across the creek: little apples drop untimely, one by one, in orchard: hawk circles slowly in the blue, up and up, a mere speck, finally lost to sight in the fathomless air.

Down in the 'gulf': Laurel tree over the spring, its gnarled trunk polished smooth by the grasping feet and hands of little climbers, restless while mother washed on the stones and boiled her clothes on the rude furnace.

Wild bees in the canopy of blossom flung by knotty-fingered boughs over the spring. Fair bosom of drooping clusters where they tremble happily, their hum drowned by the gurgle of the spring branch. Clouds of bloom, billowing up the steep sides of the gulch, under the hemlocks and liriodendron.

Piano-tinkle of drip on pool. Delicate silvery nocturnes of the frogs.

May 31, 1908

Spent Sunday at Alford's. Midsummer day, cloudless but for small tinted puffs that hang just over the blue rim of the world that shows between the forest tops. Breeze tempering the heat, except in the hollows that seem to boil like a kettle, steeping the motionless leaves. Hum of bees in persimmon tree. Sundrops: Moth mullen; catchfly or fire pink: umbels of milkweed, white and purple, narrow three week blooms: laurel about gone.

Young people all out visiting by eight or nine o'clock, in their brightest frocks and shirts. Boys in couples, lounging and talking in the edge of the woods. From porch to innermost cupboard niche, the house is in speckless Sunday order, with an air of expectancy; its floors are sand-scoured until the pine boards are worn into hollows between the rounded knots! Front yard with pink hollyhocks. Boys tuning fiddle & banjo under trees in corner of the clean-swept yard: over them the oak's passion of strength fling at the sky. Children roll in grass, swing under tree, finally scamper away to build a playhouse. The "fryin' size" boys pitch horseshoes in the barn lot. Turkey struts before the gate—a lustrous purple-legged baron, every feather iridescent: "hatched from a wild egg." The house mother has received a letter from her son-in-law in Georgia: it is brought out and passed from hand to hand to be deciphered. Baby bounces on its father's lap.

Dinner announced: The boys bring in the chairs & place long bench for the small-fry. On a cloth of bleached and well-ironed flour-sacks are placed bowls of cabbage & new potatoes, corn pones & soda biscuit, & lettuce, radishes & green onions from the garden: a huge service cobbler for dessert. Second table of children, except Foster, who is as usual sick, drugged with cheap medicines, and lies on a pallet in the entry. Then late-comers of the family, with other guests for whom the table is laid anew.

During the work of cleaning up the men adjourn to the oak tree, whose spreading roots are polished seats. Banjo & fiddle again: pitch horseshoes. Newcomer—a noted banjo player & singer—is hailed with shouts of welcome: he shambles into the circle, takes banjo and "makes her talk." By and by the women join them. 4 married men joking the 4 boys about one's rumored wedding to a sixteen-year-old girl. The crowd at the barn grows by twos and threes—at last a dozen are counted, with laughter. Boys take banjo and fiddle out to watch the game. One or two return to drink at the water shelf by the kitchen door in the shade. "Let's go git a fresh bucket." Below the spring, across a field of glistening, waving, whispering corn-blades, is a tract denuded of timber and grown up in brush: here a fellow and his girl may get lost in a few steps, among the bee-haunted skull-caps and primroses. Hot sun. . . . .

In the cool inner room, shut from the glare. Buzz of flies sounds faint from main house: dim light falls thro' door. Newspapered wall: boys' clothes hung below gunrack, and their box trunks: mirror on old bureau. Stately cat visible in loft, looking for mice: lizards hunting flies. Old four-poster: the pillows where heads shall be laid tonight, the coverlets woven, the quilts honestly stitched. Child in a rosy sleep on other bed. Sounds outside— children at play: angry gobble, and yap of scared puppy: laughter: murmur of talk under oak tree. Sudden warble of wren at eaves' corner.

June 9, 1908

Frank [Miles's husband] called a partridge within twenty feet of my hammock. The dulcimore, whittled of brown oak, unvarnished, rough. The one I saw had the head carved curiously into what the maker said was intended for a woman's face, but turned out to be a cat's. Three wire strings—played with a horn plectrum. Music faint, monotonous, strings weave shadowy melody. Like that of insects. Low, wild plaint, similar to that of Oriental sitar, sarnisen, etc. Sometimes angular in shape, like a little coffin: from 2 1/2 to 4 1/2 in length. Often played with a bow, like a viol.

Soft slither of bat's wings. Dusk thrilled with lightning:—gray blank, vast, mysterious,—cloud-palaces fitfully illumined, then instantly vanishing. Thrum & twangle of guitars.

June 14, 1908

Sensitive plant just beginning to bloom: ladies' tresses a gleam of white here and there: redroot & madder through all the open woods. Bee-balm, pale lavender & white heads of a pungency not to be endured on the tongue. Wild sunflower on brushy hillside Sourwood, just strung with first white bells,—like sprays of lily-of-the-valley.

Children at play in the fine clean sand, the rain-washed, sun-bleached, wind-sifted sand. Elder child shows them how to print "fox-tracks" with the finger-tips, and "baby-tracks" with the heel of the hand, pointing the toe-marks in delicately. Primitive sand-pictures. Plow with crooked stick, plant little garden of bush-clover, Frog-houses, wells. Water-parsnip bloom.

June 28, 1908

An annular eclipse. Begins in mid-morning heat & light, an ashy darkening of the sky. The medallion of flickering leaf shadows changes to one of crescents. Dim sudden fading light. Preacher Scott, wife & 3 children, comes to spend the day with his brother-in-law. Host meets him outside gate; family go in, men, after unhitching Pete the mule and turning him in the lot, lean against the trees & fence talking elections: saunter over to inspect a wrongly dished wheel on new wagon: are joined by Sunday-shirted neighbor; at last it occurs to one of the group that it is as cheap sitting as standing, and they sit on stacked clapboards by the fence. Finally, in deference to the preacher's habits, they retire to long front porch, talk church news, all local affairs, weather & crops, which last subject presently takes preacher & host out into garden. Wives in kitchen compare babies & sandwich gossip with dinner-getting.

Afternoon. Clouds again ride dazzling against a vivid blue. Men on porch, talk all the blessed Sunday afternoon! About three "ketch out" the mule & round up the kids to go: Little girls, Ruth & Naomi, aged 6 & 4. [Daughters of Preacher Scott]

Evening walk. Children race along road, rub sand in their hair, turning handsprings & summersaults, 'sic' dog on each other: big boys challenge, 'bet you can't turn a summersault with your eyes shut' & then sprint towards the house. Bet you cayn't walk across the road on your hands. How many times can you chin a pole? Climb trees with true monkey-like agility, bend thirty-foot saplings to ride down to the ground in their swinging, crashing tops: skin a cat, hang by the knees fanning the air with hands & yelling 15 feet above the ground; cast off shoes. (They wear no stockings, their overalls are their father's old ones, worn out at the bottom & turned up.) They assume incredible altitudes swinging hand over hand thro' tree tops, grasping trunks with knees & feet, firmly: graceful & quick.

July 1, 1908

Went to make a blackberry camp at the old Raul Brown place—tracking for miles into the woods with a loaded wheelbarrow and a boy's little wagon. No matter how far one goes into these ridges, one never feels more than about so far from home. Except along the wild laurel-tangled creeks, with their rocks and pools and falls, the landscape does not change much. There is always the blue distant hill, with its forest-trees dimly rounding through blue haze: always the same forest foreground and underbrush, the trail, a streak of sand, running through greenery of sedge-grass and huckleberries: always the official illusion of a clearing in the hollow below. The Raul Brown cabin itself is the most unexpected beauty-spot discoverable.

The children found butterfly-pea, tick-trefoil, white morning-glories or man-of-the-earths, a slender St. John's-wort: loose-strife (?) white lobelia: a deep yellow pease-like blossom—might be a small vetch or [illegible] common enough. Wild hydrangea along the brakes: first Sabbatia and last camellias. Redroot faded: madder holds its own even with the wild sunflower just coming into bloom.

Oh, these long-abandoned mountain homes! Silent, lonely, beautiful! The Timesville place, the John Price place, the old Edwards place, the old Lewis Smith place, the Wash Vandergriff place, the Winchester place, and so on without end! In this cabin no one has lived since the builder died, ten or twelve years ago. The freestone spring is choked but its iron-tinged mate still runs, cleared perhaps from time to time by wandering cattlemen or hunters in a heavily shaded hollow almost tropical with ferns. Stray cows still come to lick the earthen floor of the crumbling smoke house, where Jean [Miles's daughter] found four rings of iron—the boxing of an old-fashioned "tar-grinder" wagon, and the broken lid of a huge oven. For some reason the timber in this spot has not suffered perceptibly from the sleet of 1905: the yard slopes down to the spring, shaded and almost swept by the boughs of black & white and scarlet oaks: superb poplars down by the clearing's edge, where the thicket runs down to the old fence and stops as though chopped off with a hoe. All round the house, over the old garden and fields, like the matted briers: bowed over, sometimes lying flat, under the weighted wealth of winy dark fruit. An old appletree in the midst bears faithfully, the last of a forgotten orchard.

In the dark, cool interior, briers and vines wander, bleached like ghosts and seeking the ruddying beams. The fireplace is wide and high and deep: arched with a bar of smoke enameled black-smoked oak: the roof runs out past the rough stack-chimney, to keep the rain from the daubing, and making incidentally a shelter on each side for stock or dogs.

The night was wonderfully silent. After the whippo 'wills had sung their evening-song there was not a chirp nor a murmur. I walked in the early dew, before the others woke, to hear the chorus of birds—chat, redbird, raincrow: no thrushes, nor catbirds, robins, nor mockers—these prefer a sort of distant companionship with man. The creek bottom trees are tangled with skeins and veils of thin mist; our breakfast-smoke presently mingles with it in the still air. Pine needles beaded with rain. We eat, and are out picking berries again almost by "sun-up" in the wet undergrowth. All the cans are filled before dinner-time: how long, long the day seems in such a silent place!

We leave the cabin swept, and stocked with matches, soap, salt and pepper for the next owner, and wire the door against the cattle. It is to be hoped that we shall return.

July 17, 1908

Breakfast-smoke rising straight into the dawn.

Every day has a morning of hot still sunshine; after the early thrush-song all remains quiet, into at noon or a little later. The growing clouds begin to send forth long diapason tones of thunder. Then a grateful shadow overspreads the panting earth: a breeze comes across the woods, turning up the whitish undersides of the leaves: and at last then the cool and thrilling touch of the rain's quick fingers puts new strength into everything. The sun shines out again, however, before evening.

For years I felt rebellious and bitter at not having a home on the face of a hostile earth, at being obliged by move from shack to cabin and from cabin to shack, each evening more dirty and dismal than the last. But now I am become like the Arab who carries his tent and furnishings from oasis to oasis, and regards the whole desert as his home. When I remember all the beautiful, silent, sylvan places wherein we have nested for a season, I love the whole vast wild mother-land. I should feel at home, I think, if cast tomorrow into any lap of the hills or beside any spring-fed branch, in a "scope of country" where the contours of landscape are broadly familiar. Home is to me a matter of atmosphere and flora, instead of being confined to a particular roof and lintel. How much more precious is this state of mind than any ancestral mansion and acres could ever be. May it not come to pass in the end that no private ownership of land shall be permitted, and that every man shall feel an exquisite harmony of spirit with mere outdoor life everywhere?

July 20, 1908

To grandmother's. [Jane Winchester Miles, Frank's mother]

Queen Anne's lace: starry campion; tick-trefoil: butterfly-pea: madder: yellow fringed-orchis: white milkweed: "wild hop" in husk: wine weed: Sabbatia: lobelia: white & other morning glories: smooth gerardia: meadow beauty: a yellow desmodium: St. John's wort, large and small, with 4-petalled sulphur-colored flowers: three plants, insignificant enough of the same family as thoroughwort and stately joe-pye: milk wort, purpling certain glades: a small marsh-plant with a compact head of purple tinged scales, of which it seems no one knows the name: black-eyed Susan: wild lettuce: self-heal: the first ironweed turkey-peak: a few brightening tips of goldenrod: passion-flower.

Hills deep-blue: tinted clouds hang motionless over the motionless treetops. We rest by the way, in a cool hollow, in a couch of ferns and mosses "quite over-canopied" with alders dark as the tents of Kedar, through which the past makes a green vista. Is there a pleached alley in existence that would compare with this place?

August 1, 1908

The children bring in whatever of curious or beautiful life their hands can hold: and these clear hot days and delicious nights bring a-plenty. Monstrous green frogs and warted toads: terrapins quaintly freaked, no larger than a coin: lizards like the finest jeweller's work, done colored lustres of unknown metals: woodland insects, fantastic creatures of the green shadow: elfin snails and armored beetles: owl & woodpecker feathers: malevolent black-eyed snappers: shells chipped and cast out from the nest:—all things fragile, exquisite, or odd,—of phantasmal beauty: or the curious horror which is to natural creatures a sort of wild-flavored delight. This morning it is a gorgeous moth of a kind I have not seen before: slow, heavy, silent, downy thing, whose color might serve as a model for decorators. He is not perhaps quite so heavy-bodied as the Luna: his feathery antennae are narrower and he has not such flimsy spread of wing. His body is freaked and mottled with orange and cream: the ground color of his wings, above, is olive, with veined stripes of the same deep orange, and roundish shots of cream in two rows. Beneath, they match his body; and his muffled legs are orange: He hangs on the wall apparently asleep, a glowing spot rich as a painted leaf of autumn.

August 23, 1908

Here is a portrait:

A man of three or four prime instincts, and incapable of erring from these as is an animal or tree: to whom, in consequence, an honest, life long love is as inevitable as a large appetite at meals. A man whose mental processes are simple and direct: though chance had given him education he would still be unused to intellectual subtleties or to intricate moral balancing. He never speaks when he has nothing to say: and his words are sincere: the most cultivated mind may find real pleasure and profit in looking through his eyes. He takes a wholesome pleasure in his daily relations with employer, neighbor, and fellow-workman: he is fond of his parents, his wife, and his children: he has pleasure in his wages on pay-day, and likes to rest on Sunday as well as he likes to work through the week. He is capable of anger and quick blows, but, not being particularly afraid of anything or anybody, is not given to fighting. Coercion is apt to encounter in him, quite unexpectedly, a stubborn and unreasoning power of resistance, the more surprising by contrast with his usual easy goodnatured carelessness. He has probably never been more than twenty miles from his birthplace, the roving instinct having been overweighted from boyhood with home duties voluntarily taken and faithfully kept.

This type occurs not infrequently among the mountain people: while not often found in perfect development, still there is a strong tendency toward it. Add but the breadth of education to the inheritor of three generations of such men, and you get an Abraham Lincoln,—if only the latest of the line be a mother! . . . It is good to be mother to such a man, or brother, neighbor, son, employer, servant, wife, or friend. He brings one near to the heart of things as God set it beating.

September 2, 1908

Laura's baby died.[2]

For a day it seemed better: the unmistakable intelligence of sight was in its sunken eyes. But now, in the gray dawn, the deathlike whiteness returned, and the cheeks and throat were again horribly drawn and hollowed. A face older than extreme age could make it. The eyes became set with the look of death. . . . . At breakfast we were startled by a noise of wailing, high-pitched and long-drawn, and knew that death was upon the house: I ran, and found the mother sobbing, leaning against the back corner of her kitchen, outside. That tiny creature on the bed was drawing the slow stertorous breath of the dying: the eyes under lowered lids were set and dull: the chalk-white, ghastly-thin hands were growing cold. There was no longer any hope.

Slower and slower came the rattling breath. The grandmother and a neighbor hung over it, with the passionate pity of womanhood in their faces: but the mother could not bear to look toward the bed. Two hours later it was dead.

Two neighbor women were already with the mother. The father spent most of the day sitting behind the house, speaking to no one.

Almost as if by magic the house leapt into order, by the women's busy hands; but the business of the men's day came to a stand-still that messengers might be sent, one to notify distant-dwelling kin, another to buy the coffin in Chattanooga, a third to arrange with the strong young men of the family connection to help dig the grave. All the white phlox blooming in the yard was gathered and laid round the tiny corpse: the wee face was covered with a wet cloth, then a sheet laid smoothly over the whole mound. The mother, having put on a black dress, could only wail, numb and stony-faced now, in the back room.

Flowers were sent from neighboring yards, red & yellow & purple for the most part: a big bunch of crape-myrtle, a few white asters. Women came and went, and girls with wondering faces. The expression of elders is one of mournful acquiescence,—We understand: this is as it should be, and common to all. But the young faces are touched with awe and questioning—what is this, what does it mean. . . . .? Young girls run away to seek ferns in the low woods; they find relief in making a wreath of ferns and asters.

One woman drapes a sheet over the looking glass, lest some one glimpse the dead reflected there and become "the next to die." As the day wears on, another stops the clock.

After dinner hour, the kin begin to arrive, some talkative and excited; some grave and hushed, others weeping. The greetings are spoken in low tones. The mother speaks to all, a word or two, from a kind of remoteness, her hands folded over a cheap handkerchief in her black sateen lap. She is rapt in the mystery of pain: she rouses only to give needed directions now and again, when inquiries are made as to the whereabouts of this or that.

Old Grandma, versed in tradition, orders everything in accordance. "Frank 'n' Emmer ortin to move today: if they do somepin bad 'll happen to 'em, now you'll see," she says, and Frank and Emmer hasten to assure her that they have no intention of moving.

In the afternoon the coffin is brought by two men in a wagon. A sheet is borrowed to drape the rude little table, and on this the little body lies in state. Visitors speak admiringly of the silver coffin-trimmings, the "natural" appearance of the corpse, the clean ironed slip, the mound of bloom. The day drags its length: "Have they sent Alford's folks word? Does Larnce and his wife know yit? [Lawrence and Mary Freudenberg Miles. Lawrence, referred to here as "Larnce," was Frank's brother] Is Mary a-cryin'?" [Frank's sister, Mary Miles Vandergriff.]

"Said she'd be here to set up."

"Why, she ain't able."

"She done a big washin' this morning—and she'll hafto carry that big baby down here, too."

Nevertheless Mary came. After supper men and boys with lanterns arrived, ready to sit up after their day's work. In the house were only women and children: for death and birth are matters on which men cannot bear to look. The watchers appear to be neither young nor old in the lamp-shine: they sit silent and grave, their shadows motionless on the bare wall. Neighbor women, their hands still damp from washing the supper dishes, come in to proffer condolence and conveniences. From early candle-lighting till near the turn of the night, the house is full.

Then one after another leaves the indoor circle, and friends try to persuade the mother to take an hour's rest.

"Hit's the last night I'll ever be with the pore little thing," she answers, "I'd rather set up." Reminded that the three living children have need of her she still demurs, "Oh, I've lost so many nights' sleep now that I've got used to it: one more won't hurt me." And sister Mary, who is certainly tired to exhaustion, also refuses to lie down.

But out on the porch one lad after another stretches himself on the boards, and taking his elbow or a feed-sack for pillow, listens to the crickets and katydids and the murmur of talk a while and falls asleep. Two or three men remain smoking on the steps, and talk in the desultory fashion of mountaineers.

The night wears on: the lamp burns strongly, the air is thick with sadness, drowsiness. . . .

The midnight supper is welcome to all—biscuits & stewed potatoes, fried pork, a can or two of fish from the store, and many cups of strong coffee. Later they sing a wake of hymns. . . .

At last the gray dawn glimmers against the smoky lamplight: the watch is over. . . . . .

Two, faithful and weary, drag themselves across the kitchen floor and begin to get breakfast.

Coming and going increases with the rising day. A sister-in-law brings a hastily-ruffled cap for the dead baby: a cousin is sent to borrow a black veil & belt for the mother. Men stand and lounge among the shackly, dingy rigs in the horselot. It looks much like any other gathering, but one misses the shouts of hail and farewell.

Imperceptibly the stir increases; at length about eight or nine o'clock the gathering is ready, and after much consultation and argument as to who rides where, the coffin is placed in the most respectably looking of the buck boards; the mother, black-draped, comes out of the house, wailing and crying now, and takes her place: the others climb into wagon and cart; the family almost crowded out, as usual, by the loafer contingent eager for the ride: and I see the sad little procession go, each driver careful not to break the line lest he be next to die, on the Fairmont road—to where those four little graves lie in a row. . . . . .

" . . . and looked like all the time, in their little half-open eyes, she was wantin' me . . ."

September 8, 1908

A perfect evening, for the young folks' party—cloud-roses blooming slowly in the late light over the hills: a sudden shower just after sunset.

The house was cleared, like a deck for action, of all furniture that could not be sat upon, and these chairs, boxes, and bench were arranged along the wall out of the way. They were more than sufficient; for the young folks did not come to sit, but to play. A little after dark they come,—first, big dark George [George Levi, a neighbor], whom no one would suspect of a real passion for frolics: then Dock [Arthur "Dock" Miles, Frank's brother], the banjo player: Rose [possibly Rose Anne Hatfield, sister of Frank Miles' brother-in-law, "Ab" Hatfield] in a white dress, curls, and string of beads, petite, fair, and smiling—a little peach: a half-dozen lads, cousins, from a family 'colony' on another road: the demure young schoolmistress, with two boys from the valley: the Catlows;[3] then George's brother and sister. There being already three girls in the house, this number was voted a quorum, and a ring presently formed. The banjo had been ringing for some time, and Barney [son of Lawrence "Larnce" Miles] presently passed another through the door; but still there was a hitch and a shuffle lasting five or ten minutes before "Jolly is the Miller" was started, no two voices on the same key. Round they circled, two and two with arms, prettily linked, so as to turn at "turns right back" without loosing hands; the banjo is not needed for this play.

Another hitch, then another game. Then "London Bridge"—"Shoot the Buffalo, Fire on the Mountain, Stealing Partners," which is really a dance, and went most merrily to the tune of "Greenbacks" on Dock's banjo, glided imperceptibly into a reel: and Ada, discovering her error, too late, sulked and pouted thro' all the rest of the party.

The little ones, who had been allowed to sit up, now began to nod and had to be put to bed. The usual contingent of bad little boys arrived and began to shout at the players. The fun waxed furious; the figures wheeled and swung and eddied: coats were flung off, feet stamped heavily. Rose and Mary and the schoolteacher went through the measure like ladies, Lassie like a hoyden,[4] Tressie like a kitten with a ball, Walter like a half-grown Newfoundland, and little Floyd like a pup with an old shoe: but whose head just cleared the rafters, but big George danced like a mountaineer— dancing all over, with solemn intense enjoyment, swinging his shoulders and elbows no less than his feet. Ethel would not dance, preferring to sit and look on, refusing one lad after another: but she presently became interested in the banjos, and Dock, although he had left a wife and first baby at home, was like to forget his duty to the dances in teaching her to play. Hand-clapping and stamping increased as the whirling grew more rapid: calls were shouted, laughter was continuous. Poor Barney had come in his working clothes, splashed with plaster: but he finally edged in, irresistibly drawn, and Mrs. Catlow took pity on him. "Will you be my partner?" he asks, leaning forward, hands on knees; and they join the rest laughing,—gray woman and half-grown boys.

At 10:30 a basket full of large ripe apples was brought in, and eaten during an intermission of about ten minutes. Then the Virginia reel—disguised as a game to save the scruples of the church!—was begun. Faster and faster rang the banjos; wilder romping, madder fun!—and the merriment ended at last with a shout as Cahill laid his hand across the strings!

Then farewells, and the melting away by two and two into the moonlight. But first all are bidden by the general invitation customary here, to a similar party Thursday night at a neighbor's. For at this time of plenty & fine weather, the dance, picnic and box supper are abroad in the land, and continue until the preacher starts a "big meetin'" and shames them all into remorse for their harmless fun.

September 29, 1908

Last night, the first frost. Yesterday morning it was raining when we woke, but the temperature fell as the sky cleared. The air is cleared and sweetened by this cold touch: the sky intensely blue, the hill shadows nearly as luminous. Golden rod a little past prime; the gold & blue of Sept.—inclines toward the purple and scarlet of October. Greens, reflected in the pond, russet and olive toned.

Saw at sunrise a magnificent head of goldenrod standing alone in a single shaft of sun, swaying slowly and trembling like a flame against the deep morning shadow in the forest, over the cool meadow grass. I never saw a more emphatic exclamation of light and color.

Occasional banners of crimson in the maples; purple-dark boughs in sweet-gums. A white storm of asters by the garden fence.

George caught a hog snake in the field and carried it up by the tail. It proved a terrific bluffer, snapping right and left with almost toothless jaws, swelling and flattening in vicious-looking imitation of a deadly snake, and finally rolling on its back and playing possum with amazing accuracy & persistence.

October 13, 1908

After the thicket, the woods behind the field behind the field open out and into calm and lofty spaces, hung now with gorgeous tapestries. Between the trees the purple distance glows. Here the man took me walking in the pleasant autumn afternoon carrying the little maid, and delaying his feel for mine. We sat with our backs against the big tree and looked at the dazzling color: sour woods split open with rich cordials: maples a rosy flame; hickories done in old brass; crimson and scarlet of tupelos; the waxen lustre and perfect modeling of single catbrier leaves & background of olive and umber and amber and russet made by the whiteoaks. Flowers are few: goldenrod faded except for a small imperfect head here and there: asters less each day: once in a while a little gardenia blossom close to the ground. This is the time of the turtle heads and closed gentian by the mill-creeks, and ripe spice bush and arrow-wood berries.

Many birds in migration: such as stay the winter seem mildly happy—notably the redbirds who sing like April.

This month spreads scarlet like a woman and heaps her gold on the purple banks.

October 21, 1908

Writers of fiction ought to know that each species of hard wood tree has its own peculiar individual color in autumn, and its own time for turning. The idea of the frost turning the leaves is a popular fallacy, more idle than most such. Now this year there has been no frost yet except a feather-touch around the pond on two nights; yet the forest is painted with all the ochres and cadmiums and lakes in creation. My own idea is that the trees know when it is time to withdraw through the leaf-stem all those juices of living matter and of nutriment which the leaves have held through the spring and summer; and that this process of storing precious substances in the trunk and root for winter entails a change in the pigment of the shriveling leaf-cells. Possibly the chemical action of the different colored rays of light have something to do with it.

If a little real attention were given to this subject we should read less of "scarlet beeches" and "crimson hickories" in the October woods, or "an oak bough here and there in gaudy colors while the rest of the forest remains" green.

These are the principal trees of our woods, and their colors in shedding:

White oak: Scarcely yellowing at all: turns quietly from green to russet & raw sienna. Most hang on branches until pushed off by the swelling of new buds in spring.

Red oak: Deep crimson, without a trace of yellow: one shade from top to bottom. The last tree of our woods to turn: a rich dark red.

Black & post oak: Indian red & burned sienna, shading to maroon as it falls. The carpet under these trees is purple-streaked with frost & morning shadows.

Sour wood: First to turn entirely, in a wine red, almost one color all over: in August.

Black gum (tupelo): Upper leaves reflect sky. Most intense note of color. Glossy, varnished leaves, rich crimson & scarlet; a little orange in the lower boughs. This tree has an odd habit of hanging out an occasional red banner now and then in the summer for now apparent reason. Each separate leaf has the gloss, the richness, & the bloom of a wild goose plum, ripe or ripening.

Tulip tree (poplar)— Yellow, rather duller than that of the hickory, and turning patchily- some brown, some yellow, others still green. Soon bare.

Maple— Yellow, orange, flame, scarlet, deep crimson: maples in shaded hollows turn yellow, those exposed to the sun go to reds. Most writers call this tree the queen of the woods: I should rather give this name to—

Sweet Gum, which turns more different colors than any tree of the woods, crazy-quilt of colors; all that the maple has, with the addition of a glossy dark plum-color like the plumage of certain birds, produced by the blending of red with the green: this color clarifies into dark red as the season progresses.

Chestnut, patchy yellow, soon turning brown & falling.

Beech, yellow, turning coppery brown, remaining thick on lower boughs.

Hickory, sunshine-colored—the most perfect mass of pure yellow in creation; one shade all over.

Sassafras, no reflections, salmon—from yellow to deep orange. Old leaves turn early; younger, on upper boughs, still green.

Sumach [sic], deep red—one color mostly: turns fairly early. Underleaves glow scarlet, upper reflect sky—purple.

Some of the wild lianas are also gorgeous, notably the Virginia Creeper, which novelists call wood bine (not the true wood bine), whose leaves become rich scarlet; and the catbrier (alias horsebrier, greenbrier, bamboo, or saw brier) which bears perhaps the richest single leaf in the woods. It is modeled on lines of perfect grace, thick and waxy, and gorgeously painted in yellows and scarlet mingled with green.

October 28, 1908

There are but two classes of people in the mountains: those who are in constant dread of being caught by the nip of winter without cornmeal or meat; and those who are not. The former are likely to be in the habit of frantically chopping wood as the snow begins to fly: the latter spend the snowy weather in mending harness and half-soling the children's shoes.

November 13, 1908

Thin piercing sleet in the early morning, turning into a fine steady snow under the even-gray sky. On the brown leaves, dry as paper, it whispers, whispers: through the clinging white oaks it is loudest. One draws breath as at the end of a pageant: for this is winter, "nunc plaudit" [Latin, "now applaud"] the glory of the year! On coming into the house one instinctively seizes the poker and draws out beds of rosy embers, and shells rattling coals from off the half-burned sticks like kernels off a cob.

No stranger knows the beauty of these cabin hearth-fires which at the first touch of frost leap up exultantly,—the unfailing charm of their glow and motion and low cheery music. A northerner would start back as from a real conflagration. The mountaineer's ideal of home comfort is that of the Indian Esquimaux: let furs and violent exercise warm a man out of doors, but in the house at home he wants to sit comfortably in shirtsleeves, toasting one side at a time, eating, singing, jesting, carousing, with open doors that mock the storm. He delights in the gorgeous crimson of firelight, the soft roar of burning, the laughing sparkle, the flicker and blue flutter, the quick fusillade of hickories, the "treading snow" of brands half consumed, the clink of the falling ash at sleeping-time. He is extravagant in the matter of logs: his fire grows in glory, fed with heavy oak and fat knots and roots of old pine,—flowing over stones mossed with suit, split by projections, licking the full kettles, whirled against the soot-mossed back of the fireplace, displaying rainbows of strange color, and pouring finally into the black throat of the chimney as a waterfall disappears into a sunless gorge.

They are all romance, these luxuries of the mountaineer,—music, whiskey, firelight, religion, and fighting: they are efforts to reach a finer, larger life,—part of the blue dream of the wild land. Who knows him? Who has ever understood the devious approaches of his mind to any subject? Who has tracked him to that wild, remote spot, echo-haunted, beautiful, terrible, wherein he dwells? Who has measured the rock foundation of his home, or tasted the water of his unknown well-springs of desire?

November 15, 1908

Clear, and so still that the day seems not cold, although the pond was skimmed over with ice in the shadows, the snow lies "waiting for more." A long, silent mountain Sunday, peaceful beyond description.

Once in a while we have a visitor on this hill top. The preacher spent the day with us not long ago. Apropos of the heavy mast he told a story:

"I bought me some o' them fool town hogs, been corn-fed, and didn't know a acorn when they seed hit. Well, I 'lowed to learn 'em better. So I called 'em out under a big white oak that was hanging full, and scattered shell corn all over about thirty feet thar. They commenced a-pickin hit up, and I clumb the tree and commenced to knock acorns with a stick. The surveyor he come ridin' by on a mule direckly, and he holled, 'Why, Brother Lou! What air you a-doin' up in that tree?' And I told him, 'Why,' I says, 'I'm a-learnin' these here hogs from whence the blessin' cometh.' I says: 'I'm a learnin' em to look up.'

A keenly sweet, peaceful evening; the silence of the mountains in winter: clear pale sunset behind the spiritualized winter woods: fresh breath from off the last gleaming tatters of snow. Only cowbells, or a far call, faint and musical, in the vast outer hush: within, the laughter of children, the comforting whisper of fire. Trees naked now, except those which retain many of their leaves through the winter: drawn in sepia against the sky with the vigor and delicacy of an etching: vine leaves whisper against the chimney.

November 19, 1908

Woods afire down Suck Creek: trees drawn in dusky blue on a dun sky. Clear and warm, sunshine struggles faintly through the smoke. Hear a bee-like drone of talking to the accompaniment of cowbells: two riders pass; dim in the haze,—an old man in a faded, flapping hat and cape, bent, humped; forward thrust of head accented by beakish nose and bushy gray beard: His son beside, taller and darker: they are driving a bunch of spotted yearlings- shaggy hides clustered with the valley's roadside burrs. "Law, they'll keep on a-bringin' up stock as long as they's a bunch o' grass or a acorn on the mount'n," says old Lucy. [Possibly Lucy Miles Levi, an aunt of Frank's.]

Low fire flickers in the great chimney; doors wide open, letting in—the silent day. Red bird sings from time to time, and this is the only sound.

Sun sets in a strange blaze of cottony clouds behind the naked trees.

November 27, 1908

A brilliant winter dawn outlines Chilhowee, low behind the naked forest: long-spun clouds drawn taut across it turn to threads of fire. The day is fine, but too sharply clear; surfaces glitter, with neither frost nor rain. It will be cold, say the mountaineers.

Toward sunset a curdled film of tiny mackerel clouds and finely shredded cirri spread from east to west, blowing over like a tissue thrown in dreams, widening miraculously to entangle the world. Over the brown woodlot, over the gray forest, and the toneless fields rough with kecksies and stubble [weeds], a tender shadow steals.

Night brings with it an apparition of spectral beauty,—an emerald crescent in a bright veil: the moon is "wadin' water."

November 29, 1908

The locality has three special characteristics which distinguish it from other lands, features which taken together, are perhaps not to be duplicated in all the world. They are silence, blue air, and an endless variety. The woods are approaching the minimum of interest now: one sees nothing at first glance but low rolling hills, hollows that scoop no color, horizons like an old-fashioned pencil sketch, painstakingly and delicately detailed, foregrounds gray and dun, thick-strewn with faded leaves, and underbrush shrill-whispering in the winds that pass. But here broods a vast wild mystery of silence. The whole place—a table-land, an area, just here, many miles in extent, a mountain-top big as a county—is elevated above the lower strata of air, lifted quite out of the seething, busy valley, safe and still as an enchanted isle. The rest of the world fades to a dream; its sounds reach you echo-thin and sweet, its lights are a necklace of jewels on the dusky velvet bosom of the hills—all fairy-like unreal and dim.

And here in the loneliness one passes from surprise to surprise. Now it is a half-glimpsed unrecognized creature, a stranger in migratory flight, or fleet and shadowy, richly clothed in fur: now a flash of summer color and charm lingering in the lap of a rock: again a pocket of some rare fern, or a wild fruit shriveled and sugared by frost; or a bluff rising or dropping sheer from your feet, or a creek "breaks" abrupt through the bare winter hillsides embowered in more greens than you had supposed in existence: or most wonderful of all, a change in the dream, an aerial miracle of shifting light and atmosphere, swift and astonishing, a mighty transformation scene.

With the passage of a few months and the return of the sun, the marvel is multiplied by freakish growth. It is part of the variety of the region that the fauna and flora are unevenly distributed. You chance on a red lily in a thicket one day, a cup of delight with crimson petals finely recurved, a vision of splendid sin; you may seek for years before finding a similar group. You encounter a number of orchids under the dark hemlocks—there may not be another colony of the same plant within ten miles. Jasmine, which grows in the creeks of Lookout, our sister mountain, is unknown here; one of their commonest ferns is not found here at all: Sabbatia is never found in the valley, liverleaf never reaches the top: there is a patch of spring beauty at the Sivley gap, dogtooth violets in profusion at the falls of the Foust Mill Creek, and a handsome yellow trillium at Edwards Point—nowhere else: the walking fern is apparently imprisoned in North Chickamauga Gulch, and bloodroot keeps to the "Fur Top" and Sequatchie.[5] Along the valley streams "the touch-me-nots hang fairy folly caps;" and so without end. Birds also, a few at a time. I suppose if one were to watch long enough during migration, almost any variety native to the eastern half of North America might be catalogued as "found here," although, as we are betwixt the great feeding grounds, our habitant species are comparatively few.

December 13, 1908

Sunset lights of amethyst and emerald as on an enchanted shore, on the desolate heights above the woods. Shadows, as concealing caves. A

haze of legend and of poetry lies over their rigid outlines; they appear
more & more uncertain in the fading twilight. As the world rolls down into
shadow a horn is wound faint and clear, somewhere in the hollow of the
hills: its last note's dying echoes fall & waken images of things long gone,
lives lost in the gloom of time—of Cherokee myths and they yet more
ancient, "little" peoples—remote and vanished.

December 19, 1908

After a clear afternoon, just bracingly cold, the scale-tips of cloud
were brushed with flame over half the sky, sending back a refulgence
over the already shadowed land. It was spectacular, fantastic—one might
almost say sensational.

Today is the Saturday before Xmas—in a Southern town a phenomenon
picturesque, unique, like the old-fashioned Kentucky fair. The streets are
now thronged with country people and mountaineers as on no other day in
the year. Many who scarcely quit their own neighborhood the year round
come now to see the holiday display, having ruthlessly spoiled the home
creek of its glory of green, uprooted whole areas of "pinies," and wounded
or slain the noblest hollies, in order to take home a Christmas jug. One
sees now, on the streets, the wildest types of the region,—lean young
hawks, profiles like those of the eastward bluff, girls with the woodland
gaze of chamois, children like lemurs & lorises clinging on the top of a
load and staring at the shops: strange wild-beast or Indian glances meet
yours from the depths of quaint calico sunbonnets, and 'possum eyes fix
you from a bush of gray furry beard and eyebrows and hair: warlock faces,
& Rip Van Winkles awakened. Last year at this time I took the twins to
town, mountaineer fashion, in the back of a road wagon. On Stringer's
Ridge we passed two old women wearing aprons and rough square
breakfast shawls over old fashioned calico frocks, and each with a bandana
handkerchief tied under her chin and almost concealed by her long-caped,
deep hooded bonnet. One wore square-rimmed brass spectacles, and
carried a napkin-covered basket on her arm: the other swung a covered
tin bucket. Butter and hominy. The old faces, gnarled and shriveled as
a limber twig apple, seemed like an old Cherokee's, were alight with
anticipation. The raw fog and the frost had made their cheeks rosy; they
were talking in the sweet monotone of the mountains. Judith [Miles's

daughter] looked up with a smile, as if she had espied some one she loved: "Grandmothers, ain't they?"

That is a notable type which a child of five has learned to recognize with affection!

December 25, 1908

A glorious day, not springlike, nor like anything else but a Southern Christmas. Boys out hunting in the sodden woods, the gray and dulled copper woods—Children at play in the sun all day long, riotous with the Xmas toys. The wind is like a dancing faun, rough, but living—almost warm. Masses of cloud fly over, trailing their violet-tinted shadows.

Wind blows stronger and colder toward night; clouds spread and thicken, covering the sky.

December 26, 1908

Last night the wind was as strong and wild as it is likely ever to be here. A "little skift o' hominy snow" fell, and was blown into crevices and hollows.[6] There was one long smooth cloud across the sunrise like a mountain; the sun soon climbed it, and thenceforth the day was clear, and sharply cold. Clear silent evening: a glittering scimitar & blue-white diamond points swing in a steely sky. Last night was fearsomely noisy: tonight we hear only the putter of low flames.

January 20, 1909

Two days of clear sunshine, warm and hazy like spring. Lizards out in the sunny side of rocks and fences: I saw one on the doorstone—a dark brown fellow with a zigzag line of white down his backbone. Honey bees astir.

January 30, 1909

And colder. Kitchen full of tchink-tchinks of freezing levels smoking with sifted snow, little drifts to leeward of every projection, and smooth places swept bare. The wind is a threat, menace, a curse, a whistling scourge, a malison [curse] of terrible hatred; a visious [*sic*] weapon searching the vitals, a shriek of spite over the guardian chimney, a monster grip that rattles the windows and the doors.

Where now are the birds, and the small furry wild creatures? Oh, where the children I saw last week, pinning their rags together, tying their shoes on with strings? At this time last year, in a plank shack on the Side, a woman's feet were frozen while she was sick in bed. The misery, the misery of such time!

Toward noon the sun looks out from a pallid sky; everything appears bleached. The pond remains frozen. The cold grows more intense and cruel with the passing of the hours, falling from 12° at daybreak to 9° and then lower. Men and creatures alike think not of work, enjoyment, nor even comfort, nor cleanliness—they strive only to live through, to hang on— sitting humped and sullen by the hearth, or shivering and shrinking about the tasks of feeding and getting wood and water which may not be shirked. They say there has not been such a cold spell since that of '95—thirteen years ago.

February 1, 1909

Cold and still, crystal-clear—night-sky cold and bright as an unwinking diamond, slowly yielding to dawn. Sun leaps Chilhowee, bright as at noon, blinding, stabbing the cold with long rays.

On the breaks of Middle Creek near the headwaters, where we see it yonder by Freudenberg's farm, is an odd shaped rock, like the head and shoulders of a sphinx. The morning light causes it to stand out in bold relief against the dark soft gray of the woods, and the long blue shadow lies to one side along the hill. A strange, big rock strangely upreared from the low wall of the breaks: I want to go and look at it more closely, sometime.

The afternoon is really pleasant, indoors and out. There is an unwanted amount of visiting and going to and fro, prompted largely by an instinct like the mechanical recoil of a bent spring, but partly by a real sympathetic interest in hearing how the other fellow got through the cold spell—whether he had feed for his stock, and whether his wife's canned fruit burst in freezing. Some come here, two with the same trouble—Out of wood, for my sake will the man haul some at once? Others to borrow meat or whatever. An old man, a battered and blanched relic of many such winters, with a shrunken face and mild eyes half hid by brushy white hair, eyebrows, and tobacco-stained beard, clad in garments which seem to have grown with him a part of the weather and the woods, happens along about dinner time, having walked all the way from the Foot. Invariably fall short of the mountain code of hospitality on such occasions, not thro' intent, but simply, I confess, thro' lack of breeding in the particular regard. But he remains for an hour after dinner by the fire, talking with the man about horse swaps and the interminable vexed genealogies which are a delight of the mountaineers. Afterwards he takes his way down the gulch to visit an opossum-like kinsman who is said to live in a tree there.

February 7, 1909

Since the man killed hogs I notice we have a good deal of company.[7] Today came, with his wife, a man who has during his life assisted at the making of many a run of moonshine whiskey, and, after reforming, in many a revenuer's raid. He described to me the apparatus and process of making in details as follows:

The still proper is a copper vessel almost round, with a capacity of from 100 to 300 gallons. It is set on four stone pillars, and the whole enclosed, nearly to the top; by a rude stone furnace. This is built sloping inward, but nowhere touching the still, so that the heat may pass freely all around. A door for firing is left open in front, and a flue built up at the back, something like a peach-kiln.

The worm, also of copper, connects with the close-fitting round cap of the still. It is coiled inside a barrel—about a 40 gal. barrel—the lower end protruding about 4 inches from the bottom. All this must be located in a place not only as secret as possible, but handy to a good spring. Chestnut wood, which makes next to no smoke, is preferred for stoking. Several deep "mash tubs," a funnel, barrels and jugs to contain the product, and troughs to run into and out of the still, complete the outfit.

To make whiskey, soak corn in water till it sprouts: dry it, and have it ground into meal at the mill. Soak ordinary meal in tubs about 6 days, then stir into each tub a double handful of the malt: let stand for three days more, or until it sours, making "beer." Fill the still with this, and plaster closely round the lid and joining of the worm with [illegible] reinforce the latter with rag wrappings. This is to prevent the least entrance of air, which could cause the boiling brew to "puke" and ruin the entire output. Fire up: in about an hour the "singlin's" begin to run off, and three still-fuls may be made in a day.

This process is known as "making a run," and is kept up till enough singlin's are run to fill the still. The beer, after each run, is emptied through a pipe and faucet in the bottom of the still, carried down the hill by a series of small troughs, and thriftily collected in a larger trough in a pen where pigs are fattening on the waste.

The singlin's are now ready to be run through the worm again, and filtered, through a funnel full of charcoal, into a large barrel—say 25 gallons. The first liquid that comes through, during this second run, merely drips, and, being pure grain alcohol, is poured back into the still. It is called "first-shots" or "backin's." After it the whiskey begins to come in a thin stream. From 15 to 25 gallons are made at a run.

Apple brandy is made by grinding the apples in a mill—"a big cask concern with [illegible] and knives inside" and a lever pulled round and round by a horse, as in a sorghum-crusher. Pomace and juice together are turned into to mash tubs and left to stand till sour, then poured into the still and treated the same as beer.[8]

Sometimes the liquor is retailed by this trick and that among the country people: sometimes it is carried to town and smuggled to the liquor dealers there, who are glad to pay $2 or $2.50 per gallon for it. Thus the distiller clears a handsome profit, and the dealer, having no tax to pay on it, makes even more. He usually adulterates it to double the quantity.

Methods of transportation vary. Sometimes a man loads a pair of jugs or small kegs one in each end of a feed-bag on a jack or a mule, and takes an infrequented bridle-trail. Sometimes barrels are concealed under a wagon load or a boat-load of country produce. I learned with surprise that a man now living near the Fur Top is believed to be running a wild cat still.

"He's always got money, though, he never works out from home. And my brother seed 30 bushel more or less of apples in his barn this fall; he took away jist one load and sold hit, and when he went back nex' day or two they was gone—and they hadn't sold 'em neither. Now them apples must've been made into something!"

February 10, 1909

Cleared in the night after twelve hours of steady rain, thickened into fog toward evening. Bright, colorless, and cold: a whooping wind that smites the hilltops.

The man has been telling me of old wild days,—of campfires and killings. Of a camp under the creek hemlocks, out of the storm's strength, made by his brother & an old hunter—just two blanket rolls & a fire that reached thin fingers toward the stars and sent up flying sparks among the pendent, cone-belled boughs. How the younger man, a novice in the real woods, was kept awake half the night, unable to sleep for the pitch of the ground: "if he laid down above the fire he'd roll into it, and if he laid below, he'd slide off into the cold."

He told of the old time deer-hunts. "The old man had a rifle he'd take down every time he'd hear the dogs running, and he'd go up the hill to where there was a 'stand.' Sometimes there'd be four or five come through, one after another. Venison wasn't no rarity them days."

Of old-fashioned hog killings, when each man laid in his winter's supply of pork. "The boys'd haul up a load o' green wood the first thing of a morning, 'bout the first hard freeze o' the year, and pile 'em up like a log-heap, layin' stones in as they built it. Then again breakfast was over, the hogs killed & water drawed, the stones would be getting' hot. They'd have a platform made ready, to handle the hogs on, and have a barrel of water set slantin', with the open end handy to the platform. Then they'd put in them hot rocks, and take 'em out as they cooled. Five or six would bring the water mighty near to boilin'."

"They'd scald the hogs and scrape 'em, and hang 'em on a pole, between the apple-trees, like enough. Then in the afternoon they'd cut 'em up, send spare ribs and backbones to some o' the neighbors, give the young ones the tails to roast and the bladders to blow up, dry, and paint with poke-berry juice or something, and turn the chit'lin's over to the women to render into lard. They'd bile the heads—as many as eight or ten if they killed that many—in the big wash-pot out-doors, and make 'em up into sauce; then they'd make liverwurst, and try out the fat and make fatty-bread" (shortenin' bread) "of the cracklin's; they'd have a big mess o' brains; they'd pickle the tongues, and maybe the feet. They'd grind sausage, and put 'em away in clean corn husks and tie 'em tight. After the hams and shoulders and sides had layed [*sic*] in salt long enough they'd hang them to smoke; and oh yes, they'd cook the jowls with turnips or greens, or else bake 'em. And whatever scraps was left went into the soap-grease kag."

I wonder if the great packing-houses have got it down any finer than that!

He added: "When a man stole a hog, or killed one wild, some wheres down in a creek, he'd scald it right there, in a hole in the ground. A hog's so much easier to work with before it gits cold."

February 14, 1909

To Signal Point in the wagon.[9]

At the Point the wind is caught as in a bellows by the funnel of the river gorge. One has to shout against its voice in the pines. We take shelter in the lee of a hillock, and hear its sea-like roar above, below, and all around. The children, entirely unabashed by so much grandeur, make playhouses on the altar-like stones the soldiers piled here during the war, or watch the maneuvers of the many blizzards and chicken-hawks that sail out from these bluffs, where they live, across the river in the teeth of the wind.

The Tennessee is swollen and muddy; the jade-colored, foam-laced water of Middle and Suck Creeks make a sharp line at confluence. The steamer Patten, toy-like diminute in distance, whistles by the tree-fringed island: she is returning from the Gov't lock and dam at the Suck below.[10]

Through the blue dusk of Raccoon's afternoon shadow the bare treetops round so softly,[11] like the hair of young babes. The little river-bank farms, thick-sown with forbidding rocks and huge boulders, are now being plowed on dry days. From then the forest sweeps upward unbroken to the towering palisades at the mountain-top that face each other tier above tier, under black brows of pines, sternly as colossi.

March 5, 1909

Brush-burning, manure-spreading, plowing for field and garden. The ground is in excellent condition, dried out at last by wind and sun: the weather cloudy and still, chill but not cold. Frogs begin to ripple towards evening.

There are two or three houses on the mountain built by northern country people after the northern country style, which makes next to no provision for the army of toddlers planned for the native cabin-raiser, but invariably includes a closed parlor, which is used only in courtship or on state occasions. How well I remember those silent, stately northern houses set in the midst of wealthy farms—the porchless walls, blank and grim as a castle; the silent, draughty hall through the middle—first door to right opening into the carefully darkened parlor, first to left, opposite, into the spare bedroom with its enormous feather-bed and black mantel set with vases. Oh, what chill dignity as one contrasts it with the happy double cabins, half porch, that overflow with children into these woods!

Tonight a neighbor has dropped in to consult the man about the obnoxious new cattle laws, and they have run on into ways & means of breaking cows that suck themselves, thence to stump-sucking horses & trading. A story of how One-Eyed George once swapped with preacher Pryor just before church time: swapped a stump-sucker and got a stump-sucker, giving five dollars to boot. Both men carefully hitched their beasts to swinging limbs throughout the cautious negotiations—"and soon as the money was passed," complained One-Eye in his well-known whine, "I'm blamed if he didn't go right into the church-house and take his text 'Blessed are they that mourn for they shall be comforted' 'n by God, he knowd he'd left one man to mourn!"

March 24, 1909

Eight days of beautiful spring weather, beginning with the 16th—the day the baby was born[12]—and ending today in clouds and thundershowers with falling temperature and rising wind. Orchard buds swell and glisten; the plumtrees are in bloom. Treetoads sing by night a long-trilled, cool nocturne; porch wrens twitter a sunshine-warble for each hour of the day; a mocker greets the morning from the top of the giant gum by the pond. Every old grandmother in the country is hunting through her collection of broken coffee-pots and baking-powder cans on top shelves for garden seeds; hens cackle in log stables; little "weedies" fill the back yard of every cabin: young lambs lie together in sunny fence corners, their heads resting softly & prettily on each others' backs; colts and calves gambol awkwardly on unmanageably long legs, or fold themselves like jackknives into the lee of a stump: even the cat goes with a kitten in her mouth seeking a corner which shall be safe from the children's affectionate persecution. All of these no less than the rosy-blown peachtrees pray for the blessing of sunshine till the danger of frost shall pass.

April 4, 1909

But at last the real spring warmth. This is the first of many days of happy wandering, as I have planned for the summer: for at last we are able to think of pleasure. The woods are burning on the Signal Point road, filling all the country with smoke—a strange red thread of destruction creeping through the dreaming forest growth. Everywhere a tinge of green steals upon the gray winter color. Sunny banks and whole hillsides facing the sun and aflutter with bluish and black-velvet wings of tiny butterflies are starred with bright points of bluets, cinquefoil, and wood violets. There are purple knots of bird-foot violet under the oaks, arbutus along the creeks, yellow violets in low places, spring beauty at the Gap, and a little rose-colored sorrel. Birds everywhere: bluebirds, wood hens, cardinal, wood thrush, phoebe; a wee bird answering the description of the black cap, but smooth instead of downy and a small thrush—either an olive back, probably a hermit or a veery. Hear a whippoorwill this evening.

April 11, 1909

Easter: cold wind blowing, but the ground warms in the sunshine.

The first faint traceries of spring color on the gray fabric of winter are delicate as the forgotten cunning of old-fashioned needlework—orchard spray against the sky, maples in the dark lowlands, starring of houstonia and violets among the moss—brilliant as Oriental silks.

Of the making of a cowbell by a native smith: He'd make ready a thin sheet of iron, cut it into shape, and bend it round on the anvil, seam the sides, and rivet the seam: then he'd fix a kind of staple rivet in the top to hang a clapper to: then put on the bar to run the collar strap through—and then it was ready for brazing.

"He cut the brass into little bits and laid 'em all over the outside of the bell, and then wrapped a wet rag all round it, and packed the whole bell inside and out with clay. Then he fired it a long time in the forge; and when he took it out the brass would be run in a thin coat all over it, and it was ready to put a clapper into and hang on the cow. They put copper on them now, instead of brass, because brass has got to cos'ly. This one's been coppered, see—and the copper's all wore and knocked off. I'll bet it's travelled a man a hunderd miles through these woods—followed the cow into wild places."

April 18, 1909

To Edwards Point.[13] The woods are still in their wintry transparency, but budding and bourgeoning to the wide-flung largesse of the sun. From the rim of Middle Creek's "gulf" one still sees the noble contours of the land, its swell and dip and rise, as of some great cosmic music, sounding grandly like the muscled sides of some giant creature of a Hindoo myth, on whose surface the forest is but so much gray down: Middle Creek's beginnings outside the Fairmount group of houses, dipping and deepening between rugged "breaks" to this spot, where it is crossed by a rude pine bridge. The water slides heavily and darkly under the heavy hemlock shadows, among swart mossed boulders: its song under toning that of the trees, which stand thick and perfect, as yet untouched by the greed of the devouring saws. There are a number of large pines farther up. It is to be hoped the Company will be successful in maintaining its preserve. It ought to be a strict one, and made to include at least the hollies and rhododendrons.

Cabin folk behave as if a passing wagon were an event—Well, it probably is. Far be it from me to grudge them a single moment of staring! I too have lived the gray life of the gray wintery wilderness.

The old Edwards place is an oasis of summer green. Of the loghouse itself nothing remains but the chimney stones, in a pile like a ruined altar. At our approach a blacksnake slides under, like a slow rivulet of oil. The fields are grown up in seedling pines and winter-bleached sedge-grass: but the orchard holds its own, with falling snow of petals and the booming of more bumblebees than ever I saw in one place before.

Under the thickest shade, and in the spot best sheltered from the wind that blows continuously off the valley yonder, is a shapeless shed loosely built of rails, the roof of scrap boards too low for a man to stand under. Inside are potsherds scattered amidst the char of long-extinguished & forgotten fires, and the remains of a bunk of boards. Wash Lusk camped in this while tanbarking: the shelter is joined by a small close where he kept his mules, feeding them from a dugout trough: another of his camps was on the hither side of Middle Creek, lying out in the waste woods, but near a spring: one would consider a hollow tree or the shelter of turned-up roots a better habitation.

Trek on to the Point. None of us had ever been there, and we had received all sorts of answers to our inquiries about the way. The mountaineer's ideas of distance are vague and confused: and we began to think we had lost the way for a logging trail. This feeling of uncertainty, protracted over a mile and a half of difficult going, added somewhat of the charm of discovery to the journey's consummation.

April 30, 1909

Last night a great storm passed a few miles south of here; between gusts we heard its terrific roaring. The play of lightning was almost continuous: a fearful light came and went continually through all the house. This morning the garden is drowned: much of it must be replanted. But the sandstone bulwarks of the mountain are an effectual barricade against such storms: the wind divided strewing considerable wreckage along Sequatchie and blowing several houses down along the foot of the mountain here. Two old people were killed in a cabin on the Side, and the schoolhouse there is a ruin.

The bluff, while it affords the best possible protection against wind, exposes to another danger, that of lightning: especially at the "gaps," where a stream of heated air, rising continually from the valley, forms a "conductor" which purchasers of the coveted brow sites would do well to take into consideration before building.

Once, however, a storm was caught in one of the creeks as in a funnel, and directed over a stretch of forest here which today is still called the "Harricane." For many years the uprooted trees all fallen in the same direction, lay over the ground, their roots, flattened over strata of surface rock, standing in the air. Old people still tell of that time: the grandmother's story is of darkness falling before five o'clock in a terrible sudden storm, and the door blowing in, sending objects whirly, bumping, clattering, round the hut. When the light returned and she could venture out she found the baby, still asleep, rolled in his blanket, in the fireplace, and the young calf curled in the lee of a stump: but her washtubs and fences she never saw again. Rails were seen afterwards by wandering hunters, five miles from any fence.

May 8, 1909

Storms pass and repass along the horizon in the evenings; but none approach—nights of the "Moon of Leaves." Tremendous bellowing resonance rising from the pond, not steadily, but performing at intervals an astonishing crescendo and diminuendo.

The porch is alive with birds: wrens looking for a building site, chippies pecking crumbs, humming-birds in the blossoming woodbine, and those two big brown birds—in color and movement like a thrush, in size and energy resembling a robin, in song like a mocker, familiar as a sparrow—are building a great ragged nest in the thickest tangle of the vines, almost over my head as I lie in the hammock. I was afraid the cat would catch them: she patrols the wall tirelessly hunting lizards, and brings in from time to time a field or a house mouse, even sometimes a young rabbit or a mole; but does not appear to notice these newcomers. The pair are very busy building. The first day they placed only a couple of crooked twigs, a purchased option, probably one of several, as if to hold possession-right; next day they worked for fifteen minutes or a half-hour, with a low, charming song, before disappearing for the day: today they have been hard at it for hours, with occasional delightful warbles of joy. Catbird sings in the orchard.

Life, life, life: everywhere thrilling to million-tinted splendors of growth, of procreation, of abundance and beauty. Oh, home! Oh, forest loom of life-stuff! Oh, holy world!

May 15, 1909

The half-completed nest in the porch vines seems to be deserted: the birds flash in and out among the scarlet blossoms, but sing sweetly and low, but seem no nearer the actual business of the season than at first.

A number of pretty warblers—one colored much like a miniature jay—flit about the yard. The old cat caught a couple of chippies and then a squirrel for her kittens; I thought the thrashers would probably be next, and so sent away all but one kitten today.

The baby sleeps and grows, waking at intervals to cry and eat and laugh, stare and ponder for a while, and sleep again.

A new bird in the cherry-tree: I heard the stranger voice, and going to see, was rewarded for having followed up a not specially attractive call, by a good look at a really beautiful little fellow, bright red as a cardinal but not much over half as large. His wings are somewhat different in color from his body, but not black as in a Tanager which the mountain people call the "woods redbird." His tail and his beak are also red. I could not be certain whether he has a crest or merely raised his feathers occasionally. We watched him eat a cherry, then he flew to the woods.

May 22, 1909

Three days of rain—a "May freshet" that sends the river backing out across the valley, foot by foot, to drown the young crops. Lookout props the sheeted clouds as though they had been tent-canvas.

June 6, 1909

There used to be a wild-rose bush near the school house, a wild wayside thing, and all the little boys going to church would pin a rose or two on the clean fronts of Sunday calicoes. They wore rings of bone, nickel or gutta-percha; the young men festooned great watch chains across their fronts, stuck bird-wings in their hats, and displayed whatever pins they could get or make. Natural masculine attribute. Now the old horn tucking-combs are seen no more: there is no church to go to—at least not eaten with dry rot and the jealousies of the faithful (!) few; and the young folks care only for borrowed peacock feathers of the city people. Whatever is to become of this neighborhood?

Today is the first, for the year, of those calm and drowsy Sundays of the country which almost every one remembers as knit with youth & childhood: afternoons linked with the droning of hymns, the quaint ceremony of country parlors, and the heaviness succeeding chicken dinners topped off with pie.

June 7, 1909

Woods dark with summer. World buried under riot of growth & leafage. Virile trust of growing things.

"Hear tell" of old Allan Pickett, bear-hunter, who lives at the foot of the mountain just where Falling Water comes down. He is now too old to see well, and his famous rifle—one of the last made by old Joe Winchester, carrying a one-ounce ball—hangs useless, with shot-pouch, powder-horn, and bone charger: so he keeps bees—a score or two of gums and raises everything he eats except sugar & coffee. He is wont to rise at three or such an hour, kindle his fire, and sit playing the fiddle until the household awakes to work.

Concerning bees he holds the belief prevalent in Shakespeare's time. The queen is the king-bee: the drones are supposed to lay eggs and the workers are males. Compare the passage in Henry V: "Don't want none o' these here book bees," says old Allan: "don't want to know nothing about book bees."

The second swarm here settled admirably, after the hive, which smelt musty, had been rubbed inside with peach leaves: but the queen of the third is injured, so that a successor has been ordered from Cincinnati.

June 17, 1909

Violet ground mists, showing indistinct & softened against the brilliant rose-dawn of the day; trees immersed in a lake of it. Rolled & wind plucked upward from the blue breaks of Middle Creek, like a ragged fleece.

Tired of the long confinement I walked a little way into the woods. A path chosen at random led me to the head of a hollow that had been burned over and was grown up in brush and bunchy trees among the standing dead wood—a wood pecker's paradise. The whole hollow was aflutter with wings, thin as the fluttering leaves. I walked up on a little beauty feeding a nestling in a bush. It was generally olive above, bright yellow marked with black about the throat & breast, and not as big as a chippy. Kentucky warbler?

July 6, 1909

The second movement of the summer's great sonata is begun. Haze and heat in place of the piled clouds & daily showers. Earth is pressed into silence as by the weight of a full Pacific tide as we approach the year's noon.

The children catch June-bugs and tie them by the leg to hear them hum—beetles wrought of copper and ormolu lustres [ground or pounded gold].

July 11, 1909

A still midsummer Sunday. There was a great deal of talk about huckleberries during the morning and Flittermouse [a nickname for Katharine (Kitty), Emma's fourth child and third daughter], after joining the children in a futile search round home, departed on a quest of her own. She was gone about three hours altogether. I had dug & washed some potatoes, and put them to bake, when I missed her & instituted a quick hunt. The combined effort of two families having failed to find trace of her round home, we sent word to the neighbors & began to beat the woods in all directions. At this time Kitty must have been asleep in the bushes, for we passed along the road & missed her. More people gathered & joined us—grandpap & grandmother, uncle Dock & any number of cousins, and children of the town people. Passersby were asked to keep an eye open for a two-year-old little girl in a white dress: and one of these it was, a young fellow from the valley, going to see his girl in Sunday clothes, who at last appeared with the dirty, berry-stained, scratched & tangled little maid, very wide-eyed, in his arms. He had heard her crying, in a sand-flat towards Middle Creek.

July 15, 1909

Much of the mountain woman's housekeeping—most of her daily life, I do believe—is a matter of "muscle memory." Even in a strange house she cleans, cooks, takes care of milk & food & kitchen gear, precisely as she has been drilled by her mother, precisely as her grandmothers performed the same tasks. This gives her an immense advantage over one who, like me, is obliged to experiment, or to reason out each new problem as it arises. She knows a hundred tricks for outwitting insects, sweetening vessels, substituting in times of scarcity, making the most of the crude mechanism of fire & water and a few utensils which furnish her home. Outside these few objects she is at sea. Her mental equipment is almost instinctive like a cat's or a wren's; but it takes in a quite wonderful working knowledge of the chemistry & physics of her immediate world; and she knows it all perfectly, or almost perfectly.

August 1, 1909

A summer Sunday in the country, what a perfect day! Men getting together by twos and threes all forenoon, just to talk,—a tall dark bachelor and a freckled, flaxen boy of eighteen come to visit the man, who sits in the back yard house shadow with the baby on his lap; and so here are four of the simplest, kindest hearts in the world together. The bachelor pokes a quaint brown finger at the baby, who stares and crows, looking from one to the other of the men and tasting one fat thumb and then the other, with an occasional bounce of delight.

"Growed, ain't he?" says George. "Never saw a kid grow so."

"He don't fuss much," comments Cess.

"He's been asleep since daylight until just a few minutes ago," says the father, with admirable restraint. "That's what makes him grow so much."

"He shore is good-natured."

The tick-inspection law comes up for discussion, the state of the roads, coming elections, and the killing of Uncle Taylor's shote: then a watermelon is cut in the watershelf by the kitchen door. While I with the little girls pick beans in the garden where the sun beams are rapidly drinking up the dew from the crab-grass tangle, the men melt away into the woods.

Afternoon clouds pile higher and more dazzling beautiful, over the blue-velvet hills' half-circle against the horizon light: our world seems to float in the vast gloom of noon.

August 2, 1909

Cross the hot field of glistening, warm corn-blades, climb a rail fence splashed with foam-like elder bloom, pass by a small glade vibrant with sunshine and little motions of bird and shadow: then here is the dark Gothic arch of the forest entrance: entrance to a mossy, branching way, in a world of trembling leaves. Dim place, green and flickering: soft shack of change & readjustment: sudden spell of secrecy and silence laid upon one's being. Rich is the life of the forest, not with the flaunting, lavish display of gardens, hastens to bestow itself, exhausted in a season, but with the better guerdon [reward] of hid treasure which must be desired & sought, faithfully. Forest flowers subtle-colored,—purity shows streaked in one light with pink, in another with violet—gentle dream-things, faint in the broad day of shadows as those films and skeins of starlight the moon weaves above the black tops of pine trees.

August 9, 1909

Here is the perfection of summer; with long days of blue, or clouds soaring beneath the sun. Black and yellow sulphur-dusty butterflies over the field's primroses and white weed; birds busy in the orchard; crickets in the grass. Beautiful rustling cornfields, broad lustrous blades, frond-like tassels shining high against the blue: so straight a plant, dark and luxuriant—so truly the offspring of the mother valleys. True to the soil. Droop of boughs against the shadow; green shimmer of leaves; dark depths of shadow in the pond's pure mirror, and the shining sunken moon by night.

August 20, 1909

At dawn a vast overhead of "dominecker" clouds, flush like scattered rose leaves. From east to west they spread, but melt like foamflecks in the burning day: then the great cumuli spread vast wings over the purple-shadowed horizon. At sunset they float against a sea of golden light.

Standstill noon of summer;—the "set" of the year's tides. Insects are happy in the heat; weeds are a jungle; grass hoppers rise & hover clicking in the sun above hot grass; lemon-colored butterflies flit across the garden; chickens drowse in the afternoon shadow of the porch. Long dreamy days. A scornful hiss of grasshoppers in the roadside weeds,— "T-T-T-T-T-sha-a-ame!" mocking the summer's dusty skirts! There is a high-pitched rustle amid the stiffened oak foliage; single leaves everywhere are the worse for wear, like the wings of belated butterflies. Yet the heat is no longer oppressive; its reign was broken by the "cool spell in August" last week, which almost never fails: and the days are tempered by cloud-shadows and breezes.

Harvest moon, a globe of transparent gold, filled the veiled shapes of mysterious treasure, half revealed.

September 20, 1909

To spend the day with an old schoolmate. Such a bright, simple, cheery disposition as she has—faithful wife & mother (that she is hard-working goes without saying) clean, hospitable, childlike easy to make happy, and too polite to be quite truthful—like a Japanese woman—as incapable of great virtue or anything approaching thought as she is of spite or real sin; would there were more such. In consequent her unguided passion for pretty things has covered her walls with magazine covers, cheap chromos, paper dolls, post cards and illustrated papers, tacked & pinned up helter-skelter; her treasure is the old piano, for which she washed out ten dollars & on which she cannot play a note; her hope is her pretty, capable daughter, who tries to play and sing and draw, but can indisputably cook and iron shirts—at twelve years of age! A doll-home; but one into which the tragedies of life seem not likely to enter, because the head of the house is of a piece with the rest—simple to shallowness, cheery almost to virtue, but with no conception of real truth or honor, tho' a clever workman. A little nest of content, on the wooded slope above the creek spring: chicken-shed, paled garden, a few peach trees, shotes in a pen, kennels of three hunting-dogs, old fashioned shrubs in the swept yard.

October 5, 1909

The last rich rays of sunset strike upon the heads of the five children at play in the yard: against the green dusk of the woods they glow as ripe as the red pomes in the orchard.

All passion of growth came to a stand last month; Nature is now giving the last leisurely touches of maturing to seed and nut and fruit everywhere. Leaves drift down the wind; there is a deep glow of reds and purples and plum-color and gold in the ring of trees round the pond.

Just read a singularly suggestive story (by Josephine D. Bacon) of a woman who escapes from the body, and wandering in some realm of the unapparent, meets a son who might have been. "But that was all so long ago," she says. The Hostess of the place replies: "Here they grow very slowly, for they are nearly soulless when they come."

It reminded me of a belief of old Lucy's that at the Last Judgment every woman will be confronted with the children she refused to bear. I liked her word for them,—"the Nameless." As if she thought of creatures without a name, almost without a soul, yet human in a formless sort of way—robbed forever of the race-life, but doomed to live out an unshapen twilight sort of existence somewhere beyond space & time.

October 22, 1909

To Sawyer Springs, through such a part of the country as that whole must have been before the war: mile after mile through the rich woods, never seeming to get anywhere, because as fast as one blue hill is put behind another takes its place, swimming in the same gold light and purple haze. Crossing the creek a house is glimpsed, very tiny, far & aloof, alone on the top of a ridge—a log house with fruit trees and a truck-patch: one wonders how on earth it is approachable—yet no doubt, like every other in the mountains, a perfect spider-web of trails radiates from it under the cloaking treetops. There are other houses a many in the neighborhood, as neighborhoods go here, but they sit aloof to right & left of the road, wherever is a sheltered lap of the hills and a spring hollow. Nothing is visible for miles except the gold and scarlet glory, the beauty and mystery of living trees, the magic of the wilderness in its veil of blue. Once in a while a group of cattle is met, the gaunt, shaggy, unkempt beasts of the region, enjoying a brief day of plenty during the ripening of the "beggar-ticks"; their bell's deep brass comes pleasantly to the ear from far down the slopes.

Our destination turns out to be a cabin buried in the woods, invisible two hundred feet away from any direction—truck-patch, log stable, and all: wagon & mules enjoying a noon rest before the gate. The women & children once conveniently fore gathered in the house, the men are free to go forward with the matters of trade—looking over the horse & team, calling up shotes from the woods, even driving up a cow to be passed upon. Others join them, one with a bunch of squirrels at his belt. They light pipes & talk, as only people can to whom talk is almost the sole entertainment & diversion of the days:—sounds like a murmur of running waters,—such leisure of utterance, such masterly moderation of expressed opinion!

In the windowless interior—lighted only from the door & from a small square cut each side of the chimney—there are two great dark beds, covered with patchwork quilts: on one a banjo lies face down beside a fiddle. Splint-bottom chairs, polished & darkened with long use. A lean to kitchen in the rear, containing just the least possible number of utensils a pair of deft hands can get a meal with. Few too are the possibilities of cooking—meat salted into a stone jar, meal in a bag, a gourd of salt, dried apples & pepper hung in strings by the stove pipe.

November 2, 1909

Orchards colorless, fields dun and tawny, grizzled with naked weeds, amid the still glowing forest: the far hills luminous with that indescribable color, like the clear heart of an amethyst. Looking westward in the morning, one sees the brown oaks, gilded by the sun, upreared against the blue; and eastward, a winking of innumerable spider threads among twigs & weeds, under a sky of white haze.

George is our only near neighbor. Two days after the baby was born he appeared in the kitchen door as the Man was cooking breakfast, among the children. They spoke of the weather then, " I come to see the baby," said he quite simply.

"All right—He's in there with his mother," said the man, motioning with his head as he turned a corncake.

So George came stalking in, all six darkly-bronzed feet of him, in shirt and overalls and stogies: and I, lying on the rumpled bed, where four had slept, held up the wee "bunch of nothing" and we tried to make some remarks about it. But neither of us found much to say, though neither of us was in the least embarrassed. There was the new baby: that was all. It was really much like any other.

But George has a deep and abiding fondness for everything that is helpless and little—the great dour bachelor, with his black humors of contrariness! Who would suspect it?—and he came to see the baby again and again. By and by I put the little dumpling into his arms one day, and bade him carry the baby for me, along the road. Often now he holds out his big arms for it, in the midst of a conversation about stock or farming. He boasts about the little fellow's crawling abilities for more than the proud father would dare, and chuckles with triumph when the crawler overtakes an unwary kitten and crows as he pulls its tail. Only after the baby is asleep in the trunk-lid cradle he draws a deck of cards from his pocket and starts a game.

two

Return to Walden's Ridge

Emma Bell Miles and her family spent the last months of 1909 in Miami, Florida. She and young Frank Mirick (Mark) were in delicate health and she felt that spending the winter in a warmer climate, rather than on Walden's Ridge, would be better for them. Accompanying them was a neighbor and friend, Edith Catlow Stroop, who helped finance the trip. During this time Miles contracted out for the spring to work as author in residence at Lincoln Memorial University, in Harrogate, Tennessee. The president of the university had been impressed with *The Spirit of the Mountains*, which she had published five years earlier. Frank would tend to the president's cattle. They arrived in mid-March. The family remained there through the spring and into the summer. Miles's health suffered during their stay in Harrogate, preventing her from working much while there. In August 1910 they were back home on Walden's Ridge, where the journal resumes. This chapter picks up after the family's return to Walden's Ridge.

August 13, 1910

Tranquil summer, when no rain falls from the soaring clouds.

With return of health after a long period of depression or illness, how one's interest in life, just the ordinary every-day round of ordinary people, flames up with a passionate joy! How avidly the heart seizes on even commonplace details of the home! Life throbs warm as the lips of a lover: the earth is full of milk and beautiful as a young mother's breast. Every impression comes to the senses with a freshness of morning in Eden: all the sounds and hues and delicate forms of summer being every grass blade, painted with a dew drop, quivers with pure vitality. Most of all the elemental attraction of the voices, faces, bodies of well-known men and women and children strengthens its old appeal; one is filled with a curious sympathy, youthful and ardent, for the mere tone of a familiar voice, for the set and turn of a head, the slue of a torso on its hips, the texture and fragrance of hair, breadth and slope of a toiler's shoulders, the articulation of hands and feet that so wonderfully epitomize the grace and significance of the whole frame. One discovers unsuspected charm in homely faces; a new pathos and mildness beams in eyes that have seemed only dull. Ancient energy of sunbeams flames in the veins; the influx of glowing health, irradiation of hope. Such a recovery is a rebirth, a globing anew from the sea of existence, a rescue from approaching dissolution.

The act of refraining from looking at the addresses on letters handed one to be mailed is only courtesy in town; in a country neighborhood it approaches heroic self-denial.

August 15, 1910

Walked this evening through low woods where the black mold is padded with moss. I never saw so many yellow orchids or such beauties— the yellow fringed-orchid, the lion's beard. One deeper glen filled already with twilight at sunset, and thick with tall cinnamon-fern, was lit with ghostly candles of the white variety, dim in the stillness, seeming to float above the fern like ignesfatui [a "ghost" or "phantom" light that hovers over the ground], delicate pallid lights.

September 11, 1910

Such an atmosphere of sunny peace over all the land. The forest is steeped in it—bright light and green shadow which is only less vivid. Silence but for the thin shrilling of crickets and grasshoppers; the long drowsy sigh of a breeze in the treetops, or the whir of a cicada, or the sharp croak of a "barkin' lizard."

Blue lobelia; gerardia, yellow and rose-colored brook sunflower; early asters, blue and gold; bluebells among the rocks; goldenrod brightening the upland open woods: the last fading orchid.

Step after step of the stone descent into the spring emerges as the water is lowered by this, the "dry time o' the fall." The bottom of that quivering pool of morning essence never appears; it remains a veritable fountain of life to man and beast like Jacob's well. The roof above is dark and cool; and on its timbers, among spider webs and lichens, a host of names are cut and scrawled. Names twenty years gone and more; names of the dead, names of those who have risen out of humble ken, and of some now lodged out sight in dens of infamy, girls now staid mothers, boys grown to bearded men.

October 11, 1910

Beautiful, warm, late-summer weather again. A single sweet gum darkening to plum color, among the ring of green trees round the pond: one or two tupelos make ready for winter, more by fading embers than the usual blaze of color.

The children have such a cunning tiny pet. Coming home from the store with his father Joe [Miles's oldest son] picked up, from the dry leaves, by the road near Hutcheson's rocks, a baby ground squirrel, nearly dead and covered with ants. It is about as big as a mouse, but with a larger head; its eyes are not yet open, but its coat is velvety and beautifully striped. Jean insisted on feeding it and I, thinking it could do no harm to a creature so nearly dead, prescribed some warm milk & water in a teaspoon. It swallowed feebly at first, but soon began to revive, and after a night's sleep in well-warmed flannels is quite lively. It drinks eagerly from a spoon, or sucks at a wee bottle, holding the rag nipple tightly with its forepaws. What astonishing, tenacious vitality these wild creatures display.

Last night I dreamed, I think, the most horrible dream of my life. As I have never heard of one like it I set it down for the psychological interest.

I thought that in excavating for a cellar we came upon a dead man beneath the floor,—probably the grave of a forgotten soldier. I looked down into the obscurity below the opening, and the corpse bestirred itself, rose to its feet and turned about. It was not ghastly in appearance, but rather worthless and sordid looking, like a dried and blackened mummy.

A charred and roughened pot was inverted over its head so that the face could not be seen. Then I was afraid, and fled the house, with all the children. I came to my man where he was at work in the barn shed, and told him there was something dreadful in the house. He went at once to investigate, bidding me herd the little folks safe in the shed, but I was uneasy, and followed at a little distance. I saw him stand before one of the dimly lighted windows, looking in. The light grew brighter, and I know that something was in there moving about. He stood, I watched, and knew that something terrible beyond endurance was about to come upon us. The light suddenly glowed, and I perceived that it shone visibly through his body and clothing; it shot up to an intolerable radiance. I saw the palms of his hands translucent crimson red as a child's held in a ray of sun. And then he disappeared, melting through the wall and into the house like figures in an old Japanese ghost tale . . . I awoke shivering.

No doubt the dream was induced by much thinking over the problems of immortality, and the relation of body and soul. Its peculiar horror was, of course, the same as that of all death,—the very present personal relations it had for the setting.

November 25, 1910

Judith and I walked to the Nelson spring, sketched among the big rocks, and found witch hazel, the last flower of the year, a clear pale gold illumination in the gray underbrush along the watercourse. It has been, except in a few places, a colorless autumn; the trees went from summer to winter, the black gums & hickories simply faded from green to brown.

December 3, 1910

Moderating after a three day's cold. The pond is still sheeted with thin ice, reflecting the neutral tints and pale gleaming branches of the ring of trees round it. A typical Southern winter day, such a day as is chosen for wood chopping and hog killings. Gray transparent woods, carpeted with brown leaves; distant tap of an axe through the frosty bush, colorless, quiet little homes, sitting among the forsaken fields outspread in the pale sunshine, send up each its thread of blue smoke. Dreamy but joyless they sit, wistful in their pitiful need. A wintry pallor over-spreads earth and sky; the hills are so softened as to seem unreal, downy with feathery treetops, or veiled in haze. Never a note of color or an accent of light or shade,—only forms innumerable, anatomies of oak and hickory bared, contours of gray bluff and brown curving hill fields, blocked shapes of unpainted shacks and cabins and roofs silver gray with weather,—everywhere form, delineated with infinite delicacy and precision; as in some fine half-tone plate, mezzo-tint, reproduced from a perfectly detailed photograph.

January 7, 1911

Deep frozen earth; below-zero weather—everything frozen solid. Yesterday, in the profound hush following long-continued rain, the snow fell, lightly, softly—over the colorless dark woods, over the bare forsaken fields. Today piercing cold; cattle stand humped and shivering, their shaggy sides hung with tags of ice. A light sleet of snow lies over the ground; trees everywhere glitter with a sheathing of sleep, not heavy, but sufficient to sparkle with all the jewels of Aladdin. Sunset spreads in pale gold behind the dark etching of forest, above the shadowed snow.

Inside the house load after load of logs is fed to the singing fire, round which the children scuffle and shout. Though all else in the world is bleached and wan with age and winter, here beats the red heart of home.

January 28, 1911

After days and days of fog, and mud, and drizzling rain, clearing at last in the night—and warmer! The sun falls warm on the face, the wind is a gentle breath, the ground dries rapidly.

Such vistas of happiness open before me as the children grow, reaching out toward their world. My youth is gone; while other women were taking care of their teeth and complexions, I was taking care of rosy little bodies. Now I renew, through them, the freshness of first impressions; I see through their eyes, feel the exquisite sentiment of first contact with the lovely things of life, with music and flowers, with light and joy.

I shall be so happy! If God grant me old age—if I may be a grandmother!

February 15, 1911

A spring-like day; the sun falls warm, bluebirds warble and twitter on orchard twigs, the Carolina wren shouts his 'jubilee.' The pines sigh softly all along the cliffs, their purr mingling with the higher note of spilling waterfalls. The valley is colorless with gray haze. One discerns dimly the nearer features of green-tinged fields cradled ever so softly between dreamy hills feathery with treetops. Faint and small and far, its sounds rise to the listener,—cockcrow ever so tiny, lowing of cows, bells of varying tones. All vast, still, and dim, bathed in the gently afternoon—a wide light drenching the lonely steps.

The purple shadow creeps slowly down from the edge of the rock over the Side; innumerable small copies of it start at the same time from the crest of every hill, the point of every haystack, and every ridgepole in the valley.

The full moon makes such a night,—with the piping of shrill frog voices in every marshy hollow, and the distant roar of the creek, fed by recent snows. George says he heard a whippoorwill.

February 21, 1911

A sword of winter has cut the gentle weather off from us—the first bitter cold since early January. Two of our new-hatched chicks died: the ground is frozen; green shoots frost-nipped.

Jean found the first violet today, and I noticed in the sheltered thicket below the spring a catbrier whose broad green leaves have hung sort all winter long.

March 16, 1911

Yesterday a sudden whooping wind interrupted the spring's third advance. The temperature fell rapidly; the fire, so long merely smouldering, [sic] leapt higher and higher toward dark, and we were glad to draw closer to it.

This morning we find everything frozen—the peach and pear blooms, and tender sprouts everywhere. The lilac and woodbine leaves, however, are unhurt by the freeze.

The day continues cold. This evening a whirling springs up in the woods across the wall, and with a light clatter & rustle casts the dry leaves higher and higher, flying, twirling, glittering and winking against the blue; edging in wide circles, so that the sky seems to deepen as one looks. It fascinates the children, they follow it away over the hill.

April 16, 1911

Easter—After long weeks of bad weather, cold rain, and wind, clearing fresh and sweet. The children, after finding all the red and blue rabbit-eggs under the altheas and in the briers, set off for Aunt Laura's to spend the day—happy as only children visiting their cousins can be, and all fat and rosy with new milk and mother's loaves and God's fresh air. What does it matter, after all, that we have not three meals ahead?

April 19, 1911

A rainy month, making up for the dry winter. Men plant potatoes hurriedly on the occasional days when the ground is fit, and milk between showers half the time. Not being able to do day's work, they are running into debt for food and going without clothes. Children are sickening from running barefoot on the cold ground; they can have no new shoes—extra expense is not to be thought of.

Mirick has a penny with a hole through it. He carries it in the pocket of his rompers, and shows it to every body, saying, "Money:—'ole innit;"—and turning it over add, gravely, "'noder 'ole-in it!"

April 21, 1911

The mother hen sits in a sunny angle of the crooked stone wall, in the first flush of reward for three weeks' sitting in a dark box. Two others come and stand with heads close to hers, comically, listening to the peeps of the horrid chicks. "Mamma," says Joe, "She's a-secretin' to 'em about her babies."

Having nothing but bread and milk, we kill the big rooster; and it happens that company comes to dinner—a cattle-man on horseback, from the valley, with a bag of salt on his saddle. He is faded as only a man who has weathered the changes of sixty-seven Southern winters can be; his eyes are dim and his right hand half palsied from a minie ball lodged in his elbow. But there is nothing colorless or shaky [sic] about his talk. Stammering, cursing, gesticulating, he gives the story of Murfreesboro, the Mission Ridge charge and half a dozen lesser fights, and best of all, of how he captured Champ Ferguson.[1] It is all true; he will lie about his possessions, and is master of the curious interlocutory jiu-jitsu of horse-trading, but he has really been a wild fighter since boyhood. All afternoon he sits on the porch under the blossoming woodbine, and talks and talks, in the warm, eager, happy-go-lucky Southern fashion.

April 25, 1911

To "Topside" with Judith, where some ladies have a house-party.[2] Why, when the weather is mild and the tinted woods are full of dogwood & azaleas, should people sit and play bridge from breakfast till midnight? One girl had found a pink moccasin orchid at Mabbit Springs. I did a color study of the plant, and several copies were ordered for souvenirs.

May 11, 1911

To Davidson's place on the brow, where the men-folks are making a tennis court. Went with the children sketching; we drank at a spring that trickled out among boulders and moss, and afterwards climbed down the bluff to a little rock house. In the warm shelter of the rocks the laurel is in bloom, and the mountain ash in full bloom; rhododendrons opening. The season has jumped to summer this week; and the young leaves of the woods, so long held back, are out thick and bright, a sunshine color that dazzles the eyes.

All day the tan bark wagons go by, the driver of each sitting half asleep on his creaking swaying load; a dark cube passing thro' the bright spring woods.

May 28, 1911

To Shoal Creek, all of us, with the team & wagon & a basket of bread & butter & eggs.

The brow laurel is faded but here it leans over the singing water bursting white from its dark glossy leaves, drifting from its cluster on the surface of the pools like rosy foam. Rhododendron too in full bloom— purple tiaras on the acknowledged green of the woods. Besides there are sweet-bubbies, pink root, fire-pink, spiderwort, partridge berry, star-root, phlox, the early and the tall varieties both; mayweed, white weed, milk weed, blue linaria, skull caps, ladies' tresses, arrowwood,—brightening the green gloom.

The full summer heat has flashed upon us out of spring's delay. Almost in a single week we saw the prevailing color pass from the gray silken sheen of winter, carrying only an embroidery of leaf and blossom, to the shadowless gold of early foliage, and darken to the depths of summer. Now it is 90° and above—as hot as it commonly gets here.

Hens are hatching all over the place, but the heat seems to prevent their doing well.

June 4, 1911

Sunday. Breathless, summer heat already. The house becomes uncomfortable in the afternoon, and I and the children lie on a pallet under the trees. The man, while out hunting the colt found a bee tree, and returned after dusk, he and George, to cut it—with bucket, axe, netting, and rags for smudges; George took also a hive. Near midnight they brought back two or three pounds of honey apiece. Not very good honey—full of bark slivers, bee-bread, and bees.

What a glorious thing the night is after such a day! The cool glory of moonlight flows up to the windows, and through them the air, exquisitely pure and gentle, pours over one's whole body. Whippoorwill and frogs— fireflies, crickets.

June 10, 1911

While I was gone to the post office Jean took the baby walking, and found an orchid perfectly new to me,—a delicate greenish white and purple-veined thing, three slender olive sepals rising from the top of the ovary over the tubular flowers: rose-pagonia?—adder's mouth? It was in a somewhat marshy meadow under a maple tree. (Spreading Pagonia.)

The heat is phenomenal for this early season. The ground is baked: gardens at a standstill, all crops suffering.

June 18, 1911

The long drought breaks at last in a good hour's downpour. How glad I am that I and the children carried water evening after evening and kept the tomatoes etc. alive, though many people have abandoned their gardens. Trees have died in the woods; there are big patches where the grass & undergrowth would blaze if set afire.

I never heard so many "barkin'-lizzards" as this summer. What can they be?

Found a cuckoo's nest in a blackjack, a loose affair of crisscrossed sticks—one can glimpse the two pale blue eggs thro' its mesh.

September 9, 1911

Judith and Jean went to a schoolmate's birthday party—a great event. The hot weather is holding late; the man comes from his work almost exhausted; cattle are dying in the woods—a murrain [an outbreak of disease in cattle] feared! Much of the garden is dried up; the tomatoes ripen day by day in their juicy tangle, and great golden pumpkins glow through the dusty green. No fruit this year. Clouds swell and soar grandly over the woods, but bring no rain. At night, happy young creatures go skylarking and singing through the moon's cooler glory, impartially to church or to a dance or a candy-pull.

Night of singing wings.

Mark [Frank Mirick Miles, Miles's youngest child] shouts, holding up his arms to the pink glowing east, "Oh, look at de summer set!"

September 26, 1911

Still the hot weather, like midsummer with pearly thunderheads soaring beneath the sun with no rain. Clear starry nights with streaming meteors from time to time flashing across the sky.

Last night, had some of the young folks and young married folks in to play flinch. Today I and the stout, goodhearted, headstrong girl who helps me round the house hitched up old Green to the wagon and drove to Summertown, visiting Laura and Mrs. Poindexter.

It is wonderful how happy we are, my Man and I. What good times we have had, in every breathing-space! All through our youth we were sickly, lonely, starved for the fun young people have as a matter of course; we have found happiness only through each other. Each of us opened for the other a gate into a great still land of mystery and joy. In our daily lives we have worries and cares, but our love dwells forever in that place. It is our island, girdled by a stormless sea, whose fronded palms whisper forever to us of romance and treasure, whose sands are strewn with shells of the deep. It is not a matter of similarity of tastes or of education—these are perpetually conflicting. The bond is far stronger than any more intellectual affinity; it rests on the eternal verities.

I was taught that love would fade and change after marriage!
Why, it changes only to strike down its roots deeper, and reach out
its branches wider, and bloom with new beauty. The sex-magic is
evanescent as a baby's dimples—at best it comes and goes; but oh, the
blessed certainty of finding perfect sincerity, patience, forbearance,
unselfishness in one's mate,—the inexhaustible boyishness, the
unfailing humor that helps over all hard situations! The thought of him
brings a sense of warmth, actual physical warmth; and if I were to pray
it would be the prayer from the book of Tobit—"Mercifully grant that
we may grow aged together."

I have had more visitors this summer than ever before, though I have
not been doing any brilliant or even creditable work, for lack of time.
I believe very few folks come here for the sake of beholding a ten-cent
celebrity; hardly to look at my pictures, which are for the most part not
watercolors so much as local souvenirs. Some come perhaps because
I always make them welcome; some to talk of things that are hardly
ever talked about—except in invisible quotation marks, or by formula,
anywhere but on my front porch. But I like to think that many come for
the sight of simple human happiness that is here laid out in the sun for
all to look at. They warm their hands at my life's fire.

There is "great argument about it and about" being true to the
highest, in love, and in other things; meaning that the desire of the body
is not to be weighed against the ruling of the spirit. But is there not a
duty to the lowest as well? This divorcing of flesh and spirit is all wrong.
In the flesh begin those laws whose obedience makes the harmony of life.
For example:

I heard a woman who is called refined and cultured say, in
company, that in her opinion the ideal marriage is to be wedded to
[a] man who is extremely fond of one, and to have no children. But I
could not help remember that, in the street, a woman who demands
love and shirks its responsibilities is given a name neither cultured
or refined.

The drought in the valley is terrible. People are drinking out of old
ponds; some wealthy farms are hauling water five miles. Stock water
not to be had—a dozen families using from one well. But the mountain
springs still run, clear and low, filled with the essence of morning.

October 2, 1911

Only a little cooler, with clouds that bring no rain. A pleasant wind, making a high pitched autumnal rustle in the leaves. Hardly any leaves have turned except sumach [*sic*], sourwood & sassafras, and some gums & tupelos.

Today completes the trade of all Frank's stock for a little home of our own. Here we are out of money, with only a few pumpkins and chickens to eat, in debt, and winter approaching. However, we have rounded harder corners on a can of Hope Deferred smoking mixture. One begins to dream on it, of a bath tub & sewing machine as well as another cow & horse—perhaps even an organ, so that the young folks may come in and sing together.

October 7, 1911

Moved into temporary quarters, a three room shack in the woods. Still the hot weather and dazzling sky. The full moon rises cloudless and splendid.

Lippincott's accepted "At the Top of Sourwood" and paid cash—thus we are saved out of the racking worry and strain.[3]

October 12, 1911

Clear and cool; the first real autumn day. More visitors—a neighbor woman with three babies, and two bright-faced girls from town.

How often it happens that when one has learnt to be happy without the object of one's desire, then it comes. Now that I have come to feel that home is anywhere with Frank, and learnt to make the children feel at home anywhere with me, we are at last to have roof and lintel of our own.

October 15, 1911

The children went to Ida Hullet's wedding in the morning—the little bride, very sweet & pretty, only 14 years old. In a [illegible] to a baptizing in Middle Creek.

October 22, 1911

Dock had a candy-pull last night. Mostly the young married couples went. Today all the children go sucking a grimy chunk of taffy.

Went to grandma's and got some fresh butter milk and a basket of turnips and greens. The old man cut his hand severely with the axe, and cannot cut a stick of wood. How does he manage? I inquire. "Ehlaw," he replied, "me and her been together long enough to learn a heap o' tricks! I hold the head o' the axe, and she hits it with the maul."

A cold wind blows between the low clouds and the earth today, but still there is no touch of frost, and the woods are green. I found a little cluster of blackberry bloom; and peach and cherry blooms are common.

October 26, 1911

Spent the morning doing a watercolor head of old Grandsire Nixon, he is 72, and his hair is so ashen-blond you cannot tell it is gray. He sat very nicely, his beautiful curly beard wagging to his tall tales of adventure, or drooping as he dozed. Yesterday did a very good head of his niece, Nora.

Looking out into the faintly paling east at 5 or thereabouts, I saw Venus glowing in a bright cloudy veil, like a young moon; and a comet with a long tail, have not been able to learn its name. Tonight dark and cloudy, with a drizzle setting in.

October 29, 1911

The Wheatleys came up in an auto and met us at the Nelson Spring.[4] They brought quite a feast, and we added our plebian but solid corn meal muffins and fried chicken, and made coffee over a camp fire. The sun shone warm and clear. We stripped the children and rubbed them with oil to prevent their chilling, and photographed them in a variety of poses, among the rocks and trees. They behaved beautifully and posed surprising well. Ever since I was a girl I have had a pipe-dream of picturing beautiful children running nude in the forest like fawns,—a dream which I successfully passed along to them, so that they enjoyed it as much as anyone. I would have declared its fulfillment impossible; but here were a most artistic friend and an imported camera at my service, no less than his own, all afternoon.

But no photograph could be half as lovely as the real maize-tinted late sunshine on those plump limbs, the shadows reflecting the deep sky color, the scarlet and rose of the vine leaf crowns, the autumnal glow of the background.

After the first, at which the children & their father tasted things they had never heard of before, it was discovered that a gallon and a half of ice cream was left over—as well as grapes and almonds, cake, and three boxes of candy. All this was given to the children, to have a party with.

How tired and happy we all were, filing home along the moonlit path. Katydids still chirp occasionally, from the hickory's golden tower. Uncle Taylor says there was such a season once, thirty-five years ago.

November 1, 1911

Moved into the new house.[5] All tired out.

November 14, 15, & 16, 1911

Nov. 14, 15, & 16 are clear cool Southern winter days, perfect for outings—perfect, for that matter, for staying at home, for walking about the garden's colorless stubble in the sunshine and enjoying the new sense of possession. I never go to get a meal without thinking, "My own kitchen— God Bless it!" This afternoon as I sat painting doing some art at twenty-five cents per sample—turning out card after card for the Y.M.C.A. Bazar like a machine made for the purpose, the children came home from school accompanied by a party of people from town who had some difficulty in finding my place. Mr. & Mrs. Frank Fritts, Mrs. Mynders of Knoxville & her son, Mrs. Milton of Knoxville & another lady. Mrs. Milton is most interesting & intelligent. Told me what I have longed for fifteen years to learn,—the whereabouts of Mary Applewhite Bacon whose few exquisite studies of Georgia country people appeared in Harper's and unaccountably ceased, years ago.

November 19, 1911

Heaven bless Jim Slimkin for building this house as he did, setting good doors and windows, flooring it neatly and all,—but especially and particularly for planning this back porch so that it gets no wind and all the morning sun. I sit here warm and comfortable, breathing the air off a thousand miles of wooded mountain slopes and writing letters to distant friends. I think I shall never be lonely again; I am sensible of vast over-human reservoirs of intelligence and sympathy that make our individual lives seem like ephemeral buds.

This evening, walked with the man and babies to grandma's for buttermilk. Called on Mrs. Lane, who showed me her chickens and presented me with a bottle of wine. Uncle Joe was seated by his father's hearth, as bright as ever and full of the Irish charm. Why is his life such a tragic failure? Flawed in firing, I think. Was something left out of him when he was made, or was it a lack of sympathy and intelligent help when he was a boy?

November 25, 1911

To Mrs. Lane's this morning, to telephone concerning a packet of pictures mailed to the Bazar a week ago. A beautiful morning, after a cold night—roadside banks are slick with an icy fleece, crumbling under the sun—leaves and all surfaces in hollows furred with hoar frost.

This evening Floyd Guess shot his first turkey—probably the one I saw, quite near home. So many have been seen in the neighborhood of late, and other game as well, even a deer.

December 18, 1911

Clear again, but cold. The children all at school. It is a pity they cannot be regular in attendance, but I have not the heart to send them on a walk of two and a half miles through the mud, or if they complain of headaches or growing pains; a fact of which they are, child like, quick to take advantage.

Jean fainted away in class, one day last month; I suppose she will be like me,—the spirit half out of her body through intense concentration. It is a temperament which accomplishes. One habitually works from above downwards,—drawing more of spirit into the realm of heart and mind, more of love and intelligence into the management of material things and contacts, and so more power gathering into one's hands at every turn.

The man says that the little folks were wonderfully good during my absence in town—that Kitty in particular has a lovely disposition. This is hardly a discovery, but a gradual revelation like the unfolding of a rose.

We have had plenty to eat for a week, and new dishes and clothing in sufficiency as well. Still I have not found time to do any really good work—only filling little Xmas orders that bring me a dollar at a time. O well—three years more and we may begin to forge ahead, as the babies get out from underfoot.

Poor dear old Mrs. Barnett has just left for Knoxville, to end her days in her daughter's house, taking care of the baby—a perfect haven after the hard years she has passed.[6] It is outrageous that a woman should work hard all her life, raise a healthy honest family in the highest religion she knew, and come in her old age to washing shirts and overalls of strangers. I know so well the deadly exhaustion she feels, the weakness and hopelessness. But I tried to fill her with faith and joy when she spent the day with me, and, thank heaven, I was able to pay her cash for her canned fruit & jellies, and give her a couple of waists.

December 19, 1911

The girls and I have had the time of our lives. I have not had such a holiday since I married. The first day and night we spent with Cousin May,[7] in the two little rooms at the back of the store, that look so unprepossessing yet contain so much that is genuine and good. Next day worked on a picture in Mabel Van Dusen's bedroom. Set out with the children, rather late, in search of a room, and chanced upon Cornett Hatfield's rooms in time for supper. We slept there the rest of the week. Emmons [Freudenberg] took the children to several moving pictures and a vaudeville. The third day lunched with Mrs. Patten, who presented me with several beautiful & serviceable dresses and some children's clothes.[8] Then called on Mrs. Wheatley who gave the girls a dollar apiece to buy their Xmas with, and bought several watercolors. Friday went shopping, and the girls with much deliberation chose their dolls. Lunched with Carol [Carol Wood Morrison, a writer friend of Miles]. Mrs. Snyder most kindly took them to a vaudeville. At evening I wished to spend the night with Mr. & Mrs. Rains and got as far as the Ridge junction, but was disappointed by a breakdown on the track & had to return to town.[9] Met Mrs. Salmon & Mrs. Parnell on the car and had a charming conversation with them. Took the children to another vaudeville.

Cleared $20 by the trip to town—also $20 from the Bazar.

December 23, 1911

Frank took Joe to town. The clouds did not part once all day, and the temperature did not change. But the fog and rain held off, so that all the country people got their precious Saturday-before-Xmas chance to go to town. The man could not collect the wages coming to him—some obstinacy on Mrs. Rawlin's part—and had only a dollar to spend.[10] However, Mr.—D—gave him a new suit of clothes for a present.

I took the children all over to see Uncle Joe's little girls, who are very playful and friendly.

In the afternoon Lily Underwood brought five of her little brothers and sisters to spend the afternoon. The baby seemed croupy, so they could not play out, and though I had a headache I made them a pan of candy. It sugared for some reason, so I added chocolate and turned it into a sort of fudgy compound, and they had a delightful time after all. One almost always can, with the will to do so.

Frank says our Xmas will be slim. I don't care. We will not let that spoil our happiness. We have been happy all these years, through all the hardships and very present dangers, if we had but realized it, and been kinder to each other.

You will hear plenty of people say that I grew old before my time. Daughter, the reason some women look young at forty-five is that they have never lived.

December 25, 1911

Mrs. Carothers sent up some tinsel & ornaments which, with what I saved from last year, made the little tree splendid and there was no lack of pretty dolls and toys. But the groceries failed to arrive in the rush of Xmas hauling, so there was no candy nor fruit. One neighbor sent a plate of cake & pie, and Joe's wife sent five eggs so I made cake of my own. But it was two o'clock before I got out of the kitchen, very tired.

All went over to Joe's house and spent a pleasant evening. The children had a grand romp. The sky cleared at noon and the ground dried enough for them to run on, but when we got home at 8 o'clock it was already thickening and drops beginning to fall.

January 5, 1912

Sparkling clear and cold—the coldest night of the winter so far. But the rain is over at last.

The sacrifices a woman makes in marriage, the pains she undergoes, are not for the sake of her man and should not be charged to his account. They are for the home, and the family in the home. She must expect to sacrifice her personal interests utterly for this; it is her business, her ideal, her trade, her life work, her art nobler than marble and more enduring than bronze.

5° Fahr. this morning—and Kit & Mark taking whooping-cough.

January 7, 1912

I got up with the desire uppermost to do some watercolors of the silver forest. But Jean had got at my new Chinese White, wasted half and mixed the remainder with red, so that only a pastel was possible. I felt so disappointed that I scolded all morning. If I could only quit painting for the next five years I would be glad; but these wretched little daubs of souvenirs are almost all we have to live on.

There is absolutely not one thing in the house to cook except baking-powder biscuits and a few canned berries.

Outdoors all is beautiful—a white forest glittering against a blue sky. But I don't know when I have felt so discouraged. I try to work, and have done some good designs for the Nautilus,[11] but the house is upset from end to end and the children have to be whipped all round whenever I draw or write. I could be a good mother if I were not obliged for the sake of food to be a workman too. Yet the dear man's patience and kindness in these hard days is an example and a help to us all.

The whooping-cough does not seem to inconvenience the two little ones much. It is something to be thankful for that the rest are well—though this miserable food is hurting Frank's stomach—and a call from a creditor has not improved matters.

In the evening Judith goes for water, and falls into the well. Frank heard her screaming and tore out of the house and down the hill, I following with the first life-line I could catch up, which happened to be a bed quilt. I fell down a time or two, and arrived just in time to see him haul her out, dripping and gasping and crying. She had caught to the well rope and then to a crosspiece and clung till help came.

"I thought that was a dream," was almost her first words. "I thought nothing so bad could really happen. It must have been a dream!"

The shock of it hurt Frank worse than her. I soon had her changed and wrapped in blankets, but he was almost unable to speak, and felt badly all evening.

January 8, 1912

After a nearly sleepless night Frank set out before day in a freezing rain, called to serve on the jury. I dressed and fed the children and went to ask Uncle Taylor's [Frank's uncle] boys to cut some wood, as there was not enough for the day. They were full of promises about what they would do when the rain quit. I turned back almost ready to do something desperate, and met Larnce's boy, whom Frank had asked to stay with me the week. What a relief it was to see him. The weather grew worse and worse. He and I and Joe went away off in the woods and sawed several cuts of wood, keeping our hands and feet from freezing over a little fire kindled against a stump. He started it from a handful of coals brought from the house in a pan. When he had split the blocks we tugged them all the way to the house on Joe's little wagon, trip after trip in the slushy snow, stumbling and slipping and falling. It was as hard a day's work as I ever put in, and resulted in a scarce thirty-six hours' supply of wood that does not burn well.

Hourly the trees grew heavier, bending to the road till we could hardly make the last trip. Such a peculiar white shadow lies over the world— sheeted ice, plumy trees that do not sparkle on account of the heavy mist. Dogwood buds like little glass apples. Azalea bud clusters like a flower.

I was too tired and chilled to cook any supper, but while the coffee was warming Frank walked in. He had come all the way back to see how we were faring, and his feet were somewhat frostbitten. We had good news; we had found a chance to send for a few groceries, and better still, the long-expected check came in today's mail.

January 9, 1912

8° Fahrn this morning.

Again the man left us before day, after a night of worry and sheer suffering. The sun rode up in glittering splendor; the tops of all the trees flamed against the sky. Again, the boys & I went to the woods, but everything was icebound till we could neither saw nor split, nor persuade the little fire to do anything, but smoke. The woods are a vision, a wonder—every tree sparkling with a thousand rainbow-colored facets against the deep blue sky. When the wind blows the tops swing heavily, and fragments of ice come tinkling to the frozen crust, jingling like crystal balls rolling together. It is beautiful, but I can't see it. I cannot get warm; there is no stovewood and not enough heater wood for twenty-four hours; the children are much of the time too miserable to play, and we are so tired of baking-powder biscuits. I can't keep things clean or orderly, let alone make any thing. The money will be gone in a little while, and I don't see my way to earning any more. I don't know what to do, and the worst of it is I feel so angry it makes me miserable. Oh, if the weather would change! If we could get some washing done—at least for the baby! and most important of all, if only Frank may get through the week without frozen feet or an illness!

Evening brings a measure of peace and confidence unknown for days,—as the sun sets behind the forest veiled in its magic web, as the woodpile grows under the boys' hands, and the room grows warm, and the children become quiet, absorbed in a fairy-story. My heart expands, the racking anger and terror fall from it; I look up, and reach through the lonely darkness toward those warm faithful hands. My dear, I am so sorry I was cross! But he is in town and cannot get home before Saturday.

January 10, 1912

In summer the conventional town people come to visit me, crowds of them, hopelessly bound by their class philosophy and bourgeois ideals, with the cramp of their own psychology ineradicable in their minds. I am always glad to see them; the precious gold of humanity is in them all. How kind and good their hearts are! One can always talk to them of things they do understand, and let the rest wait for the fuller development which a few hundred years will bring.

At this time of year my visitors are, for the most part, sodden with ignorance, and the horrible superstitions of it,—heavy with poverty and the mire of it: filthy in habit of body and mind. I am glad to have them. I do wish I could make it a little pleasanter for them while they are here. They are so easily made happy, and so on the alert for every gleam of fun or beauty, when one talks to them of things they understand. That they are not always kind, not always generous or true, is due to the want they have endured ever since they can remember, and to the cramp of their class psychology. The gold of humanity is in them all, warm and bright and wonderful, waiting for the purification of generations and centuries.

My children at least will never grow up with that smug bourgeois idea in their heads that poor folks are different—that they get used to cold and hunger and ugliness and dirt, and are not hurt by it. Whatever comes to them in after life, they will not forget this. The truth about elementary things like this, is educational in the highest sense. It will make up to them for their winter's schooling.

January 12, 1912

A rainy, muddy morning, soon turning colder; the ground and the wet trees freezing rapidly. All the wood is wet and the fire does not burn well. It is good of the children to be as cheerful as they are.

Brick [Frank's nephew] gets up a lot of good firewood with some help from a neighbor boy, and we are quite comfortable in the room this afternoon.

I feared I should never be able to write verse again, but managed to scribble "The Open Door" today.

January 19, 1912

Cleared at sunrise after a bad, wakeful night. A beautiful day; the sun falls warm, the air invigorates. But I feel weak, frightened, angry, and discouraged—quite at my wits' end. For dinner we cook the last mess of food in the house, and cut Kitty's cake. Nothing but bread & coffee remains. Sending to the store at noon we succeed in getting two cans— they are "out" of other provisions.

The sun is like spring. After dinner I and the boys saw up a hickory. I'm tired, half sick.

But the Man has come home tonight!

January 27, 1912

Last night I and the Man sat with Joe's folks till ten. Sleepy today, the more reason of the warm sunshine—A gentler, hazy spring like day. Brick and another nephew are out with little Joe, doing their best to break their necks jumping, and sipping maple sap—every body is happy in his own way, the Man digging stumps out of his garden spot. Went to Joe's twice, and tried to take something the girl could eat.

Only Browning, Walt Whitman, and Stevenson have written of life as I feel towards it, or try to feel,—glad, with a hearty heroic gladness that becomes at one with sorrow and pain, and then rises again like the waves of the sea.

February 1, 1912

Joe is seven today. He cut his cake with the remaining Xmas candles burning on it. A snowstorm blows up suddenly this evening—the ground whitens rapidly but soon melts, and the moon shines tonight. But we are wretched on account of an abominable occurrence of the afternoon. Will have to keep the neighbors' boys run off the place. I shall never forget how well my Man met the situation.

February 14, 1912

Snow in the night, turning after daybreak to steady ice-cold rain. The children, disappointed about their valentines, are fretful and quarrelsome. Kitty had a hot fever all night and has been in bed all day, and I am almost sick with a cold. We have not a day's rations in the house, and are all bilious from eating beans too long. I make cards all day in hope of further orders. It is quite cold, and the Man is all out of heart. This dreadful winter, will it never break!

February 17, 1912

A gray day, the sunshine dim with haze. For us as for the earth, it is an effort to rally. But we are helped by the arrival of $4 in the mail, unexpectedly. Kill one of the few remaining hens, and afterward send to the store for groceries. The children make a readier response to this relief; they frolic and run, they go visiting, they build playhouses. They are happy, and what more ought we to ask—for today?

All through the hours of afternoon the day seems fainting, fading, making imperceptibly toward night. Dim and unreal, like a memory, a regret—the ghost of a day.

February 22, 1912

Sunrise through breaking clouds, over hard-frozen ground white with snow: very cold, but moderating.

Mailed Clay's Marget to Miss Holly.[12] She has now seven stories of mine: Clay's Marget, Cometh Not in by the Door, The Healers, Thistle Bloom, Cost What it May, The Great World, Enchanter's Nightshade.[13]

February 26, 1912

Rain in the night with distant thunder and lightning: clearing after sunrise, with a high, gusty wind that tugs at the trees and strips all but white oak bough of the last leaves,—the wind that gives the woods their early spring or late winter transparency.

Joe to Brick, in bed at night: "If you'll tell me who you're goin' to grow up and marry, I'll tell you who I will."

Brick answered: "I'm goin' to marry Callie-O."

Joe: "Well, when I'm old enough I'm goin' to try to marry Ruth Underwood." I hope he does no worse!

Frank swapped his watch for parsnips. He is morose and moody, unlike himself—unable to sleep, half sick.

Here is a bit characteristic of the difference between us; When there is little to eat, he stoically declares he don't want any, but I wait and take what [illegible].

I see the vision of a planet swinging sunward, recovering after some cosmic disaster, awful beyond conception. For generations no seed-time or harvest has graced its bosom; it has rolled thro' unbroken twilight, shrouded in thick cloud, rent and drenched by terrific storms. All the higher types of animal & vegetable life have succumbed to the prevailing desolation and become extinct: only Man, unconquerable by virtue of his alliance with eternal spirit, survives in scattered bands, half underground, finding sustenance from the bowels of mountains and of the mother of life, the Sea. At last the drowned valleys emerge, vast dull areas of unproductive half frozen mud; the mists rise and cling to the mountain-tops; the swollen, dark rivers thunder toward the ocean. Lighter grows the hours, till at last a gleam of sun—the first for years—pierces the clouds. Then those naked, lean, degraded, diseased, shivering wretches, creeping forth to the icy & all but lifeless surface of the world, peering, pointing, blink and stare at the dazzling phenomenon. They have not strength to understand what has passed, still less to divine what is coming, lost sense of color—blue sky means nothing, but their elders begin to repeat, in such poor words as have not been lost with the pride of forgotten civilization, the story of Light, as they received it from their fathers; some go to bring forth the few sacred seeds and a plan or two of some nearly indestructible sort that has kept alive, in their simple hearts, dim hope of they know not what; and looking into each other's ugly, dehumanized faces, they smile, fleetingly, hesitatingly, like young babes in the first flicker of friendliness & intelligence & returning joy. The broad golden beam sweeps across the plain, ascends the ghastly, scarred slope, at last floods the spot where they stand; they feel its caressing warmth, their souls are filled with its glory; and one and all these poor bearers of the sacred torch fall on their knees in the presence of the Sun.

February 28, 1912

I have tried all day to do little souvenir landscapes, but can have no luck, and tonight I feel so weak and chilly that I can not do work. My teeth are sore and aching, poor worthless, ugly, broken things. If I do not get to town soon I may be too ill to go. Fire out. Mirick tumbled off the high back porch; luckily no damage but a bruise on the leg—feels the hero of an occasion.

Frank is cutting bean poles, burning brush and otherwise making ready for spring. I feel as if a spell of sickness were coming on. I never saw the children heartier or happier—full of play, tho' we have only toast and mint tea, parsnips and bean soup for them.

He is a touch stone: all things are tested as rung against the perfect sincerity of his nature.

I wish that those who blame me with throwing away my life could know the utter loneliness in which I grew up. I am lonely enough now, but it was ten times worse when, if I tried to talk of anything vital in human or spiritual relations, I was brought face to face with barren formula, or else my father tramped out of the house and slammed the door and my mother burst into tears. I am making mistakes enough with my children, but at least so far they find home the most interesting place in the world. They are not lonely, and their souls at least do not starve.

March 1, 1912

Wintry cold, but clear. The ground thawing; frogs singing. I got up with the plot of two stories in mind, and immediately after breakfast sat down, regardless of the state of the house, to rush them on to paper: The Magic Casement, and In Quest of the Fountain.[14] By the time they were hastily put down it was dinner time. Again sitting down as soon as the bread and gravy was cooked & eaten, I did some more watercolor splashing to take to town. Then seeing that the girls were too eager to get out doors to make much headway with the ironing, I did up all the difficult pieces for them. Had a letter from Cousin May inviting me down for a visit; hope to go down in the morning. She writes of her little girl's outcry of consternation when one morning she teased them by refusing to get up: "Now, Mama, God made you to be my mother, and you <u>must</u> get up and send me to school!" How often do circumstances, which is another name for duty, speak to us women in those imperious words!

March 11, 1912

Went to see Mrs. Andrews—who gave me a nice present of new stockings, and an order for cards. Then to Mrs. Wheatley's, where we had a perfectly delightful visit. Kitty made up with Miss Katherine Kaufman [niece of Mrs. Wheatley] and was so happy. Just made the hack;—and came on home. The children, all but Mark, met us at the top, wildly excited and <u>hungry</u> in spite of the groceries I sent up. Caroline sent them one of the Jungle Books and some others.

Misting again, and a sharp wind blowing. So much colder on the mountain.

March 22, 1912

Cloudy after a rainy night. Such a lot of young hoodlums have been rioting in and out all day that I dismissed Mamie [a girl who was helping Miles around the house] this evening, giving her my hat and a gingham dress by way of wages. I did a thousand word story for a medicine company's advertisement today—against my principles, but the devil drives. All tired out. Feeling better this evening, but Frank feels worse.

March 25, 1912

Still colder; a bleak morning, with quarter inch ice. The field covered with flitting, pecking winter birds. Brick went down the mountain before breakfast. Mamie says it will break her heart to leave, and makes so many promises that I let her remain, giving a dress of mine as wages.

I coughed all night. Perhaps I shall not last long. That will be best. I will arrange for the children to be taken out of this gang of thieves and strumpets, and educated and cared for by those more able than I. They will not forget me, anyway, tho' on the material side of motherhood I have wretchedly failed them.

Put in the whole day with paint brushes, doing little cabins etc. but this evening I did achieve a little bit of pure beauty, a small decorative panel, the Spirit of the Heights. If I could only send it do New York to be sold!

March 26, 1912

Frank went to Davidson's. I borrowed flour from Aunt Jinny Guess to make biscuit for breakfast, and every mouthful we have eaten for weeks we are in debt for. The Fairmount store threatens to sue.

Heard the first thrasher this morning, singing over the frosty field. Went to the post office to order seeds, and Mabel came in—all on the Ridge for the day. Her friend Miss Terwilliger ordered a book & paid for it on the spot, so I sent Frank a good dinner by Jean and Joe, and bought enough groceries to last a few days.

Grandpap's mare has twin colts—one dead.

March 27, 1912

A spring day, just pleasantly cool. Finished my illuminated book in time for the mail.[15] Frank took Buzz [nickname for Joe] to Davidson's with him. I feel better than I have felt for weeks. If we could only pay the grocery bill. Frank brought in a handful of arbutus in bud, of which I made a drawing. Aunt Jinny sends us a bucket of new milk for supper.

Just before sunset a peculiar spot of light appears in the gray cloud-veil that is spun across the west,—like a short segment of a rainbow, but quite near the sun. What is it—a sundog?[16] Like some strange lines from a French poet—

> "Large masks of silver, by mists drawn away,
> So strangely alike, yet so far apart,
> Float round the old suns when faileth the day."[17]

Tonight a white circle round the moon.

March 28, 1912

Raining: very dark.

Jean finds a picture of Kipling at his desk in a magazine and explains it to Mark, who tells me: "I said 'Man, what you doin'?' and he said 'I'm writin' a Mowgli story.'" He has all kinds of funny little conversations with his underfoot world, animate or otherwise. Riding through the woods on papa's shoulder, he told us: "'ol branch said to me 'you can't go on, you can't go on;' and I said 'I will too!'"

I lay on the bed most of the day and Mamie sewed on the girls' new gingham dresses. The rain came down in floods; there is more water in the hollow than I have seen at any time this winter. For the first time, the cellar floor is wet.

March 29, 1912

Clouds breaking over the path of the rising sun, but closing again and thickening as the day advances; cold and blustery. Good news—twelve dollars in the mail, from the story sent to the Medicine Co. Frank & Luke cut wood all day, and I did some rather creditable little watercolors.

April 1, 1912

Rain, with fog. Frank & Mamie spend the morning telling ghost stories—some good ones. Of lights following one home from meeting; of a baby buried in a cellar that cried all night; of a skeleton that rode behind Preacher White; of a ghost that told a man where to find the body of his murdered brother; of a boy that half tore the chimney down trying to see his sweetheart in it on the first day of May, and was fooled by a stick; of dumb-suppers.[18]

Frank's tales are of a different sort—of a man that spoke to a gigantic dim shape that walked beside him, & receiving no answer, whacked it with a stick and nearly had to fight an inoffensive pedler [sic] of splint baskets; of a ride of his own past the haunted Hanging Rock, when a drunkard asleep in the leaves scared him and his mule; of a house that had a still concealed in the cellar, where a barrel rolled about at midnight; of a carpenter who, carrying a new-made coffin to the house where it was wanted, in passing a graveyard called to a passer-by to help him carry it and nearly scared the fellow to death; of honest farmers "haunted" out of the prospering crops by the envious; of old Joe Winchester's rocking-chair that rocked at night until proved to be manipulated by a worthless son-in-law of the old couple who had bought it; of "a little gray man" walking round the floor at night, like a kobold [small goblin], that turned out to be a 'possum: featherbed witches, and "crowns" in the pillows of the dead.

Clearing at noon: Frank and Luke go out to hunt service trees. I do feel so much better, ready to work at anything that comes up, and to face life again.

Some of the young folks and Mamie try to set a dumb supper in the kitchen tonight. They take off their shoes, fetch the water and start the fire, and prepare to make the table ready with bread and water and salt, all backwards—when the old cat jumped into the window and scared them, and the thing broke up in shrieks and giggles. Floyd was quite pale. His mother had just come to the porch and bade him have nothing to do with it.

April 3, 1912

Have sent MSS of "The Mystic Words" and "Dream of the Dust" to Carol.[19] Feeling bad again—probably on account of lifting stone yesterday. A chilly morning, but clear, warmer at mid-day. I had fifteen minutes of severe pain this morning that upset me for all day, but did some verses with small decoration for the Chattanooga News.

April 7, 1912

Easter Sunday. Rain. We have never had two week's supply ahead of debt, scarcely a day's, one time since last Easter. What an awful strain it has been—and no prospect of anything easier, and we are both about to give way. Cloudy this afternoon. We all went to Joe's and the children had a merry time with the Easter eggs.

April 8, 1912

Pinching cold—the Easter snap. Frank went to the valley to hunt Grandpap's strayed mare, and took Buzz with him. They went by Morrison Springs, and brought home strange flowers from the Side—delicate things, but withered before I saw them. I went to Mrs. Lane's and telephoned to various people. Then to the post office. Mrs. Andrews wishes to buy my Signal Mountain picture—for five or possibly seven dollars, I suppose.

Warmer this afternoon, calm and clear. Plum trees are, as Grandma says, "so white it makes you cold to look at 'em" and peaches blooming. Sunshine warm—green grass in yards and patches. Mamie washed, and afterwards went home. The girls with her—for an hour's visit.

April 16, 1912

To Chattanooga. Frank borrowed the mare to take me down for the one chance to see Mrs. Cooke.[20] Lunched at the Read House with Zella A. [Zella Armstrong (1872–1965), Chattanooga writer and historian] & her mother, Carol, and Mrs. Cooke and Katherine, who is a lovely girl. Afterward we planned a summer's work together.

April 20, 1912

Spent the night with Mrs. Wheatley—and never had a more enjoyable night. Part of the time in Mrs. Starr's [Mrs. Wheatley's mother] room, where a trained nurse moves about among bowls of tulips and lilacs. Katherine Kaufman played me to sleep with the pianola. This morning I got up and had a delicious bath—then breakfast, during which Frank telephoned for me. Mrs. W. sent me to town in a taxi,—a splendid ride. She most cordially asked me to stay a week, and have my breakfast in bed; I wish I could, and get well at my leisure. Got the groceries at Freudenberg's and lay down on May's bed till the hack came. Rode up beside Miss Mary Key.

All the hillsides are lit with white flames of dogwood. But the mountain-top is still gray above the valley's green. The children met us, shouting and waving at the Top—overjoyed to have mother back, bless them.

April 24, 1912

I did think that after this smash-up I should be taken care of;[21] but I am obliged to be up and down with the children all night, and then be waked early just the same. One has no recourse against such unconscious cruelty. And the money has to be earned by day, just the same. It does not seem possible that I can live through another year of it.

Frank plowed and planted potatoes and beans. I lay on the bed after dinner and tried to take a nap, but was disturbed by the children time after time, and finally began a short story for the News, as the nearest short-cut to cash. The children play Hi-spy by moonlight, with Brick, and get so excited that they can hardly be got to bed.

April 28, 1912

After getting breakfast I was too done up to eat, so in desperation I insisted on being taken at once to Mrs. Sarah Patten at Topside. I knew I should get some orders for cards, and I thought she would help me; and she did; she gave me a check for $30 so that I can go visiting in town, rest, and get well. What a relief it is. Then I had some tea and an egg; and we went on to see poor Laura who is expecting a baby any day, heavy and suffering. When we got home Joe's wife & children came— and she offered to comb Kitty's hair while I am gone. How kind every body is to me.

April 30, 1912

To visit Mrs. Wheatley. I thought I should drop before I got here—but on coming into the house I felt the strain of the past months letting down, down, into ease and comfort. These dear people—their kindness is greater than their wealth; by which I mean that it is not only more conspicuous but more real,—would be there if the wealth were to vanish.

I am lying in a large, airy room with long white curtained windows and a thick carpet. There is the most restful little picture I ever saw, directly over the bed,—an opalescent, misty spring twilight over some marshy place that might be the Everglades but for some low blue hills in the distance: and a Card-reproduction in sepia over the mantel—The wall is finished with a border of lilacs. I was given wine, and then a little bowl of broth, when I came. How many people would have welcomed me and taken such thought for my welfare on the eve of a splendid musicale? They have put up tents on the grass, and innumerable seats & tables, all set about with pines—evidently expecting a crowd. Her mother's illness also makes extra trouble.

May 1, 1912

6 o'clock and I am still peacefully enjoying the hemstitched linen of my bed. Lookout Mt. slopes directly up from my windows, and a wonderful

chorus of birds rings from its steep woods—thrush & mocker cardinal, catbird, grosbeak, tanager—everything large enough to whip the St. Elmo sparrows. The sun is shining brightly, though we looked for rain. I have let go of worry; slept like a top till 3 this morning, and then dozed till daybreak. I do hope Frank will not ask me to go home Saturday.

All day a great scurrying rearrangement of the already perfect house—arrival of cut flowers in boxes, fresh embroidered covers on every bed and table and dresser, palms and ferns in posts, a hundred chairs to reinforce the already numerous seats. The nurse volunteered to help in the kitchen. Only I and Mrs. Starr were out of it. The weather was perfect, and at two Kosmos began to arrive in its best frocks and new spring hats. I went into Mrs. Starr's room, and we watched them come up from the car lines, shining in the delicate silks of the season. Later we sat at the head of the stairs listening to Cadek's orchestra—Polish & Bohemian music; and gypsy songs by Rita Faxon Pryor.[22] Katharine, sweet in a linen dress, was assisted by four girls in gay gypsy costume, serving punch before a screen of dogwood boughs. The chairs all filled, and I, who had come down at Mrs. Wheatley's urging, went with others to sit on the broad stairs. After the music there was a dance on the fresh turf—a most graceful dancer, in costume—Maud Leeper [illegible]. I thought I should not know any one present, but met a number of acquaintances and was introduced to a hundred or so more, most of whom I cannot now recall. Mrs. Wheatley in her simple dress of embroidered linen kept rather in the background, looking after every one's comfort while every one was saying what a wonderful woman, "with a heart as big as Lookout Mountain." Katharine was a study in tact and winning gentleness and courtesy. As I would have none of the ices & salads, she brought me wine. I meant to keep well in the background, but found myself shaking hands right and left, and talked till my hair came down. The sun went behind the mountain, and the hostess stood for half an hour under the tent, saying good by [sic], while the deep cool shadows of Lookout crept down and enfolded the house. At last all were gone; the negroes began to gather up chairs, and Cadek made his adieux; Mr. Wheatley came forth, found Katharine dropped beside her aunt, both tired out. As the rose of sunset flamed up over the mountain we all had a plate of salad, and said what a success it had been.

May 2, 1912

Today at my request one of the "gypsies" came back and posed in costume for a couple of watercolors. Mr. Wheatley got out his camera and took a number of her graceful poses—on the green grass and rocky terraces behind the house. Afterward he got his paint box and did a very creditable sketch of my old-rose silk dress and the hammock. Dear Katherine visited in my place tonight and showed me her imported frocks.

May 3, 1912

Spent the morning doing a head of Mrs. Starr—not very successful, as she was too frail to sit long. Afterwards cut the MSS of Thistle Bloom— then loafed in the hammock and looked at books.[23] But I really began the day by running into Mrs. Wheatley's room and telling her how happy I was. She kissed me and said, "Well, we're very fond of you."

What a wonderful thing it is to have such friends. I spoke of leaving tomorrow, but was urged to stay.

May 4, 1912

I thought, perhaps Frank would be in town, so went to Cousin May's and had them put up an order of groceries, and as it was raining, arranged for a wagon to take Joe home—he has spent the week alternating between Brick & Emmons. Then I was tired and went to sleep on Cousin's bed. Waked up at dinner time and ate with them—then back to St. Elmo. Had quite a jolly time with Katherine and two young girl visitors. Afterwards came the miracle.

The house was all quiet: I was wrapped in a steamer rug in the back-porch hammock when Mrs. Wheatley came out and sat down with her knitting.

"You're going to stay with me a long time, aren't you?" she said. And suddenly she laid down her knitting, came over to me and took both my hands: "Don't you love me as much as Miss Sarah? Won't you stay with me?" I put my arm over her neck and said something inane about how good she was. "We're not," she said. "You don't know how fond Ted and I are of you. It's not your work, though you know we appreciate that: It's yourself. We like to see you come down in the mornings. When you told me yesterday how happy you were, it was one of the glad moments of my life. I felt I had won something." She sat close by me, patting my worn-out body with her warm hands, and said such lovely things about my work and me, the tears came into my eyes. There were tears in her eyes too, and she became rather incoherent. I felt the old wounds and bruises healing, knots and tensions relaxing, washed by deep warm waves of kindness and love: I talked to her of all things next my heart, freely—When I came upstairs I was crying with happiness and relief. Katherine found me, but she is young and did not notice. It is wonderful to be loved like that!

May 5, 1912

The new photos came before breakfast—one of me, and several gypsy poses. I drew a while and then rested till dinner. All afternoon I loafed, while they played clock-golf and read together from Barrack-Room Ballads. Walked among the green terraces in the evening, picking roses and strawberries, and at dinner I told them the story of the dumb supper and some of Frank's funny ghost stories—and they tried "asking the ring." Then we sat in the Green Room in the dark while Mr. W played Lucia, and Hungarian Rhapsodies. Mrs. Wheatley came into my room to kiss me goodnight.

I never dreamed I could so attract and interest the best and brightest people.

May 6, 1912

Tonight all the fibres of my being are loosened and quivering, exquisitely in tone with such music as I have dreamed. It is now late, later than I ought to be up, but sleep is not for me. That such things should come to me, should be poured out at my feet!

When one is regaining strength after a period of illness and depression there is a joyous uprushing surge of vitality: one hears truer, sees clearer, grasps at life with a quick insatiable eagerness. I am prone to distrust and check any feelings of undue warmth—but surely this is partly accounted for by the reaction from long strain.

Anyway, the gods have sent me this: I will take it with both hands.

Carol spent the day, and was happy, dear caged songbird, in the society of wealth and talent. I tried to work a little, but felt at once restless and drowsy with new happiness. After dinner we went to the library, and I was carefully placed on a couch under the electric light, rolled in a rug, and given my choice of the books; but again, I could not read. The sense of romance and wonder, the beauty and the mystery of my life, and of all my life, was vividly present with me; my heart beat fast, and I laid down the book. Then Katherine, who adores her uncle, whispered that he was about to sing, and we tiptoed to the Green Room and composed ourselves to listen. He sang "Ah schönen" and I shut my hands tight to keep from sobbing. Song after song, till my heart was out of its shell. Then one to that appealing air of Stephanie: and German lieder, and Irish and Scotch airs; and tried "Afterwards" but found that he did not know it well.

Is it a golden voice, or am I unusually sensitive just now? Or is it because I am so poignantly touched by any attempt to please me? I don't know. I am as wildly happy as a girl.

May 7, 1912

"It is not real," I heard the dawnsong of the thrush thro' the steady rain. "It is not real—" after a sleepless night, a white night of magic.

Yes, this is a gift of the gods, this beautiful illusion of an hour. But I must receive it only for what it is. Nothing in my life is real but the children.

I had a letter from them in the morning mail. They are lonely, struggling along without mother. There is the heart and the treasure—this is a beautiful dream.

The Wheatleys went to town in an auto this afternoon, and I slept for an hour and a half. On their return he brought me a present—a portfolio of engravings. How he is always going out of his way to make some one happy! The overflowing warmth of his nature!

All the men in St. Elmo were at a meeting to vote the pigs out of the streets tonight. After a delightful quiet hour in the library Katherine came up with me, walking with her arm around me like a pair of girls, and showed me some things for her "hope chest"—two beautiful night gowns she handled like the sacred robes they are. Then she kissed me good night oh, so sweetly.

May 9, 1912

"Not real!" says the thrush up the mountainside. "It's not real."
That cool clear tone seems at times to penetrate and dissolve the spirit's

connection with the material world—or perhaps rather, to fuse and kindle into identity the flesh and spirit—interweaving, blending.

O spirit Singers! Life flows round us in sweet mysterious currents, round and through us with the nightwind and the bounding blood. And afterward how many little soulless people are getting up to buy and sell and chase about on meaningless errands! What have we to do with them?

In the night I woke with a sense of something wrong. Burglars, I thought, and slipping back the bolt of the door, listened at the stair-head a long time. I could not sleep again: and at breakfast I could not eat a bite. They sent me a poached egg and a glass of milk, with a rose, on a tray to the back porch; and I choked it down some how. But immediately after, I received a letter from home saying that Joe was coming down with measles; and Jean added that Charly Brock was threatening Frank again. In an instant I was torn from the dream of these gentle days, and strung like a bow for action. No fire-horse could have leapt quicker at the tap of the gong.

But so disappointed over having to leave that I could hardly speak the few inane conventional phrases of farewell. I don't know what my lovely hosts made of my behavior; but who could get any thing but a brutal wrench out of such a parting? Their sweet kindness followed me all the way with new manifestations. But I could hardly breathe; I was torn in two,—so fierce was the urge to reach and to help my children and my man in need, so keen the longing to remain in the sunlight. All the way into Chattanooga I sat with closed eyes; and through the street I walked in a daze of misery, rigid and pale, hardly seeing the few things I had to buy.

Every nerve in me cries out against having to hear the little talk of little people, or to look at anything sordid or ungainly that may blur the impression of that music, of light and warmth and laughter. I had not realized how utterly without these my life has come to be.

And so home:—to find that the sacrifice was for nothing—nobody sick or in danger, Charley having waylaid and half killed another man and then disappeared. Only their inveterate habit of complaining to me, of throwing on to me every possible bit of worry or responsibility! For this I was called back out of the first comfort and happiness I have ever known for years! I don't feel angry, but as if something were broken.

May 10, 1912

I have dropped back into my familiar place again: I am the drudge, the ragged, pinched, worn-out slavey: Oh, the pity of all I have missed—half of life! Oh, the pain that sleeps all day heavy on the heart, and wakes at night to draw blood!

I have eaten no solid food since yesterday breakfast and all night I see the vision of a joyous acceptance of day, a free and gracious habit of living, a spontaneous and continuous kindness and bounty, a swift and sympathetic intelligence. My chance of living on that plane is gone long ago. Out of the sunshine forever.

May 11, 1912

Poor Frank has been trying all day to comfort me, because I cannot rouse interest in anything. A letter came from Grace MacGowan—on her way back to California, thus knocking out my hope of placing my novel while she is in New York.[24] I am all in: I am beat. Money gone, strength gone. I can't live through another winter; I am very sure I don't want to try. And I don't want to eat. I have been worried for years, without ceasing, about food, food, food. Now I don't want any more. They want to send for a doctor, but I would rather die than be worried about another ten dollars.

May 19, 1912

I thought surely, surely, some one would come today; listened sharp every time an auto went chugging along the Signal Point road. Such a beautiful Sunday—there must have been hundreds of people on the Ridge. But not one came. I'm hoping, longing, praying for a chance to get away from home long enough to get well and do some real work.

Brick took Mirick in the little wagon, and he and Joe brought me a great sheaf of laurel from the swimming-hole—mostly buds.

Typed the first draft of The Woman Interferes.

May 24, 1912

Back to town. I do so want to make a success of this venture. Went to Carol's and we talked story plots till after lunch. Met Katherine K. & sent some laurel to Mrs. Wheatley, who is still abed. Then went to D.V. Stroop's office and asked for a corner in the office to work in.[25] After supper C. &

I called on Mrs. Cantrell. We talked about Tennessee laws on women, & as Cantrell is a lawyer it was very interesting. Then we all went to some moving pictures & had a sundae round in the drugstore. I am tired, but not sick; I have taken heart o' grace with the chance to get some work done.

May 26, 1912

Sunday. Got up an hour or two before any one else and sat writing in the cool, silent house. After breakfast Carol & I went over a story. This evening we walked out on the lighted streets & had some ice cream.

Yesterday D.V.S. brought my typewriter down for me. Lunched with Mabel. Met Dr. & Mrs. Rathwell & Carol had my photograph taken for the News.

What ugly things people are willing to imagine & to say of each other. It passes comprehension. Such dirty gossip. If ever I write my novel, Flower of the Sun, I shall take Katherine K. for the heroine—or one similar.[26] Some girl whose every action is watched by a lot of narrow, dirty-minded people. Well—the Lord save us all from Grundy! I never had but one lover in my life, but I have managed to stir up as much talk as the next one.

Then that is why the tears were in Mrs. Wheatley's eyes. Oh, I shall love her all the better now.

Walking on Market St. [downtown Chattanooga] this evening, enjoying the crowds and the lights, I came to the railroad tracks—I like to see those emblems of power, the engines. Came to a demonstration car from Oklahoma & went over it, meaning to tell Frank about dry farming alfalfa & milo maize. Walked back to Carol's & read Aglavaine & Selysette.[27]

May 27, 1912

Monday. Typed the rough draft of a story for the News—the Cookstove.[28] It is a good story. Borrowed a dollar from Dave for MS paper & a new typewriter ribbon. Went over to Hill City at noon to send my folks some groceries.[29]

June 2, 1912

Sunday. Had an indignation meeting on my hands. Grandma exhausted her eloquence trying to persuade me to stay at home. Oh how they all pity

my children—not to the extent of doing something for them in my absence
however. And what tales are being circulated! Grandma can't read but
she knows that literary folks will do to watch—"these here writers and
typewriters" is her phrase.

June 3, 1912

Monday. Back to town. Finished the story, but the News did not want it
after all. Lunched at Carol's and lay on the bed with a headache until the
inevitable "Now don't you ever tell I told you this" became worse than the
pain, and then went to Cousin May's for the night. I told Cousin about the
hornet's nest of gossip on the Ridge, & she, becoming very earnest, laid her
hand on my knee & said: "Don't you care. Not one of the women of our family,
as far back as we know anything about them, but has been above suspicion."

June 4, 1912

After doing all errands I had still a few hours, and wanted so to see
Mrs. Wheatley that I telephoned & asked permission. I found her ailing,
but radiating the same quiet goodness & warmth. Katherine very sweet &
merry. She said Mrs. Patten told her I had such beautiful manners—which
surprised me, for it never had occurred to me that I had any. They kept
me to lunch, & I rode back to town in their auto. Mr. W. said my booklet of
verses which I sent them was nearly as good as Kipling.

Miss Gregg gave me a box of odds & ends of very nice slightly worn
clothing. Called also on Mrs. Atlee & Mrs. Van Dusen—two blessed
women who never spoke an ill word of any one.

Had a pleasant conversation with Miss Lenoir coming up in the hack.
This discovery of a talent for making friends has rather gone to my head—
As if I were to find out I had a fine singing voice or something wonderful &
new.

Only Joe & Jean meet me: Judith is abed with the measles.

June 20, 1912

Frank has been telling me tales of his boyhood: of the murder of John
Pickett the moonshiner, not twenty minutes after the boy and his father had
left him on Market Street: of whole nights spent in a bar-room, watching
his drunken father play cards, sleeping on a table and subsisting on what

sandwiches and soft drinks the bartender gave him; of a runaway on the Side in the dark, when he, all alone at twelve years, guided the team home through the burning woods; of his early acquaintance with all the vice in the lowest dives of Chattanooga. Oh, that lonely neglected, disillusioned little boy, how my heart goes out to him! I have made a promise to that far-away little boy that life shall never cheat him of anything through me.

June 30, 1912

Carol asked me to do some verses celebrating the occasion of the druggist's powwow next week in Chattanooga, for the Lookout. I remained in bed till nearly noon today, writing while the little girls & Frank got breakfast and straightened the house. "The Chemist" resulted—a poem of sixty four lines. Mrs. Dabney called, then Mrs. Talmadge and two friends, then grandma came to dinner. Cloudy & damp.

July 1, 1912

To town again. Typed the new poem, helped Carol with one of hers, and rough-drafted a new one—The Alchemist. Robert Strauss,[30] who is producing a vaudeville with certain features of his own, sent me two tickets, and I took Emmons Freudenberg this evening. All local talent and very good indeed. Showery.

July 3, 1912

As the Lookout could not pay cash I meant the new poem for a gift, but Zella had me measured for a corset on an advertising account. I took the other poem to the News—then as all was done I went to see Mrs. Wheatley. Found her alone and had a delightful hour going over my poems with her. Home on the hack—everything too crowded to bring my groceries. But Mrs. Wheatley gave me two dollars to celebrate the Fourth, for the children, and I bought the girls each a dress of India linen. Walked part of the way up with Cadek the violinist. He does not talk nearly so well as he plays.

July 7, 1912

In bed nearly all day with a sick headache, and Frank moping about very discouraged. I think however it was given me for once to say the right thing. We both feel better this evening. Mrs. Rawlins sent me a dozen eggs.

There is a nest of young chippies in the pine tree, and since we sent away the cats, the parent birds have become very tame, camping continually on the childrens' trail of crumbs.

Caroline is a complete victim of the masculine system of ethics as ever I saw. We get into an argument over some question of right & wrong every time we meet. Seems to me that women, women past the climacteric but not dotaged, mothers of healthy honest humanity, women who have never been dependent on any man for "support"—such only are fit arbiters of the moral standards of the race. I understand that certain notions of old gave such power into the hands of a few old women, setting an almost supernatural value on their counsel in affairs of peace or war. (What would be the Latin title, feminine gender, for an Arbiter of right and wrong?) But this cult became entangled with moon-worship and hysterical manifestations as the Arbiters became prophetesses and priestesses. Then the rivalry of the male began to assert itself, as the priesthood came into being; so began the religions of the world, and waxed mightily on belief in supernatural power on the one hand and the strength borrowed from the moral code on the other. But side by side with the domination of the priest has persisted that yet more ancient feminine moon-worship, traceable to this day in curious rites pertaining to feminine affairs like the care of the new-born and the planting of garden truck.

It is inevitable that systems of ethics & morals should change and modify with changing circumstances. The needs of the race are different at different times and in different parts of the world. All moral codes have some good in them; all are open to improvement. None should ever be accepted as final. The real purpose of laws regulating social purity, for example, is the breeding of greater men and women; but it is quite subject to alterations and modification. Polygamy was right for the patriarchs, when the actual first commandment, "Be fruitful and multiply," was of prime importance in the unsubdued wilderness of earth; and no doubt thievery was right for the Spartans. Ruth was a great woman, or she could not have uttered the beautiful text of her faithfulness to Naomi; and certainly she gave birth to a line of great men. David must have respected his great-grandmother profoundly, else he would not have enshrined her memory for all time to come in a special book. That her marriage would be impossible in any but a savage tribe today is no argument against the wisdom of Naomi's counsel. No experience qualifies better to mete out justice and judge right & wrong than that of raising a family; she who has done this well is more fit for the bench or the pulpit than many a man in robe or gown and bands.

Perhaps no woman really respects the law. Caroline believes she does, but what she really respects are her own men folks. A real live, thinking, feeling woman of any experience & character sees that the law is an inconsistent, feeble convention, a compromise between what ought to be and what the race has out grown, only tolerable because it is in process of growth & adaptation.—Why is it that women are the chief support of religion, the chains of their own enslavement? Because piety is a by-product of sex?

July 15, 1912

Drowsy, quiet, hot noon; only the tankle of cowbells and the zz-ing of insects, or the distant thrush-note from some coolness that lingers in the thicketed hollow. Hourly the garden-tangle thickens and deepens; the green tomatoes and peppers swell, the cabbages harden between broad bluish leaves, lettuce and mustard run gaily to seed and coquet with butterflies, sunflowers erect and lusty push great rough leaves to right and left, arrogantly overtopping the young fruit trees; the corn whets its glistening blades against the streaming air, each stalk cradling its milky ear like a babe in a robber's den; beets and turnips suck, through their muzzling roots, the juice of the soil, transforming it by the mysterious chemistry of vegetation into what shall feed us through the winter.

Frank comes to dinner tired and wet with perspiration: it is very hot. After this the sun is shouldered out of the sky by wrestling clouds, and the continuous mellow rolling of far away thunder sounds louder and louder.

The children seem to grow more interesting every day:—though there is now no baby among them. "Aw," says Mirick scornfully, "I ain't no baby; I'm done and bee'd a baby—I'm a boy!" They are "liable to say anything." They speak the dialect much of the time; Mirick shouts "Wait, you-uns—wait!" as he tugs at the little wagon in the rear of a prancing line: and

Kitty persistently says "Elf," like an old granny. But in the next breath she informs me that the new bush beans (white wax) are "almost transparent colored," and that she has found a new flower up the branch and "thinks it's a pencil-drania," meaning nobody knows what.

Last night we were all tired and went to bed early; but Mirick for some reason refused, probably because he wanted to sleep with me. He sat on the floor in his nighty, his yellow head bobbing drowsily, and replied "Naw; aint—gona—dewit" to every possible proposition.

"—Don't you want to sleep with sister?"

"Unh-huh; aint—gonna—dewit!"

"Want 'o sleep with papa? Want 'o rock in mother's lap?—Mother fix a pallet on the floor?"

Same answer. "Ain't—gona—sleep with nobody!"

Again and again he dropped off to sleep and either fell or was laid down, and each time performed a swift gyration amid flying legs and arms and came up right,—much like the little tumblers called roly-polies or McGintys, that are weighted with a marble inside. The girls meantime were giggling themselves limp in their beds, and the light was turned very low for the night.

"Put him outdoors, Emmer! Put him Outdoors!" his father commanded at last, and the spanking could be no longer delayed. But it took four or five on end before he finally subsided on his pillow.

July 16, 1912

Rode down with Cesnor Vandergriff; had breakfast with Cousin May and lunched with Carol. Went with her to a meeting of a moving-picture club among ladies, chiefly of St. Elmo. Met Lotta Anderson in at Loveman's. Met Katherine Kaufman & gave her Jean's honey-ball flowers for Mrs. Wheatley. She took me to some moving pictures & we had a glass of something cold. Back to Hill City and trimmed a nice black-and-white turban for Cousin May.

July 18, 1912

A cloudy morning. Wrote eight verses before getting up—The Candidate at Caney's Cove,[31] suggested by Frank's remark about the candidates "shaking the calico" the Fourth of July. Sold it to the News as soon as I got it typed. To Cousin May's in the evening, with two library books—Swinburne and Lafcadio Hearn.

July 23, 1912

Frank and Uncle Joe went to the valley for peaches. I mailed nine pages of notes for Grace's novel.[32] Where is the month gone to? It scares me to set down a date. Here's blackberries, peaches, and green beans to be canned—a two weeks' washing in soak—three orders for pictures waiting—a hill of sewing piled on the machine—Carol awaiting my collaboration on a story—the house upside down, and three meals a day going right on just the same! Not a promising outlook for literary labors. How much can I possibly get done? And Frank is as busy as I, with outdoor work. It is now too late to plant late potatoes; we are eating up the seed—that two-dollar bushel!

Canned peaches all afternoon, and ate too many. Such a headache.

July 29, 1912

Finished a booklet for Edith.[33] Frank got another bushel of peaches and we began to put them up. Mrs. S.A. Patten walked in about noon, accompanied by an Iowa clergyman who bought a small picture & kodaked [photographed] the house. I feel rather bad and look worse. Began a study of blackeyed Susans this evening. Brick stopped by with the horse & buggy and took Mark and Joe to the Valley with him—Mark particularly delighted with the prospect of his first visit from home.

July 31, 1912

Judith and I went to Capt. Hutcheson's after dinner to begin a sketch for a watercolor for Mrs. Dabney.[34] On the way I found the most beautiful moth, I think I ever saw—apricot-colored upper wings marked in faint brown like a Chinese character, the under wing beautifully circled with black and tinted like the riper side of a peach.

A storm came up suddenly; the wind beat the rain into white mist and drove it in great waves through the tossing trees. During its course, or after the down pour had somewhat slackened, Mrs. Dabney put some five records on the phonograph, and we heard some good music. Judith behaved beautifully, made intelligent and quiet answers when addressed, and looked her best in the white dress and pink tub-silk bonnet I just made for her, and long black stockings.

It has turned quite cool this evening.

August 1, 1912

Election. Frank walked to Fairmount to vote. Lassie Hullet came this morning. The children played with her fine-looking little "woods colt" [illegitimate child] while she washed.

August 4, 1912

I was preparing to get breakfast when an old man walked in at the gate, and it was my father.[35] He ate with us and shaved with Frank's razor, but went away in haste to get to a singing at Mountain Creek. He is exactly the same old sixpence; has flattered all the children as neatly as he used to me, and I must e'en let them find him out by experience I suppose.

It is so cool we had to make a fire this morning. Cousin May left her little girl here while they drove out to Signal Point. The children all went picking flowers in the hollow, and brought in a white Sabbatia, and the first yellow fringed-orchis, and several of the green.

August 15, 1912

Telephoned again, and Frank & I & the two babies got caught in a storm at Mrs. Rawlings'. When the electricity crackled on the telephone Mirick, who was sitting on a lounge, kicked up his heels and waved his legs about so that he nearly fell backwards, shouting: "Striked the house again! Striked the house!" He said of a short stump in the patch: "That's a little bad-boy stubby-toe place."

Sunflowers in the edge of the field, standing high in sunshine, blazed vividly against the purple curtain of the storm. Their broad leaves were beautiful as a carving in jade & crystal, till riddled by last week hail.

The green passion-flower is in bloom in the woods, the purple one in the fields. Capt. H— rides a-hunting of evenings, with a lantern hung to saddle & a horn slung round his neck.

Day by day—the sun gets up to fill the world with the laughter of light; the dew-silvered shadows shorten, turn, and flow eastward; and a thousand forms of life issue from the infinite vitality, a thousand curious beautiful manifestations of the world-spirit.

August 17, 1912

To town on the hack. A hot, hurried, worried, unsatisfactory day. Two books from the library, a bird book & the Century of the Child.[36] Judith quite ready to come home—in an auto! Carol says she has been ever so good. Brought the typewriter home. Saw Mrs. Wheatley, but she was disappointed in the figures for the cabin—more than she expected or can afford. Mr. Wheatley showed me a canvas he just bought from N.Y.—a painting of a wonderful cloudy sky by Jacob Maris [Dutch painter (1837–1899)].

August 21, 1912

Spent the day with the Atlees, most pleasantly. Mrs. Atlee has hit on the delightful idea of a guest book illuminated on several pages with pen-and-ink sketches, very tiny, of things about her place Ridgewood: from a frontispiece of the log house embowered in trees & vines, to bits of characteristic still-life & wild flowers. I got only a few done today.

Hunting orchids with Mark in the marshy hollow: "Mamma," he said, looking all round anxiously, "we don't know where we're at."

"I know where I am," I assured him.

"Well," he protested, "I don't know where my-self is."

Frank planted a small patch of turnips.

August 24, 1912

A storm is moving up the valley, accompanied by a continuous roaring, and deeper detonations that roll across the sky—a "proud music" indeed.

The Anderson girls drove over again, with a friend, and Annie Keith Frazier—the most beautiful girl I have ever drawn, I think.[37] I did some little pencil drawings of the three older girls for souvenirs, and a larger one of Miss Frazier for myself. It is reminiscent, in this line and that, of all I have admired most in types created by various artists, and yet plainly a native growth—a product of Tennessee valleys, blue air & clear springs. The full and strong modeling of the forehead; the wing-like sweep of the brows from a short high-bridged nose; the eyes deeply and exquisitely set, with dark-lashed, graciously curving lids; the flow and shining swirl of light brown hair, storming round the tinted ears and long thick neck: the peachy rounded chin, the sweetness and animation of the whole face—O that is a divine thing, such beauty; a gift from heaven! Such inspiration there is in Nature's poems. I wrote this evening a poem, If I were Spring, that is, I believe, very good. Bless the girl!

August 26, 1912

Walked up the brow and did a color sketch in front of the Patten house. Met Senator Frazier & his wife & son; took lunch with them. Very kindly & intelligent people, and more than handsome. Had a most delightful visit of half an hour with Mrs. Klaus. Her little boy, five or six months younger than Mark, talked a good bit with me—told me about Peter Rabbit and the "choo-choo crain." Mrs. Frazier gave me a bucket of sugar for the children to make candy, as I had made them laugh over Jean's experimental fudge, and some eggs & sardines. Annie Keith played the Spring Song for me. Rode part way home, after doing some pencil sketches along the brow, in Grandpap's stylish new rig. Jean is home this evening. Rain & cooler.

August 28, 1912

Lassie washed. Kitty went to school with the others. I suggested to Mark that he play with Lassie's baby, but he said, "No! I'm a man; I take care of you." Got out another poem—The Nameless, begun in a St. Elmo street car weeks ago. I should like to write one about Market Street.

It is quite true, as an ancient thinker once said, that the united opinion of fools does not make a truth; but it is equally certain that from their conflicting opinions one may arrive at a general truth, by a process analogous to that of the astronomer who determines the height of the atmosphere by observing the divergent courses of meteors. By some such a calculation I reach the conclusion that something is wrong with our civilized regulations concerning love & marriage; less because I have been reading Ellen Key than because I have been studying Lassie and her so-called illegitimate son, together with certain mothers of legitimate children & others who have no children at all.

August 30, 1912

Last night something—a hard word—the most uncalled-for, unforgettable thing. I could not sleep after it; I began to chill, and afterward vomiting set in, and pains in my bowels. I have been abed all day, though the children went to school and Frank to work. This evening sat up and ate a few bites.

September 1, 1912

Considerably better—sat up part of the day, and ate something at table. Judith has done most of the cooking but they have let the house get into such a mess. Mrs. Hutcheson & Elizabeth D. & Rosalie called, brought me some papers & the children a really good simplification of Malory's Arthur—and borrowed some of my stories to read.

My dear man will never learn to take care of me, I see that now. What had I better do? It is true what he says, I do not do much and am always complaining. If it must be one sickness after another, the writing and everything dragging along half done, would it not be better to go where I can have my health and do my work? I could visit them and send them enough, I think, to live on.

September 5, 1912

Typed on Dan Riley all morning.[38] It seems to me there is a best-seller in that idea of Frank's of a one-man home-insurance-&-detective agency if I could work it out. O for time, time! This everlasting cooking—and my stomach is so bad that the mornings drag. The fence corners of the place are gay with a tall, hairy, dark-stemmed wild sunflower, and with lettuce-birds scarcely distinguishable from the blooms. The air is thick with fine azure; the horizon glows with a wonderful warm gray made of all the spectrum intermingled, "woven and molten in one sleight of amorous color and implicated light"—and the mid-blue as it were bleached and tarnished by the breathless heat.

September 8, 1912

The twins' birthday: 10 years old. Made them a cake and some pretty whitecap cakies [*sic*], and a pitcher of a sour drink of the bottled peach syrup. The Underwood children and Virgie came after dinner, and played all afternoon. Jean came home from Aunt Laura's, in a red dress which Mrs.

Williams gave her, carrying 5 yards of pink gingham which Aunt Laura gave her for helping. Dr. Barrett & Miss Maud came up & spent an hour or so—talked ginseng with Frank & tasted the cakes with the children.

September 19, 1912

A beautiful cool autumnal day, followed by a beautiful moonlight. I worked at little pictures all day, and when the children came home from school I took them all down to the post office for a treat of soda pop. We all stopped in Wood Thrush Hollow to admire an effect of singular beauty—a single slanting shaft of sun that pierced the dim green twilight, lighting sharply the maple trunks here and there, and spreading the brown sloping earth with a soft splash of gold. I sent them home from the store with a basket of food, and went on to see Mrs. Atlee. Had a pleasant visit, & perhaps sold a picture. Coming home through the darkening field I stopped to listen to the fairy music of the crickets—a steady trilling, the only sound, in all the dew-chilled earth.

63° F. this evening, still and clear.

September 20, 1912

Frank went to town, but got almost nothing done that he went for. Lassie washed & told me the whole story of her little woods-colt. She seems to look at the matter very sensibly. I wish her luck with him. Yom Kippur.

Frank brought Judith her new third grade books, and she is reading stories from the reader to Mark. She reads, I think, uncommonly well, with considerable expression. Mark has a sore throat something like Jean's—has not been well all day. Mrs. Bachman & Mrs. Hyde called.[39]

One finds in the garden a few last least tomatoes glowing like red coals in the fading grass; the whole weedy tangle is sun-bleached, and embroidered with blue & yellow asters and tufts of goldenrod in which the lightning bugs crawl & tumble luxuriously. Some few pods of okra on the tip of climbing stalks; sweet potatoes, spindling & stringy; a few late sweet peppers. It is all one tangle of crab-grass.

September 23, 1912

Such a scurry and scramble to get off to school—"Shall I have a clean dress, Mamma? Now my hair's all right, tie me a big fluffy bow, won't you,

Mamma?"—"Aw, I can't find me no clo'es; I just ain't goin' to go!"—"Now, somebody's had my reader; I laid it right here!"—"I can't never remember what is seven times seven!"—"Juju, did you put in some bread 'm' shrup for Joe & Kitty to eat at rec-cess?"—"Seven times nine is sixty-three; seven times six is—is—Mamma, <u>how</u> many is it?"—"Joe, I do wisht you'd g'wan to school and git out of everybody's way!"—and so on till they trot away through the cool, cloudy morning.

I finished Dr. Fifer's book,[40] while Frank cleaned house thoroughly for me, like an angel—then went to Mrs. Atlee's with it, and talked with her about the chances of bringing out my book of poems by subscription. I do hope I can make it a go. She bought a Signal Point watercolor, and gave me a small check, most of which I spent for groceries on the way home.

That old Hutcheson field—I am beginning to love its waste acres. The narrow path weaves across, nearly hidden among weeds & sedge grass. In the daylight when the wind blows, one hears the voices of various growths—the long dim sigh of a seedling pine, the almost articulate whisper of large—leafed, stunted hickories or gnarled and dying Limber Twigs of a forgotten orchard. Toward nightfall there are only the steadily singing crickets. In the edge of the woods, at the head of the hollow, is a group of well-nourished, well-grown trees—quick-growing maples and poplars that have recovered an almost perfect symmetry since the 1905 sleet; the deepest shadows cluster in their hearts, shrinking at noon, expanding and flowing across the field toward evening to blend with the advancing darkness. The path approaches this splendid group, sheers round it as though afraid, skirts a great dark mound of whispering vegetation, and timidly enters the woods, accompanied at first by self-heal & sunflower & poke weed, those inhabitants of edges and corners, and followed farther by the sumachs, red-berried now before their leaves catch aflame. Then quite suddenly it is swallowed by a dark mouth of leaves; the field-growths and the field-lights are left behind, and here is the forest indeed—high and dim, in a perpetual twilight, closed in with its own dreams and its own shadowy ways—darkening down to the little stream that slips silently over the mossed tree-roots. That is Wood-Thrush Hollow.

September 24, 1912

To Summertown. Nora Renshaw—such a dear, childish slip of a woman—walked over with me. I called on Mrs. Poindexter and gave her a little watercolor of our house. Then stopped a short while at the temporary orphanage, and talked to the poor little tads about the mountain flowers: left them two little sketches for souvenirs. Then to Laura's—Her poor baby is like a skeleton, but I think it will live. After dinner she gathered a sack full of apples & pears, for me, from their trees which are hanging full to breaking. Then we sat on the porch and worked buttonholes in Little Ab's waists till Frank came for me with Grandpap's rig. A most enjoyable visit. Sold $2, pictures to Mrs. Read [Reed]—matron of the orphanage—and spent it all for groceries on the way home.[41] A beautiful day, and a most enjoyable visit. But Kitty is sick tonight—the same sore throat Jean had.

I keep thinking of what Laura said when I asked her to come and spend Sunday with us. She said, "Why, Emma, I haven't seen a Sunday in sixteen years. I told Ab so once when he was shavin' to go to an all-day singin' out at Lone Oak: I said, 'I wish I could go too.'[42] He told me to fix ready and go. 'By the time I got the young 'uns all ready to start I'd be ready for bed. I ain't seen a Sunday in sixteen years.' 'There's been a plenty passed,' says Ab. 'Yes,' says I, 'but I ain't had a one.'"

September 30, 1912

To town, got breakfast & combed Jean's hair, and feared I was too late for the hack, so rode down with Cessnor in the wagon. On the side of the mountain are so many clumps of French mulberry, rose & white berries growing close together. I got an armload mixed, to take to Mrs. Wheatley. She was seated at the sewing machine, evidently feeling very well, making cradle sheets for her pretty little namesake who was cooing and crowing in the back porch hammock. She looked at my summer's verses and said lovely things about them. I met Katherine's mother, a real New Orleans creole. I had chosen Wheatley's as the first place on the list because I felt that courage was absolutely essential to my quiet, and knew that they would put me in the right frame of mind for success. Staid for lunch and afterwards Mrs. W. bought some watercolors & Mr. W. ordered five copies of my book of poems. Then walked down to Mr. Patten's house. Found Mrs. P. packing Charlotte's trunk for school. She never once stopped but we had a delightful conversation & she bought two little pictures & also ordered five copies, & gave me the address of a printer she could recommend. I took the car & got off at Main St.—found the shop after considerable search. The printer turned out to be a really charming little old man; he & his wife working together in their tiny shop, continue to put out some very craftsmanlike work. They were setting up, from a bale of the "blindest" pencil-scrawled copy I ever saw, a Southern epic—! He looked at my work & seemed to admire it hugely.[43] Mrs. Patten's name on my order list seemed to carry conviction enough; I asked if I should go and scare up some sort of security, but he said it was unnecessary, and promised the proofs within a few days.

October 5, 1912

The most perfect weather imaginable. Treetops reddening all along the hollow—maple & sourwood & black gum—and one yellow hickory on the hill. Frank swept out a room in the empty house over the fence & helped me carry my things over. It will make me a delightful study if I can contrive to keep it reasonably warm on cold days. The children & the dogs have frolicked together all day. I have made a handsome cloak for Judith out of a velvet skirt & lined it with another old skirt and am now making a hat out of the scraps.

Lassie tells me that the Fur Top Church has just baptized 16 new members—Arren, the father of her child, among them. What is a church supposed to be for anyhow?

October 9, 1912

There were no hacks, so I sat pencil-sketching by the road, waiting for a ride. Most beautiful weather, the treetops turning on the Side, the pines immersed in a sort of blue dusk. Mr. Sim Long came by with a handsome gray horse & buggy, and took me clear to the Read House.[44] He was much pleased with my drawing for the Lookout, and ordered 25 similar of his house as souvenirs for a house party. Zella Armstrong and her mother were delighted with the drawing & the story MSS. I brought, and had coffee & rolls sent up for me. I then went to the News office—but Mr. Johnson did not care for any verses I had, and asked for something specially written for the commercial edition.

October 11, 1912

Called on the two Miss Greggs to see about the sewing machine they promised to give me. They hinted at a probability of the Pattens helping me to send Jean & Judith to the Athens school—a comforting prospect. Spent the night with the Atlees, and a most delightful visit it was. I have had very little sleep for a week, being worried & anxious about my book & other work, but last night slept well & on waking, put together the remainder of the verses without trouble. By noon Carol & I were pretty well satisfied with the poem—Warden of the Southern Gate. The News paid me $5 for it. I then dictated to Carol the revised MS of Dan Riley & the Devil, which we think is a rattling good story in its present form. I intended to go home today, but finished the poem too late to make the hack. Mrs. Miller called with her big luxurious Nyberg and took me & Carol for a long ride—out through the new additions and along the Mission Ridge boulevard, through Rossville, clear out to the army post, round it & back home.[45]

It was a splendid holiday for me. Saw the printer & bought some beautiful cover papers.

October 15, 1912

Clear & cool. Frank went to shuck out some of his corn & took Mark with him—so for once I was alone in the house, & improved the chance to attend to a small order—very pretty things in sepia. After dinner the old folks & Nora Renshaw came home with Frank & looked at Lyle's cow with a view to buying. I didn't encourage them too much, for I want her myself. Afterward I was in the garden picking the last of the okra & tomatoes, when I heard a strange cry from Frank & hurried to the house. He was sitting on the bed with one hand on his heart, very ill. I gave him whisky & hot water, put his feet into hot water & got him to bed, but it was dark before he was able to rest. I gave the children a soup of vegetables & milk, & sent for Uncle Joe, who came & sat a while after dark, but seeing that Frank was resting well, went home.

October 18, 1912

Cloudy, thickening to rain. Frank is 36 today. Apropos, Judith said to me: "I can't express myself how much I love papa. I don't want to hurt anybody's feelings, but I do just love him better than any one else!"

He & I walked down to the post office—my proofs arrived; I corrected them then & there, telephoned the printer, & sent them back by return mail.

But I feel so afraid.

This evening the girls insisted on making a birthday cake for papa's birthday & mine; it turned out very well.

three

Tragedy and Heartbreak

By 1912 Emma was frustrated with Frank's inability to earn the money required to raise five children. They began to argue about the issue. She self-published a booklet of poems, *Chords from a Dulcimore*, in hopes that the sales would provide for them. Unfortunately, the sales did not. The situation grew worse in early 1913 when their youngest child, Frank Mirick (whom they called Mirick or Mark), contracted scarlet fever and died after several agonizing days. Emma must have found it cathartic to write about the ordeal; she filled several pages on the day he died. After the shock and grieving wore off, Emma and Frank still argued, and Emma grew more resolute to find a better living. She also began to think Frank was turning the children against her.

October 19, 1912

I am 33 today. Last night we lay awake, hearing the world fill with rain, and wondered what to do. Today I rough-drafted a poem, The Dulcimore; but it seems no part of a solution. I have a toothache this evening. It is clearing, turning colder. The children have been so good all week. Kitty is not well.

A golden-gray light wells up in the west, enriching the color of the maple & red tupelos; and eastward hangs the half-moon, an emerald drowned in bright mist.

Mark was swinging in the new swing papa put up, when the gobbler, side-stepping Joe's hoop, got in his way & was bumped. The little boy was so tickled at seeing the turkey's dignity upset that he laughed until he tumbled out of the swing forwards; and this further amused him till on getting in again he immediately tumbled out backwards! He even laughs in his sleep.

October 20, 1912

A clear, cool, delightful morning. We killed a chicken expecting Aunt Laura & family, and all five of the children helped pick it, sitting on the ground—Mark rocking to and fro shouting, "Oh, ain't he long-legged! Ain't he big-long-legged!"

Ab & Laura came with all the children but Chester [Laura Miles Hatfield's son], and we had a good visit and a good dinner. Laura brought me a small jar of her apple butter & a basket of fine apples. I gave her a blue flannel wrapper for the baby, some sweet peppers, & a brown winter hat. I have lent her 5 empty fruit jars & Grandma 3.

Tinte & Lassie & their children came after dinner, & three of Joe's girls & Lever Brown.[1]

Frank has felt badly all day.

Judith struck Kitty this evening and made quite a bruise—apparently with a knife, though she denies this. I do not think she meant to hurt her so. I whipped her and sent her to bed without supper; afterwards we talked it over and she kissed Kitty and begged pardon with such a sweet graciousness that the little girl & I could not find it in our hearts to blame her further.

October 24, 1912

Last night was one long misery. I somehow went all to pieces yesterday; could not stop crying, and he and I had a frightful quarrel. I don't know what either of us said; it was awful. Did not sleep more than two or three hours. It was quite cold, and it seemed the morning would never come. I had not supposed I should ever cry that way again.

Frank proposes that we go down tomorrow and rent two rooms of Larnce, and live in Hill City, sending the children to school & him to hospital. I am sure it will not be best for him; I know he will either take some back-breaking factory job & wear himself out at it, so that he will be sick again, or else sit and mope with folded hands all winter. There is no getting him to do the one thing that would help us out of trouble; namely, take the house & children off my hands.

October 25, 1912

We got up in the gray dawn and hustled the children into their clothes; sent the three oldest to school & took the two babies with us to town. We all rode down with Grandpap and Dock. I left Frank & Mark in Hill City & went to get the first four pages of my book from the printer, taking Kitty with me. We went to St. Elmo, but Mrs. Wheatley was in bed with a neuralgia and Mrs. Patten not at home, so we rode back with Miss Parker in the auto—I did not know what to do next, but meeting Mrs. B. J. Brown & Genevieve Wilson at the Live & Let Live [Chattanooga drugstore], went home with them to lunch & sold them a picture of Wood Thrush Hollow. After lunch I went with them out on the heights behind the house, and saw one of the little known & less appreciated sights of Chattanooga—the factory town in full uproar & activity; spread out along the hither side of the river—such a contrast with the peaceful wooded hills across there, and the distant Ridge & Lookout. The lumber mills, the steel mills, the pipe kilns, the brickyard, the bed spring works, and whatever else I don't know—the raw material of the globe being hammered & sweated, with almost the effort of warfare, into the stuff of prosperity that makes civilization. Tannery Flats is worth seeing.

Afterwards we went to see Carol, & I went over her insets for Dan Riley. Then downtown with Kitty, in whose pocket a dime was burning a hole; and then back to Cousin May's. Frank & I then walked up to Larnce's house, & spent a very pleasant evening. I played the guitar & Mamie the organ, & Frank talked with Mary and her three big boys.

October 26, 1912

Last night was awful—neither I nor he could sleep. The clock ticked so loud that I finally got up & stopped it, about 1—then Frank went to sleep but I did not until the town was beginning to stir towards morning. Then we got up before day. After breakfast went to town together & as Dr. Ellis was not in I was obliged to leave Frank in his office, & go in search of a possible dollar, for I was afraid to go home without it. Mrs. Patten was very gracious

& helpful but had a houseful of other folks, and I think she must be getting tired of me & my pictures. She bought $3.75 worth of them, & promised me the boys' old printing press, which ought to be of considerable service to us. Then I went to Mrs. Wheatley, but she was asleep & I had to wait nearly three hours, in a perfect frenzy of anxiety. At last she waked, but sent word to me that she must dress. I heard the clock strike half past twelve and flew upstairs and knocked on the door. In a minute she had on a kimono and I was seated, telling her all my troubles. She had sandwiches & milk & wine set for me, though I insisted I must go, and said I should have the ten dollars for my books in advance if I would wait to see Mr. Wheatley. At last he came, and we had time for a few words; he seemed very glad to see me and to help me. They had intended to come to the Ridge for one photographic picnic tomorrow, but I had to call it off on account of Frank's condition.

I just had time to buy the children's garters & make the hack. Frank was stunned by Dr. Ellis' verdict: I cannot make out, from his account exactly what is wrong, but it seems his heart is in a serious condition and cannot be cured, only perhaps relieved.

Instead of unnerving, this news seems to steady me. I can always get through a trouble if I know just what is expected of me.

October 27, 1912

Sunday—such a beautiful day; it is a pity we could not arrange for the Wheatleys to come. Frank & I had a good night's rest & feel better. Jean came home from Grandma's after breakfast, but Judith is still at Aunt Laura's. Brick spent the night with us.

I trimmed me a winter hat today and worked on the covers of my booklet. Uncle Joe called, & Frank walked to Grandpap's with him. Willie Lyle [a neighbor] came & sat a while, talking of the Osteopath who is treating him; he thinks they might help Frank.

"How do you feel about it?" I asked Frank when we had our usual confidential talk in the night—when only the quiet breathing of the children filled the walls—"Do you feel frightened much?"

"Not particularly," he answered. "I feel as if it was something I'd sort of known for a long time. . . . You will get along better without me; but you'll miss me, you and the little chaps."

My own man, my poor man!

October 28, 1912

I went down and telephoned the Dr—to make sure, and he told me that he examined Frank thoroughly and that he found nothing wrong with his heart! I mean to go to a better doctor at once—one that will say a thing definitely and stand to it.

Mrs. Pyott called & bought two pictures. Beautiful autumn weather; I would like to go sketching.

November 9, 1912

Saturday. Frank came down with his father & brought Buzz with him. I went to the doctor's office with him, but was not alarmed by the doctor's rather rambling talk. Then went to the printer's & Mr. Meere gave me the 5 pages—must wait for the remaining 4. By the time I had done some shopping & got back to Cousin's I was very tired. Also I called on Mable Van D. Found the hack ride very tiring; have taken a cold & feel almost sick. Lassie seems very appreciative of the leggings & mittens I bought her baby, along with Mark's & Kitty's. Tinte and her children came in tonight & Lassie went home with her.

November 11, 1912

A clear, perfect day, ending in a rich deep yellow sunset in which the new moon glitters, erect as some pale girl. The group of oaks around the house is red and red-brown now, and the hill tops are fading, though some splendid maples remain on the Side. It seems that certain trees brighten to a particular glory in certain autumns; this year it has been the hickories & maples; I have seen few of the red trees,—tupelos or red oaks, and no remarkable sweet-gums.

Received $5 in the mail from Grace Cooke & some orders for work. Grandpap, in view of a prospective pension increase, has offered a small loan. So our minds are at rest for the present. Lassie proves to be good help; the folks say that she was very faithful & industrious during my absence.

Worked some hours on my books, but was troubled with nausea all day & finding myself unable to work well, cut out a dress for Kitty & one for Jean from a beautiful white suit, somewhat moth-eaten, which Mrs. Rawling's daughter gave me. Too fine for little girls but will be pretty.

I feel sure that this book will prove a money maker. It should provide the winter's living, perhaps pay us out of debt & improve the place. If I can only make good on the advertising order, we shall have a larger house & comfortable furniture, & a barn & stock as well.

November 14, 1912

After a wretched night with the children, bad dreams, & a miserable stomach, I walked over to Grandpap's with Frank, & telephoned from Mrs. Lane's. Mrs. L. gave me a glass of wine & I felt better. But at Grandma's the talk is all of Dock's proposal to run away with Lassie. I suppose I will have to send her away if the racket keeps on.

If this book brings me the $500 it ought, I will try to sell out & buy a place in St. Elmo—where the children can grow up in a good neighborhood & attend a good school.[2] Frank agrees that this is by far the best plan.

Having placed the remaining pages in & illuminated a copy or two, I begin to be well pleased with the book.

November 16, 1912

Where I looked for help in my trouble Frank has given me curses. I do not know what to do. I cannot stand this. I worked all morning on the new books, but I ought to be in bed, and did lie down most of the afternoon. Sallie came over & prescribed burnt whiskey, but I was afraid to take any. I have only eaten one biscuit in 24 hours and it made me sick. Frank says he is going to leave; but he is talking wildly about so many things—saying anything he can think of that will hurt—taunting, accusing, complaining, threatening.

November 17, 1912

Sunday. Worked all day on the books. Frank accused me of being in a conspiracy with Carol & Dr. Ellis against him, and I asked him to take it back. When he insisted I told him I could not live with any one who thought so low of me. And began at once to put my things together to go to town in the morning. Then he began to threaten, and soon I saw that it was all talk, and felt for the first time that I am really stronger than any trouble or any one. I said I would take three of the children to town with me, and if he would take charge of Joe & Kitty until I could arrange for them it would be the last favor I would ask of him. He sneered at that, but after a round of threats and abuse, to which I made no answer, he suddenly softened and said he was sorry and begged forgiveness.

I wish I could see clear what is best to do. I think he dreads me because I have supported him & the family for so long, but he is vague and contradictory about what he wants to do—says he will not say. After hours of milling round and round I finally made out that he wanted my consent to get a job, and of course I gave it, freely; which leaves us exactly where we were before, except that he has some vague idea of doing something. He is not strong enough to do hard work now.

November 19, 1912

Frank got the mare and we drove to town. Both went to Dr. Ellis, whose treatment seems to be helping Frank. The Dr. told me to go home & go to bed, & take his medicine & I would be all right. He assured me that I am not pregnant, but I think he is mistaken. I spent part of the day in the printer's shop, putting my books together—then took three copies to Mrs. Wheatley as an earnest of good intentions, but could not see any of the family. Mrs. Patten advanced me $10 and was pleased with the two copies I brought her. Have had some pain all day, but got about fairly well. At Larnce's for the night.

November 20, 1912

Went over to the Read House to see Zella Armstrong & walked right into a stunning exhibition of portraits etc. by Miss Hergesheimer [Ella Sophonisba Hergesheimer, American artist]—the finest pictures I have seen in Chattanooga. The artist talked with me for a long time— told me exactly how she made her beautiful flesh tones & rich blacks; & much to my surprise she presented me with a set of oil tubes & two excellent brushes, which in addition to those I have should enable me to do something worth while when the Xmas rush is over. I gave her one of my books.

By that time it was too late to see Mabel or Mrs. Milton or any one. I did manage a little shopping, rejoined Frank & the two babies at the stable & bought them some lunch, and we drove out.

November 22, 1912

So dim a day that one can scarcely tell the sun is shining. I worked on my books. Lassie has left on account of an ugly quarrel among the Mileses. I don't know how to get along without her and finish these books in time. And Frank says I must pay the Lyle debt. He seems to have quite given up all responsibility. It seems I will have to leave here, to get a chance to work & support us. I feel sick as ever.

November 23, 1912

The children have been so good all day. Frank and I and the babies walked to the post office, and got several interesting things in the mail— Major McGuffey's Chattanooga book,[3] with a very pleasant note; and a copy of the Standard Designer with my illustrations in it. I worked the rest of the day.

We thought it would rain, but it is still clear & beautiful, with pink suns & moons rising & setting in gray smoke.

November 28, 1912

Thanksgiving. I ate my dinner most thankfully, with returning appetite & digestion. We killed a young dominecker rooster, and George Levi ate with us. Something delightful in the mail—a letter from Miss Ricketson,[4] from whom we have not heard for years—enclosing $5 in advance for two illuminated books. This enables me to go to town not quite penniless.

Lily Underwood home on a Thanksgiving visit, came this afternoon with her three little sisters. I was glad for the impression she made on my twins,— very fetching in the neat blue serge uniform of the school. "Ah," sighed Jean happily, "I shan't be here when I'm fourteen!" I hope it may be so, but warned her that she would have to make her grades faster than she has been doing.

Joe tumbled off to sleep on my bed, and only half came to when papa said, "Wake up, and go to bed right." Placed in his own bed he tried to dive under the covers, but lost his bearings and got hold of a pillow instead—He turned it over and over with his hands & feet in the vain endeavor to draw it up over his legs, blinking & nodding like an exasperated tumblebug with a ball, and we finally came to his assistance & turned him round.

December 1, 1912

Went to the M.E. church with Mrs. Atlee and the little girls in the carriage. I had no idea of taking part in the service—but at the moment of rising Mrs. Atlee begged me to join in communion with them & the little girls pulled at my hands, and the first thing I knew I was kneeling to receive the bread & wine. Little Lupton Patten came home with them to dinner.[5] These children of the rich are as unlike ours as if they belonged to a different race.

Wrote letters & rested in my room all evening.

December 12, 1912

Had a bite <u>today</u> right out of a slice of life. The story begins far back—twenty odd years ago, when Mary's [Mary Freudenberg Miles] first husband lay dying, & wishing his six children brought up in his own church, had them taken from her & given to a convent at Nashville. Mary tried by taking in washing to hold the family together, but misbehaved signally with Larnce, and was forced to yield—the Sisters persuaded her to give them willingly. Then she married Larnce—after Barney was already born. They came through hard years, and of the five children born to them, one died, and the others have grown up ignorant & rough though good-hearted. Last week she received a letter from Eddy, one of the older boys, saying that he would come to see them "next week." She fell to and scrubbed the floors & scoured & polished as only a German can, partly to cover her nervous excitement & to put over the time of waiting. Since he did not immediately come, every book agent or collector who has rung the doorbell has called her heart into her mouth so that she came back weak & trembling after each encounter.

Today when the doorbell rang, every one was out, Frank & Mamie playing in the back yard, & Tiny having gone to visit her brother's new baby, and I was working steadily on my books. Mary opened the hall door; I heard a greeting in a man's voice, then from Mary—"This ain't Eddie, is it?" with the strong German accent of excitement. A silence, then she broke into wild weeping and incoherent words. At this I put my books by, rose, & stood waiting. They came in to the sitting-room fire—Roesslein, a big German baker, introduced the younger, an intelligent-looking, well-mannered man in a nice looking overcoat, his teeth heavily filled with gold.

He had no recollection of me, it appeared; and to judge from his manner, scarcely more of his mother. They remained for a little while talking principally of the inherited bit of land which he had come to see about; but Mary, after a few rational sentences, would burst out "Oh, I didn't know whether I'd live to ever see him again!" and cry, with her apron over her eyes. And as I was about setting the table, having taken up the dinner lest it burn, they rose to go. Against her entreaties, they left, giving us a reason that both were obliged to go to the court house about certain papers connected with the land, and that Roesslein must go on his wagon at three; but Eddie promised to return & spend the night.

Mary could not eat. A tempest of unhappy memories shook her to the soul, and she must recount them to me. All afternoon as I worked she told me of sins and sorrows twenty years gone by, and every now and then questioned anxiously whether possibly Eddie would not return for the night. At last she came in from some outside work, trembling, and dropping into a chair, wrung her hands: "Emmer, I've just thought: do you reckon he thinks hisself too good to stay all night in my house? For what I know he may be just like Nettie."

Nettie is the only one of the six whom Mary has seen all these years. She spent a summer on the Ridge with the well-to-do family who took her as half ward, half nurse girl, and was not allowed to visit or to receive her mother at all.

"Nonsense," I said, of course. "Men are not so finicky about themselves; he's got no such idea in his head." But I could not help reflecting that Eddie might have heard the same ghastly tales I have heard about her.

But he came,—a cheerful, courteous stranger, a man who had scarcely known the meaning of home, behaving as he might have done in any other house or in a boarding house. The land & the law was their talk, the law & the land. And the thought went through me, a bright sword of fear, "If I should be forced to the wall, if my children should be taken from me, and one of them were to come back like this?"

I worked on until the light began to fail, then I got up and put my things together for departure, she helping me half absently. I had paid for my stay, and now thanked her for additional kindness; then I came close to where she stood on the hearth and laid my arm over her square little shoulders.

"Eddie," I said, "you don't remember ever seeing me before, and I'm going now, and unless you come to visit us on the mountain next week I guess you'll not see me again; and meantime I aim to say something to you that's none of my business." We all laughed rather nervously. "I want you to be just as fond of your mother as you can! She's a good woman, Eddie. I've known her for twenty years. There ain't a day since you all been gone that she hasn't thought of you and grieved about you,—I know, because I've talked with her about you so often. You'll never regret it, Eddie; it won't mean much to you, but it'll mean a lot to her."

With the words I kissed her, and she burst into tears. I quitted the house, for I was in haste; but she followed me to the porch with protestations of willingness to house me indefinitely, and then stood twisting her apron & smiling shyly down, like a girl.

"Well—and thank you for your—kindness," said she.

I hope it helped!

An hour later I was telling the Wheatleys about it before the library fire. That was an unsatisfactory visit. No sales, no quick warm kindliness either, which is what I am starving for. It was better with Mrs. Rawlings, farther up the line. I got to the house late—about eight, with two books finished during the day.

December 19, 1912

Mailed Miss Wells & Edith Stroop some books yesterday for Xmas gifts.

Last night was awful—I tried to straighten things out with Frank, who was muttering to himself like a madman about drowning himself in Marshall Creek and all the dark sayings he could think of; but I was led by his bitter reproaches to answer him in kind, and things were soon worse than ever. I admitted that I am afraid of him; and he proceeded to justify my fears by threats and ravings, leapt out of bed with fierce gestures, and drew on his clothes. My silence seemed to infuriate him more than any words. I chilled, and got out of bed to sit by the fire he had built. He was by turns fierce and anxious about me, with long sullen silences, while I sat rolled in a quilt & sipped hot water. At last I went back to bed, and after some entreaty he too lay down—about 1 o'clock—he reproaching me with having broken his night's rest by a quarrel, and threatening what he would do if I ever did it again!

I have been sick and feverish all day. Have made several attempts
to make peace with him, but in vain—I know it is trouble that speaks so
harsh, and not Frank. But this can have but one ending.

December 22, 1912

Snowing this morning. Frank seems to have recovered his usual spirits;
but I never expect to see health or happiness again.

Mark has a new game with his papa: he climbs into his lap and says,
"Now you be my graphophone: I'll grind (wind) you up," using one arm for
a crank, and poking with a fat finger by way of putting in a record. Then he
cuddles down and demands Steamboat Bill or the Preacher and the Bear.
Maggie Brown has a little boy.

Three of the little Underwood girls & Jamie spent most of the day, and
what a riotous good time they all had together. It was almost pure suffering for
me, for I had to finish an illuminated book to be sent to Mrs. Atlee tomorrow, or
lose two dollars. I gave them a bowl of soup around at noon and worked on.

Cold, cloudy weather. I feel very weak and bad. This is 8 weeks of
almost steady waste & no end yet.

December 23, 1912

Sleet set in at daybreak. Frank and Joe set forth in it with more holly
for Miss Gregg. I think it was very inconsiderate of her to oblige him to
make two trips, when she herself set the appointment for last Friday; but
she cannot imagine what a hard trip it really is, or the kindness of her heart
would have prevented.

For the first time since I was a little sick girl, I have no stomach for
Xmas goodies. No words can express the misery and degradation I feel.
That I who dreamt and worked for such noble things, for a high ideality of
conduct, should be brought to this slavish pass! But, thank God, the wild
tears are past, and I feel strong to bear my lot with fortitude. Whatever
comes, I am resolved not to reproach Frank again by word or look; I am
satisfied that there is no reason in him. Charley Brock is his cousin, John
Pickett was his third cousin, and how can I tell what may be in that wild
blood, waiting only the provocation of my sickness and unhappiness to turn
on me with any weapon that comes to hand? It will be better to yield to his
demands in all things without demur; though it kill me by inches, it will

bring no shame to the children. Yet on the other hand, if he should do the grand John Pickett act, the law would in that event surely put the children out of reach of this lewd and drunken crew of his kin. I wish I knew. For the present I am determined that he shall have no cause to complain of the way I treat him. He by turns declares that I must and shall "treat him better," and then admits that my treatment of him is quite right, and says it is my contempt and that of others that he cannot endure. This is probably true. Also he complains of a lack of passionate love on my part, and this I cannot find it in me to simulate; that my physical sickness serves as a present defense. I do not see how he can possibly ask it of me, or my confidence or respect either but he demands all as a right, and I give them as far as possible. However, I can be kind to him, and hope for a death that shall free me without bringing any more shame on the children.

Hour by hour the field whitens as the rain freezes on the dry weeds; at two o'clock it ceases to fall, and a fog steals over the icy gray world. I did some Xmas cards for an order, but fear it is now too late to deliver them—also seven little 25 ct watercolors. Judith & Jean did some cunning Kewpies to make into New Year calendar cards. They really do remarkably well at this sort of thing.

December 25, 1912

Such a houseful of Xmas. Aunt Laura & all her family, except for Chester, came, and brought some cake & pie & jelly in a basket. Her baby is so little and bright, like Jean used to be. The children had a riotous good time, and the dinner was, I think, the best ever served on my table. I found some extra toys for Ab & Helen & Libby, and gave Ab a cap and Laura a short coat & a corset which are too large for me.

While we were redding up the kitchen I told Laura as far as I could in a few words about our trouble. She could not help me—seemed to think it was the family disposition to be unreasonable in anger. She said their mother was so worried and ill-treated by their father during the years when they were born, that she "marked" them all, and so bred the endless unhappiness that oppresses all the five homes.

Jean went home with them, and I sent old Mrs. Crosier a lot of the magazines. It has been a beautiful day, and a particularly jolly Xmas but for the shadow of injustice that lies across my heart.

January 1, 1913

Last night, the last night of the old year, we did patiently and kindly try to reason things out. I gave up, yielded every point, gained nothing, yet the atmosphere is better today, and I can but hope the new year is well begun.

A beautiful day, clear and still, not too cold. Frank worked at clearing Lyle's field all morning, then went to the store. The girls understood that they were invited to a New Year's dinner of roast goose at Freudenburg's, and I hurried all morning making Jean a new dress; but they received no welcome on arrival, and turned round and came home. There must have been a mistake somewhere. I was sorry on their account.

Frank met Mr. Atlee and they went hunting for hemlock boughs with pretty little cones, and holly and winter ferns, for a party Mrs. Atlee is giving. Buzz was delighted at being allowed to go to Shoal Creek with them.

January 13, 1913

The sun comes out this morning and thaws the ground, making everybody feel better. Several little cousins came to play. I finished a booklet—so much toward paying debts. Two duns [debts, or bills] in the mail, and a letter from Edith advising me to keep on pulling my load, up hill & down. It is good advice—but how to do it? I still don't get well, and we have nothing to live on.

January 18, 1913

A rainy night and dark morning, clearing beautifully at noon, very warm. Frank cleaned up the two front rooms thoroughly in the morning, and after dinner went to Albert's. The mail brought a letter from the Montague Co. and 26 copies of my "Brothers" story written for them, in dainty little booklets—such a clever advertising idea. I do hope it will amount to something—but Frank will not talk of it at all. I feel better this afternoon, and scrubbed the kitchen.

January 22, 1913

Frank helped straighten up the house and then went to help Willie Lyle. Mark was sick all night, so that we had little sleep, and I could do no work but a little sewing. He ate nothing all day.

What a bitter thing it is that through all the years when I gave my love and trust to the uttermost, Frank never cared what he put on me or how he made me suffer; while now that my health & spirit are alike broken, and I preserve the quiet of indifference no matter what he does, he is learning patience and consideration at a rate I should not have believed possible. How happy it would have made me then—would now, if I could believe it would last, or had anything to hope for from him.

January 23, 1913

Last night the moon glowed white thro' a heavy mist and looked like a translucent globe, lighted from within—a strange, ghostly thing, white-ringed. Today is all fog and drizzle.

Mark was sick all night, and has broken out a rash this morning. Seems to be worse today. Throat swelling, tries to vomit every little while; takes only a few spoonfuls of condensed milk. I wish I could afford a doctor.

Frank went to help Joe with some interior work. He came home to dinner in high feather, because he has the promise of work all spring.

Turned very dark at 4 o'clock, so that I lit the lamp, and directly down came a rain that washed away the fog. The little straying watercourse below the well is swollen to the dimensions of a creek, and thinking itself to be one, goes roaring through the woods.

January 24, 1913

Mark is worse—a bad sore throat & a red rash; can hardly swallow; eats nothing. If I had any money I would send for a doctor.

A thick, rainy day. When Frank went to work he saw that Will Lyle's big Angora goat was down, & sent Buzz to telephone. Will came up & fed & doctored the creature amid a great excitement on the part of the children. Then he & Frank came to dinner. I had only my pickles & preserves, a rice pudding, some soup made of the leftovers of several dinners & coffee & a little salt pork; now there is only one mess of beans & a little meal. These mountain winters are something no woman ought to be called on to undergo. Unlike the prairie or western or Canadian winters, they promise no ultimate reward of prosperity. Everyone who stays here grows poorer as age comes on.

January 25, 1913

Mark seems rather better. The sun came out this morning. Frank went to the store & got some few groceries on credit, then worked with Joe till noon. Mark wants to lie in my arms most of the time. His throat is dreadfully swelled and his breathing hard.

January 26, 1913

We expected Frank would be paid today for his week's work, but the man failed to bring it. Willie Lyle brought some more oranges and Mark sucked a piece. He grew worse, and at last Frank telephoned to Dr. Peay,[6] who arrived at about 2:30 and immediately pronounced it scarlet fever, and said that the little boy is in a dangerous condition. We could pay nothing—must borrow to get the prescription filled. We are sitting up tonight, and hardly expect the baby to live till morning. He struggles dreadfully for breath, and moans and cries all the time he is awake; his heart runs like a millrace.

It rains steadily all night; the fire burns softly, and the child gasps and moans. We have given all the medicine and are helpless. We have moments of hard-won hope alternating with despair. I told the children to pray for him when they went to bed.

January 27, 1913

The little sufferer was easier all forenoon, taking a little and breathing better; once when I lifted him he threw his little arms round my neck and drew them tight. Dock sent the required prescription out from town, but I fear too late. The little fellow is starving to death, if nothing else were wrong.

The rest of us fare well; Joe brought a big ham & a jar of jelly, Grandpap sent a half-bushel of potatoes, and we got some flour from the store.

In the middle of the afternoon Frank's heart breaks down from lack of sleep and overwork at cutting & carrying wood for this night & day consumption, and he is barely able to get about. Uncle Joe comes in with another armload of food supplies, and I ask him about getting into the pest house. He don't know; but later in the evening Buck [Frank's nephew] comes to say that he has telephoned George Freudenberg, who promises to send us a trained nurse. I wonder if it can be true!

Tonight we got the little boy's bowels to move, but he is weaker & utterly stupid.

After midnight, weakening. Uncle Joe sat with us till 12. The awful struggle for breath goes on he tosses and wrestles with astonishing strength.

Three o'clock. He still knows me, but his eyes remain closed. Just now he whispered, "I'm gona—I'm gona—I'm gona go to some other house;" and then he actually added, a little more distinctly, "I'm—gona—die."

"Going to die?"

"Ye—h, I am, sir," he panted, with the feeblest effort at emphasis. I said what I could,—that mother would stay with him and God would take care of him; but no words could soothe that extreme anguish; I doubt if they reached his understanding at all. The labor of his tiny chest shakes the bed. It is dreadful to realize that this is my little Mark, my baby, suffering so horribly, and I unable—for the first time in his life—to reach him with any relief.

His strong constitution is only prolonging the agony, making its gallant struggle against certain death. I am alone with him in the night. God forgive me for having brought into the world these children I cannot take care of.

January 28, 1913

He breathed his last, after a frightful convulsion, about ten o'clock. I think he knew me, knew he was in my arms, until that convulsion. Joe came in and stood by the bed, though I begged him not. I told Frank, but he did not come in. Joe told me how to straighten & cover the body. Then I told the children that the little brother's sufferings were ended; they began to cry, huddled in the kitchen; I comforted them as best I could, covered the poor little face, and then Frank & I began to straighten the room.

Presently the doctor & young nurse, sent by Mrs. Patten, arrived. I told them they came too late, but if they would tell me how to lay out the body. Dr. Peay said to leave it to the ladies who would come in. I assured him that no one would come; he then requested the nurse to wash the body, which she did; and also instructed me about laying it out, and disinfecting. They went away, promising to report to the Board of Health.

Uncle Joe borrowed a bottle of carbolic acid for us and later in the day I prepared the whitest of his poor clothes, and made ready a ragged winding sheet. But the little shoes, that no one but me could ever fasten because the button hook pinched his ankles, I set aside; and Frank, passing them, cried out suddenly: "I wish you'd put them shoes somewhere else!" He cleaned the yard, while I rested on a pallet in the kitchen.

In the afternoon the white coffin came. Joe had ordered one, offering to pay for it himself, and was told that one was already on the way, and no charges. I think from Mrs. Wheatley; she telephoned that she was coming to the burial tomorrow. Oh, I hope she will, for I am all alone.

"Mother, I would help ye," said Frank, "but I don't want to. He may be—changed. I want to remember him happy and like he always was."

So I went to lift him in my arms for the last time. But what a surprise met me when I lifted the cloth from his face! The dreadful agony was gone; according to the Gaelic phrase, the Smoothing of the Hand. The piteous gasping, straining mouth had eased into the old sweet petal-like curves; it was the mouth that had drawn his first life-milk from my breast, the lips that were always kissing me. Such a faint mysterious smile, as when I have heard him chuckle in his sleep, and turned to wonder what he could be dreaming about.

He was beautiful. The cowlick stood up from among the damp hair on his brow; the hands that patted me softly in the night, the little feet were chill and white. Rigid like a marble figure he lay on the white sheet; only the head, as I raised it, turned a little in my hand. Carefully, by the failing light in the west window, I drew on the clothes. Not the losing him, so much as the thought that I had not been able to help him in his bitter agony, was breaking my heart.

And suddenly the remembrance came to me of Mary Mother she too saw her son die under torture, slain by the ignorance and selfishness that lost me mine. Nail and spear and thorn! It comforted me more than anything else has been able to; and though not a Catholic I prayed to Mary from the heart, while Frank walked up and down the porch outside.

Then for the last time I took him in my arms, and laid him into his last little bed. My baby, my baby.

To the others he is lost; but to me his perfect little life, unstained by sin or sorrow, is a precious possession, sealed to me for a joy forever.

He loved us all. Never was a friendlier little heart. But more than the other children do, he loved me.

Come back to me if you can, O little son! Asleep or awake, in shadow or substance, come when you will. You cannot come but I shall welcome you; you will always be my little boy.

The father lit the lamp, and brought the children to see him, except Kitty, who begged to stay in the kitchen, afraid perhaps. He asked me to pray. I put my arms around the little children, and they clung to me, sobbing softly while I tried to lift him and lay him on the knees of God. The wee face smiled from its white satin nest, calm after the great passage. So we gathered once to watch his first slumber, after that other passage to this known shore of existence. He was reluctant then as now, till the waiting welcome clasped and comforted him. Who knows? I can't even say I believe, for I do not know. Neither does anybody else. But in that prayer I gave the children the benefit of the doubt, and prayed with all the faith I could summon.

We did not look on him again.

Belief is not a virtue, but may be a comfort—may be founded on constructive & helpful or destructive & vicious ideals. I would rather know what is true than believe what is comforting. But there is little we can know about that other house to which he told me he was going.

I can bear to lose him; but the memory of his frightful anguish is beyond endurance. My baby, my baby, imploring me, screaming for my help, in the last torture! and I could only squeeze a few drops of water into the ghostly orifice, all distorted, scabbed, and swollen that was his sweet mouth! At the last I failed him—could not help, could not reach him. That is the sword's edge, which Frank is mercifully spared; he does not seem to feel that part of it at all.

Joe came, after his day's work, and sat with us till far into the night. We had to make pallets in the kitchen, as we are bidden to let the rest of the house stand till the health officers come to disinfect. It is very crowded & ill convenient. Joe! What a big-hearted, brave, simple man he is.

January 29, 1913

Willie Lyle brought some flowers, and Mrs. Bennett sent some. After the children had had their breakfast I put things straight hastily, and as John had come with the mare & buggy, I gathered us all on the front porch for a funeral service of our own. It was the only way; there was no one else to do it; we were not to be allowed to go to the burying, and I could not bear that nothing should be read or said. I do not know much of the burial service, and we had no prayerbook; but I never cared for the book of Job except as literature, nor for the word that came to John in the isle of Patmos. So I read "I am the resurrection and the life" and "Let not your heart be troubled," and tried again to pray. But I could not say much.

Then they lifted the box and carried it away. I sent the children into the warm kitchen, and went off and sat on a stump in the gray field. I could see the little feet making tracks in the soft earth there,—could hear his soft, slow, singularly distinct utterance, as he prattled along the rows of sprouting seeds last spring—sprouts that stand thin & stark now, winter-killed. When I could get hold of myself I went back to the children, and read them stories for an hour, by the kitchen stove; then we played a game of flinch; then I put on dinner—but all at once it seemed to me that my heart would burst if I did not give tongue to its pain, so I went away to the top of the hill and walked among the trees. Could not pray, could only squall like a brute.

I had dinner on the table when Frank returned. I looked all day for some one to come; but the cold wind in the pine tree was the only voice we heard, except that Joe brought the mail. There was plenty of work—everything to be gone over with carbolic acid solution, and loads of infected things to be burnt, and his toys to be hid away. Even the health officer don't come.

January 30, 1913

Boiled bedding all morning, & other clothes. Then made ready for fumigation—wrapped the children warm, lit the formaldehyde burners & went out. We were almost too tired to drag along, but the children enjoyed it. At last we stopped in a pine thicket that shut off the cold wind; Frank built up a fire near a log, and we warmed our feet and hands. All about us were broad rocks covered with the richest moss, and pine trees & the dark green tangle of cross-vine. We found arbutus with pink and white buds, and much that was interesting and delightful; but I was thinking—and I know Frank was too—of the picnic we had near this spot with the Wheatleys, and how Mark would have enjoyed being with us now—out in the woods as he loved to be.

When the fire burnt down to a bed of coals and the stars were pointing through the pines, we went on to Uncle Joe's; he had bidden us there for the night. I had put all the children & ourselves into fresh clothes, and had tied a cloth tight round their heads & mine, because they all had slight colds & I was afraid to disinfect their hair—the more by token I don't know how. I was so glad to see Sally, though ordinarily she gets on my nerves; her kindness is like water in the desert now. It was our intention to keep the children separate, but they rushed together in the wildest merriment before I knew, and Sallie would not countenance parting them.

January 31, 1913

Rained hard all night & morning. Kitty seemed sick the first part of the night but afterwards fell off to sleep; then Frank's heart began to act badly, and I got up and prepared hot stove lids & hot toddy, and rubbed him with liniment. He went to sleep about one o'clock, but I lay awake nearly all night.

The letters of condolence have begun to come in, but no one comes— except Uncle Sam Pyott, who brought a gift of $5 from Mrs. Atlee. Mrs. Sarah Patten sent $6, most of which I gave Sally as some slight return for her trouble. She passed the snuff, saying, "It'll be company for you."

Frank keeps telling me to put on a different face—that it makes him feel bad. He does not see that he has put all the hardest of this trial on to me. I asked Sally if Joe would be willing to speak a word to Frank about his ways: she replied that he certainly would,—would "find out his soul." I hope so. If any one can it will be Joe. She added, however, just what Laura said—that the five brothers are alike in thinking that a wife should stand any abuse;—Joe, she says, had his lesson and is a changed man.

I received in the mail a letter from Mrs. Vaughn & some copies of the News containing a short poem Mr. Lon Warner has written on my little boy's death.[7] This made me go to pieces again—till the girls patted me and begged me not to cry any more.

Little Virgie put her arms round me and said, "Oh, I just love you, Aunt Emmer, I just love you. I wish I was your little girl!"

No child can ever be so dear to me as that one who must be a child forever. And no one, no one, knows the core of my sorrow. His suffering, the agony that tore him, helpless and imploring me to relieve him—through those dreadful hours when the labor of his brave heart shook the bed. He loved me more than any of the others—they have learned from their father to sneer at me; but I made his whole life for him, and he saw that it was good, and gave me only love.

Well, we opened and aired the house when the rain quit, and went to work restoring order enough to sleep in: Frank complaining with a bad heart, and Kitty with a sore throat. We think she must be taking it too. Must telephone early tomorrow if they will let me.

February 1, 1913

Kitty was fretful all night, but better this morning. Mr. Miller was most obliging about the telephone, and I heard several voices I longed for—Mrs. Patten, Carol, Mrs. Wheatley, Cousin Mary. Could not get the Dr. so came home—to find the little maid eating quite a hearty breakfast, able to laugh at our fears. They all feel badly, but that is easily accounted for. Still, we are living under the shadow of the sword. And alone.

There is great washing piled up which we can get no help with: today we have cleaned and sprinkled carbolic acid solution in every corner, and disinfected our hair. I cut off Jean's—her one beauty. We put the clothes to soak, and Frank cleaned out the cellar. I made Joe some gelatin, because he is eight today.

February 2, 1913

The ground hog may have glimpsed his shadow, but I doubt it. I went to the post office right after breakfast and telephoned. Had a long & satisfactory conversation with Mrs. Wheatley—& was glad to be able to repeat to everyone the doctor's words, "The little fellow died just in time to save the others"—that is, before desquamation had set in.

Returning, I met Mr. Padgett, who had called at our house, and reassured him about our disinfection. Got dinner, sewed, and wrote a letter. Joe called, & said his children are well but for colds.

I hoped that the little brother's death would be a warning to Jean about teasing & deviling the younger children; but she is worse than ever to Kitty. We spoke to her several times during the day, & finally I thought a whipping could no longer be put off, and cut a peach tree limb. She screamed so that her father came running. It was very bad for his heart. He scolded me, then declared he would send her to Bonny Oaks.[8] Afterward she told me she didn't care,—wanted to go to the reform school; didn't want to be anybody's little girl.

I don't know what to do with her. Frank insisted on holding family prayers last night. But nothing of the kind seems to influence Jean.

Yet afterward while I was cooking again, I asked if the beans were too salt, and Jean said no—"It'll be all right if you cook it, mama. Anything you do is all right with me." And she put her arms around me.

"Is it all right when mother has to punish you so?"

She nodded with eyes closed.

My pulse has gone very bad this afternoon. Frank is not well at all either, but keeps on carrying heavy wood. Frank holds prayers at bedtime, and what big, simple satisfying prayers he makes. I think he is trying to do better than ever before, but he will never understand how to help me.

February 3, 1913

Ice-cold rain all night, so that washing is out of the question. I feel too bad to do much. This afternoon we were much surprised to receive a visit from Dr. Brooks—Mrs. Patten sent him as a precaution against further cases. He examined the children's throats, reported a congested condition of Joe's & Jean's tonsils, and gave us very little hope of escaping further trouble. He left some medicine, and a tonic for me.

I received several letters of condolence in the mail, and a box of Mecca [either tobacco or a first aid ointment] from Edith. The fog has cleared tonight and a cold wind has sprung up. How desolate the world looks, with danger lurking unseen, and no hand to clasp and hold to.

I thought I knew loneliness, but this is beyond anything I ever imagined.

February 7, 1913

A delightful rest in bed, with first Judith & then Jean beside me. The nurse wants me to go to hospital. Meantime expenses are mounting.

Mrs. Donnell sends a sympathetic letter, and $5. And the Designer accepts "Falling Weather." So much to the good.

A clear, cold day.

February 12, 1913

I felt better until mail time—received a dun from the printer, which upset me all over—and Frank went to pieces because I did. Mrs. Cooke sent me a kindly letter & $10—so I should have felt better. But I can't see for my life how we are to go on with it this time.

February 13, 1913

Last night was the coldest night yet—16°. All night we heard the drinking frost at the buckets and vessels. No one slept well: I dreamed again and again of my little boy, and woke up trembling.

Some one sent the children a very pretty valentine apiece in the mail. The cat has disappeared ever since her bath in carbolic-acid solution.

February 14, 1913

I feel better after getting out of bed, but very tired; and never have I imagined such a grief as now tugs upon me. Whether I cry out or keep silent, there is no relief; but the least complaint brings down a scolding. He does not care how I suffer, if only I do not worry him with complaint. Joe and Jean went to Uncle Joe's early, with a valentine, and did not come back all day. No mail. Frank worked in Albert's orchard after dinner, and Judith & I made her a dress out of my gray skirt.

Everywhere I see a little fair head bobbing about; every hour I hear some of his baby words, and then I remember that if I had had a little money he might, might have been saved, or at least would not have died in extreme torture. I am ripped and wrung with the pain of it. My baby, my little boy.

He was Balder the Beautiful to us, the beloved, the little Sungod; and he is dead.[9] He was the son I looked to, to make up to me with his brave heart and willing hands for all the ignominy and hardship I have endured. But that is the least of my sorrow. That he should have suffered and that I could have got relief for him with so little money—Oh, my heart is breaking. And to Frank I dare not say one word of this, lest he start on a tirade about my blaming him with everything. He wants me to go to hospital or on a visit; but I told him outright that I would never hear again the bitter and insulting words he gave me about my other absences from home.

How can I save or help the others, bound like this? Oh, merciful God!

February 15, 1913

Last night Uncle Joe came in and told us inspiring news of sales, plans and developments on different parts of the Ridge—notably a Chatauqua concern of some sort.[10] He sat for an hour talking; racy and modern as a story in the Sat. Evening Post are his yarns—of his quarrel with the city water company; of mending a memorial window; of how knowing the square of the hypotenuse once saved his job in a tin shop; of his experiments with his gasoline engine—he believes that the component elements of water can be separated to produce a hydrogen explosion, like a miniature boiler explosion, to run an engine: he thinks he has done it twice, and that this will finally become the great motive force of enginery everywhere, because it is cheap & inexhaustible. I have never heard him talk so entertainingly; I was surprised at his knowledge of chemistry and physics, and was at length roused out of misery, and enjoyed the evening as much as the two men. It enabled me to get a good night's rest and wake ready to take hold this morning.

Frank went to work. I began at last with the oils Miss Hergesheimer gave me, and did a small portrait sketch of Jean, and then a quick landscape. Neither was satisfactory; the coloring is heavy and dull.

Virgie and Icie [Frank's nieces] played here all day. Ended up in a grand row about stockings and mittens. I think they carried off Judith's.

Beautiful spring-like weather.

Mr. Dewees sent us a nice little box packed with various groceries. Oh God's mercy! if only all this help could have come <u>before</u> my baby got sick, I could have had a good doctor!

February 19, 1913

Clouding. Frank worked in Lyle's field & around the place, then after dinner went to Albert's. For the first time in my life I dread being alone, so I took the three girls over to Uncle Joe's. We carried over a mess of parsnips and some of Mark's clothes which may fit Hunkie: only I put away his shoes, the battered little horse he chose himself the last time he went to town, his knife that he asked for and held in his hand before he died, and a few other toys and garments that he liked best. I cannot bear to be alone with the thought of him—and I dread still more the nights when all that is hard or coarse in Frank's nature come sharpest against me. I see it is impossible that he should ever understand; but he is trying to be kind in his way—and working every day.

We heard the first frog, coming home.

February 23, 1913

Clear and warmer. Kitty had the croup and both Frank and I felt badly all night, and got up before 4. He went to the store for groceries. Miss Varnell [Anna Varnell, a nurse] sent us some medicine. Frank rode to Fairmount with Willie. I gave Buzz a much needed bath, and found him to be quite plump for the first time in several years—ever so pretty.

To my astonishment, Willy offers us the organ & a mattress for $10. We went and looked it over, and paid for it at once. This leaves us $11. but the organ is worth double the money.

Began on a new picture. I do hope this new line will sell—cabins and "points" hastily slashed together. We walked over to Joe's this evening to see Icie, who is sick.

February 24, 1913

Kitty had the croup and is abed today. Colder, but clear. Frank went to work at Albert's and Buzz, who is holding his very first real job—painting the sawed limbs in the orchard—went too. Jean went to school in spite of our better judgment, & Virgie with her. The principal sent them back with an ungrammatical & misspelled <u>scrawl</u> to the effect that they are not to return without an order from the doctor. Mrs. Clark, who is going down unexpectedly, gave me half a bushel of potatoes & several loaves of bread. Turning very cold this afternoon.

February 25, 1913

Willie brought down the organ, and he & Frank placed it in the house. It has lost a screw or two on the way down and is not so well toned as I supposed. I wish now that we had not committed this extravagance,—we who have not paid the little boy's doctor bill. I wanted it so bad—some music, any kind of music—and now I have it, it seems to me like a piece of almost criminal foolishness, like that winter in Florida.

March 3, 1913

Warmer and cloudy. I felt better all day, and the children, though coughing badly, are at least out of bed. This afternoon we all gathered a mess of "sissles" and a few leaves of lettuce & mustard that have come up under the crab-grass. Something is wrong with the organ's bellows; I am afraid that was a bad bargain. I wrote some dialect verses—A Sunbonnet at Big Meetin.

March 4, 1913

Woodrow Wilson takes his seat today—a cloudy day, thickening to rain. Frank spent most of the day at his father's. I and the girls filled the new ticking with straw, then I typed my new verses and "The Dulcimore" and sent them to Mr. Milton of the News, and afterward spent a distracted hour trying to improve the condition of the organ. I do wish we had not bought it—it will hardly play, and the leak in the bellows is out of my reach. But I wrote a little five-finger exercise and taught it to Judith. I suppose that what happiness is left to me in this life will come through the children just in proportion as I teach and develop them and hold them to me.

March 14, 1913

Things came unexpectedly to a head last night. Frank's rudeness and crossness suddenly became simply unbearable. I spoke quickly, firmly and to the point; I said I will give him six months to show whether he can and will do better, and then if there is no improvement I will leave for good and take the children. He was utterly taken aback—went through three hours' hysterical moods, varying in the wildest way to abject self abasement, then threats, then pleadings and tears. I held quiet, and I do believe won my case so far as it is possible. I know better than to look for a decided change. I know now why so many country girls go wrong.

However, the relief is great. If I could only keep from thinking of the little boy's death, I could stand it now. This blank unresponsiveness, this harsh monotony!

Fair and warm, windy; a real spring day, $5 in the mail from Elizabeth,[11] in payment for Ragnarok—one of the best things I ever wrote! She says she knows it is not enough, but they cannot pay more.

March 16, 1913

If he had lived he would have been four years old today, and I would have made him a cake.

Freezing cold last night and snowing a little this morning; clearing later, but a cold wind still blows. I am in a worse condition than I have been yet: this is the worst day I have had. Frank cut some white oak bark, peeling it downward according to tradition, and made an infusion which I have begun to drink.

Mrs. Lyle & Faith came to see me this afternoon. It was more than good to have a visitor at last. Junni & Arnold stayed some hours and the children had a great time playing.

March 22, 1913

Tom Scott & wife, an old looking pair of valley people, moved into the Barrett house. She gave me a bucket of buttermilk that is a treat. The girls & I washed a few necessary clothes, & prepared some colored eggs and a rooster for Easter. A clear, pleasantly cool day. The children put some early bluets & trefoil into a bowl for a table centerpiece. Tinte—Dock's wife—lies at the point of death.

March 23, 1913

The spirit of Easter has taken hold of us, my mind is at last clear of bewilderment, fright, and pain. It is given me to see my way. Not poverty, not overwork is the enemy, but despair and all unhappiness; it is the paralysis of discouragement that brings our best efforts to naught; it is the weeping and bitter rebellion that drains one's forces, and this more than even overstrain that is putting me in bed every so often. I will not give in again. I will not be overcome, now that I see the face of the enemy and know what to guard against. I will meet it with courage—no, with light and joy and love.

I said to Frank, "Listen: it's like this. We must be kind to each other; must consider each other's welfare & convenience in every word, in ten thousand ways, right along every day. Whether we feel like it or not. Feelings have nothing to do with it: we've got it to do. Just like that—see?"

He nodded. Oh, does well to gain a nod from him at such moments. But what a gift for prayer he has! Those simple, sincere words, touching

only the everyday affairs of life, illuminating like a sunray! He prayed for
Dock whose wife is dying, for the ignorant & careless, for the perplexed
and defeated—for the people he knows and the things he knows: and the
children murmured Amen.

I ought to be thankful that so much of spirituality is here to leaven
the harshness & coarseness of our daily lives. Jen, whom I have perhaps
envied on account of her material welfare, writes that her husband, my
uncle George, has broken her heart. He is running a saloon.

Certainly I have to be glad that my man is at least faithful, honest and
thoroughly good.

Now let the light shine! Open all windows to the Sun of God!

Frank hid the children's Easter eggs and they had a merry hour
hunting them. Then he went to Dock's. The Lyle children came to play,
dear things. Brick drove by & and brought me [illegible] arbutus. Frank
and I walked over to Joe's but it was almost too much for me.

March 26, 1913

Washed the colored clothes with the girls' help. Heavy, driving showers
this afternoon. The children all went to play with Faith and Jamie, and
Frank being unable to do more than half a day's work, stayed in the house,
and we had such a good long, quiet, friendly talk as we have not had for
years. I am surprised to find my spirits rising:—and I begin to realize that
I shall have more time at my disposal henceforth than for the past ten years
and more to think & work in.

Perhaps he does not remember his torment?—perhaps he
remembers—if anything—those hours of almost delirious gladness when
I nursed him, fed him, played with him, taught him, led him through the
woods and the garden? God knows! I remember it all, God help me.

Good night, my little boy, my darling. My heart is no longer in the
grave with you, but in today's life and work once more.

March 30, 1913

Sunday. Uncle Joe stopped by to show us a drawing he made for Mrs.
Long's log barn & garage. Judith & Kit came back accompanied by Little
Ab & Helen. After dinner we walked over to Grandpap's. Laura was there
& we had quite a visit. She & I went to see poor Tinte—who is now sitting

up. I made potato soup for supper & Sent Tinte some, then walked over to Joe's to see how the little chicks were faring in Sally's absence.

April 4, 1913

Cool & cloudy—a rainy morning. Uncle Larnce stayed to supper & all night. His folks have had a round with smallpox & other illnesses, but he is quite brave about the debts & trouble that follow in the train of illness in a workingman's family. Wants to come back to the Ridge. Frank plows for his father & is to have seed potatoes & a load of manure in return.

Some one, we can't discover who, left a suitbox full of nice clothing at the store addressed to me. It contained some small jap trinkets & post cards for the children—and a fine pair of shoes that Judith can wear. A splendid corset almost new, and only a little large for me, a silk gown I mended into shape, and some white shirt waists new and nicely done up. I searched carefully for a laundry mark, but could find no clew.

Mrs. Scott sends me some buttermilk nearly every day, in addition to the sweet milk I buy from her. It makes easier living. I asked her to come over today and gave her some good worsted clothes.

April 10, 1913

Two days I have lain in bed with a pillow under my hips listening for the thrush's song, those faint far exquisite tones; through the wind and rain. I try to read, try to write or sew—have been some time reading the history of Rome to engage my thoughts out of reach of torment; but at the most unexpected moments I hear that sad and terrible murmur with its strange import,—"I'm gona go to some other house. . . . . I'm gona die." And the heart-sickness seizes me again.

That cool pure strain—is it not like a voice out of the unknown? O singer, winged like a soul! If you could but convey to me some hint of how he fares in that other house! Has he forgotten? Is personality, the individual life, a figment of the temporary consciousness? I thought so—but my hold on thought is slipping. I cling so to that little life, that we by our clumsiness and carelessness allowed to die. My baby, my little boy that never lived his life!

I read the folks funny stories, read my best and sent them all laughing to bed; then I must lie silent and let the tears fall in the dark, for the little boy that loved me so.

April 12, 1913

Five dollars in the mail from Elizabeth; and a lovely letter. Bless her.
A cool, fair day; the young leaves and blossoms laugh in the sun. Jean went
to Aunt Laura's, Frank & Buzz to Grandpap's. I had a happy thought, and
unscrewed the drop-leaf from the old sewing machine, painted a sign on
it—Emma Bell Miles, Sketch Classes—and nailed it to a tree on the Signal
Point Road. Have cut down 3 of my last summer dresses for the twins.

I have at last determined what to do—an undertaking that required
strength, judgment, and courage to carry out, but I feel rather weak. I
must do it—must save enough this summer to take me to Hill City, open a
sketch class & put the children in school, by the first of Sept. if possible. It
will be difficult, not to say dangerous, what I have in mind. But I must not
falter nor be content with half measures. The children must be fed, must
be educated, must have better associates—and there is but one way. They
will soon have no mother if the present arrangement is persisted in through
these dreadful winters.

April 13, 1913

A cloudy, cold day. Everything is behind. The hen did not hatch a
single chicken, and none of the others will set. Frank & I walked over to see
the old folks. Found them sitting one on each side of a fire almost gone out,
shivering and asleep. He cut a backstick and put on a good fire, enough to
last them till morning. Larnce's folks have just moved up, they had a house
full—rowdy boys & girls, & a drunk man. The young folks all went off to
the woods & asked Judith. I was so proud of her refusal that I let her make
fudge when we got home. Jean spent last night at Aunt Laura's.

April 18, 1913

An unexpectedly delightful day. Frank went to help Grandpap make
garden. I took Kitty with me to hunt for poke greens, and met her &
Mrs. Bachman—the dearest people—and their little daughter in cowboy
shirt & trousers half way up a tree. They want a painting of the house &
blossoming orchard—so I went to work on it after a hasty noon lunch. Tried
a large canvas & succeeded fairly well. Kitty found a thrasher's nest with
eggs, and came running under the trees crying, "Aint' I lucky, oh, mamma,
ain't I lucky!" After talking about it for some time she began to look

doubtful, and said: "I <u>hope</u> I ain't fooled. I—I <u>saw</u> 'em, but—sometimes I get fooled." Back she went to make sure, and presently reported: "Now I <u>know</u> I ain't fooled, because I took one egg up in my hand."

Afterward we sat under the tree in Mrs. Bachman's yard and Kitty got very well acquainted, and told Mrs. B's fortune, and said some of the quaintest things. I spoilt the poke, though, in cooking it for supper.

April 24, 1913

The gray haze thickens at last over the clear cool weather—haze of a Southern spring, shot through with delicious colors & notes. How many ages have perfected the thrush's strain?

I got out some of those booklets and lettered the covers, wondering whether I might sell some during the Confederate Veteran's Reunion.[12] Mrs. Lyle brought two ladies to call this afternoon, and afterwards a Miss Thatcher called.

April 26, 1913

Frank lost his temper last night, simply because I was tired out, and went through half a night of spoiled-baby raging, and the threats I know by heart. It ended suddenly about midnight in a bad heart that called, of course, for hot water and whiskey—then he very sweetly begged forgiveness, as if forgiveness had any thing to do with such foolishness. I went to sleep about two o'clock, and woke up as usual about 4:30. The girls got breakfast, and afterwards Frank went to the store. A steady rain all night made it impossible to go on with gardening, but there is plenty more that ought to be done. A collector came about an old grocery bill, and I was obliged to turn over the Bachman check in part payment. I felt very bad, and Frank began to blame me about the ironing.

"You know it's not the ironing," I told him: "it was that miserable night you gave me." This is positively the first short answer I have given him for months, but I could hardly breathe at the moment.

"Well—I'll never do it again." He was quite gentle now, and took my hand.

"That's what you said one night last August," I reminded him. The end of my patience was reached.

He was silent a while, then proposed that he go to the Signal Point working camp to get a job.

What did I think of it? I said he can not stand the day's work, and will presently be back here sick, out of a job and out of garden too.

"I won't. I'll go to hospital," he said. "You've kept me up long enough."

He went. But he begged me not to be angry, and not to feel bad at him. There seems to be no anger left in me toward him at all; but last night when he ordered me to get up and <u>git</u> when daylight came, how I wished that I could! I have been thinking of camping alone in the Chapin barn & out houses for the rest of the summer. But in that case where could I meet people or hold my sketch class? Of course, he came back unsuccessful this afternoon.

April 28, 1913

When I told Frank I wanted to go away and rest for a time, make a little money and get some sleep, he asked at once where I was going and how long I expected to be gone. I told him the truth, for I didn't know; and then he made a frightful scene, locking the door, and calling the sobbing children to witness that I was deserting him. He said it was desertion in the eyes of the law—I don't know; I only want to sleep—and expounded the code of Tennessee to me for half an hour or so, even talking divorce and making all kinds of wild threats, before he finally gave up and said I could go and come back when I got ready; but that Joe and Kitty must get their things on and go with me. This destroyed my plan for camping and sketching, but I thought possibly I could board them at Laura's for a week till I could rent a room somewhere.

We set out with the bag and basket. A fine cold rain began to fall when we were half way there, and Kitty complained of being tired. I stopped at Key's, but could sell nothing there—then saw Mrs. Poindexter feeding her White Orpingtons [chickens] and ducks, and called on her in the barn. I gave her some long promised books, and she gave me five dollars.

But we found Laura very ill, just over the worst of a serious miscarriage. It was now too late to go home, raining, and very cold—so I merely made myself useful and cheerful, saying nothing of our own trouble or Joe's. I did not get the sleep I hoped for—had to sleep with the two little boys, who kicked and snored and crowded against me all night. At daybreak Kitty cried and said she was sick, so I dressed hurriedly and gave her senna leaf tea. She began to throw up and cry harder, and I saw there was nothing for it but to go home. Mr. Long was just starting for town, so I boldly asked for a place in his car. There was just room to cling, with Kitty in my lap: we left Buzz to follow. The little fellow has shown me the most perfect consideration all through this; he even warned Kitty to say nothing about the trouble at home, bless him!

I got out at the store and ordered some groceries sent up, and left my basket. I got Kitty home some how—made a fire, put her feet into hot water, and put her to bed: we both slept three or four hours. Then I cut some wood and piled it on the porch, because the wind was blowing colder all the time and Kitty seemed to be getting worse. I thought Joe might have helped me home, but he didn't.

Mary Larnce went by with Mamie and Tiny [Frank's niece]. When I called to her to tell her Laura was sick, she gasped, "I didn't know you'd come back! Does Frank know you're here?" So I knew he had told Smoky Row that I had left him. I almost laughed; for he would never have thought so if he had not been afraid I would call his bluff.

Mary stopped on her way home, to tell me about Eula, and also, I suppose, to find out whether there was really any trouble between me and Frank; but she asked us questions and I proffered but little information. A while after she had gone, Frank and the children came. Buzz having hunted him up at Grandma's and told him I was at home. I gave the children supper of mush & milk, and after they went to bed he began, as he said, to try to straighten things out. I begged him to let me go to sleep; but he said he couldn't sleep till the matter was put straight, and went on and on. Every now and then his desire to inflict pain would get the better of him, but he would make an effort, get control of himself, and compromise with kisses. Oh, I was so tired—but at last we got to bed somehow. But not to rest—I am now up to give Kitty a bath under the blanket, to reduce the fever and quiet her heart, which is skipping beats. I am afraid she is in for a sick spell.

April 29, 1913

I told Frank last night that I wondered what the girls thought of my being shamed so before them. This morning I found out. Judith got up sulky and rebellious because her slippers are worn out; she stamped about, tossing her head and throwing her stockings on the floor, and finally said spitefully, "Papa's going to get me a pair of shoes when he gets the money; but I know somebody'll interfere."

"Do you mean me?" I asked. "Why don't you say what you mean?"

"Well, you know you will interfere."

There it was—the constant imputing to me low motives and mean actions, all either in the future tense or else made by twisting innocent words & actions. She has already learnt the tune.

"How many pair of shoes do you suppose papa ever bought you in your life?" I asked her.

"Every stitch of shoe leather you ever wore has been either paid for out of my earnings or given you by some one for my sake."

She stamped out, flaming, and sat barefooted till breakfast time, never offering to help me. When Frank came in, I held him at arm's length till I could tell him about it. He seemed to wither as I spoke.

"Well—I'm sorry," he stammered, trying to draw me into his arms.

But I pushed him away. "That won't do. I've had a public humiliation; now I must have a public apology. If you're not man enough to tell those children the facts of the case, eat your words, and make them understand, never speak to me of love and respect again the longest day you live."

"If I've done you wrong, I'm sorry, and will say so. But you always think you're perfect—"

"I don't want any ifs about it."

Of course there was another ugly quarrel. He wasn't going to be able to live with me anyhow; he couldn't make them understand; he would promise anything else under heaven I wanted; he didn't know how, etc. But in the end he went through his reparation.

It was not so dramatic as the offense had been, and the children didn't pay much attention. And all the time Kitty lay stupid, breathing heavily, only rousing to ask for a spoonful of water and a few moments later to throw it up. She has been so all day.

But at bed time Judith came sweetly and put her arms round my neck, whispering: "Mama, I am sorry. Only I didn't feel like saying so."

It almost made up for all the trouble! I was so afraid of that inflexible stupid contrariness becoming set and hardened and spoiling her beautiful nature. But she is full of genuine feeling, the dear girl.

In the afternoon I carried a package to Joe's house, intending to stay only a few minutes away from Kitty; but Joe and Sally both seemed pathetically eager to tell me about it, glad to get to talk to me; so I stayed and talked quite a while. I felt too that some explanation of Frank's behavior was due to Joe at least, (Frank had even gone so far as to try to rent the house, and the girls came home delighted over his project of taking them to Signal Point for the summer,) so in a few words I told them how Frank's bluff had been called.

Emma Bell Miles sketching at the home of a friend, circa 1912 (photo by E. A. Wheatley; Jean Miles Catino Collection, Special Collections, University of Tennessee at Chattanooga)

Emma at the age of twenty (Jean Miles Catino Collection, Special Collections,
University of Tennessee at Chattanooga)

Frank in Miami, 1909 (Jean Miles Catino Collection, Special Collections,
University of Tennessee at Chattanooga)

Emma with her youngest son, Frank Mirick (Mark), in Miami, 1909 (Jean Miles
Catino Collection, Special Collections, University of Tennessee at Chattanooga)

Hollywood, Signal Mt. May 11, 1916

To Judith and Jean and Joe and Katharine —

Dear children, if you keep nothing else of my writing I want you to keep this book, for in it I have told how happy we were. At the time I began it my stories were beginning to sell, and we were for the first and only time free of painful want. I was full of love and delight in your babyhood: and made the book of gathered hours of happiness, as people sometimes store rose leaves in a jar, to sweeten your lives.

Later, as you remember, things changed — I had resolved to live above disease and all unhappiness and shameful things; and until the terrible breaking sorrow and shame that was put on me, I think I kept my resolution as well as any one could. Often I have been too harsh with you; when you remember this try to understand that I was at the time struggling for a chance to live, and forgive me —

And O my darlings, if you learn nothing else from my notebooks, let them teach you that the happiest times may be changed and darkened by unkindness in the home, and that the best opportunities are wasted by neglect — Love one another as I have loved you, and try to be patient as I have never been — Above all things, be kind —

With everlasting love, from

Mother.

The preface to the journal, written in 1916 (Jean Miles Catino Collection, Special Collections, University of Tennessee at Chattanooga)

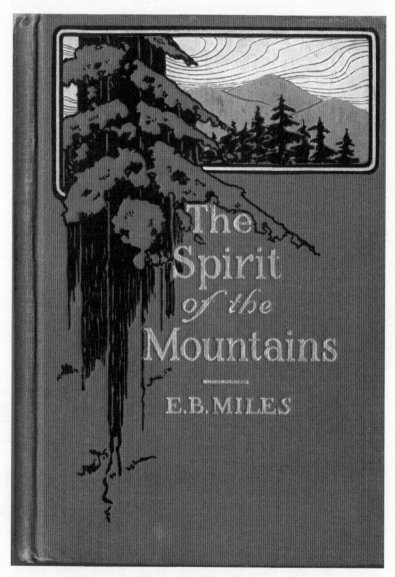

The cover of Miles's 1905 book, *The Spirit of the Mountains*

The cover of Miles's 1919 book, *Our Southern Birds*

The cover of Miles's pamphlet of poems, *Chords from a Dulcimore*

THE STICK HORSE

I went to Aunt Betty's with mother.
    We was up and eat breakfast by day,
And I was as tired as I could be
    When we'd gone only half o' the way.
I 'ist couldn't walk any furder;
    So mother she cut me a horse—
The prettiest sourwood saplin'!
    And I rode right off on him, o' course.

He tried to run 'way with me, first thing!
    But therectly got gentle and kind.
Mother couldn't keep up with my horsey,
    So I axed her to ride behind.
He wouldn't a-kicked her, nor th'owed her,
    But she's feared of a nag, anyhow;
So I come down the road 'ist a-kitin',
    And got to Aunt Betty's right now!

A poem and illustration from *Chords from a Dulcimore*

Small watercolor by Miles of a cabin on Walden's Ridge, Tennessee (Jean Miles Catino Collection, Special Collections, University of Tennessee at Chattanooga)

Small watercolor by Miles of Lookout Mountain (Jean Miles Catino Collection, Special Collections, University of Tennessee at Chattanooga)

Watercolor by Miles of her first four children, Jean, Judith, Joe, and Katharine (Jean Miles Catino Collection, Special Collections, University of Tennessee at Chattanooga)

Small watercolor by Miles of a waterfall (Jean Miles Catino Collection, Special Collections, University of Tennessee at Chattanooga)

FOX SPARROW
Length 7¼ inches

Watercolor by Miles of a fox sparrow, from *Our Southern Birds*

SPARROW HAWK
Length 10 inches

Ink drawing by Miles of a sparrow hawk, from *Our Southern Birds*

Ink drawing by Miles of a cabin on Walden's Ridge (Jean Miles
Catino Collection, Special Collections, University of Tennessee
at Chattanooga)

Emma Bell Miles's grave in Red Bank, Tennessee. Photo by Steven Cox

four

"I Must Be Free!"

In the aftermath of young Mirick's death, Emma tried to provide for her family. During this period, her frustration with Frank grew, and was turning into outright contempt. They had night-long rows, after which neither got much sleep. This was also the period during which there are large gaps between entries in the journal. Emma temporarily left the family to live in Chattanooga so she could teach art lessons and possibly sell some paintings and other work. The family occasionally visited, and she spent weekends up on Walden's Ridge. In 1914 she found work with the *Chattanooga News*. She found herself pregnant again in early 1914, and the pregnancy ended her job with the *News*. There are hints in her writing that she resorted to an abortion, possibly self-induced, and had done so in the past. In any case, she eventually miscarried. She vowed to be free of the poverty that life with Frank offered. Fortunately, the twins were sponsored by family friends to attend school elsewhere.

May 5, 1913

I could get together only 3 pupils for my sketch class, half-equipped beginners. The two Lyles are to count their tuition on Frank's debt, but I shall have $1 a week from Martha Bachman. Jean went with us, and I think she enjoyed it enough to go again.

Notwithstanding the pain in his knee, Frank plowed most of the day. We all went to Grandma's in the evening, and I asked Mrs. Lane to present my regrets to the Hill City Book Club, that I can't be with them on their Author's Day.

May 8, 1913

Frank went to town with the old man again. I tried to iron, but was slowly overcome by a dead weight of misery against which I seem to be powerless. It is paralyzing all my faculties. I can do nothing, think of nothing. Oh, what have I ever done that I must suffer like this! That my life should come to be one futile struggle to pay that nightmare grocery bill! Will there never be an end?

It seemed to me from ten o clock on that I would go mad.

But after dinner all but Judith went away, and the house became quiet. She was trying to pick out with one finger a tune on the organ; I tumbled out of bed, and before I knew it I was giving her a music lesson. She is also learning a little American history. It makes me happy, every little that they gain.

I had five dollars to send to town. Some of it paid the tax on the place, some bought groceries, some came home to pay the milk bill. The girls need summer underclothes, and we are out of sheets; I make the pillow slips of flour sacks. And we are all out of stockings. I don't know what to do.

May 11, 1913

Sunday. Frank had a bad night, I think from eating a heavy dinner hurriedly when he was tired; but he says it was the way I cooked the greens. He would not eat the toast I made this morning. I left him sitting by the stove, for it is quite cold and cloudy, and taking Kitty with me went to see Cora Freudenberg. I wanted to take Erna as a sketch class pupil on the old debt—but Erna's time is already filled. However, I let her have some booklets & arranged to do some small pictures for their new house. I think we can soon work out of debt if no more illness intervenes. We went then and called on Mrs. Miller at the store; they bought two booklets and I took the price in groceries. I tried to get something Frank could eat, but he was very ungracious about it. I think when a man marries a good woman he likes to experiment with her patience; so that the greater her forbearance the more she has to endure.

Joe and all his folks came over this afternoon.

May 15, 1913

Frank was wakeful all night, could not rest on account of his heart. I think he realized at last that he has slowly killed my love, and instead of trying what pure kindness will do, he despairs, and torments himself and me. For him it has always been easier to give up and sink than to try. Oh, if he had only helped me in my hour of need, I would now be able to help him. God knows I give him everything except the passionate love he wants.

He got up early and went to Pap's, intending to go to town, and I supposing he had gone, took the children and went down to the brow to try for one good picture—one whole morning of freedom, of letting loose all the skill and insight that makes for good work. Oh, how I enjoyed it! The resulting canvas was the best yet—better even than Judge Bachman's orchard picture. I got through about twelve, and came back to the store. Frank was there, sick and miserable. We bought a loaf & some potted meat and ate it outdoors, and came home.

I took the children to play with Martha Bachman this evening. Grace MacGowan sent me a book in the mail.

May 16, 1913

Frank had a good night's rest. He is trying now to be patient and considerate, and it eases things. The new book—The Wind before the Dawn—is a big, vital utterance, very simple, with no literary style—a protest against woman's financial dependence.[1] But does it get at the root of the trouble? Myself I was never dependent on any man for food and clothing; I hardly know what it is to ask any man for money: yet all my life, when at home, I have been at the mercy of an inconsiderate, unreasonable boss. There is certainly something inherent in motherhood, or mother-feeling, that puts one in such a position in family life.

Frank went to take his Pap to town. He got some groceries on credit. I had the class, then gave the children such food as there was in the house, and washed all afternoon. Got through just about in time; a driving rain came up and relieved the thirst of the land.

May 20, 1913

Frank went to Pap's to plow. I don't know what we are going to do for sheets and stockings; and I have used my last stretcher of canvas. But if Frank keeps on doing his best, we shall win out. Mrs. Clark came and Mr. Albert, to ask Frank to work in their gardens. Went to Mr. Lyle's to telephone. Had a long conversation with Mrs. Wheatley: I no sooner heard her speak than I felt the same waves of kindness as before, and came home with the same refreshed feeling. We planned for a picnic early in June.

May 24, 1913

To town with Frank and his pap. All the streets are decorated for next week's [Confederate veteran's] Reunion. I called on several people, did my little bit of shopping, mostly paint & paper, then went to see Mrs. Wheatley. Found her abed, resting after a dinner party. Mr. Wheatley & I had a delightful conversation about pictures etc. and Mrs. Wheatley was most gentle & sympathetic about my dreadful winter. I had a hasty luncheon with them, looked at Katherine's new Maid of Honor dress & proposed to paint her portrait in it. (I hope they will let me!) and made haste to get back. Coming out of town we were met by Judith & Jean & Joe on Stringer's Ridge. They had walked all the way—and how tired we all were, before we got home. I have a bad sick headache.

June 1, 1913

Sunday. A hot, sultry morning. We packed a basket & went walking—decided on the Levi falls for our photographic party next Sunday. I let the children strip & wade, and arranged some poses against the beautiful background of the shadow under the falls. I looked at them in a diminishing-mirror in line of a "finder"—exquisite things. We came home about 1.

I had a headache, but when Mrs. Willingham sent for me to come over to Joe's to see her, I dressed & went. Frank & I both looked our best & we had a nice visit. Mrs. W. walked home with me, the rest rode in a big Nyberg on the Point road. When they left the Grahams came & some other Hill City folks, and after that Mrs. Clark & Mrs. Rawlings. We had such a good time all day. I wish I didn't have these headaches. Cloudy & cooler.

June 2, 1913

Clear & pleasant. Went sketching with the class. Frank plowed for Mrs. Clark. He was dunned for his poll tax in the mail, and I, rather sharply, for my debt to the printer. Oh dear.

Everything has gone wrong today. I am so nervous I could scream. Jean has a purple mark on her shoulder where I whipped her—and is not behaving one bit better either, even though Martha B. has invited her to go to see Buffalo Bill Saturday.[2] I am feeling miserable again for the third time this month, and can only sew a little. Telephoned Wheatley's this evening; they are planning to come out Sunday.

June 6, 1913

So cold & cloudy, and I felt so bad, that I did not take the class out. Will I never be well again? I could, with half a chance, I think; but beg as I may, he will not change. There is no mercy in him, even when he is sick-ashamed of his own cruel sensuality. He is a spoilt baby when he is not a brute. I have spent my life following mirages; I paid all I had for a little love, and only to see it turn to dust and ashes in my hands.

Frank has suddenly taken offense about the proposed picnic with the Wheatleys; naturally enough, perhaps, he feels left out of it, and refuses to go. Of course I said that I would not go either if he feels so about it. Jean has sobbed herself into hysterics, the others are all unmanageably cross with the disappointment. Of this Frank sees nothing, for he is off at work. I went to Mrs. Bachman's to telephone Mrs. Wheatley that we probably can not meet them Sunday; how I hated to—she was so disappointed, so I temporized, thinking probably Frank might change his mood, and said I would let her know in the morning.

June 7, 1913

The children were so disappointed over Martha's failure to follow up her promise to take them to the show, and Mrs. Wheatley so alarmed over their prospective disappointment, and poor Frank so hurt, that I hardly know what to do or say. He rudely ordered me to go on with the thing alone, as I had begun it; but he went and engaged the hack and team; then I telephoned Mrs. Wheatley, only to hear that they have decided to postpone the picnic, as the paper says rain and because I am not feeling well. I felt

relieved to be rid of the affair, and promised Frank that I will never again
see the Wheatleys if I can help it, and certainly I will get out of having the
picnic as gracefully as may be; but Frank was by this time wrought to such
a pitch of wrath that nothing would satisfy him. He saw that he was making
me ill and knew that he was behaving like a brute, but as usual at such
times he seemed utterly unable to stop himself, and kept on and on with
every mean thing he could think of to say and every ugly thing he could dig
up out of the unpleasant past. I was sick and lay down; he ordered me not
to cook him a bit, and went to the garden. I got dinner for the children and
lay down again, and he came to the door and snarled at me, "Why in the
nation didn't you tell me dinner was ready?" in such a tone that everybody
in the house jumped and I flew out of bed and burst into tears. This brought
down on me a violent and shameful scolding that lasted for hours. Kitty
was frightened and cried so that I could hardly comfort her, but Judith I
think was simply disgusted. Thank heaven, Joe was gone to the show with
Jamie Lyle. I made as few answers as possible, and replied very guilty
to all his insulting tirade; which caused him to cry out—"Oh, this cold,
gentle contempt of yours! There's not a man living that could stand it!" We
had come to a deadlock that seemed to paralyze our understandings. One
moment he would accuse me of having made it up with "that damned son-
of-a-bitch of a Wheatley" to slight him; the next he would be almost on
his knees begging me with tears to love him and to be "like myself" again.
And all the time the beating of my heart was smothering me, and I heard
my little boy murmuring between agonized gasps, "I'm gona go to some
other house. . . . . I'm gona die." In vain I begged him to let me alone; he
seems to take no account of any one's physical condition but his own. It is
his own shame that makes him wish to insult me, and his own torment that
drives him to this, though he knows it must be to his own undoing. Well,
the day is over, and the children gone to rest. But I dread the night; these
reconciliations are often worse than the quarrels; and oh, those pitiful
attempts of his to revive by physical means the corpse of love—what
ordeals they are for me!

June 9, 1913

So cold and cloudy that only Jamie came to the class; I put him and
Jean to drawing a kitchen still-life study. Mrs. Wheatley telephoned that

she was sending the children some things on the hack, so they went to the Top this afternoon. Such gifts—a dainty white dress apiece for the twins, a ball, bat & mitt for Joe, and for Kitty the finest doll any of them has ever had, dressed by Katherine Kaufman in pink satin. It seems they are from her friend Mrs. Clark, whom I scarcely know. I tried to get some expression out of Frank as to how I ought to receive these things; he must see that I cannot remain in such a position. But he now denies that he accused me of anything yesterday, and will not face the issue at all. It has always been so; every friend I have had, he has divided me from in some such indirect way; yet we have all lived off the money of such wealthy people, appreciative people—I don't know how to make a living out of any other kind; I can't take a job in a factory, and he will not arrange things so that I can write.

Buzzy-boy brought in a wee fledgling vireo, the daintiest little creature imaginable, ready to perish of cold. We fed and warmed it, and will take it back to its native bushes in the morning. We hear that a little snow fell in Chattanooga today![3]

June 12, 1913

Thursday. Still cold. Frank again went to Pap's before breakfast. I have at last, ironing a few pieces every time the fire was hot in the stove, got through with the great bag of clothes. Took the children over on the brow & spent the morning on an oil sketch, 2 x 3 ½ looking from Winters Point. Stopped to show it to Mrs. Atlee on the way home, and had some talk with her about sending the girls away to school. I was afraid Frank might interfere; but I found him at home when I arrived, very good-humored and inclined to be complaisant about it. I hope and believe it can be arranged.

June 15, 1913

Sunday. Frank ate nothing all day yesterday, slept but little all night, and began on me before we were out of bed: went out of the house instead of eating breakfast, and later proposed to go away at dinner too, saying that I would like it better so. I felt obliged to take this up, and told him I was quite willing to cook & sew for him, and he must not try to make out otherwise. Hence began another quarrel. He insisted that I was "mad" and accused me of misbehaving with Wheatley again—"you've admitted that you did smoke part of a cigarette with him," said he—and threatened to throw them off the place if they came to see me next month, and all the rest of it. But so soon as I really did begin to reply to him he gave down, apologized, promised, retracted, and begged forgiveness—"only be like you were before this came up."

"This?" I said. "This is nothing; has made no difference in my feeling. You seem to forget that I would never have gone to visit Mrs. Wheatley in the first place if your moods and tempers had not made it impossible for me to live at home. It is not only friends you have taken from me; it is comfort and books and music, my work, my health, everything that makes life worth living. You have even embittered my motherhood, the most precious thing in any woman's life—"

"I wouldn't say anything about motherhood if I was you," he interrupted scornfully.

"You put me in a situation that made it almost impossible to bear and bring up children: you oblige me to do it nevertheless, and now you reproach me with not being a good mother."

"Well—let's not say any more about it, let's forget it and make up." He shut his eyes; he was really sick. "I want you—I want you!"

"This will all be to go over again the first time you lose your temper," I reminded him. "It has happened many times in the past year."

Now he was humbly anxious to promise anything. But what are such promises worth? and how am I to meet the scandal he may precipitate upon me at any day? and how am I to get well under such conditions?

I have worked all he would let me on Thrid o' Warp today.[4]

June 18, 1913

Frank surprised me this morning with the proposition that he spend the winter with John V. while the girls go to Alabama and I take Joe and Kitty to town to school.[5] I do hope he will arrange things in such a sensible and easy way. He has threatened to leave me so often, but without any intention behind the words more serious than an angry mood; but this was apparently not meant as a threat; I hope he will see the advantages of the plan. He went to John's immediately on rising, though I offered to get him a harty [sic] breakfast.

I took the class sketching, then went to see if Mrs. Atlee had heard from that Ala. School.[6] Read something about the place and got Jean very much interested. Read a letter from Mrs. Elder, the president of the home. I think it is the right chance for them. But, Lord have mercy on a fool—I have made so many mistakes! I telephoned and tried to get some more pupils from various sources, but without success.

June 19, 1913

Just a sprinkle last night with wind and thunder; but today is not so burning hot. We figure it will take $15 to buy the girls' clothes—and we are not at present keeping them in enough to eat! I must get up a bigger class somehow! Jamie asked the bunch to go picnicking which called for our last nickel. I must do something. It gets harder every year instead of better. I looked into the glass this morning and saw the ruin this life has made of me; I looked at my brown, skinny hands, all cut and burnt and bruised and blackened—and oh, God, how I longed to do some good work once again for appreciative people! I must be free of Frank Miles—I must be free. It is my children's only hope. Poor Frank!

But Jean was so good all day yesterday—and this morning Kitty put her arms around me and kissed me, a very unusual demonstration for her. These little things are, it may be, sign posts on the way to a happiness yet to seek.

Frank cut Willy Lyle's vats all morning. Frank Atlee and Jack Nicklin stopped on their way home from hunting to show me a flower, a Spreading Pogonia they had found.[7]

June 22, 1913

Judith ran away early yesterday morning, having been sharply reproved by her father and me. We did not feel uneasy until afternoon. As we knew she was not anywhere in the neighborhood we decided she must have gone to Laura's. We all set out in a drizzling rain to find her. It quit raining shortly after our arrival, and Frank borrowed Ab's horse to seek further. It was dark when he returned, having at last met the child and sent her to Grandma's for the night. We spent the night very pleasantly at Laura's and came home in the morning.

Called on Mrs. Atlee and Miss Gregg—then went to Mr. Lyle's to telephone.

June 24, 1913

Fair and pleasant. Frank went hunting early, with Frank Atlee. My class now pays $4 a week, out of which $1 goes for washing and about 75c. for milk; the rest buys enough groceries to run us. Perhaps I can get a little ahead.

June 27, 1913

The class took up the morning, and in the evening I took Jean with me to make some calls. We gave Mrs. Chapin the orchid. Mrs. Dabney was there, having just arrived from Texas, sweet and charming as ever. At Mr. Bachman's I met Dr. Bachman for the first time—one of Chattanooga's grand old men.[8] Then called on Mrs. Martin. I believe she is one of those women who have always been taken care of and cannot comprehend any but a selfish point of view. Stopped a minute with Mrs. Dugger—then home. Mrs. Chapin promised me her daughter & Pauline Megge for my class.

June 28, 1913

Mr. Padgett called this morning to ask us to sign a petition retaining him in school. I do believe I'm the only woman in this neighborhood that had strength of mind to refuse. He was very nervous and hesitating; his grammar worse than ever—he repeated "I seen they was" in several tales, and was deeply apologetic about sending the children home from school last winter—as if that were my ground for refusing.

So hot, so dry. Will there be any potatoes after all? Buzz fell in with a baseball crowd and they offered him a dime for the loan of his bat & mitt. He watched the game, and came home treading on air.

We have green beans & onions now.

July 1, 1913

Rode down the new road with Mr. Lyle in the auto. After carrying my flowers to St. Paul's, where Mrs. Clark put them into water, went to Carol's expecting to rest some hours, but finding that her chatter was making me too nervous, went out to Mrs. Wheatley & stayed for lunch. Showed them my canvases, but I guess they are not so well done as I thought. Perhaps I had better give up painting except in emergencies where I must raise a little money. Then to see Mrs. Patten. She did not come till mid-afternoon. I had a delightful visit with her on the front porch. Met Zerelda Rains, Miss Margaret Chaffee & Carol by appointment at the Live & Let Live at 4.

The lecture was at 8. I was surprised at the number of people that came, in the sweltering heat; several men even, in coats & collars stewing. Mrs. Clark sang, Carol introduced me most gracefully, and I went through my part creditably enough. My audience was delightfully sympathetic; the room was rather small, and the whole affair was like a visit. Home with Zerelda and Mr. Rains afterwards.

July 2, 1913

Telephoning all morning—receiving congratulations, briefly consulting with Frank, lengthily conversing with Mrs. Marguerite Severance,[9] inquiring after Mrs. Wheatley's health—she is nearly prostrated by the heat—and visiting with Zerelda between whiles: best of all, the Stedmans offered to bring me home in their auto, and as Frank could not come for me I gratefully accepted.

To Carol's—I was too tired to accept Mrs. Patten's invitation to lunch at the English Tea Room—afterward bought the girls' dry goods, met Mrs. Stedman and was whirled away in the big machine, out of the wilting, sickening heat of town. The ride was delightful. Mr. Stedman's face holds more of the refinement of pure goodness than any other man's face I have seen this year; and others have told me that they are just that kind of folks.

Up the new road. The line of the cliffs against the sky is magnificent. The machine got stalled on a heavy grade and Mrs. S. & I walked up to the commissary and succeeded in obtaining a half gallon of oil. I took her children to Grindstone Spring while she walked back by a short cut. Soon we were again on our way and were planning to have supper at my house, but it was rather late and they decided to return. I found the house empty, with open doors, all disorder and confusion. Mr. Scott told me that Joe had gone to where the boys are laying out a diamond to play ball; so I found him and sent him in search of his sisters. When they got back I put them to straightening the house, as I had only a few hours' sleep last night and was about all in. I did not school any one much; it was about what I expected. One can endure anything for two months; and it is such a waste of energy to quarrel.

July 7, 1913

Only the deepest, truest veins of water are running now, when the ground cracks everywhere between the wilted, crisping weeds. I lean and look into one clear pool, the very essence of transparent morning, welling from mysterious depths between harsh masses of crude planetary substance, deep-dreaming always in that dim hour before the morning-glory's frail urns of dew are shattered by the sun. Insects fill the shadow above it, murmuring in their happiness; a frog sits on the stone step; birds come to the escaping rivulet to drink and bathe. Ferns lean to the water's run, and the stones are velveted with moss and arched with the fairy grace of grasses. And drops skip one by one down the channel provided by a single bending blade, letting go with some particular twirl that sends them gliding across the surface of the pool like flying diamonds; each is sustained by capillary attraction in moment only, sinking and losing itself, for its brief second of duration, all the luminous beauty of the day—each one thrills and trembles, and pictures its world of ferns and rock and blue sky. Microcosms like those other things that whirl a little way and sink back into indistinguishability,—insects and planets and men—they have been cloud & glacier & dew & steam & ocean wave.

Over the spring is a little roof upheld by the rock walls and by oaken beams on which are cut the names of many who once loved to drink here,—young people mostly who met and laughed and quarrelled [*sic*] and courted here on long Sunday afternoons. Some are gone out into the world that is itself but an orbed drop whirling across the dark; some reflect their tiny soul-pictures of home and the new generation but a stone's-throw away; some have ceased to thrill with the sense of a temporary orbit apart from the vast spring of existence from which they rose. "Lucille"—how beautiful she was, how dear! With all the myriads of worlds that shall be born and spin brightly with a freight of souls across the deeps, there will never be another Lucille! All that grace & charm, the warm heart and clever hands of her,—gone like the warm breath held for a moment by a bubble's film! But drops will always fall and glide across the springs; and there will always be the tiny beauty of trembling pictures.

The sky today is thick with a white haze, so that the sun hardly casts a shadow. Judith posed for the class this morning, and after dinner I sewed all afternoon on Mrs. Lyle's machine.

July 10, 1913

The morning clouds hung low,—looked like rain; the wind's touch was subtly keener with damp. But the hours lightened, the sun looked out, and Tinte came to wash. Frank went to work after getting me some wood.

Ah, no one guesses that I am counting the days till I can go free! As soon as the girls are gone, then with as little argument as possible I shall make a bold stroke for freedom—put the two little ones in school, and live with them in a room somewhere where I can write all day and all night too if I wish. Oh, I shall visit with delightful people, and read the best books in the city library, and hear music and lectures—and there shall be no more of these dreadful nights, no more tobacco-spit and stale perspiration, no more cutting my stovewood, no more quarrels! Oh, God, how I count the days!

But again—where is the money to come from? I shall have to earn it somehow. And meantime the girls' clothes are to make, and shoes and stockings to buy.

July 11, 1913

After dinner yesterday I walked out to Summertown. Mrs. Andrews was lying down, so I went on to see Mrs. Poindexter and had a good visit. She told me of many offers to help the girls off to school. Then to Laura's. Judith is too busy & seems contented. I meant to go home, but tried to see Mrs. Davidson— she was out—and by that time the whole west was filled with storm clouds, and I went to Mrs. Albert Key's in a slight rain and decided to go no farther that evening than Summertown. I sold her a booklet—then saw Mrs. Andrews at last, and had a long talk with her about Mirick and her little son that died. She promised the twins some stockings from her husband's hosiery mill; when they go away. I spent the night with Laura, to Judith's delight.

Walked home this morning, in time for the class which was not very successful with but Faith, Jamie & Martha. I feel rather tough—tired out.

Rain by showers, thick fog towards evening—every leaf and every grain of sand drinking deep.

July 12, 1913

The drought was effectually broken by a damp night and rainy morning. I sewed and ironed, and helped Kitty make a dress for her doll. Clearing some what this afternoon.

Frank knows, now, what I plan to do. It must have dawned on him gradually; for suddenly, but quietly, he asked me if I meant him to go with me this winter. Very quietly and without bitterness he accepted my decision. I put it so as to spare him as much as possible, pointing out that it will be too hard on him in town. He went to bed early, eating nothing and saying little. But after night he whispered, gently enough: "I don't blame you at all. I've known for some time that you'd be better off without me."

At once I was filled with pity and tenderness—I almost loved him again. But this gentleness of his is only a mood, I know. If it will only hold until the girls get away!

July 13, 1913

Sunday. We have received so many duns in the mail that I have put aside the girls' sewing and every thing else till I can raise some money. Frank helped with the housework and I tried to do some of the cheap watercolors that sell so well, but Buzz is sick with a cankered sore throat. Judith came home for the day, bringing Ab & Helen with her, which made extra children. So I could not do much and was very nervous. Frank & I walked over to Joe's this afternoon, and he, not I, told them of the plan. They approved of it, as I expected—the sheer common sense of it should appeal, I think, to any one.

July 14, 1913

Last night the mood changed, as I have feared all along. Quite suddenly, when I had nearly fallen asleep, he began a steady fire of suspicious questions. I could add nothing to the explanation I had already given; and at the words "an underhanded, sneaking, dirty way you've taken" I tried to get up and go elsewhere to sleep, but he jerked me back, threw me across the bed and raised one arm as if to strike me. And a moment afterward he was crying and begging: "I didn't mean that the way it sounded; I'm so sorry I said it! Won't you forgive me?" I answered that he must think what he says and remember whom he is speaking to. But the night was broken with his sick hysteria, and this morning he got up early and went to Pap's for the day, leaving me puzzled & despairing.

I trimmed a hat before class time. Joe passed, and on impulse I intercepted him at the gate to ask his aid. I told him of my belief that some one—probably the old folks—have filled Frank's mind with distrust of me, and asked him to dispel this influence if possible. He assured me that he thinks I am in the right to go to town; that Frank can board at his house for nothing if he likes; and that he will take the first opportunity of talking him into a better frame of mind.

Later in the day, when I took Sally a hat I trimmed for her, I was glad to perceive that he had not mentioned the matter at home.

Everything went wrong at the class, and nothing was accomplished, then we got wet with rain coming home. Frank is in a bad mood this evening—makes things impossible. I dread the night.

July 15, 1913

Yesterday, he says, he asked the old folks to let him stay with them this winter, and they refused. After all he has done for them! This made him angry—not at them, but at me. He says he defended my course to them, but after dark he began threatening to leave in the morning, to drown himself—anything to keep me from going to sleep. I refused to talk at all until he was in a better frame of mind, which sobered him somewhat; but he kept up an utterly useless discussion for hours for all that and did all he could to be contrary—such as leaving off his nightgown, ordering me out of bed and then holding me back, threatening to take to morphine, etc. At last, when I began to go to pieces, he changed the tune to promising: He would be good,—would buy a cow & pigs to keep him interested and busy till I came back; he would be kind; he—

I paid about as much attention to this as to the threats. He has sold his pig back to Willy, and his harrow, and intends to sell the plow and his best suit. Does he not see that he is making it impossible for me to come back next summer?

I had a toothache all morning, but when the house was put straight and I went up to Lyle's to sew, Mrs. Lyle succeeded in stopping it with toothache gum and rubbing pepper mint on the gums. Sewed on her machine all morning, and this evening cut out & basted Jean's blue poplin, going by a picture in a paper. Tonight I have a headache coming on. But Frank has come home with good news. Joe has been to the old folks and persuaded them to remain on the mountain this winter and let Frank stay with them. They make him a good proposition—all he can make on the place, the use of the mare, and a place to keep a hog or any other stock he may pick up. Frank seems quite contented with this, said I hope they will all stand by this entirely sensible arrangement.

July 17, 1913

It seems strange that the morning should be clear and quiet, with a thrush and cat bird singing. Last night was dreadful. He was more unreasonable and violent than ever. Of course he had the excuse of being hungry, and sick, and very tired after a day's plowing. I reminded him that he had given me to understand he would not come back.

"I never said any such thing, and you're a liar if you said I did," was the astonishing reply.

He has drawn back his hand to hit me several times. Last night I really thought for a moment that he would. Then he begged me to love him, love him, love him—and began to make promises. At last we went to sleep; but I waked up at 2:30 with a severe pain that brought the sweat out, and before I got it cured my teeth had commenced aching. He went away at day break and I slept for an hour more. But I felt quite done up this morning, and my teeth hurt.

Sewed on Mrs. Lyle's machine, and finished the last of the new school dresses. I was preparing a good supper of some liver and macaroni, and making a pie of some berries Jean had picked, when Mr. & Mrs. Atlee and the two little girls came, and a cousin—Miss Baughman. Jean went on with the supper as best she could, while I showed my pictures: then Jean, who has been good and helpful all day, showed the new school dresses. When they had gone Frank ate his supper and seemed more like himself than he has been since Sunday. It has been a very hot day.

July 18, 1913

We actually enjoyed a peaceful night. Frank gave me two dollars he had earned plowing—and went to plow again, in the baking heat. I am afraid it will make him sick. He directed that the children should have some ice cream around, out of the money, so I let them go down to the store when I took the class out. We drew in Herron's green and pleasant yard. The Herrons gave me the order for a portrait of the baby. Called then on Mrs. Atlee who had asked me to take her & Miss Baughman to the Twin Sisters [rock formation on Walden's Ridge], but Charlotte was sick and it was 90° in their cool hall, so we did not go. She gave me a package Mrs. Patten had sent me, which when I got home I found to contain a silk dress, slightly worn, of the most exquisite soft old-rose. I spent the afternoon putting it in order for a lecturing dress—also a brown silk for Judith. Frank gave over working on account of the heat, and came in feeling better. Judith & Jean changed places again.

July 21, 1913

Last night we talked a long time. Frank explained to me, without undue bitterness, what a hard position he is in—also how the mountain people suspect & dislike me. He says my departure in company with Mrs. Atlee's boy, yesterday evening, scandalized the Scotts. Well, I shall never be able to please such people and it is not worth while trying. But I wish I could make things easier for him among his kin. Why can't they accept a perfectly sensible explanation of a commonplace arrangement?

Took the class to Herron's again. Six pupils besides the Lyles. That does well—if they will only pay.

July 25, 1913

Cloudy and cool. Only three in the class besides Faith & Jamie. They drew a very pretty group of peaches in a bowl.

From the garden we have onions, beets, okra, beans, and potatoes now: no great plenty of anything however—it is dried up.

My baby, my little son! I have not forgotten,—not a touch nor a word of you. For your sake, if for no other,—that your suffering and death may not have been given in vain,—I am going. I will put your brothers and sisters in school; and I will work, oh, how I will work, to win out, to make a way for them all, that their fate may be kinder than yours or mine.

To town early, with Frank, who took Long's mare down to the veterinary. Went to dinner at Mrs. Crutchfield's boarding house with Mrs. Vaughn and a visiting artist who is a friend of hers—and discovered how vain & stupid a distinguished painter can be. Then to meet Margaret Severance. I have fallen in love with her intelligence and courage, & her expressive beauty; I hope I shall be able to work with her, for I value her friendship. Kitty, whom I was obliged to bring, trots contentedly & quietly about the house.

July 27, 1913

Mrs. Severance worked hard all morning getting things ready for a dinner to Mr. & Mrs. Lon Warner. I was ashamed to have brought a barefoot child to a party of grown people; but no little lady could have behaved better. She sat at a little side table within reach, demure but cheerful, like a little bird or squirrel. Our clothes got quite wet coming down yesterday morning; but fortunately I had kept my drawings & a white silk dress out of the rain. It was a delightfully Bohemian affair—the pleasanter that we had all helped to make the salad & freeze the sherbet.

After the guests' departure Margaret Severance undertook to teach me what I need to know about lecturing. We talked till ten o'clock. If I could look like her, lecturing would be easy. . . . . Well, she asked me, and I told her more of the truth about things at home than I have told any one else, but not much. She promised to help me find rooms.

August 2, 1913

The girls were looking forward so to their visit with Mrs. Stedman that I could not disappoint them; neither could I leave Kitty at home with such a wrist. So papa took us all to town. The girls took lunch with Carol and played with the Johnson children till time to meet Mrs. Stedman. I first shopped some few necessaries for them, then went to look at some rooms on Vine St—that looked very good to me, then to lunch with beautiful dear Margaret Severance, taking Kitty. The tired little girl, who had but little sleep last night with her wrist, went to sleep immediately after lunch, saying that she was going to stay with Mrs. Severance this week. Then I had such a delightful visit, helping Margaret Severance get her peach jelly to jell, that I did not notice how the time was going till Frank telephoned that it was three o'clock. Then I did the Cinderella act—Kitty changed her mind at the last moment, and we hurried to catch a downtown car. Frank should have been ready, but still had to hitch up & buy some feed—and it was half past four when we crossed the bridge. He had to ease the mare by milking her, and she kept calling for her colt all the way home. I felt so sorry for her, because I remember how I felt the time I lectured in town when Kitty was a baby, and had to walk home the next day.

Frank has been quite himself all day—not only patient & lovable, but regaining his own quiet, delicious humor. Perhaps he begins to feel the approach of relief as I do.

August 4, 1913

Judith was sick last night, so I called up Mrs. Stedman this morning & inquired. Judith herself answered that she is feeling all right again, and they are having the time of their lives. Took the class to Dripping Spring, and a very creditable sketch they made among the rocks, where it is quite pleasant even on such a hot day. Talked with Mrs. Atlee a few minutes on my way to the post office—then went to Lyle's & made 4 crape nighties for the girls.

Only by the exercise of self-control can I refrain from calling Margaret Severance on the phone every day. I hope the girls fall in love with her too; she is lovely, all alive with intelligence & feeling.

Huckleberries have a much longer season than other berries. They began before the blackberries and are still bearing—though blackberries have been gone a week or more. Frank went with his folks and the Longs, and brought home enough for a pie. Kitty's wrist is still considerably swelled.

August 8, 1913

God's mercy! What have I done—and what shall I do next? No sleep last night till nearly morning—the worst yet. He demanded an apology, which I gave—to no effect except that he plunged into a tirade of abuse, and threatened more than he ever has. Finding that I took it quietly, he began then to beg for money: asked me to borrow a hundred dollars for him to go away on. I refused at first, saying that it would be no real help to him. He asked then for money to get something to eat. I told him he might sell the chickens, and offered to give him half the price of my picture that Herrons are buying. Then he got up and shoved his fist into my face, glaring and grinding his teeth.

"I was just a-trying you," he said. "I wanted to see if you was that low-down. The devil's in you, you selfish bad woman!"

I asked him to let me sleep elsewhere, and he agreed, but the instant I rose he threw me down across the bed and threatened to beat me. I turned quite sick and began to chill, which angered him again: he threatened to kill himself and me.

It lasted till one o'clock. I believe the real trouble is that his folks don't want him this winter; they have decided to sell.

Everything is wrong, everything. My heart is sick. Oh, the things he said last night!

"People that live on charity can always act independent like you!" But I must forget what he said. No, I must remember, or else in pity for his distress I might return to him.

But whatever possessed me yesterday? O good Lord! I might have known better. If ever I was lonesome and sick and frightened in my life I was this morning.

I had but three in the class. Got dinner, then tried to take a nap but had to telephone. Mrs. Severance wants me to write a play with her, and suggested that Frank keep the two children two weeks and let us get it under way as soon as the girls are gone. I don't know what to say when people want him to help me out; I can't explain.

Went to call on Mrs. Arnold & sold two booklets. Then to Herron's and did a preliminary sketch for Mrs. H's portrait. They gave me $10—for my Martin's bluff picture and said I might ride down with Mr. Walsh any morning. As Frank told me I had to make my own arrangements about getting to town hereafter, I gladly accepted the chance. Then called on Mrs. Atlee & talked about various things connected with the girls' going away.

August 10, 1913

But he came in late, and angrier than I have ever seen him—began at once to cross-question me fiercely as to where I had been and why I did not meet him. I told him he had not mentioned my necessity for meeting him, and he replied suspiciously that he had telephoned to all those places & others, and been told I was not there. Even the dentist's. I made no reply, thinking if he would rather take the word of negro servants, he might. He said he had been with Atlee, to a ball game, and to a saloon; and I judge he may have been drinking. He said such dreadful things that I was thrown a little off my poise, spoke rather slowly in the effort to retain control of my nerves; so he pounced upon me and shook me, and jerked my head back by the hair til my neck hurt, saying he expected a prompt answer.

The children were in the house, and we in the yard. I thought I would keep things as quiet as possible till they went to sleep, and then try to slip into the woods for the night. But when they were asleep he seemed quieter, and I did not quite want to leave them alone with him; so when he commanded me harshly to come in and go to bed, I went—still in two minds about it. It was not long before he ordered me to get up and dress; but the instant I rose he jerked me back, and holding me by the arms hard, said—"Oh, Ben Bell you, Ben Bell, you've ruined my life."[10] He kept saying everything he could think of that would hurt me—the most outrageous things; and threatening to stop the girls from going to school, threatening to make every bit of the horrible [illegible] public. I agreed with him that this might be best, and when he found I was quite ready to go him one better he ceased to talk in such a strain. His mind ran on divorce, and at first he assured me that any jury in Tennessee would bring a verdict in his favor; but afterward his bluff began to break and he told me—what I never had thought of before—that the children receiving an education without any help from him gives me an immense advantage before the law. I tried in every possible way to reassure and soothe him, but he got worse. It was in the midst of a perfectly gentle answer to one of his insults that he caught me up with a jerk that threw my head back and snapped something in my neck most painfully. My nerves gave way completely; I screamed, and began to cry out loud, horribly, hating to hear myself but unable to stop.

And suddenly, instead of the curses I expected, a torrent of pleading love-words broke from him; "Oh, did I hurt you, my girl—my darling! Don't cry so—don't cry—listen, you're scaring the children! I never meant to hurt you—I don't know what made me! Oh, I'll never lay hands on you again, my dear, dear wife!" And he too, began to sob, with his arms around me: "I've done something I never would have thought I'd do. . . . I'm a dangerous man. Oh!" he moaned bitterly, "I'm homeless. I'm an invalid. I—"

But it was ended for the night—at one o'clock in the morning. He went away early; and I, feeling quite ill, let the girls get breakfast. I had not risen when Joe came in, and I called to him to be seated till I could talk with him. I told him about it, and asked what should I do.

"Well, I tell ye, Emmer," he said gravely. "I believe Frank's a little bit jealous."

"Jealous of what?" I asked.

"He hasn't anything to be jealous of; he probably couldn't tell you himself. But he feels—"

"I know," I said, "he feels bad because I run with a different class of folks than he does."

Joe nodded, yes.

"But you see, Joe, I can't make a living out of any other kind of people?"

He went in a minute, promising to see the old folks and try to get them to make Frank welcome. He was not out of sight when Frank and his mother & father came in. And to them I told a part of the truth—that Frank was not letting me sleep, that it was making me sick, and that while he is welcome to stay with me if he will be good, he must go to them or let me sleep. I explained that I was not trying to do them or any one any dirt; and turning to Frank I added, "Now if I've said anything you don't agree with, this is the time to object; don't come at me with it tonight."

They were extremely complaisant about it, and we parted amicably; but I could feel that the situation was unchanged. He was good till evening, even saying I had always been a good wife and kissing my hands with thanks; but toward nightfall, when it was time for him to leave if he meant to carry his bluff, he went to pieces again—saying that I had arranged for the girls' departure without consulting him, which is utterly false, and that he would stop it if I didn't do to suit him. I told him very well—in that case I must warn Mrs. Atlee to forward no money till his mind is made up, and give her a full explanation.

Finding his bluff called once more, he began to accuse me and call me names: but he seemed at last to see the futility of this, and cried out— "Well, you've got me blocked at every turn, and the only redress I've got is to go and do something mean! I warn you I'm desperate: now I've warned you, don't go too fast—" he shook his finger and glared—"don't you go too fast, I say, about sending them!"

As I paid no particular attention, his mood changed and he begged me at least to say goodby [sic], kiss him and forgive him. I did. Good Lord! if he knew how little hard feeling I have time to hold against his poor wreck of a spirit!

I've other things to think of. Had company all evening; think I sold Mrs. Arnold a picture.

August 13, 1913

I was cutting some wood to cook breakfast and had bruised my foot on the axe, when Frank came in. "The way of the transgressor is hard," he sneered as he saw my plight; but as I made no answer, he took the axe and cut an armful of wood, and was good natured enough. He asked for fifty cents, which I gave him. I wish I knew whether he has paid his road tax though. He went away before the children got up. Does he suppose I did not have to cut wood while he was here? or that cutting wood is harder than enduring his insulting tirades?

Mrs. Chapin called, and afterward Mrs. Long. I have all the stockings to mark, and many stitches to take.

August 17, 1913

Such a rush as I had to get everything ready at the last. Frank took the trunk down yesterday—complaining to the last that I have planned and done everything without consulting him. Mrs. Chapin sent me & the twins down in the auto: but first they went to Lyle's to say goodbye and Judith caught my breath by calmly and sweetly promising to write Jamie. We stopped at Cousin May's and found Frank and Buzz there. I thought Frank might break down at parting, and tried to reassure him by saying that Boaz in only 80 miles from Chatta. and the fare only 2.40. "You could run down in a day."

"Can I?" he laughed. "Didn't know I was such a runner."

"Some Marathon," I replied; and we parted in apparent good spirits. As the heat of the day passed I took the girls and their cousin Dean to town, and treated them to ice cream and moving pictures while I went to get the trunk checked. Tried to buy them a sweater apiece, but could find nothing suitable at this season. I will have to buy flannel and make them some [illegible]. We spent the night with May. After the children were asleep I told her all my plans quite frankly, suppressing only the worst of Frank's behavior. She seemed to have expected it for years. I asked her advice about claiming the children; she tells me the law will give them all to the father. I then proposed to put up a bluff about abandoning them, which will I think cause Frank and his folks to throw them into my arms at once; and we decided that this was the safest way.

To Mrs. Severance's this morning—intending to go to church, but we found ourselves very tired and headachy, so I let Jean have a nap instead.

Jean was much interested in the details of a city house—the gas stove and plumbing etc. But after that good-looking, well-brought-up young man came in, Judith lost interest in every thing else; she laughed and chattered as she helped freeze the sherbet, and flashed her pretty eyes at him, and discussed O. Henry and Jack London quite like an eighteen-year-old! Margaret and I went up stairs to laugh, and agreed it was high time to put that girl into school!

My last day with my daughters is over. Dearer and more beautiful they ever seem. Jean clings to me as if she hardly wants to go; and I am surprised and glad to see that she begins to depend on Judith and lean on her judgment.

August 18, 1913

How coolly the girls took the separation—almost gaily! I could not sleep last night nor eat this morning; my stomach was sick, my throat tightened, my limbs trembling. But I put them on the train. And then weakness and weariness rolled over me like a big wave, and I got back to Margaret's, telephoned Mrs. Atlee that all was creditably seen to, and dropped on the bed.

It was three o'clock before, under Margaret's ministrations and cheer, I began to revive. Then we worked at Timber Redbird till time for me to go. I went to Market Street, and being loth [sic] to break my ten dollar check, spent my last coin for a mess of frankfurters. Had a fine ride home with Mr. Walsh.

It was nearly dusk; the big machine flew along, screaming monotonously, ripping the miles off the road and mounting into higher and sweeter layers of air every minute. Frank met me at Herron's and I cooked him some supper when we got home. The News has telephoned me asking for a G.A.R. welcome poem.[11]

August 22, 1913

Cloudy and cool as autumn. Alone again, and feel scarcely able to work. But I must; I had to break my $10 ck yesterday. Frank left early, after a very pleasant night, but came back in the middle of the morning. I was lying down, almost sick, and he began that rude love making of his: I stood it as long as I could and began to cry, which made him angry. One word brought on another, for this time I was not so anxious to keep the peace at any cost; and presently he pretended to go away, but came back. At the first note of bluster and threat I let him have it straight between the eyes. He was bristled for a great show of fight, with feet apart, glaring. I did not even raise my head from the pillow. "Lay a hand on me," I told him, "and by tomorrow this country'll be too hot to hold you. I dare you to touch me. Yes, say it; say every vile, dirty, insulting word you like to spit in a clean woman's face, and see if it helps your case any. Do you know the penalty for treating a woman as you've treated me?" (This was an empty gun; I have no idea whether there is any penalty I could lay hold of; but it sufficed.) "You want me to stay here with you, work twice as hard as you do and take all the responsibility and any talk you want to give me. You can get it out of your head that we're ever going to live that way again. The law's on my side."

He wilted; he did not even cry; all his anger went out like a flame. "I've struck a knot," he said, and laughed whimsically. But it was two hours before I got rid of him. And I told him not to come back unless he could be good. I told him that any time he goes to court he will find himself with four children on his hands to support.

I think he feels a good deal better. It was a storm that cleared the air. He is very kind. I have had a long nap, and now it is raining. We have a letter from the girls, very worried because their trunk is delayed.

September 2, 1913

Home again after a week in town. What all have I done? Let me count up: Helped Margaret Severance with her one-act play which I named A Timber Redbird; did a portrait-sketch of her & lent it to The News, as an ad for Margaret & to help out Mrs. Vaughn; illuminated two books for Miss Nell Wright @ $5 each; wrote the Welcome Song for the G.A.R. and made a capital page decoration with it for the News—another $10; rented my room, and many lesser things.

Frank, too, has worked every day. I believe his health is on the whole very good this fall. But little Joe seems puny, and just as I expected, the folks are already willing I should take him down with me! Nothing like a good bluff!

Frank and the boy are so glad to see me, and Kitty is glad to be at home. I brought some sausage for supper. I thought they might have met me at the Top and helped me home with my packages, but they didn't. The well is dry, and no wood cut except as Frank makes it for one meal at a time. I don't believe I can stay more than a few days. 3 letters in the mail from Judith & Jean.

September 3, 1913

Cleaned house most of the day. Packing my trunk I came on some of Frank's old letters, and looked once more into the gentle, faithful lover-heart of him. Dear boy, how has he ever come to this pass? The failure must be partly in my self. I should have maintained a different attitude somehow. He meant so well; he tried—he didn't try hard enough, but I could have braced him; perhaps. Well, I do believe I'm on the right road now.

We got no sleep for the chinches [bed bugs]. And this morning, when he proposed to go off to work early and leave me the whole cleaning to contend with, I—for once—came out flat-footed and told him if he didn't carry out those beds into the sun and cut some wood, he would find me gone by evening. He complied. He did it cheerfully. So I scalded & scrubbed, and put the place neat.

Buzz complains so I let him stay at home. It is a baking hot day.

September 5, 1913

Frank no longer sneers or scolds me; he looks better, and is more like himself. But last night he confessed to me, what I have suspected since the night of August 9, that he occasionally drinks too much. I asked no questions and tried to act wisely. I talked to him very straight and kindly, and at the slightest hint of losing his temper I warned him to be careful what he said, and let him see that I was not in the least afraid: whereupon he became very mild and gentle. Oh, dear! If only he wouldn't ask me for money! He went to town this morning early. I gave him just enough to get some cake & candy for the girls' birthday, and some Listerine for Buzz. I went to Herron's and did a very good portrait of the boy. Came home by-way of Joe's and was caught in a shower that made me late getting home, but Frank did not come at all.

September 7, 1913

Frank & the boy came late, after the day's work, tired, and we passed a pleasant, restful night. Frank is as one smitten on the cheekbone: he has no angry words left even when I ruthlessly check his occasional flights of sentiment. When he talked of "giving me a chance" this morning, for instance, I contradicted him with unwanted straightforwardness: "You are not giving it to me. I'm taking it by main force. You've fought me every step of the way." He made no reply. And I realized that I have fought a good fight single-handed,—that I have won for myself very much what the Pankhursts and other fighters are winning for all.[12]

Freedom for myself and my children! A new joy, a delight to which I have long been stranger, comes over me when I am with them. Joe and Kitty feel the new conditions, child-fashion; they have ceased to fret and quarrel—their eyes are like stars—their prattle is interspersed with the matchless laughter of young unconscious things. Now I am freed of the unnatural burden, they are an endless delight to me.

I went over to Joe's this morning with Sally, who had come to fetch home some housegear I lent her for the winter. Joe was sitting on the porch. "How's my good brother," I greeted him, and saw a flash of pleasure cross his face. He cut a melon; I said goodbye to them all in the dusk, and went home to give the two children their supper. When they went to bed I went to meet my man, and we walked home through the moonlight with our arms around each other.

September 8, 1913

To town in Mr. Walsh's auto. Found my room in possession of a starveling waif just from the charity ward, over which Mrs. Vaughn & Miss Alberta were hovering. I went to work and helped with it. The room is dark and dirty, and Joe does not like the place because he can find no boys to play with. Very hot. I rested most of the day.

September 22, 1913

Started Joe & Kitty in school this morning. It seems to be such a good school. I then went to the dentist's and had considerable work done on my teeth—after which I lay down for some hours. At five I was roused by a telephone call. It turned out to be from Sally. She had got Mrs. Severance a rain crow. I went right over to Hill City to get it from her sister's house, then carried it to Margaret Severance.

September 23, 1913

Took the children to school and went on to spend most of the day with Margaret Severance. I helped with the Timber Red Bird; but I begin to suspect that she don't mean to pay me anything for my help.

Buzz came home very proud of the fact that he has been promoted to the second grade.

September 25, 1913

Again to the dentist's. My teeth begin to look better, and certainly they feel more comfortable. I think I am gaining weight. I look better. Miss Berta has had the room painted in pale pink and it is clean [illegible]. Today I began a portrait of her which will cover two month's rent. Oh, I'm so comfortable and happy!

Margaret Severance has two passes to the circus tonight and has asked me, and Miss Berta will stay with the children.

September 30, 1913

How my man and I have enjoyed each other the past few days—with an inexpressible delight in each other! Last night, as it was too late to go back to the mountain, he stayed with me, and I had long, delightful hours in his arms, whispering to him. I asked how he liked Margaret Severance. I thought surely he would feel the spell of her beauty. [The rest of this entry is omitted due to illegibility.]

October 1, 1913

Painted a [illegible] into my green woods picture of May 19, which I hope makes it sellable. Worked all afternoon and called on Mrs. Atlee this evening. The Dentist put me in some front teeth. I look 5 years younger.

October 3, 1913

Buzz waked up this morning and began at once to cry; the tears rolled down his little fair face. He said he was sick—that the air didn't agree with him! Later in the day Frank came in unexpectedly, and nearly fell over when he saw my new teeth: he says I am prettier now than when he courted me first. I let Buzz go home with papa, whereupon he straight way mended, and promptly got well. Kit & I called on the Van Dusens this evening.

October 4, 1913

Stopped a few minutes to see the Wheatleys who have just moved. I found them sitting or working among towers & pyramids of packing-boxes. Sunheart like a giant baby, fair and clean. Very pleasant it was, those few merry minutes; but afterwards the realization came to me that only he had asked me to come again.

Well, I'm sorry. But I can manage without them. There are plenty of other people who do want me.

October 6, 1913

The tax collector got after Frank, and he tried to collect from Long what was coming to him for a week's work. Long refused to pay, and before the saloon full of men Frank called him a damned rascal.

"I don't often take that off a man!" said Long.

"Well, you've got your billiard-cue," was my man's retort. I was so proud of it that I promised to get the money for him by Wednesday, to pay his taxes. But oh, dear! I'm broke myself.

The studio is splendid. But I'm afraid I'll have trouble getting up a class.

Went to the dentist again this afternoon, and he gave me over 57 varieties of toothache.

October 13, 1913

Friday I borrowed two dollars of Mrs. Atlee; went to a reception and fell in love with Ida Kerr's throat & chin as she sang, and asked her to pose for me; did a stunning head of her, in sepia, Saturday morning; and Sunday morning rode up the mountain with George Freudenberg. I never saw the air a clearer, finer blue, or the autumn light a more opulent gold. At the Top store I got out, and went in—taking Frank by surprise, as he happened to be there buying his mother some medicine. Joe was there too. "This is the weather that made the mountain famous," I said to the crowd. Frank was so glad to see me. Kitty went to see Virgie & Icie and Buzz to Lyle's. I got dinner for Frank and then we went sketching. Spent the whole afternoon in the brightening woods watching the changing shadows of luminous purple. Two watercolors, one at Key's Point & one of a yellow hickory. But the best was my long talk with my man.

He was close beside me as I sketched, telling me of Mrs. Rawling's apparent fondness for him—how she frankly likes to talk with him for hours when she is lonely, and how she stands with her hand on his shoulder, and talks with him of subjects usually taboo in mixed company. I laughed and kissed him.

"You never told me all this before!"

"Well—I was 'fraid you might not like it—"

"I think," I told him, "there would be less trouble in this world and fewer assignation-houses, if it were generally understood and accepted that a good man and woman can be awfully fond of each other without getting into mischief."

"I think so," he replied, "but it depends entirely on who the man is and who the woman. Now, you take a man like Webb Renshaw—he couldn't talk to the nicest kind of woman about—those things." He steadied his voice with an effort and went on: "You take a man like—

[Next two pages missing][13]

Unclear Date

. . . lay down quietly enough, and got up this morning before day and left for home. He said it would be best for him not to come again for a long time, and I did not contradict him.

I have sworn by the death-stains on the white slips which I keep, that I will free myself and the children from this man's dead weight. Margaret Severance is thoroughly disgusted with the way he has laid down on the deal she proposed, about her Eastlake lots; of course I suppose she asked too much for them and he could not make a trade, but then he should have said so clearly.

Mrs. Milton brought me a beautiful scrap book, and a cloak.

October 25, 1913

Last night I lectured to a good large crowd at the Hill City Normal, on a collection of sepia photogravures of famous paintings. It was very interesting. I received only $5—but have got another engagement already, to lecture on Mission Ridge.

October 30, 1913

Mrs. Atlee telephoned me to come out this evening & help her son arrange a program for an Emma Bell Miles evening in the literary society.

So after I had finished a big ironing and two little school frocks for Kitty, cut over out of two old skirts, I made ready to go. The telephone rang just as we opened the door, we turned back, and it was my man—proposing to come spend the night with me. I bade him come & help himself to the hot soup on the stove, and make himself comfortable till our return—then we went on. Had a pleasant visit & a good supper with the Atlees, & helped arrange a program, while Kitty & Joe played with Charlotte & Margery. We came home at 7. I dreaded to meet Frank, as he usually blames me severely when he has done wrong; but he was only homesick for me, and so humbly eager for a pleasant home visit that I had not the heart to scold him for fumbling his opportunity to help me make a living. He coaxed me till I promised to go up over Sunday.

November 13, 1913

I worked this morning on Miss Alberta's portrait, then on my lecture, then had a scramble to get anything for the kiddies to eat. Called for the fourth time on Mrs. Will Long, and found her actually at home—and very sociable. Tried to sell her a picture, but don't know yet. I'm desperate for cash. This evening went with Frank Atlee to his literary society meeting; some nineteen young people met at the house of a bright, merry, charming mischievous Irish girl—Kathleen Stewart. I read a story & gave a talk—the boys' quartet sang and some of the girls, and then some of my poems were read, and then they served refreshments. It was a most enjoyable little affair.

November 16, 1913

Frank came down yesterday and brought me a bag of potatoes, and borrowed my last dollar to get a shave & hair cut, saying he would get his pay for two weeks' work & come back. I warned him that I was very busy, but made him welcome. He came back with 7 or 8 dollars, and made love to me all afternoon, and gave the children 40 cts to fool away, and took me to the movies in the evening & bought me enough groceries for today and a little material at Payne's. The night was very bad. He could not sleep on the floor & Buzz had the toothache so we were all four in the same bed. He could not sleep & of course would not let me, saying that he wanted to explain things to me, but that I had never been able to understand him. I got two or three hours' sleep towards morning; then he got up and went out, early, saying that he would not come to see me again for a long time. Of course I bade him reconsider & stay to breakfast; but as a matter of fact breakfast was just over when he came in with 3 boxes of matches he had bought me. I told him how important it was that I should finish writing my lecture today, and tried to write in spite of him, but on finding me indifferent to his lovemaking he worked himself up to the usual pitch—shoved into my apron all the money he had, with his knife & tax receipts, & started off to drown himself. Then he was back begging me to forgive him, & promising to help me. He really did slick over the middle of the floor & the dishes, and I, too worn out to think any more about my lecture, took a short nap. Then I had to sit up till nearly 12 to make up for the lost time. I wonder if he will let me sleep? Ever since he learnt this combination of the third degree & the Chinese waking torture, my life is not worth living.

November 17, 1913

He did, and got up early & went away without any more trouble; but he took with him not only every cent of his money but the dollar he borrowed from me. When I found this out I felt, for once, crushed. I could not think of my lecture nor of the afternoon affair Miss Alberta arranged for—to show my pictures. I went to see Mrs. Atlee, but she was ill and I would not tell her the state of affairs.

Some fifty people, I suppose, were here this afternoon. It was socially a nice affair, my pictures looked well enough & Mrs. Walsh lent us a beautiful service & I poured the tea. But I made almost no sales & the orders are few & trivial.

November 18, 1913

I telephoned Frank to return my dollar; he was very apologetic & said he thought I had kept some. I went to get Margaret to help with the lecture. It is a good [illegible] written but she proposed that I consult her friend Boddy, the lawyer. I did: I asked him what I was to do with a man that couldn't make a living himself & won't let me. But after inquiring thoroughly into it, he told me I am pretty near helpless—have no legal case unless I could prove Frank to be of unsound mind.

This evening Mr. Stedman called for me & Miss Alberta & took us to Mission Ridge in the auto. We had supper at their house, then went to Rains's. At first I felt nervous & rattled—which I seldom do; I had not been able to study this as I wished—and my voice broke and I coughed a good deal. Then as I went on, I felt that I was among my own friends, and my voice came to me and I got hold of paragraph after paragraph just right. I never before tried to get a laugh; but I got them, and even tears! And after it I was asked to recite some of my poems—unexpectedly. I have not recited in public since I was ten, but my readings & recitations to my children stood me in good stead, and I gave "The Stack Horse" & the "Banjo & the Loom" pretty well. There were music & refreshments, and I held a sort of levee among all the folks, and enjoyed it very much.

Oh, I'm tired though. I think I'll get about $6 out of it.

November 30, 1913

I'm not feeling well—but I staid up till after ten last night and got my ironing & sewing done, so as to go to church today, purely as a matter of policy, for I was sure I should get more individual good out of staying abed after breakfast & reading Lafcadio Hearn. But after all the sermon was worth hearing. It was about theological subjects, generally, but more specially about the fight for nationwide prohibition. The bishop preached as it happened; and I was horrified at the close of the service to find that Joe had stayed to church, and had sat between Mrs. Atlee & the bishop's wife! Fortunately he had on his best manners though not his best trousers; and I think he made a hit with the ladies. I don't suppose he understood a word of the sermon. This was his first attendance at a civilized church.

Kitty has made a rhyme:
"Will and Lily got into the chili,
And what do you think they did?
They ate it all up, and saved me a cup,
And saved me the Classes-lid!"

January 17, 1914

Many things have taken place which I should be glad to keep a record of, notably the visit to the girls Xmas, and one or two readings I have given; but I have had no time. Frank does most of the house cleaning for me, and walks the streets looking for a job; but he is becoming discouraged with repeated failures, slacking off, giving up. I have been quite patient and affectionate except when he dropped two or three times into ways unendurably slouchy. He is heavier than he has been since the idle winter in Florida, and his color is good. I have been good to him, oh, so good, he says,—and he was happy until he became discouraged about getting a job. We went to the moving pictures together, and enjoyed it hugely. But now he is slouchy and grouchy again. Will he give up trying? I am trying all the time, sometimes failing sometimes succeeding; I take no count of results but keep right on.

What ought I to do?

Well, it has been a happy time for a few weeks. Yesterday evening I went to report a lecture for the News, as Mrs. Vaughn found herself unable to cover all her assignments. Miss Rutherford gave "The South in History." I wonder if I shall ever speak as well as she, and evoke laughter and applause, round after round? At least I learned something from her!

Frank went with me, and I think his enjoyment was scarcely marred by the fact that he was the only man in the room who did not wear a collar. I have never been able to make my mind whether this attitude to be accounted unto him for common-sense or mere carelessness. I could gladly give him the benefit of the doubt if he would learn daintier ways with handkerchiefs, tooth-brushes, and under-clothing. What am I to think? What stand should I take? This afternoon I fairly drove him up from the bed and out to church. He must not again become addicted to the habit of unearned ease!

Not one of us has been sick at all this winter, and the children are doing well in school. I am quite justified in coming down for the winter. But only Frank remains a problem. For weeks now he has tried his best to be good; but now I can see the beginnings of the same old story—the story of winter after winter. He upsets my discipline of the children in various ways, yet when there is a decision to be made his answer to an appeal is always: "Just as you like." My authority is continually being sapped, but I must carry all responsibility. It is the beginning of the same old thing.

If he could get work it might be better. But he is not a man who can get work. He is merely one of hundreds of unskilled laborers that are seeking work in this town. With all his brain to know, and his true simple feeling! his sincerity and kindness!

I have kept us in plenty so far, but without paying my debts or keeping up the rent as it ought to be, and now we are down to ten cents.

January 20, 1914

Frank has the promise of a job next week, and my pictures at Trimby's are selling. I went to a Japanese sale, and Mrs. Atlee bought me a present—a beautiful little drawing of Fuji in the clouds—and sent Kitty some "water seeds" for her birthday. I miscounted the date; her day was yesterday; but I said nothing about it, and the little cake looked just as gay tonight and the little gifts please her so much—she says it's the best birthday she ever had.

January 23, 1914

Last night I spoke for an evening party at Mrs. Annis' house on Lookout Mt. I had a lovely visit with her, made some pine tree sketches, and sold a number of my new "Japanese Lookout" water colors. Mrs. Annis is a splendid living example of New Thought. I should write to Elizabeth about it if I had time.

There must have been some 50 or 60 people present. Many of them I knew; made friends with many more. Mrs. Annis kept me all night, with a large & fine hospitality, and paid me $5 for the entertainment.

Came home this morning. Frank had sent the children to school, put the house straight, and made all comfortable. I was very tired. He made me a cup of tea and took off my shoes.

I went to the studio & gave a lesson at 3. Mrs. Parnell sent me a huge roll of studies, odd canvases, & bits of material.

February 8, 1914

Sunday. Yesterday evening I went to deliver place cards to Mrs. Chapin. I found her abed, and had a pleasant little visit with her. I stopped to see Mrs. Atlee on the way home, and as it was about supper time I telephoned Frank that I would remain for the meal. It was about 9 when I started home, or a little before. At the corner of Vine & Lindsay a negro snatched my satchel, and after a struggle in which

I was thrown to the ground and dragged, ran off with it up the hill and disappeared in an alley. I shouted and called for help, but could raise no one, and seeing that nothing could be done there, hurried the two blocks homeward—not frightened but very angry and shocked; I could hardly stand at times, and again felt wonderfully strong. Met Frank just coming back from Jimmy Dutton's fruit stand with the breakfast milk. He took me down to the fruit stand at once, and Jimmy telephoned the Headquarters and got two plain-clothes men there in about five minutes. From my description they decided the robber to be a negro who is "wanted," but did not speak hopefully of the case—"a hard proposition," said Peace & Turner.

I passed a rather bad night. Mrs. Chapin had paid me $2.50 for the cards; there was about $4 all told, and about 15 little pictures; two larger watercolors bounced out of the satchel in the struggle and I brought them home. But there was my book of accounts, and Jean's little story, some drawing instruments, and a ticket to Melba & [illegible] concert which Prof. Cadek gave me, and a knife. I was wrenched & bruised, or rather jolted, and could not rest much.

Frank went over me with hot water & liniment this morning, and then I lay down. But about 1 o'clock they sent for me to identify a negro they had caught who fitted my description. I dressed, though feeling bad, and Frank went with me to Headquarters. Detectives Peace & Turner were with the captain in his office, and others kept coming & going. It seems this is a rather important arrest. The negro was arrested last night on some lesser charge—stealing a dollar; he is also wanted on several accounts, and was run in late last night.

The negro was presently brought in—rather taller than he appeared when crouching along last night, and in other clothes except his cap, which I recognized. He had a baleful, unwinking sullen stare. I gave my meager account of the affair, and was about to leave, when Frank asked if the negro had a knife when he was brought in. Detective Peace took him back to the sergeant's desk and they inquired. While I was waiting, Joe, who had begged to come with us, reminded me in a whisper that my knife had a nick in the handle as if some one had been driving tacks with it.

Frank instantly picked up the knife from among the odds and ends that had been taken from the negro's pockets; they brought it to me—the absurd heavy, worn thing Jean found and gave me Xmas—and I turned it in my hand. There, sure enough, was the triangular nick!

The captain said this was all the evidence necessary. They had more, however—the fact that the negro had not been working where he said he had, yet had just got three dollar bills & some change; just what was in my purse.

I came back and felt better. Mrs. Atlee came to see me, and others called over the phone.

Frank will go down and prosecute the negro tomorrow morning.

February 14, 1914

I lost one week's work in that robbery, and have been ill ever since, so I may say it set me back two weeks behind my running expenses. I sold Mr. Annis a Lookout watercolor today, and went and bought Kitty some new dresses. Frank says he will give up his job, as he is not making anything on it. That is true, he is not making his board. There seems no use in looking to him for help.

February 15, 1914

Went to church this morning. I dreamed of Mark last night, and as usual after such a dream I woke up feeling that I could not bear the sight of his father. Frank was very disagreeable about his clean shirt then, and I, feeling that I could not work, went and heard Dr. Myers preach. When I came home Frank was angry and made things unpleasant with his sneering at fashionable preaching; and after dinner he went out. I sat sewing and thinking, trying to plan. I understand Mrs. Annis to say that she wants me to spend a month with her on Lookout this summer; is it possible she has a plan to help me? Miss Coleman has offered me some rooms cheap, in Highland Park.[14] Frank is determined to have me at home this summer. But I won't go unless there is a living in plain sight.

Unclear Date

Frank has broken up everything I tried to do this winter; he kept me so uneasy I could not write, took up my time so I did no good painting, and hung around in his greasy rags till pupil after pupil went to Miss Weatherford's studio instead of coming to me. I do so want to give up and die; I have carried him on my back till I am sick of life; my life has no plan, no hope, no meaning.

Today I tramped about, trying to get a steady job. I applied for the position of cartoonist on the news, and received a lecture from Mr. Milton about scattering, when I ought to be devoting myself to my work. I told him my work is dead—a thing of the past. At last—for he is a just and kind hearted man—he said I could bring a few drawings to try. I went to the library and tried to get some notion out of the recent papers; but I could not understand what I was reading; I could think only of the fact that one of my children is dying, and another is conceived into unspeakable misery and degradation.

Then I thought of suicide, and wrote a letter to Frank. But I don't know what my poor little sick children would do without me, just now, if I were dead.

I have tried to get various people over the telephone, but could reach no one I wanted. If I only had some one like Edith, sensible and brave, to talk with. Mrs. Atlee won't listen: well, certainly it is asking a good deal of any one: but I am losing my mind.

I only wanted a separation, and Frank has hung to me like a spoiled child. It seems the law will not allow me a divorce. Is God dead?

March 28, 1914

I have not suffered since Mark died as I have this week. If I try to paint I cry till I can't see and my throat cramps and I have tramped the town over looking for work—newspaper work, architectural work, advertising—but don't understand any of these well enough to get a real job. Today I went to see Supt. Graves in his office, but he tells me that the teacher's meeting has been postponed and I can't get to talk "chalk" for them until June.

I met Joe on the street and was very glad to see him, though he urged me to move back to the mountain. Mrs. Wheatley is the only one who does not urge it. I called her for a telephone conversation this evening; she asked me to come and see her—talked as though she had thought of a plan to help me. But it seems to me that help from outside only makes things worse at home.

But when I came in this evening I found a postal from Jean—a very weak & shaky little scrawl to say that she is better. Thank God for that!

March 29, 1914

The worst day yet. Frank promised to come down today and take the children up with him; they counted heavily on it and so did I. Also I had decided not to put off any longer the murder that will have to be done, and I wanted him here to share the responsibility of the danger and pain as well as the sin. It is not pleasant, this killing his children before they are born.[15]

But the day went by and I could not even get him over the telephone, though Mrs. Stanfield told me he passed their house twice. The children cried and fretted all day. Mrs. Stanfield wanted me to go to church in the auto with them; but I was expecting Frank momently, and did not even take them for a walk. I washed some clothes, and began on an advertising drawing; & got the children to bed by promising to take them sketching tomorrow if the day is fair.

If there were only some way of making him understand the wickedness of breaking promises!

Now the horror of what I must do is almost swamping me. I must think of something else. . . . I will go to the Wheatley's tomorrow: there is the only gleam of light and warmth that I can see.

April 15, 1914

Never in my life, with all its emotional contrasts, have I ever experienced such a change from despair to security as this. I was in the depths when a telephone message came from Mr. Clark, managing editor of the News, offering me work on the staff. I went down that same day with whatever scraps of verse & paragraphic comment I could get together, and took the job with a thankful heart.

At first, ignorant of the first principles of newspaper writing (aside from brevity), and distracted by outside troubles, I made blunders at which every one in the office laughed. I never had time to worry over mistakes, though; and one day Mr. Clark walked me all around the place & pointed out to me the difference between a news item, a feature story, an interview and an editorial. Since then I have got on better.

Only one of my woman's page editorials has gone into the waste basket—I never could find out why. One day they sent me out for an interview with the police matron. I watched her at work among the wretched and fallen of the city for a while. This was not society news. This was something I understood. I packed that story full of human interest. Next day the entire staff (with the single exception of the society editor, Miss Kerr, who is a chicken) woke up to the fact that I can write.

I don't over value any praise given me down there, for I have much higher in letters from Mr. Alden of Harpers,' Mr. Johnson of the Century, etc., put away. But, oh, I am so grateful for nine dollars a week. No matter if I do have to earn eighteen.

That is one good thing. Just when my trouble seemed deepening to tragedy—this came. Then Jean grew better; then, oh relief! the threatened illness passed me by—I suffered of course, but I did not miss a day's work. Now all is well, the danger gone by.

If only Jean were safe at home. And if I knew that the family could get along this summer without me. Can Judith keep house? Who will take care of Jean in her delicate condition? Will Frank stay with them as he says—or will he manage to make me lose my position?

I will not worry over these things till they are at hand. Meantime I am taking good care of Kitty through the last of the whooping cough, rejoicing in the independence this work gives me among the people I was of late almost begging from, and paying out of debt on my nine a week.

There is the debt for my teeth—I hope they will take it all in pictures. Mrs. Atlee has just paid $54 dollars to Jean's nurse, and the doctor bill is yet to come in. No doubt it saved the dear girl's life—that's something I can never repay. But the Atlees have fallen out with me entirely since I told her some part of my real trouble. These comfortable people cannot bear anything but a smooth appearance, no matter how good they really are.

I have not got to go visiting at all yet, to the Stedmans nor the Wheatleys nor anybody else. One day Mrs. Montague invited me to a rendering of Verdi's Requiem at her house, and I started, but did not after all get to go. Perhaps I can visit a while later on.

May 3, 1914

Sunday. Rode up on the new car line yesterday, to spend the weekend with Frank & the children at home. The trees are covered with young fruit, and Frank is putting in a garden. I do feel so glad & hopeful.

Work on the News is delightful. It has pushed me into the center of the suffrage controversy in Chatta—but I feel that this is where I ought to be. I am too busy to know from day to day where I am "at."

May 25, 1914

Time was when the beauty of the woods and wild mountains was all my thought—all my joy—so constantly was my mind fixed in contemplation of this one thing, so earnestly did I seek to understand and to know ever more and more of it, that the beauty of nature seemed to clothe me as a most intimate garment. During the years when most girls crave only pleasure and young companions, I asked no other satisfaction of life than in the worship of wild beauty and in my own efforts to represent it in drawings and words.

Then like a revelation came the beauty of the simple elements of home, a thing I had scarcely known; and in the years of motherhood I found delight in these.

It was not to continue. The pinch of utter abject poverty became harder and harder until, as the children's demands grew with their growth, its misery and shame grew insupportable.

After the terrible struggle of last year, which threatened to engulf the entire home, it seemed that nothing was left me. But a readjustment and a new start on a different basis have been granted us, and now I behold new and wider fields of beauty opening before me, in larger relationships and limitless hunting-grounds.

My position on the News enables me to come in touch with large and vital issues. I do not care to read the average newspaper, but have felt for years that I should enjoy working on one. This position is one which seems to others underpaid and insignificant; but it allows me to express myself, and with some hours of extra outside work which I do as I can, the pay of $9 a week permits us to live. So it looks like a heaven-sent opportunity to me.

The News is a small paper, quite eclipsed by its contemporary the Times, but it has the essential quality of being sincere.

Yesterday I spent at home on the mountain. The children and their father are, I think, doing very well: the house is clean and not too badly upset to live in, and the children's bickering and complaints are not serious. Frank is lonely and misses his wife. Worse still, he told me last night, that he feels like a thief whenever he takes my money. I hope he will get over that as conditions improve. Perhaps he can get work later in the summer—but it would be hard for the children to manage without him.

Yesterday morning I did a water-color for the Herrons, for which I expect to receive $5. I have also $5 earned by tinting a large photo for Ferger Bros.[16] This amount should settle all outstanding debts this week and leave Saturday's wages clear for expenses. I begin to feel very much encouraged.

Rode down in Mr. Walsh's auto. He is not conversationally inclined, but talked interestingly of John Barleycorn and suffrage, also of his niece and nephews, the Herron triplets, on the way to town. What a big, hearty household they have. These Catholics, who play cards all day Sunday and drink when they feel inclined can teach a good deal about wholesome human feelings to plenty of good stilted and deadened Protestants.

May 28, 1914

Eds. were "A Song of Shadows," and "Introducing Budding Talent"—anent [about] the office boy's verses, very funny I thought. Both were left out of today's issue, together with nearly all the news I turned in, leaving only "Poor Tired Mother" and the Fountain Square story.[17]

Hot and dry—headachy.

I sent the children a basket of groceries by Mr. Stanfield. Spent most of the afternoon in the city library; they are all delighted with my library series of feature stories.

Spent the evening getting acquainted with some of the Willard Home girls in the rooms around me.[18] They are fine true specimens of the Southern working girl, who is not so hard as her Northern sister. They are religious, honest, humorous and kind.

But I like my roommate best of all—dear little salamander! She keeps every one responsible for the house in terror for her reputation; but there is really nothing wrong with her except the rebellious spirit of youth. She is a bubbling fountain of joy, like a crowing baby, in spite of her harsh drawl and her cheap slang and constant "Hevins" and "doggone" and "I don't give a kitty." At sunrise I fall to dreaming over her beautiful body, lying outstretched in its rich vase-like curves on her white hard bed opposite mine; at breakfast time she smiles at me, drowsily, showing all her beautiful teeth and coral gums before she is fairly awake; at the end of her day's work she comes in dancing, laughing, exultant over a meeting with the boy she "goes with." I suppose she will make dreadful mistakes and the social conventions will crush all the beauty and spring from her body and the song from her heart, sooner or later; but for that I shall blame society, not gay little Annie Jordan.

I like Mrs. Stamper, the Madonna-faced matron. I like the girl who is cashier at the ten-cent store and studying to be a teacher; I like the girls who are studying shorthand and come to me for definitions; the widow who sells shirt waists at Miller's (but not her little girl)—deliver us from a child raised in even the best Home with a capital H! It's almost like a big family here.

June 3, 1914

Frank drove me over to the car line and Jean picked me a great bunch of flowers on the way—spigelia, indigofern, lamb's tail, blue linaria, peppermint, sundrops. I wrote only my editorials, and after eating a good solid plate of roast beef and potatoes at a lunch counter (I wonder if that was an outrageously unconventional thing to do—I couldn't have got it elsewhere for the money) I went to discuss my chalk talks with Prof. Lee.[19] Fortunately he knows a good deal about what I can do, and gave me the chance at once. So I shall make $20 extra, teaching the teachers this chalk work.

Still hot, but with great temple-like clouds.

July 24, 1914

All is lost now; my hope, my health, all sacrificed to a man's pleasure. This is the destiny of women, under the laws and customs of our mad and cruel civilization.[20]

God deliver my daughters from such love as has ruined me.

Since I left town about a month ago, I have been too ill to earn a cent. We are living very close indeed as to food, and our clothes are not being replaced as they wear out. Frank is doing the best he can. Jean and Joe and Kitty help me, unwillingly as children do, with the housework, washing and ironing; Judith, my good girl, is actually supporting herself working at Mrs. Stanfield's and putting her wages by for school clothes. She works well, and looks well, for she gets three hearty meals every day.

I do not visit anyone; I am too ashamed of the depth to which I have
fallen. But I called on Mrs. Atlee and told her that the girls can not go back
to Boaz this year. I quite agree with Frank that it is not best to accept any
more gifts from anyone. If we have brought four children into the world
whom we cannot support, we must bear the punishment.

I have no books, no associates, almost no appetizing food, not a single
pair of stockings and not a dress that I can wear during the next months. I
have tried every way I can think of to escape what is coming, but for some
reason the usual methods failed. I think of suicide day and night, and day
and night I see my children's need of me; I am in two minds. But certainly
the winter will save me the trouble of putting an end to myself.

It drives me wild to remember how, from the time Joe was born, I have
begged Frank not to lay this burden on my sick body and overworked hands;
and how at each of the two births and three miscarriages since then I have
tried to make him understand that it is bound to kill me sooner or later. At
present he is kinder and more reasonable than he has ever been, and very
sorry for what he has done so far as he is able to comprehend it. Now, when
it is too late, he begs me to write a story. But I can think of nothing but what
is before me, and what will become of my daughters if I die.

If he had only let me alone when I went to town last fall. Oh, the
madness of it, the waste of it, the infernal cruelty!

This is the first time I have given up. I will not support this family any
more. I shall sit still and await the death that is the one thing left me.

I occupy myself, when not too ill, with the cooking, washing, etc.,
and mending the children's clothes, and putting up what few jars of fruit
I can get together for the winter. The days go by as fair as ever come to
the mountain; but I am too sick of body and soul to take any pleasure in
anything. I am paying the penalty of my own mistakes and sins, and of my
father's and Frank's as well: it is not right or just. My death shall protest
this injustice.

July 25, 1914

Hundreds of white wild morning glories open every morning in the
dew—some of them climbing the peach trees to mingle prettily with the softly
ruddying fruit. Insect life swarms in armies, indoors and out; the city people,
whose orderly system of housekeeping precludes no such contingency,

are horrified at the unprecedented legions of ants and flies and roaches; mountain women who possess traditional tricks for circumventing such, get along better. Tremendous choruses of cicadas, grasshoppers, katydids.

What of our early garden escaped drought, neglect and weeds, was eaten by Hutcheson's mare. I had quite a scrape with the old skinflint about it, and proved his excruciatingly fine Southern manners to be the sham I have always suspected. But he had to pay $5 for the garden.

I shall ask no more of help of anyone. Frank has insisted for years that he can make a living if I will be satisfied with the living he can make. We are now down to 40¢ in the flush time of the summer, and only a little fat pork and some meal in the house. I am quite able to bear hunger; he shall be the one to find it unendurable. He sat on the porch and sang all yesterday evening, and has spent the forenoon visiting with the various neighbor men, going out near dinner time to find something to eat. The children do nothing but quarrel. Even Judith wishes to quit her work at Stanfield's. Their carelessness and wastefulness, which they certainly never got from my side of the house, is simply astounding: it seems almost unnatural, till I remember how hard I have tried to get their father to even take care of his own clothes and tools.

I can do no more; I give up. I have told Frank that I do not expect or wish to live through the winter, and am very anxious as to the children's fare. He has no suggestion to make—it seems a piece of foolishness to him, despair like mine.

If he can sell the place and buy some stock, he may pull us through. Or, if I could only rid myself of this physical disability, I could go back to the News and pull us through. But the hope is not to be depended on.

Well, if the State has no law to make him support the family, I feel sure there is none that compels me to do it, at least while I am pregnant. I can starve much easier than he; and Judith at least can make her way. When the raven of actual hunger comes, and he sees me perishing before his eyes, he may at least consent to give the children to some responsible and respectable people who can take care of them, and I can die in peace.

August 1, 1914

All week the children were helpful and fairly good, and I half promised that they should go to the Saturday night dance if papa would take them. He did not like to go without me, so we all walked up; and some of Stanfield's boarders went too. It proved to be one of the best country dances I ever attended. The rough, lumber pavilion—a mere roof over a floor, lighted with four oil torches flaring and smoking among the beams overhead—was crowded; as many as could dance at once were on the floor. Most were natives, but there were quite a number from the valley; the few from town were mostly native born, like Man Miles and the three youngest Woodheads.

The crowd gathered with an alacrity that some of the elders felt would have been commendable if displayed tomorrow morning at church time. These elders, with wistful young mothers overburdened with babies, and little boys and girls, like mine, too young to dance, sat on a plank bench that ran a subsidiary game resembling pussy-wants-a-corner sprang up even before the first set was formed; whenever one sprang up to cross the room, having spied a relative or friend, the vacated place was promptly filled.

From one end of the room a sort of enclosed stall jutted into the woods, separated from the dancing floor by a plank counter across which Big Gus, owner of the pavilion, served soda pop and ice cream in cones and sandwiches consisting of two slabs of bread and a split boiled wienerwurst. Being a German he made the occasion a great success without appearing to do anything. The younger married men, that is to say the boy-fathers, having come here straight from their day's labor and supperless, since their girl-wives were already looking on over lapfuls of nurslings and heads of toddlers grouped along the bench, were the best customers here.

The musicians sat on a narrow platform raised about two feet from the floor at one side, each in a split-bottom chair with its back against the only strip of wall. Jim Guess in the center led the air with a squealing fiddle; he seemed to know only three tunes, the mountaineer's versions of Red Wing and the Whistling Rufus, and Bile Them Cabbage Down, which I remember was his one tune when he used to play on a comb for us to go through play-figures when the teacher was not watching the schoolyard. There was no music about it, but the rhythm was strongly beaten by an excellent accompaniment. A trusty from the county gang, pumpkin-colored and ape-skulled, "made the guitar talk" as Dock had told me he would, and Dock on the other side knocked the banjo. Having no written score to keep them together, these accompanists watch the fiddler's fingers assiduously, taking their cue from the changing motion: they both lean a little toward Jim, who sits in the center erect, cross-legged, jiggling the bow across the strings.

The first time they played evoked no response. The crowd was too busy moving about, conversing, finding out who was present and what had been the principal happenings of the day in the various districts. There followed a halt and a shuffle, and when the second air swung into its rhythm, two or three leading spirits stepped into the open floor and began tentatively pirouetting to and fro; the ornery cuss whose reason for existence is an ability to call the figures stood forth and shouted encouragement and warnings against wasting the evening; and the selection of partners began. No reluctance or shyness was manifested. The ring, so wide that it touched all four walls, was promptly formed; the young feet could hardly keep still until the first call, which sent them eddying in an all-hands-round.

Outside among the trees were buckboards, wagons, even an automobile, and groups of spectators who edged closer.

The second call broke the great first eddy into minor rings of eight, that whirled in figure on figure, wove in and out, turned in figures-of-eight, and joined again. Certain dancers were promptly singled out for comment.

"Callie Rogers don't get a day older."

"Ain't Ethel got a pretty blue dress, all over lace."

"Mamie never misses a set. Law, watch her git about! Made out o' rubber—and she'd do the same on top of a hard day's work."

"Who's she goin' with now?"

"Another of them big long Shannons—seein' she missed getting Elmore, she's took up with the next longest, I reckon."

"Aint Amos Woodhead growed—I wouldn't a-knowed him. There, that's him stannin' behind Buck Miles."

"Buck's too ficety [feisty] and noisy; he ought to be put off the floor—look at him."

"Callie and Mamie's the best dancers here to-night."

"Lou Rogers is a good dancer, too. Look how he moves. Springy."

"The Browns is noted for years and feet."

"Who's that big, heavy fellow with the galluses [suspenders]?"

"Don't know—but he's better off than them that has to stop and hitch up their belts."

"Who's the girl in the big plaid sash?"

"Big Lil's homely, but she shore loves to dance."

"What's she done with her baby?"

"Aunt Mary Vandergriff's got it."

"She ain't here?"

"Sh' is. Yander she sets—with Hazel's baby and Lil's and Cesnor's and her own Blanche, and Walter's wife 'n' baby right by her."

"Howdy, Aunt Emmer," chirped flaxen Gracie [Frank's niece], jumping out of a corner. "Where's Judith and Jean?"

I pointed out the girls, who were spending 25¢ each of their hard earned pennies on ice cream, and she ran to join them. Mary, in whose kind, weak, care-worn face the passionate Miles blood yet speaketh, was still explaining that she didn't see any harm—

"Devotees of the tango and maxixe don't know what they're missing," declared a city schoolmarm by the door. "But—did you <u>ever</u> see so many babies at a dance!"

That is the part of the primitive hearty gladness of it—the presence of overlapping generations.

But not every one on the floor was a maid or laddie. Lou Rogers and his wife were among the most buoyant, the most graceful. In Callie's peachy cheeks the dimples came and went fetchingly as she swung through the maze; and Callie is at least as old as I am. In all that gathering she was perhaps the only woman of 35 who did not look at least ten years older.

Why?

Because.

One would look in vain for a babe of hers among the groups along the wall: that is why.

I looked at her, erect, glowing, gliding; thick haired; with rich color and perfect teeth. I looked at the drooping, sallow, overworked, underfed matrons of her age round the benches, half buried under heaps of drowsy noddles; and I wanted madly to call a hunger strike against child-bearing, until civilization ceases to penalize motherhood.

Set after set went by. During the breathing space after each, ten cents apiece was collected from the men and boys dancing. Of this $1.50 went to each of the musicians when they quit at midnight. Besides this, and the few hours' pay earned this week by helping Frank build a fence around Lyle's barn, Dock's family are now, as he put it, "living on nothing."

A sleepy tow-head in overalls, knocked sprawling by the feet of a dancer and only half pacified by a cone of ice cream, whined about in search of his mother. Two or three partnerless youths clambered up to a perch above the musician's heads, winding their legs round a crossbeam, and guyed the dancers with personal remarks. Between sets there was eyeing and comparing and discussing of the frocks that spoke of free-with-each-subscription patterns from afar—a discussion that lost nothing from its frankness.

"See, I got this on Miller's bargain counter for 5 cents; it's 25-cent a yard goods, and I got 3 dresses out o' my dollar!" says Susy triumphantly.

"Look at big Hazel; she just slumps across the floor!"

"Her dress never seed ary pattern—and look at that red ribbon around her head!"

"I bet y' anything Lily Underwood and Bob Guess marries as soon's she's out o' school. Now, you listen what I'm a-telling you." This over an emphatically pointed muff stick.

"Then what's the use of her a-studyin' to be a teacher a-tall? I was married afore I was her age." This was spoken, of course, over several small heads.

"They cain't any of 'em out-dance Mamie Tallant."

"Cain't anybody beat Lou Rogers a-shakin' the calico, neither."

I saw, in among the swinging, wheeling figures, Callie's eyes and teeth too often gleaming—saw her wink at her partner mischievously. In the local social order, this was equivalent to a declared liaison, a corollary of the fact aforementioned. Why? Because.

The more foresighted among these had brought shawls and squares of blanketing, and as their progeny dropped off to sleep during the progress of the evening's entertainment, it was rolled up and by favor of Freudenberg deposited within the safe harbor of the ice-cream stand to snore in peace. Some few of these mothers then felt free to join in the fun: but most accept their destiny, taking the consequence more or less stupidly, but not without complaint.

But we had brought no blankets, because our bunch is too well grown to be carried home asleep; and they soon began nodding; so we left early—for if Joe once went to sleep, he could not be waked up and might start off into the woods under the impression that he was going to bed.

The houses along the way were already dark and asleep; we heard afterward, however, that Preacher Scrudder's remained alight, out watching the devil with open Bible. His married daughter Callie, who led the dance, lives next door to him; so he is wont to speak of himself as living next door to hell. He has repeatedly threatened his son-in-law with the wrath of God's lightning; but oddly enough it is his own house that has been struck again.

The girls were still giggling excitedly when we reached home and found them already tucked up in bed.

August 15, 1914

From Erlanger Hospital to Mrs. Annis' home on Lookout Mountain.

A week ago today it happened. I did not think I should live through the loss of blood, much less the horror of it. Oh, the ghastly little victim, limp and cold, that fell upon the bed beside me! I fell over and began screaming and crying as I had not screamed with the pain. A little boy, they said— Mary Larnce and Grandma. Oh, my little son!

When the doctor arrived he shook his head; he could do nothing, though he caused me agony in the vain attempt to help me. It had to be an operation; we must decide quickly. Frank telephoned for help, getting Mrs. Atlee to stand good for the price of an ambulance. By the time it came for me the night had come on dark and rainy, and I had ceased to suffer much. I closed my eyes and lay quite still; the ride was rather a rest than a trial. I wondered how it was going to be paid for, but thought, "Never mind— perhaps I shall not live to be troubled about payment." I was so weak that I could not hold up my head when they lifted me out.

They did not lose five minutes getting me onto the operating table. A most excellent nurse prepared me, and slipped on the ether cap. I drank the fumes greedily, for I thought, "Maybe I shall not wake up to suffer or be shamed any more."

However, it was not to be so. I came out of it very easily, and recovered with surprising facility during the first few days. The News telephoned to ask for a poem on the war which has suddenly embroiled all Europe, and I, thinking I saw a good chance to settle the hospital bill, went at it immediately. It kept my mind occupied, and Dr. Rathmell commented that I was hard to kill. But the morning after I finished it I noticed that my breasts were filled with milk, and suddenly I realized I had lost another little boy.

For some reason it struck me as nothing short of tragedy, that my breast should be full of milk. My baby cold, under the ground. I cried till I was exhausted and have not felt so well since.

The bill at the hospital was $15. I borrowed it from the News on the understanding that I should come Monday and begin work, and they allowed me $5 for the poem. But I am not able to work. Mrs. Annis came for me and took me home with her in the auto. I was glad to drop into a comfortable bed and cease thinking. Time enough to go back on the News next week and work till all debts are paid.

August 25, 1914

Home on Saturday expecting to go to work on the News yesterday, but this Frank positively refuses to let me do. Not on account of my state of health—it is really much easier on me there than at home—but because he and the children need me. So I'm back in the same old trap, worse off than ever and more helpless.

It is a great disappointment to me, for Mrs. Annis and I had planned to start a New Thought Club which should pay me something.

That which decided me was not only my own lack of strength, inability to oppose his will; but something horrible. While I was gone, Sally and her viperous offspring got at my girls and filled their ears with the most vile and false version of what has happened. Fortunately they had the good sense to come straight to me with the story, and I had no choice but to tell them the truth—that my baby had been born before it was half developed.

I do not care for what Sally and her brood have told all over the country; no one with any sense will believe. But oh, to think of the vile slanders they have told my innocent children about me! I dare not leave them in such a neighborhood.

I have to sleep and rest a great part of the time. I read a little, stitch a little, cook the meals which are alarmingly skimpy. It is all just as it was before, but worse; and he is not keeping his promises of doing better by me—it is the same as always. Oh, I ought to have died two weeks ago; it would have been easy enough then.

September 1, 1914

The children are all at school except for Judith. For her, the same old round of disappointment and hope deferred has begun that has been my portion throughout my married years. Her little hoard of hard earned savings has been nearly all spent, nickel by nickel, to buy food for the family; and still her books have not been bought, nor her shoes. Frank works every day, but he cannot keep us enough to eat.

He has gone himself today, on business. His political affiliations have brought him promise of a steady job at some time during the winter, with the county. Until then he must occupy himself with something else that will support us, for my strength and spirit are alike gone.

We have had one frightful quarrel, some kind of a nervous smash, I suppose, in which I drew blood—more by accident than design; I don't know how it happened—both on himself and myself. If he only would—

It seems foolish to hope for anything after such hundreds of disappointments. But I do so hope, because it is the last chance, that he will find a winter's work today.

September 28, 1914

Such a great change, into peace and comfort and the sunshine of existence. We have sold the place and are living in three rooms over an empty store building in Hill City. We have visitors and good hearty food, and the children go to school. I am making them some clothes. I have done some illustrations for the Nautilus, and received for them today a very pleasant and helpful letter from Elizabeth and check for $18.00. Kitty and I were alone when the mail came; we immediately celebrated with a pitcher of chocolate.

Better still—some of the New Thought students—all ladies—today appointed me leading speaker of a quite informal but earnest little club. I made a fairly good address on the history and intent of the movement for which we stand, and it was more than well received. Frank met me afterwards and we walked about town shopping, stopping at Cousin May's on the way home, to take up a collection of the young ones. The little N.T. Club made a voluntary contribution of $1.25, which made me feel rather awkward, though of course, as I remind myself, the address is worth more. Frank had luck too—won a gray jinny on the single chance he took on Selman's raffle.

September 29, 1914

Tuesday. Laura telephoned that the baby, my namesake, is starving as so many of hers have starved thro' inability to digest milk, and asked that I find some one to nurse it. I arranged with Mrs. Arledge, next door, who has an illegitimate child and four older boys. I thought she would be glad of the change as she has to work hard. Laura came at noon. The baby seems almost dying. I don't know how to sleep 4 extra in these three rooms.

October 1, 1914

Thursday. Frank is on the jury and sends word he cannot get home tonight. Today Mrs. Reed, Mrs. Ferguson, Mrs. Wade, spent the afternoon sketching on the front porch. This class will be another help to me. The view is lovely, and the autumn color just coming.

Laura's baby is improving, beginning to laugh and make little talk-sounds. The next one, Dot, is the shortest, cunningest little chunk; her seriousness sits so quaintly on her dimples. Libby is younger than Kitty, they enjoy blowing bubbles together.

October 13, 1914

Received word by telephone that Laura's baby is dead. My little namesake [Emma Miles Hatfield]. This is the fifth she has lost. She says it is a sin, as I think.

The Photoplay Library Co., who have taken a considerable space for headquarters in the James Bldg., have asked me to collaborate with Miss McPherson in preparing scenarios for them. I do not like Miss McP. much, and some say this company is a fraud, but I still hope for remunerative and interesting work from them. Mrs. Annis came through the rain to see me this afternoon.

November 3, 1914

I held a larger semi-public meeting in the court house; made a good address to about 30 people—had them listening with open eyes and mouths. I do hope this Circle may grow into something, as it seems the Photoplay Co. is a false. I am scheduled to give a number of such talks, and have decided to call them a series of Studies in the New Psychology, as there is so much suspicion here directed against anything that smells like a new religion.

The beautiful warm weather continues—okra still bearing in the gardens. We have had only one freeze. The sun feels fairly hot.

five

Pine Breeze Sanitarium

After several months without entries, Emma resumed her journal from the Pine Breeze Tuberculosis Sanitarium in Chattanooga. She was suffering from tuberculosis, which apparently was not a surprise to her. The silver lining for her was that she was finally free of the living conditions up on Walden's Ridge, even if it came at the price of being sick and confined. She was there only a month, but during this time she unsuccessfully attempted to get the divorce process in motion. By mid-March she was back with her family on the mountain, this time living with Frank's parents, who made no bones about being put-upon. By late August she moved down to Chattanooga, her health somewhat better for the time being, and rented a room in a boardinghouse for women, in order to work and make money. Jean was now living with friends, and late in the summer Judith was sent off to a school in Alabama. The two youngest children remained with Frank up on the mountain.

February 6, 1915

Pine Breeze Sanitarium.[1]

Again I have the sensation of having fallen out of things; but this time into a haven, a clear and quiet pool of life beneath the sun. I was afraid I should be "free among the dead," but it is not like that at all.

To be free of the power of sin! Ever since Mark died—and before that, since first I realized the shame and the cruelty of bringing children into life unprepared for—I have longed to be free. Of late I have torn out of these records the pages which told the worst of my situation, for I wished to remember them no more forever, and the children must never know. But even through this last peaceful, pleasant, almost happy winter I have wished it were possible to free myself.

Oh, I am glad we had this happy winter, all together for the last time. But since it had to end, it was better that the end came suddenly.

My cold grew worse after an auto ride with some ladies, and then Frank simply slumped. He had helped through the winter about as usual, looking after the cow and the fires, and doing errands. Of late he planned to return to the same neighborhood on the mountain, to work for the same people in the same old way. I agreed to back him as well as possible and live in a tent; I believed this was the best plan he was likely to make; though it looked like defeat to me, putting the children in the same associations I have tried so hard to escape from.

In the right time Edith Stroop came back from Washington—came back to stay. At the first opportunity I asked her advice, as she is the only living person who understands the situation. She said that it is hard to know what is right, and advised me to wait patiently.

When I became sick and Frank went into the dumps so deep that he did scarcely anything but sit by the stove, I tried again to brace him up and get him to face things, but only succeeded in upsetting his nerves and temper. He went to see Stanfield, however, and arranged for his summer's job, but did not seem hopeful or satisfied.

At this juncture, two disquieting things happened: I had reason to suspect myself of being again pregnant; and Dr. Horton pronounced my lungs in a pre-tubercular state, requiring immediate attention.

Coming home from his examination, however, the solution of my problem flashed on me. The door was open at last!

My poor man met me on my return with an anxious face. When I told him what the doctor had said, he bowed forward as if he had been struck. "Oh, Emma," he groaned.

But I could have laughed for joy; I felt uplifted and free. "Don't look that way," I bade him. "If you only knew how glad I am that I won't have to go on having these miscarriages."

And we went up the muddy, ramshackle steps into the house. Edith was there, taking care of Kitty, who has a cold. She looked a question, but I would not answer till I got them both in the kitchen where the child would not hear.

Then I put the situation before Frank, thus: "I can get well if I want to. And also I can go out without the trouble of jumping off the bridge. If I'm to get well, I have to have something to live for. I won't try, unless you will give me a legal separation or a divorce."

"Oh! Not a divorce, Emma," said Edith sensibly. "You don't want to do that. You have too much affection for each other to make good on it."

"We have tried separation again and again," I reminded her. "It always leaves me in a worse shape than before. I've got to have legal protection this time."

Poor Frank leaned against the table of kitchen things, astounded and smitten. He rose to the occasion splendidly after a little, and promised anything I wanted, even giving me advice about chancery proceedings.

"But it is not true what she says about herself," he explained to Edith. "It can't be that way, at all."

"I've heard that often enough to know the tune of it," I declared. Maybe I was flippant and hard, but it was better, I think, than tears or anger would have been.

I nearly fell asleep in my chair from weakness before the conference was ended, and Edith tucked me into bed. He was about to go to the mountain to arrange for a horse trade and some rooms in his father's house, and came in for a last minute. I shall never forget it.

"Anything you want," he assured me. "I only want you to get well. And—I'm not the least bit mad about it—I don't blame you at all."

"What a good man you are, dear," I replied, and kissed him. Then he was gone.

That was day before yesterday. Edith helped me pack, all afternoon; the children and I had a jolly evening together over some library books; and next day—yesterday—Edith came back to help us through. She has only sympathy for Frank. There is no one else whom I would have trusted at such a time.

She will take Kitty home with her, and Judith will go to Mrs. Stanfield's to work for her board until gardening time. This leaves Jean and Joe to stay with Frank.

Edith and I both thought best for me to go to town before Frank's return. I knew he would be dreadfully disappointed, but was afraid I might not be strong enough to endure anything emotional. I left him what ready money paper there was, and kept the $100 note on Freudenberg and the one of J. M. Levi, which Frank had turned over to me; I guess he and Jean and Joe can get thro' the next two months on that and the cow and his labor.

In town I saw Mrs. Annis, who congratulated me on my decision, recommended Capt. [Henry A.] Chambers as a good man and lawyer, which agreeing with Frank's estimate of him, to Capt. C. I went. Found him a nice old Southerner and acquainted with the Mileses. He thinks I can get a decree in March.

Mrs. Annis gave me a lunch. I telephoned and had my trunk, typewriter, sewing machine and painting materials, sketches and mss. put in storage. Then to Mrs. Gahagan's.[2] She also approved my decision and sent me in the carriage to Pine Breeze. A beautiful hilltop. I had a fairly good night and am quite content here.

February 8, 1915

Received a copy of a bill-of-divorce from Capt. Chambers. I wonder what the children will think, how they will take it. Judith has of late accused me of having no spirit, when she heard her father upbraiding me in the night; but I fear she will feel shamed by these proceedings. Well, the sun shines, the birds sing, and spring is on the way. I feel strong and able to carry my responsibility.

"You think tuberculosis is something," I said to Frank in that last talk. "I tell you being killed is nothing to having your life torn all to pieces and ruined for you—spoilt and soured when you meant it to be beautiful and sweet."

"You have your children," Edith reminded me.

"But I had to see Mark die in torture, for the lack of a good doctor," I replied. And I afterward showed her the stained pillowslip on which he died,—the slip I have kept all these years to strengthen me in the resolution I took the day he was buried.

My little son, I have partly squared myself with you now.

Mrs. Annis yesterday asked about my plans. I have none; I am letting the Great Intelligence plan for me.

This bill of divorce is a cruel thing. It seems hard to charge poor, sad, well-meaning, blunderingly affectionate Frank with having refused and neglected to provide for me. As well blame a faithful, awkward old dog with such a failure. But then, there are plenty of charges which this paper does not name—the dead babies, the hard words, the long nights when he would not let me sleep, the deliberate refusals to share responsibility. I cannot do better than to let it stand.

February 10, 1915

My stay is being cheered by remembrances from many people. Sarah Frazier sends me oranges; Mrs. Morrison, magazines; Mrs. Richmond, a great basket of fruit; and a stranger who has read my book adds to the latter gift a box of tulips and carnations which aroused the admiration of all the other patients in our cottage. Of course I was glad to divide with them: for the thought behind the gift is the most precious part, and that I keep for myself.

Judith telephoned to Miss Plewess,[3] the matron, that all are well at home. It is almost too much to hope for that Frank will go on with his summer's work as planned, but this beautiful weather is encouraging.

How these poor invalids squabble! Like a pack of spoiled children. Miss Plewess manages them all with admirable tact, firmness, patience and perfect kindness. I try to help all I can; but the attitude of one who never gets the blues or says can't is disconcertingly new to them. Perhaps I shall give a New Thought address from time to time.

Last night I dreamed that my dear man was with me in his kindest, happiest wooing mood. I felt the warmth of his arms. They are dreadfully upsetting, such dreams. But I must remember that in fact such moods are increasingly rare—and think only how best to help him while maintaining my own course. My poor dear man! I am as fond of him as I ever was; but I have kept my last tryst with death and sin through his love. Over and over, morning and evening I make the affirmation, "I am free from the power of sin."

I cannot see a step before me: how to support the children or where to make them a home. God will show me, or my own soul's light—one is the same as the other.

February 11, 1915

Mrs. Stedman and Mrs. Bacher came to see me immediately after breakfast. We had a long, serious, comforting conversation about my own troubles. Perhaps I shall never feel so desperately alone again. Mrs. Stedman is so sincere and so good. She told me that my patience in the marriage bond has helped more than one other woman to go forward under trying circumstances—a thing I never dreamed of and can hardly believe, though I should like to! She urged me to consider well before entering suit for divorce, lest I do violence to some spiritual tie. Edith's letter, too, urges me to try some kind of signed contract of separation, quietly.

Then this afternoon Frank himself came. He was very tired and coughing—convinced that he too has tuberculosis and that all the children are due for it, of course, the croaker. He seemed relieved to learn that I have not yet brought suit, and thinks for the children's sake a quiet separation will be best. He offers to buy me a tent to let me live near the car line with Edith, and promises never to come about me again; thinks he will be able to support me, after a fashion, until I get well, or through this coming summer. How kind are his intentions, poor boy! I give him credit for them, but know better than to trust them.

We had to have our talk out of doors, under a chestnut tree on the windy hill—the cottage sitting room being full of patients and their guests. I got somewhat chilled, and I fear he did too. My temperature went a little high for the first time since I came, and my pulse was quite nervous; I could not eat. Oh, I shall be so relieved when this thing is settled. Until then I cannot get well.

February 13, 1915

Frank came again as I was making my bed this morning. I suppose he will come back every time he can think of anything distressing to tell me. He said that his lungs are very sore; that he has just missed a good job; that he and the children will have to move, he don't know where; that every friend I have in the world is false at heart except Edith, and that Edith is about done with me since I asked her to be a witness for me. I don't know how much of all this to believe. He went on with a light of triumph in his eye to say that I know nothing about the New Thought teaching beside Edith, that Edith agrees with him in his estimate of me—in short, that I am slightly unbalanced. I don't think he left anything unsaid that could discourage and humiliate me. But he spoke in the highest terms of her good sense and sincerity, and I was only too glad that he has come under a good wholesome influence like hers.

I assured him that I would see Capt. Chambers today and call off the divorce suit, and if possible, have a bond prepared for him to sign—the sort of separation he wants. I am afraid that this paper will be worth no more, in law, than his word; and what his word is worth I know by experience.

I fear too that it will be impossible for me to get a divorce. Since Edith will not witness for me, I don't believe Cousin May will either; and no one else knows, except Frank's own folks, and I cannot in decency call on them. They would not tell the truth, anyway.

If this separation plan falls through, there is yet the third alternative—the door that God has opened. If it were not for the children how gladly I could say, "Even so, come, Lord Jesus—dear dark giver of perpetual rest."

Once in his talk I had to laugh—when he told me he was planning to send the girls away to school this fall. After all his bitter opposition to my sending them, all his reproaches!

I was disappointed about going to town—no chance to do anything today. Perhaps they do not intend to let me go. It doesn't matter; only I should like to hear from Edith's own mouth whether she is really as near done with me as he says. But remembering how bitterly jealous he has been of her while he believed her to be helping me, I am bound to take his words with a grain of salt.

I lay quite still all day without eating. I wanted to scream and cry, but under the eyes of those cackling women it was necessary to use the most rigid self-control. Toward sunset I got up and walked about, and began a sketch, thinking I should keep a hold on myself. But I was hardly started when here came Frank up the hill!

I put the sketch down with shaking hands, and begged him, whatever he did, to tell me no more bad news or I should run up a fever.

His tone changed instantly, and with a visible effort he braced himself and began to talk more like a man. He promised to draw up a paper of separation and bring it to be witnessed and signed. I consented, but pointed out the fact that such a paper will be useless; that I am just where I have always been, quite at his mercy. He does seem to want to make good, but I know by experience that the least discouragement, the least jealousy, or a fit of contrariness, will end his resolution in a moment. However, to pacify him, I promised to try it.

At the beginning of the talk, he said, "We are nothing at all to each other any more."

"We are the father and mother of four children," I reminded him. And we planned on that basis. But at farewell he kissed my hands and begged me to think kindly of him. It is all sentimentalizing and weakness—means nothing, either way.

I am tired out.

February 16, 1915

Again Frank came, early. Joe came with him, the darling, fat and cheery; it did me so much good to see him. Frank had not yet received my letter, so I put my plan before him. He consented to let Jean go to Mrs. Stedman, but wishes to keep the other two. I sent the children a basket of fruit, and Joe staid with me till noon and went away laughing and skipping.

After dinner Mrs. Annis, Mrs. Gahagan and Mrs. Clift came, and talked very straight and serious with me about my plans. I felt frightened and bewildered, and hardly knew what stand to take. They offer to find temporary homes for the children on the understanding that I am to have a complete separation.

If I could only get to town and see Capt. Chambers. One thing troubles me—Frank wants one of the notes to buy a horse. I have never refused him money—how can I?

Mrs. Palmer lingered behind the others to see me alone. I don't know who told her. She said she was prying for me, and that she knew whatever I decided would be done in the spirit of striving to do right. I was surprised; I had thought hers would be the conventional view—but she has had a hard and bitter trial this winter, and understands.

Oh, I suffer. And the management don't like his repeated visits, which have such a bad effect on me. Can I bring myself to tell him to stay away? He surely understands I don't want to see him! And that $100 note—I must try to keep it and use it for the children. Oh, dear God—when will this strain end?

February 17, 1915

Miss Plewess took me to town in the Ford. I saw Bowling, Chamber's partner, who reassured me as to the probability of winning a suit. From the Willard Home I telephoned to Cousin May, who expressed herself as willing to testify, but doubtful as to the value of anything she knows. This set me wondering whether it were not one of those things which everyone knows but no one can swear to, but Bowling says very little additional testimony will be needed.

I felt terribly anxious about Edith, could not reach her by phone and dared not call. Got Mrs. Standfield, who gave a good report of Judith but Judith herself had gone to visit her papa.

Left the house feeling depressed and perplexed, and had not gone half a block before I walked into Edith herself! At the first glance into her face half my difficulties vanished. I could not forbear telling her what Frank had said; and she understood at once how he had drawn his own impressions. She walked a long way with me, giving me comfort and cheer at every step.

I could eat nothing, and was very tired before time to go home. Warned by Cousin May, I stopped to see about the bill at Freud's and was shocked to find a bill of $11.00 already run up against the note I hold.[4] I ordered this stopped at once. Frank ought not to have done this, surely; and yet he has always been accustomed to draw on me.

I came back tired out, but the long mental conflict is, I believe, nearing a close. I will have to sue for a divorce: there is no other way.

February 22, 1915

Yesterday the first spring bird awoke me,—a phoebe. This morning it was a cardinal's cheery shout. The morning was like spring; but this afternoon is wrapped in gray damp that blurs and veils all the hilltops.

It is a revelation to me how this place is filled with women who have leaned too long on the promises of worthless men. Some have laid their children in the grave, some have put theirs into the orphanage, one is expecting her sixth child. One of her children was taken by Clinton Daingerfield, spoilt for a life of hardship and toil, and then turned over to the training school: two others were taken by Bob Nixon and wife, of all people, and another in the orphanage.[5] Those promises! She had to break up housekeeping to rid herself of them. And the sweet-faced Virginia widow—her man broke her health and threatened her, and when her baby died she escaped from him, from his letters even.

Oh, poor women, poor wives. All lost and broken!

February 23, 1915

But am I not in worse case than any? He has been back twice, in the pouring rain; I had not the heart to refuse to see him. He stayed long, and talked quietly. He has indeed played the man for once, going to see my friends and my lawyer, wishing to effect a compromise. And he has sent Jean to Mrs. Stedman and Kitty to Mrs. Blair.

But he has also been to a lawyer of his own, and has found that he can divorce me for the death of those unborn children—whom I loved and would have worked for when he would not. God, is there no justice anywhere for a married wife?

I went to sleep in my chair and dreamed that he and I were hunting arbutus along the Foust Mill Branch within sound of the waterfall:— dreamed that he was kind and happy, dreamed of his arms. Then, a few minutes after I woke—he came. God knows, when he began to talk reasonably and look like a man, I wanted to come close to him and rest against him. But I knew it would be no rest—and I remembered the long, long, weary nights I had no rest for body or soul.

February 24, 1915

Today again I looked at the dark, snow-cold sky and felt the keen wind, and thought, "Today at least he will not bring me new trouble and perplexity." But as I came down the walk after dinner, I saw him waiting in the cottage door. He had a bunch of clothes from the washwoman for me, which served as well as any excuse to come.

"See if they are right," he said. "I must go right back, and—I suppose this is goodbye."

"Why," I said, dropping the clothes on the bench, "I'll see you Saturday?"

"I don't know. We haven't settled the terms of the agreement, but I'll sign anything you decide on. Capt. Chambers says there are four children, we can very easily divide them."

This was not at all what I wanted, and no doubt it showed in my face.

"Or either—you could keep all the children and I could work and help support them."

"Mrs. Stedman?"

"She will come by to see you tomorrow."

"And Mrs. Stroop?"

"She'll try to come the day after. Don't tell either one that I've been here today."

"Not?"

"No. Don't tell them. . . . Goodbye." He held out his hands, and I saw all the lines of his face give and break. I laid mine in them, and standing close to him, looking into his eyes as they filled, I told my dream.

He shook his head. "I'll never be happy again."

"No. We can neither of us ever be happy again," I agreed. But I put my arms around him, and he kissed me on the cheeks and neck, and mouth. I kissed him and whispered, "I love you, I love you."

As he turned away he said, "If things are ever different—" and broke off to begin again, "This agreement doesn't bind you. But it binds me hard. But—if I was ever to make good—"

He said no more till, at the door, he murmured something scarcely audible about my walking down the hill with him. It was a damp and biting wind, but I went. We paused by the chestnut tree, and I knew not what to say. But in him the flood of emotion was loosed at last.

"Oh, Emma," he broke out suddenly, "how do you bear it?"

But I wondered how I had stood the things that are past, and was silent.

"You can help me a lot still," he said. "I want you to help me if you will—I don't mean money," he said.

"How, then, brother?"

"Nothing that you wouldn't want to give."

"What would you look to me for? Tell me."

"Love," he said, and his mouth and chin quivered like a child's. "If you'd love me—"

"I'm just as fond of you as I ever was," I hastened to explain. "Only you've nearly killed me—you will kill me if I stay with you; and I must save myself alive now for the children. You see that, don't you?"

He nodded, his face working. "I think I've done all I can—got things about as you wished . . ."

I felt a sinking of the heart. "As I wished?" I asked quietly. "Is that all you can see in it even now—a notion of mine?"

"No, no," he agreed. "I know it's not right you should have to live with me." And then in a rush he outlined his plan. "There's nothing in this agreement against our seeing one another—meeting now and then and visiting together."

"Do you think you'd be able?" I asked.

"Yes. Oh, I ain't going to bother you any more—in that way. I don't want to—besides the agreement binds me. But if I should make good—if I should sometime have money—we could dissolve it between us. I want to take care of you and the children—want to talk to you, kiss you sometimes, like it was before we married."

"I should like that," I told him, "if you'd stand by it. But I think you'd want to get a hold over me again. I'd be able, I know; but you—"

"I wouldn't," he promised. "I'd like to meet you and take the children on little picnics in the woods, and be friends with you—like we was courting—"

"I know I'd like that," I replied, but without joy or confidence, remembering that I have longed and pleaded for such a relationship since before Mark was born.

He was hopeful, however, and went away promising to come into town Saturday; and he waved to me as he went down the hill.

I feel strangely comforted by this interview, and though I feel sure his nature, the male nature, which contains so strange and dreadful a beast to be conquered or to devour, will not allow him to stand to the terms of such an agreement except with entire separation; still it is consoling to know that to him, too, the relation of friendship colored with sweetheart's passion is at last a desirable thing. It is something that the idea, the vision of such a love, has entered his mind and taken hold there. I remember how, shortly after marriage, I tried to picture to him such a relation, and how he misunderstood so badly that I never spoke of it again. I am glad to have the children; yet I believe it would have been the right relation for us two, from the beginning.

February 28, 1915

Edith has been to see me, and Frank; and this morning Mrs. Reed and Mrs. Adams and Frank again. And the more he comes the more I feel convinced of the uselessness of all this palaver about it and about—he is the same, will always be the same.

Every man has within him a ravenous beast which if he conquer it not, devours him and all that he loves. Mr. Stedman, it seems, had a plain, good talk with Frank about this thing. I shall always be glad of that—that for once a high-minded, father-natured man has been quite plain with my man on this subject; he has heard enough street toughs and stable Negroes hold forth upon it, God knows, and never would quite believe what I told him.

He has lost seven pounds, and many a night's rest over this—yet will not his folly depart from him. Every man holds unalterable in the bottom of his heart the belief that, ornery scoundrel as he knows himself to be, his wife must be somewhat worse or she wouldn't belong to him. Frank is quite willing to say now that he has wronged me, that he is to blame for all that has come upon us; but I fear that is from the teeth out; every now and then something is let slip which shows that he blames me. This being so, if he gets hold of me again, he may be as vindictive as after that visit to the Wheatley's years ago, and take it out of me with red-hot whips of wrath for all that he has suffered of late.

I was glad to see him this morning and all went well for a time. He was telling me of the job near Crossville, which Mrs. Stedman and Mrs. Bacher have found for him. I agreed even to go there with him if necessary, though it means giving up nearly everything of my few satisfactions in life—Edith and all friends, the city library, and what little music I get to hear. Then it came to me with a shock that I must give up not only going among people but lecturing—and this for very shame. He assured me that this is true; Mrs. Stedman knows of the sin and shame, violence and misery, and while she does not blame me she feels that I ought never to teach New Thought again.

The shame of it sickened me, and the sure knowledge of another failure. My writing, my painting, the publication of my little book of verse, my studio, my newspaper work, my lecturing—one after another he had double-crossed every effort I have made, and this not because he objects to my earning money at all, but because he could not bear for me to take an interest in anything but him. Now there is nothing left for me to try.

I told him this, and felt as if I could not move, weighted in every limb by the despair of it, the deep woe. "I want to crawl back out of the way somewhere, where nobody can see me," I told him.

"I would if I was you," he replied.

And again death appeared like a door opened before me. "I ought to be dead," I said. "I want to die. I feel that I can't bear to leave this hospital and take up living again: I am not lazy, but I'm ashamed to. I always said that any woman who would do such a thing, do what I have done, ought to die. Ashamed to live, I am."

And then he slumped again, began to get angry. "Is this the encouragement you are going to give me," he began.

I lost my temper and cut him short with, "Oh, you; always you! must have encouragement and petting and waiting on or you won't try! Where shall I look for encouragement?"

Very justly he reminded me of the children's need of me. I promised to stand by them and do my best if he will only make good. "I'm willing, but I can't pretend to be happy over it."

He left, then turned back and came to me again, fearing, I suppose that I might be ill. But he was helpless before the rock of his own disposition and habits, and though I believe he wanted to, he could not offer a word of comfort.

When he had gone it began to snow, and snowed heavily all day, changing the piney hills to richer beauty. I went to bed and did not get up till supper time. I have such a bitter longing to lie down and sleep myself to death, since both love and work are denied me, and I am ashamed to live.

The money from the sale of the cow is nearly gone already. When he asks for the note again I will give it to him. If he spends my last cent and makes me pregnant again—perhaps then I will be allowed, even by Edith, to die in peace.

And all the time we were talking this morning, the patients huddled round the stove in the next room of the cottage heard only the even murmur of voices. As I came back, one young victim of a drunken husband's neglect during childbirth looked up and said enviously, "My goodness, Mis' Miles, your husband sure must love you."

I might have answered that there is a love that kills.

March 2, 1915

Chickadees on snow-splashed hillsides, bluebirds in the sun, and a magnificent pair of cardinals on the hilltop. My sweet birds! Once I too had wings.

I have been too cold to rest lately. It is not the ordinary pinch of the weather, but a sick chill that begins in the bones and searches the vitals. Last night was very bad, and this morning I ate my breakfast but can eat no more.

I know this is not real. It cannot be real, because God does not make things so, does not will them to be so. It is not true that I am in this trap; it is a nightmare. I want to wake up—to wake up as little Mark must have waked up after his suffering, in that other house where all is peace and joy—where only real things exist. I shall wake up in God's great house, and open my wings again, wide and free; and God's kindness will be round and over me as it used to be.

One part of Frank is real. I think of it and love him, though thinking of his mistreatment of me I hate and fear him. It is the look on his face when he speaks to a very small child. It is not a smile, but a slow dawn, a coming to the surface of what is fine and lovely in him. It is an exquisite thing, and unimpeachably true.

If he would only look at me like that! But for me his face is full of resentment, and anxiety, and shame.

Can he realize that all these years I have struggled and strained to make things better, carrying the whole family on my back, he has never given me one word of genuine appreciation? It was at first good for me to encounter difficulties; whether I overcame them or not, there was a song in my heart. But the last years have been one long melancolia. [*sic*]

But it is over now, I can labor no more. Now when I leave this sanatorium, in all probability I shall never sleep another night in a clean and comfortable bed, nor eat a square meal. When I have made the Freudenberg note over to Frank and spent the two dollar bills that are in my stocking, I shall probably never have any more money. I am tired out; I want to wake out of this.

> "From too much love of living,
>   From hope and fear set free,
> We thank with brief thanksgiving
>   Whatever gods there be.
> That no life lives forever,
> That dead men rise up never,
> That even the weariest river
>   Winds somewhere safe to sea."[6]

> "For each man kills the thing he loves,
>   By all let this be heard,

Some do it with a flattering look,
Some with a careless word;
The coward does it with a smile,
The brave man with a sword."[7]

March 6, 1915

I am awake now: fully awake I think.

When did I begin to waken?

I think it must have been when Kitty ran in at the door. Frank brought her and Judith, the dears, so happy and rosy and good. He said that a grown woman could not have been steadier than she since I have been away from home. Kitty cuddled against me and rubbed her cropped head against my arm, and made quaint little remarks about the place. Judith's cheeks are redder and fuller than ever. An unusual girl, most satisfactory.

I felt the tension relax, all those knots of pain and resentment and anxiety giving way. He told me what he had been able to learn about that Cumberland Mountain job, and what plans he has made. It was such a relief to find him capably planning toward a veritable livelihood that I laid my head on his shoulder and sighed, "I wish I could sleep here," before I thought.

"I wish you could," he whispered. "Feel more at home?" And I saw that he was looking at me with that immeasurable sweetness of expression which he turns to little children: and knew that whatever happens, in him is my heart's home.

That was Wednesday; and in defiance of the rules. Thursday he brought the little girls again and they staid most of the day. Edith too came, and brought me some arbutus which she found after long searching, not quite open. We talked long concerning Frank's prospects, and how his self-respect and will power had suffered from these years without occupation, and from "strangulated emotions" now freed by his talks with Mr. Stedman, Dr. Wagner, and Capt. Chambers. To my surprise she seems to think I should go with him to Cumberland Mt. O yes, I will go! If he is man enough to take care of his family, well: I am sure of health and happiness. If not, no legal process can help matters much—I am lost inevitably.

I told him so, and also that I can hardly hope ever to accomplish anything more of my own motion. He denied this, gravely, saying that my best work is before me. I wish I could think so.

Yesterday came a letter from Grace MacGowan, enclosing a $25 check for a story I had lost hope and sight of: a splendid surprise! And this morning, with his usual disregard of regulations, Frank came to show me a letter just received from Mrs. Wortham offering him a 3-year contract, $20 a month, house-rent, garden, cow. It looks good.

Just as naturally as he has told me about the two or three past occasions when he has drunk just a little too much, so now he told me of poor Mrs. Arledge's attempt to inveigle him in a secret affair which might help her to live, and of her confusion and apologies when he refused her. For refuse he did, I do not question that, as gently and respectfully as if declining an invitation to dinner; that is my man all over, with perfect chivalry toward the helpless and degraded.

"But mightn't she have been a comfort to you?" I asked.

"What do you think?"

"Well—I've refused you. I don't feel, under the circumstances, that I've got a right to say. It's between you and your conscience—isn't it?"

"I don't know. Would you care?"

I wouldn't say. "Question is, if you need her. If you can't endure it without her ministrations—I'll have to try to stand it."

He laughed suddenly. "Girl—I wouldn't fool with her for anything. Why—while she stood in the door and talked to me, I looked her over good, and thought, "You dirty, red-haired thing.""

"Such an epithet to describe that dimpled, pleasant young woman, Frank!" I laughed. "But we'll manage without her. Only—I can't suffer any more."

"You shan't suffer," he promised.

I am all happy again, all freely and ready. This afternoon made the prettiest watercolor I have done for months, and presented it to Miss Plewes.

March 13, 1915

At the old folks' house on the mountain.

I did not enjoy coming here and the old folks do not want me, but no other arrangement was practicable. And I would be contented anywhere with Frank and the children now. We are living in two rooms and boarding with Barney and his wife. Not the least pleasant feature of the arrangement is Barney's splendid baby; the girls play with her all day.

At last the weather is beautiful. It is a late spring, that is today, will be a good fruit year. Many redbirds; orchard full of bluebirds; the first chippy on the fence; friendly and brave, asking for crumbs; today the first thrasher. The spring house is walled with mossy stones, in the edge of a sedge field, a sunny hollow; and here are a number of delicate gray sparrow birds flitting, with delicate sparrowy songs, from stump to brier and back again. All pleasant and peaceful.

Of the goodness and loyalty of my man I cannot get enough. No one could be kinder or more sensible. I enjoy every minute of the time. Laura came to see us yesterday and brought the little girls. Today Frank and Judith and Jean washed. I could not help much.

I left the sanatorium before the treatment was half completed, but think I shall recover as well here, in relief at the cessation of mental pain.

What he tells me of his talks with Edith and Mrs. Stedman is a revelation of loyalty and love. I can only try to be worthy of such devotion. I did not know there was so much pure goodness in the world. His kindness to me, here to both of us—faithfulness and understanding and good will, unfailing through all these years! This alone is real.

March 18, 1915

Everyone is plowing and we have to sit still, can do nothing. Barney's wife has refused to cook for us any longer at any price, so we have made a little room over here and are scraping up meals as best we can. Everything is crowded and inconvenient; it is impossible to keep clean or orderly, and no speech is exchanged among the children without snarling and frequent blows. Yesterday and the day before we could not keep warm; today the rooms are dark—we have to light the lamp before sunset. In the evening I read to the children, but we have to quit early on account of Grandpa's bedtime. The old lady is quite apologetic about his crabbedness, however; today she brought me 3 fresh eggs and a mess of dried apples.

I do enjoy being with my good man. Never did his patient, sad, wise face look so good and dear. But how long can my digestion stand this food? And my nerves this way of living? Worse still, how long will the money hold out?

March 22, 1915

Coughed a good deal in the night, and Frank became discouraged and talked of sending me back to the sanatorium: he says it will be impossible for him to hold that Crossville job with me in this condition, and I suppose that is true; but why did he not let me alone while I was improving? If I were to go back to Pine Breeze, it would be the same thing over.

It is not tuberculosis, nor any physical condition I fear. It is not this cough that will make an end of me. There is a dark mood that comes without warning, to stand by me like the presence of the Noseless One,[8] whose counsels bind me with a horror of great darkness and a deadly calm. Like a voice it says, over and over: "No use, No use. You are only one of the millions; so little will be lost if you but cease to struggle, this losing fight which only prolongs your pain. Give up and let go. Then you will never have the shame of looking people in the face, people who have seen your failure and guessed your sin. Give up; it is the easiest way, will be the only way. All your life you have been cheated, have tried and failed, have run forward and fallen, have fought and been knocked out. Take the count, and cease to suffer."

It stays like a weight on me, sometimes five minutes, sometimes five days. I know I ought to try to overcome it, but I have neither wish nor will. And Frank is too faint-hearted and lazy to help. When I get to work with the children and start things to going, when all are active and cheerful, I have hope for the time being, and the bitter and evil mood of helplessness seems like a madness. But it is the one power that will kill me if anything does.

Such is the night. We wake this morning to find three inches of snow, sifted and drifted by a cutting wind—a fine, powdery snow that smokes along the field in every gust, and sweeps dry from off the porch. The wind is weaving a fine shroud for me—for me to lie down with my little sons.

March 24, 1915

A clear morning at last—and Frank made me a nest in the sun on the back porch by laying an old mattress over the top of a box. I have a hot stone at my feet and blankets over me, with an oilcloth for storm-sheet. It is even more comfortable then at the sanatorium, and far more interesting, since I have a splendid view on all sides—the road through the woods, several little shacks and clearings, and all the varied activities of the season; Barney whistling "All Night Long" as he hammers and saws on the boards of his new house; chickens scratching over the plowed field; women washing, a curl of blue smoke rising from the pot; wood-cutting, raking yards; and Domineckers hunting for nests among the broken furniture, barrels and packing-cases which clutter my porch. I feel uncommonly content and comfortable. A fitting place for me to end my days in.

March 25, 1915

Helped what I could with what Grandma calls "a master washin'." Frank and the girls succeeded in getting it done, but the clothes are only dingily clean. A lovely spring day, but the wind still blows cool. No letter yet from Crossville, and Frank has about given up hope of the job; he is utterly out of heart again, and I do not believe he will try to do anything.

Last night again I dreamed of my little son. I heard his laughter and prattle. I saw him standing straight and sturdy in his little overalls,—saw distinctly his beautiful hair and his mouth and eyes. Ah, well, by and by even his death will not matter to me any more. It seems strange to think that in a little while even the memory of those little dead bodies can not make me suffer.

Poor Frank will suffer, no doubt. But I have besieged him for years, begging him not to let things come to this pass. He has had plenty of warning. Now he promises to go to work if I will first get well. The old story! If I should get well tomorrow I would only have to take the entire responsibility for the family again.

For me the Wind is weaving
A shroud of softest white;
Is spreading smooth as velvet
My measure overnight.
The budless boughs are whistling,
The earth is iron below.
But O to be, my darling,
With you beneath the snow.
For me the Wind is wailing
That all your songs are stilled,
Your laughing lips are withered,
Your limbs are stark and chilled.
The night of time has darkened
Your face that glowed so fair,

Your eyes like purple orchids,
The dawn-light of your hair.
For me the frost is blanching
Your blossoms one by one,
And winged lives pursuing
Behind the flying sun.
Your feet that were so little
I warmed them in my hand,
The iron frost imprisons
Deep down in frozen sand.
For me the night is waiting;
The shadow from below
Apace climbs westward, westward,
Across a world of snow.
The wind is flagging, failing,
The dark is rising fast;
And free o' the dead, my darling,
We two shall walk at last.

March 29, 1915

A lovely spring day, warm sun and cool wind. The two old folks have
been out planting potatoes. Nanny came up on a visit to them, and as she
was rather afraid to walk back to the car line alone, Frank went with her
to town.

Birds everywhere. A pair of nuthatches searching the oak tree bark, going
round the boughs and up and down the trunk; making a sound like rubbing
a wet finger on a pane of glass. Many handsome woodpeckers abroad.

Frank is so good about tiding me over these murderous vagaries
of despair—though certainly he never seems to know when he is
overstraining me and bringing them on. I know I have made him a lot
of trouble, but he never has a word of blame for me. He says we are to
stand by and help each other through all things; and I am but just coming
to see this perfectly simple thing. When I married I gave myself with
reservations. That was certain to make trouble. I meant to reserve my work,
my brains, for myself. Also I had the idea, all along, that if one's husband
did wrong, one should deny him all support and countenance. Now that I

have myself sinned and blundered and failed so terribly, and found him right at my back through and after it all, taking his share of the blame before the world, I begin to see the marriage goes deeper than all these aberrations of purpose, these ebbs and risings of moral force. The goodness and loyalty of his heart is my main defence against the evil of the world. How patient he is with these black moods and vagaries of mine!

Mrs. Worthan has written that she is selling her farm and will not want Frank. So that chance is gone, and there is no living in sight. Always before I have pulled us through hard places, but this time I can't.

April 4, 1915

Easter. Yesterday, a high, gusty wind blew all day; today is cold but sunshiny. There is much fine weather overdue, and Frank talks of putting in a garden right away and is looking about for a horse or mule. So we are settled down finally to day labor in this God-forsaken neighborhood among the scum of humanity, those thieves, strumpets and degenerates left when the capable and normal mountaineers move away. The children hear nothing from week to week but scandalous gossip of this one's thievery and that one's lewdness, except that every evening I read them a story. The supply of reading is, however, running short. Judith has just read Zola's Fecondite, of all things, and by dint of talking it over with me has come to understand most of its scope and intent very well. I am hard put for a gleam of mental interest myself, but make out to read a little simple French, which I have no means of pronouncing.

Even the woods here are stunted and mean looking. I have some bird visitors, however—a tufted titmouse, a brown creeper, house-wrens, and a very tiny, sawed-off, reddish, perky wren, who plays peep-eye in Frank's woodpile, and renders a quaint twitter scarcely audible; one cannot say a song. Winter wren?

That thrasher is splendid; he talks, one may say, but exquisitely—delivers his message in a purer and more flexible language than ours.

In the afternoon the Stedmans and Bachers came up unexpectedly in an auto, and ate a picnic lunch at the spring, making coffee over a little fire. They brought the most delicious hot cross buns and chocolate, jam, English bread and French, and left what remained, with homemade candy and home-grown radishes, for the children's school lunch tomorrow.

Everyone was happy but Grandma and Grandpap, who sulked in the house and quarreled because Stedman's pup hurt one of their hens, and me, who am simply ashamed to be seen. Frank sings to himself about the house in an accession of hope, and affection and confidence, and the children are so glad to have seen their friends.

April 7, 1915

Smoky, warm, languid days. Frank put in his patch of potatoes, beans, onions, peas, and other garden truck, on his father's land. Lost labor, probably—either the old man or the weeds will get most of it—but it is better than doing nothing.

The sun falls to the treetops and there appears to pause, turning clear red and then fading out in smoke. Exquisite twilights, full of voices: tree toad, pickering, frogs, vesper sparrow, and the mocking bird's evening carol—the one things exultant, free, and perfect, given wholeheartedly amid all this startlified wretchedness. Among other strains he attempts the thrush's; it is rather like trying to play Mendelssohn on a banjo, but the performance as a whole is individual and true, a perfect utterance to living joy. After dark, the banjos and guitars and fiddles take up the music, answering from porch to porch of the neighborhood. Bats are out.

April 8, 1915

Frank had next to no sleep last night, but got up kind and patient as ever and went to Fairmount to look at a horse. A lovely spring morning, smoke-veiled, everything grayer than in winter. Many birds; jays, brilliant and noisy, waiting to devour the young of others; a red bird's quarrel flashes by in a vivid whirl of scarlet wings. Jean reports six of those yellow-hammers with the black V-collar. She found, in the shelter of a pine thicket, the last autumn leaf—sourwood, which had hung on all winter.

The horse, when brought home, proved to be a pitiful wreck, blind, nearly starved, horribly cut and bruised, and has just lost a colt from overwork. And that brute had the harness on her this morning to pull out a load of cross-ties! However, with the exception of her eyes, there is nothing wrong with her that Frank cannot cure. It was a pleasure to see her eat while his hands went all over her wounds with healing tallow.

He burnt off the sedge-grass field this afternoon and I and the children went down to look on. Meantime we cut a mess of green sissles and had them for supper, sharing with the old folks.

April 15, 1915

Dear, good Edith came up to see me, walking from the car line with Mrs. Bacher and Mrs. Stedman. They brought sandwiches, etc., cakes and candy, but Edith ate with Frank and Judith in the kitchen because, poor Edith, she is not getting enough to eat at home. Mrs. Stedman and Mrs. Bacher visited on the porch with me; but I could not tell them of my state or my feeling. At last I had a few words with my faithful mother-friend.

"You'll have to tell these folks how it is, Edith," I said to her. "I haven't the heart."

"How much shall I tell them?" she asked, holding my hands. "All of it? Or some of it?"

"Tell them I've given up," I said. "Tell them I don't see this getting-well proposition. There's nothing in it for me. Tell them—why, could you or they or any woman, live the way I do? It isn't a question of whether I want to; I haven't <u>wanted</u> to for years."

"I know," she answered, weeping. "But it's worth while, isn't it, to keep on trying?—for the girls?"

"It may be worthwhile—and I don't know what's to become of them if I let go. But I can't live this way; you know I can't, Edith."

"Just four or five years," she urged. "then you can let it go. But with Judith and Jean at this age, it's like deserting them—it's pretty near desertion."

"It's to lose all the years I've put in on the children—all the sweat and blood and tears. Like losing something you've nearly paid for. But listen—if I get well, I'll have to shoulder the whole burden again; and do all the drudgery, take all the responsibility, and then—another miscarriage likely. I can't, I can't Edith. And now, how will I make a living? Can't write any more, can't draw. Can't eat! I can't eat in that kitchen." I told her all, retching up the gathered bitterness and poison of my sorrow and my shame, and she kept her sweet strong face close to mine, and her eyes were stars of truth and kindness, but filled with tears.

"Maybe we can go to Florida next winter, just you and I and Kitty and John," she told me. "Wouldn't you get well for that? Wait and see!"

"I can't leave the children in this neighborhood."

"Don't I know this neighborhood? Didn't I take my children out of school here—and I was afraid to let Girlie out without two boys. I know! But," she went on, gripping my wrists, "do you know it will be the saving of Judith and Jean if they have to stay at home and take care of an invalid mother?"

I was struck by the force of this.

"Work the invalid mother racket for all it is worth," she advised, half laughing, and made me promise to do so.

Afterward, I learned from Frank, with whom she had a long talk privately, that she was wearing one of Dave's old shirts, and not getting near enough to eat; that they are behind the rent, without a stick of furniture, and have no place to go. I learnt nothing of this from her—only that Dave does not allow her to visit me, and she had to come by stealth.

O, what a place this world is for women!

April 20, 1915

I have eaten a good breakfast for the first time in weeks, and feel stronger. The last gray thicket is tinted now with spring, and through and through the morning ring thrush notes, keen and pure, keener and purer than any other sound in the woods. The bees have deserted plum and peach for apple and cherry bloom; dogwood boughs begin to whiten. Frank continues to plow and plant. The poor old mare falls over inequalities in the ground from time to time, being too weak to handle herself well; but she is gaining steadily, and is always willing, after a little time to collect herself, to get up and try again. In the dark!

Yesterday evening Jean ran away, and Judith quarreled with the others until I went into the kitchen and did all the work myself. I was tired and sick and immeasurably discouraged when I got through, and went out in the dusk and sat down on the steps by my man. He tried to talk to me about the stars and cherry-bloom, but I wrapped up in my big wool robe and sat still—one mass of suffering from head to foot.

"Come here, girl," he said suddenly, reaching his hands, "and tell me about it." His voice was infinitely tender, and I knew that this time he would understand.

"Don't you think it's awful?" I asked him. I did not cry or tremble; those things are gone by. "Don't it seem a dreadful thing to you, that I should lose everything, everything?"

"Yes, it does," he answered, holding me tight. "I can't express things as you can, I have to bear them and suffer; but it does tear my heart to see you doing this drudgery." He talked a long time, not promising much now, but counseling patience with the children.

"I thought you didn't care."

"Oh, I do care, I do! I can't tell you. I would give anything to help you— and I will help you, only it takes time. Things will be better for us . . ."

We went to bed under the misty stars, and listened to Barney and Dock playing Ole Pee Dee and All Night Long, Ida Red, Greenbacks, and Doogin-Pin, till everybody went to sleep and the whippoorwills had the night to themselves. And while nothing is changed, yet I feel now that I can bear it for the present, which means that I shall live until cold weather anyway and must plan for a summer's work.

April 21, 1915

Yesterday we set the hen. The lovely growing weather is rapidly becoming a dry spell.

It is strange and terrible to think that, at any hour, I might free myself—might step at any time into comfort and leisure, get well, and begin writing again. All I would have to do is to go down to Chattanooga and take a room and board at the Willard Home. The $3.50 a week it would cost me I could earn in two days of making place cards, with less nervous strain than the same length of time costs me here; the rest of the week I could read and study, hear music and enjoy myself at will, and perhaps as the anxieties and strain fell away and my thoughts became less confused, I could write again. When I think of the quiet, little white room, alone with my typewriter and watercolors, that I might have, it seems to me that the whole earth and sky are filled with resentment and bitterness; oh, it is not fair, not right!

I could go so easily and be free! I would soon be well, soon be myself again and win my own place as a writer! Oh, for what do I stay here in the stinking disorder of a house I have not strength to clean, in the moral filth of a neighborhood I have tried so long to escape! I suppose simply because

I have brought these children into the world and must stand by them, see them through—no matter how lazy and impudent and wasteful they are. Meantime they would only be too glad to be rid of me, so that they could do as they please; they let me know it every time there is work to be done.

I am utterly stripped, stark, robbed of every bit of pleasure and interest in life. But I keep on and on. I say to death, Not yet. But when in the next cold weather he comes for me, I shall lay my head on his knees, and say to the Angel of the Dark Draught,[9] as Judith said when a little, lost, tired baby— "Take me back to house!" To that other house of quiet and mystery where my little son found surcease of torture, among the unfathomable shadows.

What can I do while yet I linger in the house of the Sun? Not much. Poor Judith, who is a head taller than her grandma and not yet thirteen— she needs me more than she knows, yet will have none of me, considering me a harsh taskmistress who stands between her and pleasure. There is a standing quarrel about the length of her skirts; she goes into hysterics when the subject comes up, and Jean declared flatly that she won't wear hers any longer. Meantime their bare legs are a scandal to this row of shacks, and I fear the consequence, but as for authority, I seem to have none.

April 28, 1915

Cool and pleasant, perfect weather, but too dry for the garden and corn and potatoes. There is a bird who sings at intervals all through the night: song sparrow perhaps, or whitethroat. The morning chorus is a rain of delicate sounds in which individual voices are scarcely distinguishable; it reaches its fullest a little after 5 o'clock. Black gnats have come.

My health is so much improved in the past few days that I can do nearly my ordinary "stunt," cooking and cleaning and painting cards, serving out my life sentence at hard labor. I am sick with shame and horror of this life; I know now, I think, how prostitutes take to drink and cocaine. Nothing in the kitchen but a little dried fruit, a handful of beans, and breadstuffs, with a small cube of salt pork unfit to be eaten; not enough utensils and dishes to cook and serve a meal—one teacup, two plates, and some enamel cups and piepans scaling so that they ought to be thrown away. No respect from any one, my family least of all; no thanks for what I have done. No summer hat, not one thing for me or the girls to wear on our heads, not a pair of whole stockings among us!

In effect, a man says to his chosen: "I love you because you are a little finer than others,—because of your grace, your intelligence, your moral elegance, which show that you have been raised in a better place than the kitchen, in better company than that of tradesmen and laborers, and for your accomplishments which fit you to be something better than a servant. If you love me, come and spend the best years of your life in the kitchen, which I shall precariously provide for you, doing the drudgery for which otherwise I should have to hire a negro. Your hours will be from 5 A.M. to 5 A.M., your recompense will be the right to bear my name, and board rather poorer than that in the cheapest houses, and the cheapest clothes you can find. Be very humble now, and very grateful indeed; for without a man's name to yours you can have no love under the law. And in any case remember that the reward of love is mortal peril."

In talking with Frank's mother about Dock's wife, who has recently suffered a dangerous miscarriage, the subject of protection during pregnancy came up. She told me that, although for 15 years she took in washing to help support the family, she always insisted on being let alone during the period of gestation.

"I told him," she said, "that he'd have to go elsewhere. I told him I didn't care nothing about hit if only I didn't hafta see hit. And so he let me plumb alone."

I had no answer to this. It is what many women do—perhaps most. But is it any answer to the problem? Does it not merely shift the burden to the shoulders of another woman, and add shame to its weight? Yet is this practice any worse than that of shifting the family cooking and cleaning, and the care of the children, into the hands of servants?—ignorant, coarse creatures who do their work joylessly and crudely, receiving neither thanks, human interest, nor pay beyond bare living wage? Is not the servant's condition a sort of shame? How was it in slave days, when the wife of a land owner was a sort of head of his harem? I wonder what exactly the Socialists propose? I believe they alone have fairly faced this question.

Why do I think of these things? Because of my daughters, perhaps. However it coarsens them, I mean to send them into life with open eyes, that they may not suffer as I have.

Last night I told Frank that I would give anything in the world to be loved, for a little while, by one who asked for nothing, got nothing, out of me. His feelings were terribly hurt, but it is true. Until he married, his folks kept him drained, overworked, sick and penniless half the time. Since then he has drained me of my last cent, my strength and talent, the very blood in my veins. And this is Love!

Judith comes home from Laura's saying that Aunt Laura wants her to stay the summer, or until Grandma Hatfield's death, as the poor old creature is a burden to care for and makes extra help necessary. Her wages will be $1.50 a week, which should clothe her well.

She brought a dead woodthrush which she had picked up; it had flown against the wires. I made a little watercolor from it in the pages of my bird book.

Set the hen on 6 duck eggs.

May 10, 1915

The day broke cool and brilliantly sunny, like an autumn morning. I hurriedly stitched up a blue gingham sunhat for myself, and went with Frank and Kitty to Signal Point. The mare managed fairly well with the borrowed harness and buggy; she is nervous, but intelligent, and I am finding the psychology of a blind horse an interesting study. It is an interesting and pathetic sight to see Frank call her from the pasture, guiding her, by calling, round stumps, and other obstacles. His understanding of the poor creature is perfect; he warns her of every bank and stone, his movements never startle her, and even in the temper-trying process of plowing he never blames or punishes her mistakes. Her will is good, her condition improving, and he gets surprisingly good results.

The drive was very pleasant. Near the old salting-ground we heard a strange bird song and stopped. The singer was in full view—a rosebreasted grosbeak, on a bough above the road and not a bit afraid. We listened a long time to the low-pitched violin tones with such rich coloratura of turns and slides and grace-notes. Will bird-song ever come to be translated into human music, I wonder?

Kitty had her first good look at a scarlet tanager; and I saw a chestnut-sided warbler and made a more or less inaccurate drawing of it. At the store we bought a week's supplies on credit, and stopped at Mrs. Stanfiel's coming home. She gave me a bucket of buttermilk, my dinner, and an armful of Sat. Eve. Posts. Mrs. Rawlings gave Frank several dozen tomato plants.

Another "little bit helps" is that two of E. Shannon's cows have fallen into the way of stopping at our gate to be milked. Neither of them gives enough to be worth his while, but what a help to us.

May 22, 1915

Dock and a negro from the chain gang came to the yard this morning, Dock with a banjo and "Pence" with guitar; and they played Liza Jane, Old Gray Bonnet, All Night Long, Kitty Wells, Buffalo Gals, Bully of the Town, Creole Belles, and Back to Baltimore—favorites old and new.

In the afternoon, Frank and I went down into the woods, found some maidenhair fern, not much. Tonight we hear what they call here a "Dutch whippoorwill"—chuck wills widow. A little boy in the valley once told me it says "chip out o' whiteoak." The most unusual rendering of the old strain I have ever heard.

June 2, 1915

I have come to the conclusion that it is necessary for me to go to town and find work—get back my place on the News if possible. I have finished the last least order for cards, and now we are out of cash and out of provisions and supplies; the old mattresses and springs, as well as other bedding, are coming to pieces; the towels are going to rags; and Kitty had several days' illness last week, I suppose from poor feeding. We are nearly $15 in debt for groceries, and the poor old blind mare must be sold for lack of feed—thus throwing Frank's crop to be worked with the hoe. He still says that if I will be patient and hold on, he will make us a living. It sounds to me very much like, "Consider, old cow, consider." Being patient in these circumstances involves eight hours or so of steady supplication to Art at 24 cts. per specimen each day, besides the house and children. That is, when I can get orders. And no more orders are at hand.

Still he tries to make me happy. Today he found a beautiful thrush's nest in the hollow, the mother bird sitting, and having called me to look at it, begged me to stay and spend a pleasant afternoon where he was cutting wood in the thick woods. But I knew that I had no time—that henceforth the most I can do in each 24 hours will be all too little.

Judith has gone to stay with Mrs. Stanfiel. She came back today for clothes, and I explained to her that she will have to stay there whether she likes the place or not, since we cannot feed her at home. Jean has gone to Laura's, but only for a few days I suppose. Old Grandma Hatfield seems to have gone insane, and Laura at length left home refusing to return until the unendurable old woman was out of her house. So Ab took his mother to Erlanger. I am sorry for both women, but chiefly for Laura.

June 10, 1915

Lost the whole day again—got breakfast, and then as usual the children exasperated me till I gave up the attempt to paint. I wanted Jean to try for the nature-study prize in the November fair exhibit, but on investigating found that she has wasted all her available paint on paper dolls while I was in town. One or two things of this sort are the mere trifles Franks says they are, but piled up continually, day after day, they amount to a ghastly waste of energy. I feel sometimes that I am losing my mind.

But one thing promises relief. Mrs. Rains has promised to take Judith for the winter, to be company for her through the day and evening, and go to school. I am so glad. She is to go to Mrs. Rains the 1st of July, and I hope Mrs. Stanfiel will take Jean. Then maybe I can look after the two younger ones with less strain and expense.

Today we had mustard and peas from the garden—also radishes, onions, lettuce. But there is not a plenty of these, only a mess now and then.

June 19, 1915

At last the dawn of hope. First Mrs. Rains proposed to have Judith stay with her all winter and go to school. When I told Judith that she would have a dainty little bedroom all to herself, and a bath every day, she said it was too good to be true. Then yesterday evening Mrs. Graeme called on me and asked for Jean on the same terms—simply to stay with her at night and for company during the day. Of course I shall want both girls to make themselves useful and be worth their keep, though it was not so nominated in the bond.

White camellia blooms, large and fine as lilies, in thick moist woods. The red honeysuckle about gone.

June 20, 1915

Sunday. Mrs. Stanfiel sent for Judith to help her, and as she already had Jean, this left me all the work. But as I am glad for them to earn a little money I let them go. Very hot weather now, and I feel rather no-'count.

Mr. and Mrs. Graeme came this afternoon and asked to have Judith for their own. We could not consent to give her for adoption, but would be glad for her to stay with them this winter, in order to go to school.

Frank and I and Kitty walked through the moonlight to Mrs. Rawlins' to telephone. I called the Rains and Mrs. Stedman. They say it is terribly hot there.

June 30, 1915

Dock's wife found a whippoorwill's egg while huckleberrying—saw the bird fly up from her nest. Grandma says the bird turns the small or white end of her eggs to the sun,—east in the morning, west in the evening.

To Signal Point with Frank. A great deal of orange-colored butterfly weed in bloom; yellow gerardia opening; white lobelia. See a vireo & nest; and take a good long look at a Cuckoo.

See a little slatey-blue bird with dusky wings, perhaps tufted: song "twee o twee o tooley tooley tweet tweet twee," varied & indefinitely continued.

See a large bird—size perhaps of a thrush, dusky brown tail, crying "threep? Shreep?" through the trees. Yellow hammer?

Tonight Jim Guess, Dock, and the negro Pinson have brought fiddle, banjo & guitar, and are playing. A gang of boys came with them, John & Nanny [Frank's brother and his wife], and Tinte and her kids. They are playing under the trees. The lamp shines among the leafy boughs; lightning plays in the clouds. The ring and jangles of the music is like the very throb of hearts. Goodby Liza Jane; Choctaw Bill; Rubber Dolly; Jeff Davis; Big Jim!—John keeps asking for the Georgia Wagoner and this demand is taken as a huge joke. The negro, Pinson plays the guitar beautifully, undertoning the others' lead with rich bass full of runs & changing chords,—undertoning their talk with the rich good nature of his temperament. . . . Go on, boys! Greensleves—Tipperary—Old Main— Arkansas Traveler—"That there Man" and Hubey shoot craps in a patch of lamplight with 2 large whittled blacks; Ira, who is learning the banjo, leans and looks from a tree; tiny Tooley [nickname for a daughter of Dock Miles] dances like a killdee; small boys drop asleep in huddled rows along the porch. Huby slaps a bones accompaniment with sticks: "that there man"

dances "shoofly" as he throws his grotesque dice, grotesquely. The small
boys swing joyously, "pumping" to the lower boughs; Pinson's cigarette
glows against his bronze Mongolian features and blue work shirt; Ira and
"that there Man" two-step together. The silent lightnings flame behind the
cornfield. Tooby pipes up that nobody won't dance with her, and topples
over to sleep in her mother's lap.

Then voluntarily banjo & fiddle are laid aside, and Pinson plays solo
after solo to an all but breathless company—Make me Down a Pallet on
the Floor, with the oddest shivery quavers and quaint barbaric minors,
managing an accompaniment at the same time. After this John Henry,—
"whipping the steel" with a knife handle held under his third finger
with all the cleverness of a Chinaman with a chopstick—John Henry,
a strange negro air. Then curious adaptations remodeled from popular
music-hall tunes, given the color almost of native folk-song—Red Wing
intermingled with All Night Long! Pinson is easily the guest of honor; he
is begged to play again; the mountaineers revel in the barbaric warmth of
his attainments,—the dramatic color long denied them by severe living
conditions & a churchly rule. He rolls up the yellow whites of his eyes
sentimentally, like an Italian; but there is no sentiment in his talk or his
music—only good nature and a clear rippling speed and deftness. He talks
as he plays, almost too rapidly for the ear to follow at times, and again
with a slow, full, rich cadence. I have only a little of Jean's fudge to pass
the players; but Jean's temperament insists that the frugal cheer be passed
them, and the boys receive it in the spirit in which it is proffered. The party
ends pleasantly, Penson [sic] volunteering with his Mongolian grin to bring
his mandolin next time.

July 6, 1915

Had a frightful experience with the twins this morning. If Frank
had not helped me I don't know what might have occurred. Everything
is wrong: Judith has left her place and Mrs. Rains telephoned that she
cannot take either of the girls; we are out of money, deep in debt, and
living on corn bread and garden vegetables. The girls are more and more
lazy, ill-tempered, insolent and stubborn; they will not do anything but
quarrel. I have two stories ready to send out, but no immediate money in
sight anywhere.

We had a splendid rain the night of the 4th, after 24 hours of slow drizzle. It improved an already remarkable huckleberry crop. This afternoon Frank and I and the twins went picking, Kitty going off with Grandma after blackberries. So I had no sugar to cook the gallon we got, we sold them before we brought them home.

I found the nest of a thrush smaller than the wood thrush, in the crotch of an upright winter-huckleberry bush just within reach. Saw the mother bird plain—upright, with speckled breast; general color olive brown or dusky; the crest was raised in alarm and it seemed to me the chicks were different in color from the head & back. Eggs 4, beautiful blue-green. It was about 15 ft from a stream, in thick woods. The bird's note was different from the Wood thrush as she scolded me away from the place.

Jean pointed out to me this evening a Black throated Green Warbler in the trees by the porch.

I am all tired out, and still rather hungry.

July 11, 1915

Picked up a Red-eyed Vireo just out of the nest, perched on a ragweed where he had evidently spent the night. A bright little fellow.

To Signal Point, early in the morning before the hot sun quieted all bird movement. See a Phoebe by Elberfield's pond: 4 wood peewees on the hill. About 8 o'clock we stopped by the little woodland pool near Stanfiel's to watch a great deal of flitting to and fro. A pair of Long-billed March Wrens on a dead stump; a Downy Woodpecker; Chippies, one singing; a Phoebe; 2 Red-eyed Vireos; a Cardinal; a Cerulean Warbler; a Thrush; two Bluebirds on a fence—and a great many others not so much in evidence. Near the old Levi place a bird nearly as large as a Bluebird sitting on dead branch on tree top, preening his wings after the fashion of a Martin, & singing. Grayish—we could not see against the light; darker on head—perhaps a black cap? Beak glinting conspicuously in sun shine— must have been a brood, polished finch-like beak. The song was pleasing enough—6 or 8 pairs of notes, in a sequence, rapidly delivered. On the return trip we found him perched in same place.

New songs:

"zee-ee, chip-chip-chip-chip-chip-chip"—the first note a long keen whistle variations.

"Fee, fee, fee, la-la-la-la-la—" the latter notes in a descending run.

And after all this, that legal light and speaker Hon. Foster V. Brown [US Representative from Tennessee] argued to me that there are but few birds on the Point end of the mountain!

Mr. & Mrs. Lautermische & Margery came up in the their new Ford, spent the afternoon talking with us in the shade of the yard maples, and took Jean home with them for a week's visit, very happy.

Hear a nest of young Crows raising Cain over their dinner, some where down in the "gulf."

July 25, 1915

We have never had such a good garden. It supplies us with plenty to eat—beets, okra, fine large tomatoes, sugar corn, squash, potatoes, beans, sweet peppers, cabbage, rhubarb. Coming on are the cantaloupes and a few melons, pumpkins, field corn, sweet potatoes. One feels a loving interest and pride in the splendid stalks of corn standing lusty and tall, their use overshadows their beauty till it is rarely thought of—the grace and lustre of waving, whispering blades, the many changing, glinting greens, the soft dull crimson silks, and the finishing tassel in which goldfinches sing. And hidden away in a green sheath is the milk of the ear, swelling and growing richer and firmer every day.

The mysterious chemistry of vegetation is at work now day and night, that life may be sustained. Can see & smell it. Folks who sleep with open windows near river-bottom cornfields even hear it, as the growing stalk splits its sheathing blade. Under the warm ground the rich roots of beet and potato swell, storing the bounty of summer against leaner months of cold; tomatoes break the vines with their weight as they redden; glutinous & tender pods of okra must be cut every other day; string beans hang in clusters; the peanut pushes its "goober" pods underground to ripen; the crisp white heart of the cabbages crowds hard on the overlapping outer leaves; apples hang heavier and heavier, pulling their boughs lower every day; in plenty of places the juice of overripe burst plums has dripped through leaves and thorny twigs. I have put up 25 jars of fruit, mostly plums—without sugar; it is hard to get sugar for the table, with the bread and bit of fat meat and tea that we must needs buy. The berry crop is past good picking now, both huckleberries and blackberries. It has been a great growing year; now the chemistry of growth is to be supplemented by the secondary magic of cooking, and all these rough roots and greenery are transformed into smoking mounds of edible pearl and copper and crimson and gold.

Lettuce seeds are ripening at the top of their stalks, inviting the goldfinches. The Black-throated Green Warbler and the pair of Creeping Warblers continue to visit the yard trees, almost daily. A number of blue birds with darker wings & forked tail about the place; song like that heard on the S.P. road—what are they?

Yesterday Joe went to town and spent his berry money for gingham shirting—today he went home with his running mate, little Abb. Jean has been for two weeks visiting Margery Lautermische.

August 3, 1915

The excitement of the day was over a pair of Luna moths, unusually fresh and perfect, which I found this morning clinging together on a gourd vine. I made ten life size drawings in color and pen and ink, and Kitty made one too. We carried them to the porch, where one of them fell and fluttered about, and by and by the other flew away. Lovely, happy things, the very incarnation of the amorous bright morning! "Poor little things, their love-story's over," sighed Judith. I am so glad to have a complete watercolor of those broad, velvety, pale green fans with their tinted circles and tiny transparent slits.

My MS. is at last off to Houghton-Mifflin Co—with six decorative drawings.

Kitty is becoming wilder every day.

August 4, 1915

We all pitched in and washed nearly a barrel of clothes. Conditions here are becoming unbearable—the old folks crosser every day, never openly, but complaining of us to other people. I tried to get Mr. Kirk over the phone to rent his house, but could not. Frank and I were both in the tub when two ladies drove over from Shackleford's to ask me to postpone the lecture for a week, on account of a church meeting. Mrs. Raleigh bought one of the bird panels, for $1.

The red bird's second brood, we think, came off today.

August 7, 1915

Frank went to town. The Klaus girls called this evening. I am sick and tired out, and out of money. It is cook and clean, mend, wash and iron, every day, and in the intervals I must earn enough for our needs. Never an hour nor a cent for myself. I can't stand it. The place is overrun with Ault's chickens and John's and Dock's children, none of which I can keep out of the house. I am utterly exasperated, can endure no more; and yet we cannot get away without losing all the vegetables here.

A queer speckle-breast bird—I am sure, by the smacking note and jerking tail, it was a fledgling thrasher—perched in the yard.

August 9, 1915

Frank is registrar at the Fairmount polling booth, or whatever they call it, and gone all day till 10 or so at night. Any job is a godsend these times. I walked to the Top—tried to see Mrs. Atlee but she was gone—called on Mrs. & Judge Bachman, & sold a bird panel to Mrs. Mitchell for $1. Telephoned Kirk to try to rent his shack, and was disappointed. I don't know what we can do.

Saw quite a bunch of yellow-throated Vireos in some pines—also three Long billed March Wrens in a brush pile ducking in and out and warbling and chirping to each other.

August 14, 1915

Yesterday went to Fairmount with Frank and lectured at 8:00 P.M. in the old ramshackle schoolhouse. My 30 bird drawings made a fine showing, pinned up on the denim curtains; but there were not more than twenty present. The Aid Society who were to have advertised in the papers, provided lights, and cleaned the house, did absolutely nothing except bring a few smoky, smelly lamps and lanterns out of their kitchens.

We came home in the thick dark, at 11 o'clock—tired out. Got up tired this morning to see that Judith had left the whole house in disorder, for me to clean and ran away. I started to find her but seeing her at Hester Godsey's playing with the baby, I felt that it might be easier to clean the house myself than to cope with the situation, and turned back home. Joe helped me all day like a good fellow. We went over to the little 2-room shack in the woods and scrubbed it clean; I think I shall sleep and work there. It is inconveniently located but has a view and is neat and comfortable.

I want to write a book. How easy, now, if I had not this dreadful housework to contend with, to take my work over there and camp alone till it is finished! I could not get the owner of the shack over the phone, but mean to take a chance.

August 15, 1915

Today I make a dash for freedom, and am rewarded by such a day as I have not had for years—a long silent, solitary day. I simply turned my back on the housework; I love my family and love to work for them, but this has gone beyond sense & reason.

In the little house in the woods, which I shall call Bird's-Nest while I stay in it, I pinned up all my panels; laid my few sandwiches, with fresh green peppers & tomatoes from the garden on a shelf; put a pail of spring water in the cellar; placed a cushion and folded quilt to sit on and fell to work. All the quiet sunny hours were rich and lovely. Chickadee & field sparrows conversed in the woods, and there is a continuous sound of cowbells from the Hendricks farm below; and a long chirring of grasshoppers.

What a sense of blessed relief it gives me to know, in the fresh morning, that the day is before me without interruption!—and the isolation, the large silence round me, away from the miserable village of spiteful minds! Joe and Kitty came down to play and two of Laura's little girls, and they made a play house in the yard; but that was no disturbance. I draw; I write; I eat my lunch sitting in the doorway, looking at the magnificent sailing clouds and the distant hills; I take a nap on my quilt, and wake when I get rested; I sit and listen to the grasshoppers and watch the goldenrod heads swaying, and bees and butterflies flitting in the sun. A wonderful day; I hope for a whole autumn of days like it!

August 16, 1915

This morning made a few pencil sketches of a white wild lily in Lane's yard—spider-lily he calls it. Having been well cared for, this place is blooming more lavishly than in its native meadow—eight or nine flower stalks, maybe 20 white frail blooms crowning them. One of our rare and lovely wild flowers. It has been some days in bloom—possibly a week.

Saw a Chat in the elder bushes, gobbling the berries—too busy to notice me; sandwiching a worm or occasional bug, however. Why so silent after a vociferous April? Does he, after berries are ripe, conclude that this is a pretty fair world after all his scolding and fault finding?

To Summertown with Joe; gave a talk on birds at the house of Mrs. Williams. Very delightful time—$4.00 cleared. Called on Laura, and brought little Abb home with us.

First cardinal flower in bloom near Smith's road. I reached home tired out, but found Judith already arrived, and she got supper while I rested.

August 21, 1915

Frank went to town. After getting breakfast I remained abed until 9 or 10—when the Klaus girls and their nice little black-eyed brother came and brought a pretty box of cake and one of fudge, a bunch of old magazines, and a splendid bundle of clothes for the girls—notably a blue silk poplin which I will shorten for Judith, though it is rather richly elaborate for a young girl. We had a conversation about plays and books—I would have liked to talk with them about the dreadful lynching of Leo Frank a few nights ago, but was afraid we might all feel too strongly about it.[10] Then I showed my birds, and Adele bought $2.50 and I gave them each a small one. Rested all day, in spite of the upset house; bought groceries and read.

September 9, 1915

This is the first breathing-space I have had for weeks. Two weeks ago I came to town, and put up at the Willard House for working girls as before. I have had good luck ever since—more orders for decorative panels of birds than I can fill; invitations aplenty, which I turn down as graciously as may be; and quiet hours of steady work. Then Zerelda Rains writes that she has arranged with wealthy friends for Judith to go to school at Huntsville.[11] Also Miss Holly has sold a story for me—Youth's Companion—$4. for Turkey Luck. Lastly I have an engagement to lecture at the Normal Park school.

Dear little Jean is doing well with the Lautermisches. They are kind to her, and better still, quite firm; she is learning to be industrious and orderly. Judith at home is looking forward to going away. I have made her some underwear & a dress or two.

But oh, that unendurable slovenly, slack-twisted, dirty home! I have been up twice to look after the folks, and though I work all the time I am there trying to make things better, I can hardly stand it till time to leave. Poor Joe is almost sick from staying in swimming too long; he coughed a good deal, but he and Kitty are going to school. Frank has a sore place in his side, which troubles him constantly. He has sold his mule.

We shall soon be out of debt, if only none of them gets sick. It is only a question of my being able to keep work.

I have seen many interesting birds of late: a Prairie Warbler & a Nashville Warbler in a meadow at Riverview: a splendid Red-tailed Hawk sailed right across the car, going up the mountain the 7th, then Frank & I had a good look at a Red-headed Woodpecker. Here in town have heard a Goldfinch and a Cardinal and a Cuckoo called for several mornings in succession.

The W turns are banked with a tangle of bellflower & purple gerardia.[12]

September 15, 1915

After three days of hard work getting ready, blundering around here and there, forgetting all kinds of details, I have at last got Judith off on the train at 5 this morning.[13] She has been very sweet and looks lovely.

I had a hard trip up the Ridge Saturday. Thought I should never get there—but had a nice visit with the folks. Sunday we ate under the trees by the spring, and afterwards Frank and I walked in the hollow and got me a pot of different ferns, wood geranium, and heartleaf to bring down to draw. The rest of the day, and all of Monday, I put in sewing on Judith's clothes and packing her trunk.

A roommate has come in with us but she is at the Southern Express all day and I can sit and work alone as before.[14]

Mrs. Stedman called yesterday and had lunch with me, looked over my birds & bought one.

Yesterday evening had a post card photo taken of Judith. She took a lovely pose, but the photographer ruined the face at the last moment by directing her to smile—which spoiled the exquisite curve of the mouth. The hands however are fine.

six

A Brief Separation

After a break of several weeks, Emma resumed the journal. She was again separated from her family and living in the Frances Willard Home in Chattanooga. Frank had left the mountain as well and had a job in Hill City, an area today known as North Chattanooga. Emma had spent four weeks in hospital beginning on October 14, and had a hysterectomy. She would be back on Walden's Ridge in January 1916. The first news of the war that would become World War I reached the mountain, and Emma made note of it. She remained on Walden's Ridge, where her will to survive diminished. She was back in the rut of poverty and want. Later in the summer she began dabbling in Christian Science to deal with her tuberculosis, after moving back into the Pine Breeze Sanitarium. The family could not acquire the funds to have her admitted, so friends and admirers chipped in and purchased a tent so she could live on the grounds.

November 20, 1915

Frances Willard Home, Oak St.

Walked down to Market Street with Jean in the warm afternoon—the first time I have gone out, except for the ride in Dr. Ellis' auto to and from the hospital. I have been shut in for about six weeks. It has been a delightful experience in some ways; at least I have come out of it with a new hold on life and more appreciation of my kind than ever—I am proud to belong to a race that produces great surgeons like Dr. Ellis, and such lovable, intelligent nurses, and such hosts of helpful friends.

When we got back we found that Joe had come up to my room after his sweater which I had mended, in hope of seeing Jean but had gone. He left a curious note on my bed: "Jean—I have been and went. Joe."

Mrs. E. A. Wells sent me $3 which I paid on my hospital bill. The Writers' Club sent me $8. Mrs. Bacher came with Mrs. Stedman. Mrs. Ennis and another lady brought me some flowers from the Mission Ridge school children.

December 29, 1915

At John's house in Hill City—visiting Frank for the holidays, while Jean and Joe have gone to the mountain. We have had such a happy Christmas.

I have got well acquainted with Nanny. She has been very good to my boys, and I made her a purple velvet cap and scarf like my black one, for Xmas; she gave me a large crochet piece—a corset cover. I have sat by the fire, crocheting, resting up and feeding up, all week, and listening to the endless good humored banter and talk of a neighborly, slack-twisted, whole-hearted Southern Christmas.

Talk, talk, talk—all day and far into the night. Every one who comes to the door is welcome, whether he knocks or not. Children with firecrackers run in to ask for a coal of fire; children with nuts, for a darning needle or hairpin; children with dolls, for a scrap of cloth—"maa says she'd done made hern all up." There seems a boundless store of good-nature and open-handed friendliness to draw upon.

Except that Nanny; teased too far, fires now and again with a flash of jealousy that is half serious.

"What makes you think I went to the boat excursion?" he argues.

"The Lord tol' me," she declares sternly. "He ort to be keerful," protests John, the picture of aggrieved innocence.

Again, in an argument as to the pronunciation of a fruit he calls 'pananers,' she rounds on him: "Listen at him callin' me ign'ant; why, man, you was raised way back in the sticks, and never knowed geese went barefooted till I learnt ye!" All which delights him immensely.

She baked four huge cakes for Xmas, and a great number of pies. She says "'bout middleways of the street," and her good-natured drawl has nothing in common with the town in which she has lived half her life a typical valley girl.

She says, "When I was up there at yoren's house I set out on that porch and them black gnats bit me till my arms an' wrist-es was all whelped an' poned up till hit was a si-ight." All this in a monotone, a sing song drawl.

I am boarding at the Willards' and he is living at John's house till my strength comes back so I can keep house and bring the family together. Jean is with me in my room, Judith away at school, Kitty at Aunt Laura's, and Joe with his papa.

December 31, 1915

Two negroes with guitars have come in to play; both types, with narrow, close-wooled skulls and huge jaws, round small ears. They sit knee to knee, humped over their instruments, and play. First Frisco, a long jingle with odd close harmonies in the bass. Then John Henry: Old K.C.— whatever that is: & by request Casey Jones.

Pontine Nolan, the big bronze-colored, loud voiced one, whose left hand has been cut up in Loomis & Hart's rip-saws, is a singer. He says he would give fifteen thousand dollars if he could learn to play Almost Persuaded as he heard it once on a violin with piano to "second"; and he does play part of it, very softly and sweetly.

They change guitars and, like catching the whirl of a skipping-rope, the "second" picks up a new lead on "Old K.C." It is fine.

"What does K.C. Mean?" I inquire.

"Oh, hit's just a mixed-up song, lady—just a mixed-up ole song. Mostly a railroad song." He seems shy and awkward.

"You ketch pieces fo' records, lady?" And he directs black Snooze to "Play Dream." And adds, "I goin' to make you tell a story right afore all these good people." The strings begin to talk then.

"One o dese mornings and it ain't long,
You gon'to wake up and find you' baby gone.
Come here, honey, lemme tell you my sad dream,
Come here, honey, and drop down on your knees.

I dramp' one night I died in Arkansaw,
They shipped my body home to m' mother-in-law.
She refused it and thowed it in the sea,
So the fishes 'n' whales 'd make a fuss over me."

"How's that go? This box is a little bit high for my voice."—a velvety black voice it is. "I don't' believe I kin secon' that. Did I [illegible] second hit? Seems lak I did oncet on Market Street. Lawd, I don't remember what I used to do over there." And he sings "I got mine," which is from some old minstrel show.

"Now you play some, while I smoke." Some of the songs are fragments from minstrels. Here is Home Sweet Home in two-step time.

Casey Jones with quite a rag-time ring, and the big foot beating the floor, the big soft voice catching marked phrases and dying away. There is a great deal to the latter, in music & words, as these boys sing it; also "All Night Long," which is amazingly like a negro composition.

Pont tells about Georgia. "Never had no trouble wid nobody there myself. I like de money; dey pays off in gold. But haven' to git out 'n' go to wuk at three in de mornin'—and men comin' to wuk wid Winchesters on their shoulders, and dese here ahmatoor guns—Lawd! you'd start to wuk an' run on to dead people layin' by de railroad. One time we seen a big nice box 'n' went 'n' looked into hit, 'n' bress de holy Lamb there laid a boy as big as Lonny! Evy time I go round dere I hear about som-body bein' killed. I ain't got no business round dere." His big crooked hands are talking all this time. And Snooze interjects: "Dat de reason you lef' dar," and "Ain't you done forgot about dat yet?" There is a good deal of large, soft laughter and tossing to and fro over the guitars. "Tell you they won't wuk a black mule by a white 'n' down there."

Yet the white men say that Pont is not a good singer. One more he is obliging enough to give the words of—Stagalee, or Stackalee,[1] the story he says of a murder mix-up that arose "like now, if me 'n' Preacher Snooze here was to git run together about some girl we both liked the looks of pretty well. And I was to shoot Snooze."

"Yes, 'n' likely I was to shoot you," retorts Snooze.
Stackalee—
Stackalee 'fore I take this ride,
Ca'y me down on Cherry St.—I kiss my girl goodby,

Ain't dat a shame and a dirty shame,
Maggie's hung herself wid her own apron-string.
Took S— to the court house an' put him on de bench
Swore 'at he killed Bill Goliah in self defense.
Cry-me, all I got in this world done gone.
Maggie went thro the alley, she didn' go for fun,
Under her apron was a .44 smokeless gun,
Cry-me, all I got in this world done gone.
Maggie went down to the wine room, called for a glass o' beer,
Bartender, bartender, is my lovin' man been here?
Cry-me, all I got in this world done gone.
She went down to the wine-room, ordered a class o'gin,
Just about that time was when her man walked in—
("—and that," explains Pout, "is when business took place.")
"Tu'n me oveh, doctor, tu'n me oveh slow,
I been wounded in de side, killed wid a forty fo.'"
"All dat trouble about one Stetson hat" is the closing line of this song.
A variation of Penson's euphemism
:|| Make yo' babe a pallet on the flo,' ||: 3
Make it wha' the lamp is burnin' low—
:|| I got nobody to tell my trouble to ||: 3
What am I to do!
:|| I got no place to lay my weary head ||: 3
What am I to do!

At 9:15 the big mulatto says it is time to go home. "My little hen she's a-waitin' fo' me over at the stand: aw else she's went up to Mis' King's: I think they got a chick'n oveh there, in she sawta' likes chick'n."

Frank tells me that Pont's little wife pulled him out of the rollicking crowd at the stand by one ear the other day, and made him go home at her pleasure.

I wish we had a picture of Pont without the disfigurement of dirty shirt, white man's coat, and starched collar and tie. His broad face is not pleasing; but then he is so shy that you rarely see anything but the profile, which has a quaint fawn-like grace of heavy jaw, sloping forehead, flat nose and loose unmanageable smiling mouth filled with perfect teeth. "Much of a man" Frank calls him.

Illustrators make a mistake in representing primitive man as heavy, brutal and stupid.

January 6, 1916

Telephoned Frank about the witch hazel—his answer electrified me: said he wasn't a bit surprised, because last night was Old Xmas night and the old folks are looking for lots of things to be in bloom, and finding some too! I hadn't thought of the Twelfth Night legend,[2] but saw the chance of a story at once, and telephoned it to the News—also used it in my lecture at the Park Place school, where I met with an intelligent audience. I never spoke better, and the ladies were enthusiastic.

January 7, 1916

Started Jean to painting valentines and went to lunch with the Wheatleys. I believe they had forgotten I was coming, but we had a lovely visit for all that. They had the house full of hothouse flowers, but my twig of hazel found a place on account of its story. I had a set of little drawings for her birthday tomorrow, which I left, and I showed Mr. Wheatley my birds, and he showed me many engravings and photographs. There was a crab for dinner, and strawberries, and wine. We had a most interesting conversation about negro music. Then rode down with Katharine and Mr. W. in the auto. He lent me the MS. of his play, Ka—also a copy in German, suggesting that I follow the text and learn German in that way; but I haven't time.

January 12, 1916

Yesterday gave a talk at the Hemlock school on evergreens, and today at the City High. At both schools I cinched an engagement to lecture on birds in the near future. All tired out, having spent last night with Frank in Hill City instead of resting in my room, and then I packed my things all morning. To Signal Mt– in the evening, during a spring-like sudden storm of thunder and lightning and warm rain.

It was pitch dark and pouring when I arrived, so tired and heavily loaded I could scarcely get off the car. No supper—they had eaten some cheese and crackers and were nearly ready for bed. With Jean's help I soon had a nice oyster stew for a treat, and we had a pleasant evening. But why need they be so helpless!

Joe and Jean started school Monday. But Kitty has had such a cold that I did not send her.

January 19, 1916

Before it was fairly day, half a dozen Juncos were pecking at the breakfast of crumbs I had spread for them. Hear a Wren and bluebirds.

Kitty was very much disappointed over not getting to go to town as Frank had promised her, and still further disappointed over not getting a birthday cake because the store was out of eggs. Then she burnt her hand twice—the cold drives us all right on the stove. But her lovely disposition triumphed over mishap, and when I taught her to crochet, and Jean made some brown sugar candy in the evening, she said no more about it.

Joe came home in tears and had quite a spell, because his teacher is an ignorant, unreasonable, thick headed country girl whom he personally does not like. I helped him with his arithmetic, and discovered that he is being taught by the careless "add up this and multiply that, divide by the other and get the answer" method. He feels confused and angry, and no wonder. I must e'en make time to instruct him myself.

We have not had a square meal for days; it is simply too cold for me to stay in the kitchen. My digestion is all upset. I made another big rug today.

Nothing in order, nothing to work with, constant discomfort. I feel sick and exhausted. I can't stand much more of this.

January 28, 1916

Lectured at the Hemlock school and improved the opportunity to get better acquainted with Mrs. Betterton. Home, pretty badly tired. Saw from car yesterday two doves, and six or eight gray birds feeding in a field: kildees?—one buzzard sailing over the shoulder of the mountain, and a Bluedarter hawk. Frank reports three robins: Edith says the side of Lookout is alive with them suddenly. Frank saw a flock of wild geese go over, northwest.

February 1, 1916

Yesterday gave a talk on birds at the South St. Elmo school. Did not do well, on account of poor lighting which did not permit the children to see my birds. Came back in the rain, very tired and full of rheumatic pains.

This morning I telephoned to call off tomorrow's engagements, intending to rest. Had a lovely quiet day at home with Frank; the room is papered now and quite cozy. Baked Joe at his request a "whackin' big cake" with figs, dates, raisins & currants in it—an expensive & unusual luxury, but he is such a good boy.

We both jumped up from dinner to look at birds among the rocks and pines,—a flock of Juncos, two Wrens scolding vehemently, Titmice, and one Brown Creeper like a beautiful moth on the bark, velvety cream and brown.

From the car line yesterday saw a handsome Cooper's Hawk, several buzzards, and maybe 50 or more crows in a distant field.

Tonight the rain on the roof changes to the sharper hiss and rattle of sleet. Where is that Phoebe now? In a cleft of the rock?

February 14, 1916

Took some ladies of the Bird Club walking from the Inn to the Rainbow fall.[3] Mrs. Lodor, Mrs. Foster V. Brown, Mrs. Smith, Mrs. Dunbar Newell, Mrs. Wright, Mrs. Whittle, Mrs. Embrie, Mrs. Atcheson and her mother Mrs. Quintel. Saw only juncos and tufted titmice, a wren or two—but I showed them a number of nests and told them names of evergreen plants. We made a fire in shelter of a rock. I don't know how they enjoyed it. Very cold—masses of ice, and a slicing wind, moderating as the day rose.

Had lunch at the Inn with Mrs. Brown, then walked with Mrs. Brown & Smith home ward—Saw perhaps 50 bluebirds in a flock at the Inn; then a nuthatch, then a yellowhammer, then several redheads—one sitting right above the nesting hole.

I hope they were interested—they ought to have been.

Came home to find Frank with the house all nicely warmed and straightened. If the family continues to back me as it does now, we shall win out!

He reports seeing 6–8 Meadowlarks near Hill City trestle, Judge Bachman reports quite a large flock of Goldfinches near his place.

February 20, 1916

This morning warm, sunny and spring-like. After the children went to school Frank and I walked across the rocks. We set the glasses on a pair of bluebirds, male and female, eating berries from a sumach bush;

they were presently joined by another pair and then another till we counted twelve on that one bush. The males were all in bright nuptial plumage, a beautiful sight. The sky seemed full of bluebirds—must have been a hundred.

By following a trill, we got another look at the Pine Warbler. Then the song of "fee, fee, fee, la-la-lllla" lured us down a spring branch, but the singer was too shy for us. However, a beautiful blue bird took his bath in a pool before us, and then a robin walked the length of a dead log and stepped delicately down to drink.

We had a lovely day. Edith came to go to the Club meeting with me. She reports seeing a Catbird the other day, identified by several; also a White crowned Sparrow. We took the Club walking to Signal Point—about 20 ladies. Saw a few common birds. Edith stayed to supper.

February 28, 1916

Cold, frosty clear this morning; but we were too cold to look out even at six yellowhammers eating black gum berries. Kitty went to school with the others this morning. At 10 snow began to fall, wet and heavy, quickly whitening the ground. Many birds do not seem to mind it; juncos, chickadees, titmice and nuthatches in the white smother, and then the pine warbler, in the boughs over the porch, skipping from limb to limb and coming almost within arm's length, busily pecking.

Frank went to town after dinner to buy Jean's new shoes, as she was nearly barefoot. He fell on the street. Cars on all lines were blocked; the children waited half an hour or more in the cold before they could get home. I had a splendid supper, potatoes and peas, with a little bacon. How comfortable we all felt afterward, cozy and sleepy!

I finished the MS. of "A Mess of Greens" while alone this afternoon.[4] The lame, mangy pup who has taken up with us whined in the cold, and going to the door to feed him, I saw a delicate printed pattern of bird tracks on the porch, where the eaves' shelter made the snow thin, coming to the very door. I at once scattered fine crumbs of cornbread, and all evening the juncos kept coming, two or three at a time, others waiting their turn in the snowy boughs. A Carolina wren was among the logs, but would come no nearer.

Sleet at nightfall, crusting the snow.

March 7, 1916

Clear, with a rather sharp wind. Every wing a flit; the song sparrow sings. We think we saw the first Chipping Sparrow, feeding with the Juncos; but just as I got the glasses on him a Junco chased him into a brierpatch.

I feel so tired, and am not gaining weight or strength. We are down to $7 now, and nothing in sight; two months behind on the rent; Joe and Kitty and I all needing shoes. Oh I wish winter would break.

March 13, 1916

The first day of real spring warmth. Sunshine all day. At sunrise on the rocks see only two or three juncos, instead of the usual flocks; their place is taken by the chippies, whose trill is heard on every side. Tried to catch sight of a small bird that says, in comical haste, "che-wee, cheewee, why it's you!" with the emphasis on the last syllable, but he gave me the slip; then the mysterious little "come-here-to-me" alighted just over my head, so that it (chickadee) nearly broke my poor rheumatic neck to see. He is a little less than the Tufted Titmouse, and so swift and restless—never in the same tree for more than a few seconds; here, there & you over a wide scope of woods. Underside smooth gray. Another bird I think a wood pevee.

Sick and nervous all day—Near sunset on the rocks saw a pair of Song sparrows scratching like chickens, flirting up the dirt under the briers.

March 23, 1916

A lovely day for the Bird Club. I am in bed, but sent three nests for study. They insisted on paying me my next month's salary at $6 in advance—and Frank gave Edith $1 of it because she certainly deserved it.

We have Lee Brown helping with the housework, a very goodnatured honest girl, but sick, and encumbered with an illegitimate child—a jolly three year old girl. I paid her first week's wages today. Frank is working for Hardie's.

March 29, 1916

None of our winter birds seem to have left us yet. I saw a Brown Creeper and several Juncos. Cold and cloudy. I am out of bed and out of pain, but weak. I do not know how to deal with Jean. She seems possessed to lie, to filch small objects and sums of money, to refuse all helpfulness or kindness toward the family and to cut up her clothes. Concerning the latter I have adopted the plan of refusing to send them with the laundry until she takes better care of them. She positively refuses, so far, to wash them herself or even to keep them picked up from the floor. I do not know how it will end; I am completely out of heart with the unfeeling selfishness shown me by Frank and the two older girls. If it were possible I should take Joe and Kitty, who do seem to have some human softness about them, and a reasonable willingness to work, and go far away. Frank has been very kind since I became so ill; but I know by repeated experiences of this sort that as soon as I am able to work he will make things harder and harder on me until I must complain; then will come, instantly, the same loud storm of fury, the same long-driven persecution, the same brutal threats that put me in bed this time. Well, I am not afraid of being murdered; for such a release I would be thankful, nor of divorce; it would suit me admirably. Even a severe beating would not be so bad; if I could survive it, it might give me grounds for divorce. So I do not see that his threats, even when accompanied by a red face, tears, grinding of teeth, clenched fists, and growls, can weigh after all any heavier than his promises.

Only this I fear, that my whole life will be wasted, as the best of it has been in drudgery, pointless quarrels, and consequent illness. I want to get away, but [illegible] have strength and [illegible . . .]

April 6, 1916

Severe headache, chills and sweating last night, but this afternoon I surprised myself by accompanying Edith to the Bird Club. The sun shone, and we had things of interest between us, to show: dogwood, paw paw, redbud, May-apple, trillium, bloodroot, bell wort, meadow rue, the last shattering hepaticas, spring beauty, bluets, arbutus, several violets (Jean has found the long spur violet,) a lovely deep orange-yellow flower we couldn't name—we thought a St. John's-wort; and star wort, crucifer, cinquefoil, sorrel, butter cups, chickweed, service-berry, red & pale blue phlox, robin's plantain, anemones, wood betony, ground locust.

I had a wood thrush's nest, and she had the arched-over, side-entrance nest of a Bewick (?) wren, built in a rolled-up fold of their tent last summer. One dainty, freckled feather lay in it!

Most of these fashionable ladies know as much about study as a July rabbit; but all are delightfully kindly and interested. Mrs. Dobbs presided—she is uncommonly capable & likable. How strange, they recognize people readily and can't remember birds or plants. My chief difficulty is in distinguishing and remembering people.

Heard from the MacGowans about Bitter Herbs.[5] A plan begins to shape itself.

April 9, 1916

Sunday—couldn't get any of the children to Sunday school though. Clear and cold, a sharp wind blowing. Lonnie in a complete new suit came yesterday to week-end with Joe. If he has pellagra it is not visible; still I feel uneasy about the boys playing and sleeping together. If ever I can manage to get away from these Mileses—!

I feel exhausted with the cold, and lie abed most of the time.

Miss Brooke called & turned over to me $1.75 which was collected from the club.

The children brought in a branch of some unknown tree between bud & bloom with 4-parted bell-shaped corollas hanging. Leaves similar to tupelo. (Silverbell tree)

April 12, 1916

Sat in my big rocker out doors all day—tried to start rough-drafting my novel. Frank and I followed a bird whose song is "Chee, chee, chee, chechecheche," ending in allegretto—might be an Oven bird.

Walked this evening for the first time in six weeks. Saw a Hermit Thrush, exquisitely formed and colored, scratching the ground for his evening meal, flitting softly among the underbrush, and left him eating berries from a sumach bush. Then saw a Thrasher.

I am terribly anxious about affairs at home. Lee's wretched cooking is throwing all digestions out of order except Jean's; the waste is fearful too. Frank has not been at work for ten days or so, and I can earn nothing. Jean gets lazier and more insolent every day, and the grocery bill and the rent pile up and up, waiting for me to settle I suppose. I have done my best. God help!

April 17, 1916

Such a bad night last night—a little worrisome cough, then a sweat, which frightened Frank and distressed him out of reason, so that he kept me awake for hours; it was very like quarreling, but was not exactly.

This morning the first Redeyed Vireo came, and finding not trees in leaf, hunted his breakfast in our pines.

We sent to Miss Ricketson a box of wild flowers packed with wet moss & wrapped in oiled paper.

Frank & I walked to Mrs. Ellsworth's where he had some vines, etc. to set out. Saw a Raven—then a Hawk in still more graceful flight; and a pair of Redheads building, with muffled hammering, a home in an old bare pine that had already more than a dozen similar borings.

Mrs. Ellsworth's dog bit me painfully. I had a pleasant visit with her, but the walk was rather too much for me.

Received a note from Mrs. Patten inviting me for a week's visit. Better still, a lovely, loving letter from Judith so sweet & brave—offering to stay where she is all summer if it will help us.

April 20, 1916

Frank pulled up a handful of Wood Betony this morning, and there under the roots was a baby snake! He is working for Mrs. Ellsworth, setting out trees & plants. Club meeting this afternoon had but few present, probably on account of Holy Week & a Shakespeare celebration. Walked about with Edith afterward.

I believe really that tuberculosis is coming on me. This steady little cough, the night sweats, the day fevers, look like it. Well, I have long known I could not live; it might as well be this as other troubles.

April 23, 1916

Easter. Lay on a bunk on the back porch all day, while the children were gone to egg hunts—saw more birds than on any day yet. All the ordinary ones in a grand morning chorus. Then a Mountain Solitary Vireo. A pair of Summer Tanagers seem to be building in the hollow; the male came overhead and sang. Later a Scarlet Tanager. There was a lull, and I nearly went to sleep, when a group of Warblers arrived—several I think were Tennessee W. & a pair of Yellow throated Warblers, which I had not seen before. I had my glasses trained on these last, and things were getting exciting, when a Tufted Titmouse who had been investigating the porch and chairs for some time suddenly hopped up on my pillow. I "froze," of course, delighted, but what was my astonishment when he hopped to my head and began to pull my hair!

He worked away energetically, pecking and tugging and hopping about, now and then calling his mate—who came to the pine bough overhead but seemed suspicious. Twice he was frightened away, once by a child, and once because my scalp refused to bear such rough handling, and I took down my hair and threw it across the pillow. Both times he came back promptly, staying at least 10 minutes altogether.

When it was over I had to go in the house to do my hair, and found it considerably tangled.

First Black-throated Green Warbler and one unidentified.

April 24, 1916

Rain. We sent for Dr. Ellis but it was Dr. Johnson who called, and Frank went right to town and bought the medicine and some beefsteak, etc. We had been so frightened and discouraged, as I was weak and coughing hard, and unable to breathe. But after the Dr's visit he felt better.

We had been talking of the advisability of breaking up and letting me go to Pine Breeze. He said it was not intended for him to succeed at anything; that every time he got a start something gave way. Luck was against us.

I hate that word "intended." I struck the wall with my fist. "You never intended to do your part, that's all. Your bad luck is bad management, carelessness. If you had worked as hard as I have—"

And just then some one knocked at the door with a letter from the MacGowans enclosing $25 from Bitter Herbs!

My first thought was that this will give me time to get some stories ready, time to get well, to get a start. But when I counted up the rent and the grocery bill I saw that medicine and a little decent food was the most I can hope to get out of it for myself.

Anyway—we are relieved.

April 26, 1916

Still cold. Frank carried to Mrs. Ellsworth the maiden hair and jack-in-the-pulpit which Jean brought from the valley. She has a new fern too. John A. Patten is dead.[6]

I was in bed most of the day, with rheumatism. The Cleveland City Beautiful has written me to lecture for them on birds in June—but I'm hardly going to make it.[7]

April 30, 1916

Frank bought a hen with some of his week's wages, and we had a fine dinner. Then I had a nap, and on waking up saw a beautiful rose-breast in a tree near by.

Mrs. R.B. Cooke called on me to ask for some points for a speech she is to make—How the Clubwomen can help the women of the mountains.[8]

The Nuthatch still runs up and down the trees. There is an owl—or is it?—who sounds by night a sad tree-toad-like trill, more lonely, more richly mournful than any I ever heard, and shadowy with the mystery of the woods at night.

Such crafty, cruel robbers are these Blue jays! Habitually noisy, when out looking for birds' nests they become silent, flitting through the thickest growth like smoke. Parent birds are seeing them set up a distressful chipping, but are helpless before those murderous black pick axe beaks. I noticed one in the pines, looking for a chippy's nest, utter a series of notes that well imitated the chirp of parent birds to young: was this with a view to rousing the nestlings to answer, and so betray the whereabouts of the nests? No wonder the woods are silent for an hour after the passing of these Villains!

May 5, 1916

Mrs. R.B. Cooke and five ladies from different parts of the State, attending the Federation meeting in Chattanooga, came out to see me. I had helped her with an address on the women of these mountains; she had probably given me more credit than I deserved; and these ladies being interested in mountain school & settlement work found it worth while to come and talk to me. I received them in bed, on the back porch. We also talked birds; they looked at my few bird pictures that are left, and bought several.

Frank is still working every day on Mrs. Ellsworth's pergola, evergreens, & wild garden, and having a most gratifying success. His pay is as yet but little higher than that of a laborer, but that will be amended when people find out his skill and special knowledge in these things. He is very much interested, and I am so glad of the whole business—on the children's account and his and my own.

May 6, 1916

Three more clubwomen from Morristown called, looked at my things & talked, and after leaving sent me from the store a quite large basket of fruit, which gave us all a treat for dinner & me what bananas I need for a day or two.

These mountain folks are becoming a constant worriment—always sitting round with a batch of meddlesome children who spit on the floor & carry off things when not watched. I sent a great bunch out of the house today. They will not take a hint.

May 7, 1916

A long, lovely, quiet spring Sunday—heavenly. The Titmouse comes to the porch, and as we all instantly "freeze," makes himself one of the family circle, pulling first Jean's hair and then Lee's. See Bay breasted and Chestnut sided warblers, and a Cuckoo. But I am no longer able to keep a close watch on the birds.

I am dying. So far as I am concerned nothing could be pleasanter then to die quietly, here under the trees. I am not afraid of death—it seems to me a worth-while experience, on the yon side of which I shall learn all sorts of things I want to know. I believe that after the Change we shall find that the universal life of which we are a part is much more beautiful and full of significance than we can imagine here. How I shall want to come back and tell my darlings all about it!

"I have many things to tell you, but ye cannot bear them now." For pathos and profound significance that sentence stands, unmatched in all history. Jesus knew: knew all about the nature and progress of the future life; but he had not the terminology to explain—and those Galilean peasants would not have understood, nor, on that distressful night, have remembered ought of it. It would have been like trying to explain the Fourth Dimension to a child. So He used the words "place" and "Mansions" in default of any better. How could he have described to them a form of existence in which, being out of the body, relations with space and hence with time should be utterly different from these, perhaps cease?

I am well content. As for my anxiety about the children, that is another matter.

May 10, 1916

I am trying hard to put my affairs in order and do every thing possible to help my children. I looked over the clothes, laid out some to be made over for Jean; but I cannot make them. There are letters to write, and Frank keeps urging me to get them done, but it is a task. He works every day, and gets but little sleep at night. I am afraid he cannot stand it long.

May 13, 1916

My father and his wife and boy came from Graysville to see me. I was feeling better, and talked a good deal with poor Maggie, who is afraid for her life of the ill-natured scalawag. I counseled her to try making fun of him, as I always found that course to work best; but then I was never afraid of him. I fear nothing can help her much. I was sorry to see too, that he is much more severe and unreasonable with the boy than he ever dared be with me.

May 14, 1916

Dr. Wagner came this evening—thinks I may last a long time or, by going to Florida in winter, even get well. But I have been too often deceived by false hopes. I know it is true what he says, that I have not enough tuberculosis to make an end of me; people with worse lungs than mine get well every day. But what he does not know and Frank won't admit is that I have plenty to kill me without any tuberculosis.

However, if it makes Frank feel better to pay for a doctor and medicines and fruit and eggs and milk, I am content. He is taking such good care of me—never too tired, after his day's work, to bring me something to eat and make me comfortable for the night; and he sleeps on a straw pallet within arm's reach of me, on the back porch. Dear man.

May 20, 1916

I do wish Frank would not be so friendly and sociable with my father—today he came again. I was obliged to listen to the usual tales of his prowess in threatening and overriding people, and other uninteresting yarns. I feel sure it will end in trouble if he continues to visit here.

Mrs. Stansell & baby also made a visit—we tried to hire her to stay, but she seems to have promised her present employer. Every one is so kind—Mrs. Haskell sends me sweet milk every other day.

May 23, 1916

I shall be a long time dying at this rate; I lie quite comfortable except for some soreness in the left lung, and only grow weaker by degrees. Today I am on a cot in the house, as it still rains. Frank is imprisoned too, earning nothing, and expenses piling up every day.

So I have hit on the expedient of having Jean letter the covers that remain unfinished of my booklets of poems—poor booklets, buried in a rat-eaten old trunk since that winter when I thought they would be successful. Maybe they will still sell at 50 cts and bring in enough to get the girls off to school and pay the arrears of rent.

I do miss Edith Stroop dreadfully—can't think what has become of her, but probably she is not allowed to visit me anymore.

How strange it seems, looking out into the happy green woods, that these May days, slipping by one by one in sunshine and glad rain, are the last May days I shall probably see; and that when I no longer count them the May days will still go on, will bring the green shadow and bloom of spigelia and linaria by the path, and the cheery preaching of the vireo.

I regret only that I have not spent more time in merely appreciating the loveliness of this world!

I have no pain, only some soreness in the left lung; feel very tired; sitting up half an hour or writing a letter tires me out. I feel contented and somehow happy. Three years ago when I realized that all my endeavor must end thus, I was cruelly disappointed; but my grieving is all over now; I am content.

May 25, 1916

Today I felt very bad and restless, until evening—then peace and comfort. A present came for me, such a warm bath robe. Had a letter from

Grace MacG. Enclosing the other $25 for my Bitter Herbs ms. I suppose now we shall send for Judith to make her visit home, then I must say goodby [*sic*] to my girls forever, and send them back to school.

Oh, my little Flittermouse! if I could make any provision for her future! I can't bear to think of her lonely and neglected. Joe will be constantly with his father, and will get along all right; but Katharine will be neglected.

May 26, 1916

Very hot. The discomfort and restlessness of this disease overcame me today for the first time, so that Frank staid with me nearly all day. I do wish there were some sort of provision made for incurable consumptives; I ought not to remain here, hindering and endangering my folks.

Mrs. Ellsworth is sending the children a year of the Youth's Companion. Miss Ricketson sends me a package of writing materials and a light bathrobe, very convenient and comfortable. So much kindness—

It is God in his world, God's work, the expression of God's will.

May 29, 1916

Had company all day—first Miss Brooke—then my father, the same old wearisome braggart and chatterbox at 69 years.

Then this evening, Mrs. McGuffey whom we knew some twenty odd years ago. I was so glad to hear of Preacher McGuffey again—the one preacher I ever met in my life who really helped and taught me. I sent him a copy of my little booklet of poems.

May 30, 1916

What I take to be an enormously important invention is announced in the papers—a very cheap substitute for gasoline. I should like to be here to observe the effect of cheap power on the world. It should revolutionize industry and commerce.

Also the dream of harnessing the atomic energy is engaging the attention of this chemist & others. It will be an absorbing problem—I wish I could see it worked out.

Mrs. Blocher, the osteopath, gave me a fourth treatment today. These treatments are a considerable relief, lowering the fever and preventing night sweats.

June 3, 1916

Frank took Joe down and had him examined by a specialist. The boy has incipient tuberculosis and will have to take the first vacancy at Pine Breeze. The doctor says the chances are all in favor of his recovery, but that there is no certainty about the progress of the disease in a child.

Our "help" left this morning—which should materially reduce the cost of living, as the waste has been fearful. Jean is so far making a pretty good shift at keeping house. Should say that Lee left very unexpectedly to herself. Frank simply gave her her time, and she packed with a disappointed face.

June 7, 1916

Wednesday. Frank took Joe and Katharine to town, prepared Joe's clothes and outfit and sent him to Pine Breeze—where he is to stay till Sept. He did not want to go, poor dear boy. Frank also paid to have Kitty examined; she was pronounced as sound as a dollar.

Very sick all day.

June 22, 1916

No one at home now but Jean, who helps with the cooking and is very good, but will not keep anything neat or clean. Frank works as the mood strikes him, and Katharine is safest at Aunt Laura's where she has milk to drink.

People continue to send me gifts and to keep a little heaven of kindness round me. I am content and fairly comfortable, and my general condition is considerably better. Hard coughing, however, brings up blood.

Bird Club day—though I think the bird proposition has been dropped as too difficult; they walk in the woods, pick flowers, learn the common English names, and imagine they are studying botany, bless their hearts! Jean had Vaccaria last time, the cow-herb pink, new to me; and today a plant of the wild portulaca now in bloom.

Edith brought me a lovely new lily from Lookout Mt., not like the Red Wood Lily here though related—seems to be a southern variety of the Turk's-Cap, the Carolina lily. There are three crimson blooms nodding on the stalk, about half as large as the red Wood Lilies I have found here. In the jar with Queen Anne's Lace and Butterfly-weed they are lovely.

I suffer with the heat these days, but so does everybody else. From time to time heavy showers cool the air. Last night a tremendous storm. Jean stood a long time by the window in her night gown, while the house quivered to the thunder and the hail cracked on the roof, telling me from time to time what a fine spectacle it was. I am so thankful to find her appreciative of such things.

June 24, 1916

Judith came home from school last night, large and beautiful and warm and energetic—a splendid creature. Today she has been cooking—cocoanut cookies and a fine dinner.

I am surprised to find her so well clothed and cared for at the Mossop School. I don't see how they do it. More of the work of God—God expressing himself through the medium of His creatures, all more or less imperfectly, but always with a divine gladness. Surely He looks on this world and sees that it is good, new every morning!

June 25, 1916

My father's wife and boy came yesterday, stayed all night and until noon today. It is our belief that this poor good woman has tuberculosis almost as bad as I. She and the boy are both terrified silly, afraid for their lives of the old man. We are so sorry for her. I tried my best to put some spunk of independence into her; but she is an old fashioned woman, loving her martyrdom, on whom the "new thought" of courage and hope takes no hold at all.

The girls both liked their little uncle, and had a good time playing with him.

July 2, 1916

Arch deacon Claiborne very kindly offered to baptize the children after the Episcopal ceremony. As he is the only representative of any church that has taken any notice of my long illness, and as it would be an advantage to them and a comfort to Frank, I gladly agreed. He also proposed, with the Ellsworths, to put Jean in St. Mary's.[10] I have felt for some time that she ought by all means to be separated from the other children, so have agreed to this also. Of course we have had trouble about this, since all Frank's folks subscribe to the popular notion that 'Piscopals is just the same as Catholics. Good old Mr. Fowler, whom we had not seen since leaving Florida, even came this morning to plead with us, he having heard that we were sending Jean to a Catholic convent school. And Judith and Jean have had one spell of hysterics and contraries after another. Only Kitty mouse announced quietly that when the Bishop came she was going to stay home and be right good. Nobly she stuck to this decision, and was rewarded by Dr. Claiborne's telling her a jolly story of a rabbit that was chased by a fox and took refuge in his kitchen (this at Sewanee, on the country place) only to fall into the cat's claws. Kitty breathed easier on hearing of the rabbit's subsequent rescue & return to freedom, by the Bishop, and dimpled and smiled, and asked questions, and made a new friend as usual.

The ceremony was the first of almost any kind the children had ever seen. The bishop looked very impressive in his robes, in spite of the sweltering heat in the little room; the girls went through it well enough, and were glad at least to have Mrs. Stroop and Mrs. Ellsworth for godmothers. Mr. Ellsworth stood godfather, and made out the certificates. He also offered to place my notebooks in his vault. I don't know what good those notes will ever be, except for the children to read; but I can't rid myself of the persuasion that they are valuable and ought to be carefully preserved.

We all had a good sociable visit together, except Judith, who was too contrary to speak; I don't know why unless a recent visit to some of her father's folks. The bishop made himself at home and we all fell in love with him for a big, jolly good Irishman. Afterwards Jean, who was the difficulty we had feared all along, seemed entirely content and cheerful; but Judith sulked and had hysterics. Poor child—no doubt I should have felt the same at her age.

July 4, 1916

Old Mr. Fitzgerald sent us a fat hen. Mrs. Stansell cooked it and made pie—a regular good dinner, and we all ate so much. Afterwards all but Frank and me went to the barbecue.

Edith came by and told me that the thing is all decided at last—Jean is to go to St. Mary's, and Father Robertson of Trinity church will arrange for me to go to Pine Breeze. I am glad: it will relieve Frank, and I shall be able to help Joe—perhaps to write something on Tennessee birds.

July 5, 1916

Judith and Katharine left this morning for the Mossop school. I have made up my mind not to grieve at all over the separation, since it is the best practicable arrangement. Separation, like most other troubles, is not real.

And they too went cheerfully, quite delighted with the trip and their new clothes. Judith alone was still fussing and sulking because she had not got much pleasure out of her visit; but that is because she does not realize yet that this is the final break-up of the home. Poor Frank will undoubtedly grieve and suffer enough for all of us.

July 8, 1916

Jean left this morning in the steady rain,—the last fledgling quitting the nest. Frank took her to visit Mrs. Stroop and others until Monday, when she leaves for St. Mary's. She insisted on taking her favorite pot-plants wrapped in paper, and seemed quite happy.

Edith thoughtfully had her examined at St. Luke's clinic and pronounced O.K.

Rain all day. The News is out with 3 columns–padded of course with lengthy quotations. Fortunately they said very little that we would not have wished to be said.[11]

Mrs. Stansell is cooking for us, very nicely, and I think is regaining her health in spite of having the blues.

July 10, 1916

Steady rain all night, slackening toward noon. The valley and in fact the whole South is flooded. A postcard from Judith says that all is well and Kitty seems happy.

This was the time I had set for letting go—in fact I intended, so soon as the children were safely placed, to quit eating little by little, and so make an end of this long process. Not that I find it tedious, but I thought it would be best for Joe and Frank to have me out of the way. But I have got so much better of late, and Frank so much worse, that it upsets my plans. Frank is despairing and helpless, while in me the physical will to live has come up strong; I sleep and eat well. Perhaps I can help more by hanging on to write a little book on Tennessee birds. If I were sure of finding some money, I would know what to do.

July 14, 1916

Clear and hot again, to every body's delight. Frank said he felt better, and went to work for Mrs. Ellsworth. Mrs. Stansell also took a walk in the afternoon.

My appetite is so keen that I find it hard to limit myself to two small meals. But I feel it ought to be done—otherwise they might send me to lie at Pine Breeze indefinitely and leave Frank out to die, and then what would Joe do. The good Bishop says he will send Joe to St. Andrews.[12] That might be best. If I don't go to Pine Breeze I shall be simply making things harder on Frank. He is already too ill to support himself, me, and Mrs. Stansell. As for recovering completely or partially, as people urge me to do, I cannot bear to think of taking up that burden again.

This afternoon Mrs. Palmer came, and with her a Mrs. Mann of Idaho, and Mamma Reed of the orphanage. Mrs. Palmer has been through so much trouble, so much like mine: I am always so glad to see her though we never speak much about it. Mrs. Mann showed me a great pit on her arm where she had been healed of necrosis of the bone by faith alone. She and Mamma Reed urged and pleaded; but Mrs. Palmer knows better.

They bought some of my booklets and a drawing of a mocking bird, so that I am able to pay Mrs. Stansell and buy food. I felt so much better that I went in the kitchen and ate supper at the table.

Sometimes when I hear katydids or see the full moon or early dawn, I am grieved, because the days of my last summer are going by one by one. But this sadness is only a shadow. Sufficient unto eternity is the glory of the hour. Summer with all its rich loveliness is mine for a permanent possession; I am the summer; I am the fireflies and the moon, and the rain on the leaves, and the swamp orchids and black berries.

I listen to a thrush in the cool evening, after rain—probably the last song of the season. Perhaps I shall hear that song in another existence.

July 16, 1916

Mr. and Mrs. Ellsworth called. Mr. E. and Frank sat outside on the Company's crossties while Mrs. E. & I had a most interesting conversation in the house. She told me about St. Mary's and St. Andrews, then we talked of wild flowers and of the Gospel of Luke which I am now enjoying so much with a modern Commentary she lent me. Then of Joe—Dr. Claiborne wishes to take him to St. Andrews' as soon as he gets out of Pine Breeze. I know he needs good schooling; but I know too, and explained to her, that if all of us are taken away from Frank at once he will surely die. More as a joke than anything else I suggested that Frank would have to go to the St. A. neighborhood and get him a job; and was surprised when she said of course, that would solve the difficulty. Dr. Claiborne would speak to the Fathers of the Holy Cross and they would put Frank to work on the grounds. She then gave me $5 from the Writers' Club telling me that as Dr. C. had provided for Jean's tuition, this money was to provide for me personally. I threw up both hands crying: "What kind of people are you Episcopalians anyway!"

She said it wasn't the Episcopalians, it was Dr. Claiborne. But we talked a good while about their church and its ministry.

My fasting brought me nothing but a bad case of constipation that I had some trouble to correct, and seemed to be pulling down Frank's condition faster than mine, though he could hardly have guessed my purpose. Then the thought came to me, that I would not dare deprive another of food under like circumstances, for fear of shortening his rightful term of experience and learning on this earth in the flesh. In other words, what I am doing and thinking is wrong.

Having considered this for some 24 hours till I was sure, I went into the kitchen and ate with Frank, telling him that I want to get well and mean to try. And that I mean hereafter to live with natural enjoyment, taking a sufficiency of rest, keeping Sunday, and ceasing from worry and resentment.

Dear heart, he ate four baked potatoes as if he enjoyed them, got over his headache and quit moping.

In the evening he read a chapter of the miracles of healing, and we prayed: it was a prayer of joy and thanksgiving, and an appeal to be cured of this disease.

July 18, 1916

Sultry, showery, thunderous weather. I heard this morning that Mrs. Mann went to St. Mary's with Edith & Jean yesterday; that they will remain there most of the week and stop over at some place in Sequatchie on their way back. I am so glad on Edith's account as on Jean's—Edith will enjoy the trip and get our peculiar little genius bunched into the school just right.

Frank has not coughed much for several days now, and feels better all over, and is brighter. I put on my clothes today for the first time since about Easter. I feel quite well, though not strong, and still coughing some.

Lady Snowball sometimes forgets that her kittens were taken last week to live in the store, and bringing in a lizard or young rabbit which she has caught in the woods, calls them persistently through every doorway in the house.

This illustrates what is to my thinking one of the strongest and most significant facts of the animal creation,—the slightness of the individual recollection contrasted with the deep strength and infallibility of the race memory, ages old, which we call instinct. She cannot remember that her kittens are no longer here;—she remembers perfectly how her ancestors caught game in the jungles, countless generations ago, and she patterns her skill upon theirs.

For that part of her being which is a cat, our cat, "Lady Snowball," is weak and temporary, vanishing in a few years—in other words is not permanent or real. But that part which is not any special cat but the Cat, the graceful, cruel, skilful Cat of age-long habit and unbroken memory of other existences, is immortal.

To follow a little farther: The individual cat is not real; is but a temporary and more or less fragmentary and imperfect expression of the Cat-type, the ideal which exists in the universal mind. That type, that ideal is real and enduring.

Or is it? As Tennyson says, "a thousand types are gone."[13] But have not the lost types left something permanent in the structure of our world,— left whatever was best and fittest in themselves, whatever approximated or even tended toward the ultimate ideal at which nature was aiming? Could the Cat and its royal relatives have come into existence without a long line of ancestral types, bequeathing as they vanished each something of fitness for survival to the future consummate huntress?

And if in time to come the various hunting types shall likewise vanish, as blood-lust and terror disappear from the earth,—that the lion of the future may lie down with the lamb, when that which is perfect is come and that which expressed the cosmic ideal but in part shall be done away; then, in that far future, what of Snowball and her kind will remain?

Nothing real can ever be lost. In that day the generations will still value grace; and patience, persistence and skill may yet win food when a lack of them means failure; and mothers will call to their young in tones of love.

There you stand, little Lady Snowball, dimly white in the open doorway beneath a rainy moon, calling and calling in a soft trilling coo, proud of your successful hunting, glad to have found food for your darlings.

May I too contribute, in the course of a life-span but little longer or more important than yours, something as real, as unperishable, as impossible of extinction, a worthy of acceptance in the divine and universal plan!

July 25, 1916

Jean writes that she is "having a fine time" at St. Mary's; she has got the wish of her heart about dancing,—the Sisters let them have the Virginia reel and other old square dances quite often.

Frank seems pretty well and quite cheerful. He has a new job, nearer home.

Mrs. Stansell went picking huckleberries with that "hoss in the cane," Sally Brown, and was walked off her poor old legs. I hope it won't make her sick. She is positively the best help we ever had in the house.

July 31, 1916

Edith came this morning and we had a good visit, but I felt very selfish when I had to relinquish her to Mrs. Ellsworth.

Jean, the dear, writes that she is lonely and unhappy. I have hoped that loneliness would teach her forbearance toward others and turn her proud little heart toward her brother and sisters. She adds that when she feels bad she goes to work in Sister Martha's garden—So she has learnt a great lesson—my treasure, my darling. So much willing personal service she gave me this summer!—and then, one bad morning when I was all but crushed with pain and sorrow, lost control of myself and could only cry out loud—and Frank stood around and scolded, being dreadfully unsympathetic at such times—it was Jean who ran in her nightie, put her arms round me without a word and simply held me till I came to myself. Edith herself could hardly have done better. Oh, I am sure our little troublesome girl will make a great woman, rich in heart and mind.

Tonight arrives a box from her which some one must have brought down on the railroad—a box of flowers, fresh and sweet, quite different from those of this mountain. May the breath of Nature be always to her the comfort in loneliness and the rock of trust it has been to me.

August 3, 1916

My cough has changed for the worse—worries me down. I feel the need of some sustaining help, some one to talk to and lean on. Frank and Mrs. Stansell are like two children when I become really ill. Such visitors as still come are no help at all. O for intelligence and sympathy! The Presence of God is with me, but oh how I long for the presence of a good sensible woman. Edith's time is so limited, and there is no one else who comes.

We have again run short of money in mid-weeks. That Club of which the paper spoke, I wonder if there was nothing more to it? And for all I can make out, the plan to send me to Pine Breeze has fallen through entirely. Well, the children are taken care of, and that is all I could reasonably ask.

But I do wish the papers would hush talking about Chattanooga's appreciation of my pictures. At the price they paid for them! They may yet allow me to die in the poorhouse.

August 6, 1916

Sunday. Edith brought me two books from the library, as I am starving for something to read: one of Bennett's novels and Bergson's Creative Evaluation, which I find hard reading in places but feel sure is worth digging after. I feel sure that if one could know the true metaphysics of evolution—if one could once understand completely the mind or spirit part of a ground-squirrel, or an ovenbird, or even of a service-berry tree, one would have the secret of existence now and forever.

O how glad I was to see Edith even for a few minutes. I have been rather lonely and discouraged; and this has made Mrs. Stansell and Frank give down in health and spirits—dependent like children. But Frank finds today that he has gained several pounds—so I am not so anxious about him, although he still coughs. Might it not be a sympathetic cough? He went today to see Joe, and found him better contented and doing very well.

August 7, 1916

Frank has finished at Ellsworth's. He expected to begin work for Mrs. Foster V. Brown, who has been greatly excited over plans for a wild garden and some landscape work; but she has gone back on herself entirely—will have no wild garden, and has a gardener from town to do the rest. She is all talk, that woman. I should think these rich people would be ashamed to let me die unnoticed at their very doors. Their ignorance of the value of art is appalling.

Frank spent the day in a futile search for immediate work. The weather is still hot, with thunder-showers.

O the futility, the emptiness of these days! Would it not be better to make an end of them?

August 9, 1916

Yesterday afternoon Frank's old folks stopped by on their way home from John's house, and we prevailed on them to stay overnight. But this morning the old man was taken suddenly very ill, and it was late in the day before he felt able to ride home in the jitney-bus. He had just drawn his pension, and magnificently gave Frank two dollars.

Grandma told one of the best stories I ever heard—such a perfect thing that I don't care how much or little of it is true:

[Emblem drawn]

Sandy Smith was knowed by every body to be a truthful man. He told this tale for the plain fac's; and to the ind of his days he believed that he had seed and talked with Jesus Christ.

It happened at Caperton's Ferry (Jackson County, Alabama], in the last year o' the war. I've been to Caperton's Ferry; hit's near Vy-anner,— or is hit?—anyhow I recollect hit's just like Sandy said at the landin'; there's a bank, and a'ter you're up hit there's nary thing but a plain straight road, with a big high hedge o' these here thorny hedge bushes on each side. Not a stump nor a bush for a man to hide behind,—like Sandy said; <u>that</u> much I <u>know</u>.

They was about to cross the river, Sandy and his horse and the ferry men, when this here stranger came down and called on 'em to wait, he wanted to go across too. So he came aboard, and they shoved off, and he set by Sandy and talked with him. He was a tall, good-lookin' man, in the Federal uniform.

And Sandy Smith declared that all the sermants he had ever heared in the whole course of his life didn't do him so much good as the few words that stranger spoke a-comin' acrost the river.

He told him, for one thing, to be careful how he spoke to strangers; that for what he knew he might be speakin' to a Angel. Sandy said he never seed a sign o' wings on this one, though; ef he was a Angel he didn't have any wings.

He spoke about faith. Said faith is what men live by; if it wasn't for the faith that's in 'em they couldn't live . . .

Sandy said he never thought about that before. He thought he'd go with this man along the road, and hear more. His mind was completely took up with what he'd heared, and that made him slow a-makin' change with the ferry man. Oncet he looked round, and seed the stranger had left the boat and was climbin' the bank.

Well, he got his horse ashore and clim' the bank too, 'lowin' to overtake him shortly. But when he got on top the bank, the man wasn't there! No, sir; he wasn't nowhurs in sight!

And there wasn't a place he could a-got through in the hedge, 'cause Sandy hunted along it; and nary a bush nor stump that a man could git behind. He went back then to whurr he seed him last, and tried to track him. But he couldn't find no tracks. The feller hadn't made no tracks!

Sandy said that he never heared a man talk like that one before or since, and he blieved hit wasn't a man. But he said he couldn't a-been a Angel without any wings to fly with; and ef he wasn't Jesus Christ he didn't know what hit could a-been.

August 10, 1916

Frank had a day's work at Ellsworth's—and in the afternoon Mrs. Ellsworth made me a nice long call. I am greatly helped and cheered when the right kind of folks come in, but some ladies talk of nothing but symptoms and illnesses; while others insist on lending me the Christian Herald.

Bad news this evening: George Levi has at the last minute cut Frank out of the Thompson job, which he depended on. Why do all these women call themselves my friends? They have always beat me down to ridiculous and humiliating prices for my pictures; now they promise and promise my husband work, and then turn the job over to someone else. What sort of friendship is it that rolls in ease and plenty, and condemns me to want like this?

August 11, 1916

Frank is out of a job and out of heart; says he will never set another flower for anyone. On top of this comes the news that the wretched shack in which we live is to be forthwith torn down over our heads. I do not believe they will actually do this, but if they do I am going to have the occurrence thoroughly aired in the papers.

Frank talks of moving in with the old folks again. There is nowhere else we can go, I suppose. Lower depths and ever lower. I cannot submit further. And certainly Frank cannot make a living for himself and me and Mrs. Stansell. I must put an end to the situation.

I have found the way out, I think—the only dignified and helpful thing to do. Today I was alone, Mrs. Stansell having gone to town and Frank in search of work: and I dressed myself and went out on the ground.

Below the Dewees stable lot is a thicket of Stramonium. Its pale trumpets open in the evening and send forth a rank odor; they are moons of peace to me, white poppies of perpetual sleep. I managed to reach them without being seen, and gathered a quart of the green thorn-apples. Datura: narcotic poisonous, says the botany. A clear and certain relief.

Still I put if off. Joe is to come home for a day's visit Wednesday; I do want to see my little boy again. Oh! I do shrink from the last parting from these my darlings. But life has become impossible; and anyway it is only the difference of a few months.

How my head swung and rang, and how the thorn-apples stung my thumbs and fingers! I thought I should fall among the broad, pointed leaves. But I got back safely, and put the jimpson apples in my trunk. Perhaps I shall never set foot on the ground again.

August 14, 1916

We heard this morning that Mrs. Stansell got hurt in an auto wreck, and had about decided that she would not be back for a long time, when she walked in. Frank had bought a catfish with part of his last dollar, and we had a good dinner. I am become a mere animated stomach; nothing to read, think or talk about. Here I am, in transit between the wonderful past and the unimaginable future, anxious about next day's meals!

Well, it will soon be over.

But what if the stuff does not work! I have no idea what quantity will be sufficient. Kipling's description of this plant as "the readiest poison in all India" proves nothing: I know how unreliable a fiction-monger's statements are apt to be. Or worse, what if it were to make me frightfully ill, or cause death by agony and convulsions!

I will have to risk it. Narcotic, the botany says. Few things in this world are trustworthy, but the conclusions of scientists are probably the soundest things we despised, defeated, deceived women have to go by. Narcotic sounds good; I shall lie down and go to sleep, and never wake.

So Frank will be free, and can bring Joe out of Pine Breeze and make a home for him. And I shall not have to dread the cold weather, nor hunger and neglect. I shall be free from hope and fear and disappointment, out of humiliations and anxieties. Narcotic sounds good!

I bit into one of the thorn-apples out of curiosity. So tasteless was it that it does not seem possible it can be poisonous. If indeed such a convenient and simple "euphasia" for earth's miseries grows at every barn-door, it is strange that so many should put themselves to painful and troublesome deaths each year,—by drowning, by drugs, by hanging, by casting themselves from heights. Yes, considering people's ignorance and appalling heedlessness of the facts of nature, it is not incredible.

My hope is for a perfectly simple and quiet end, which will pass as heart failure, and not get into the newspapers.

August 15, 1916

I am counting the hours until Joe comes tomorrow. But Mrs. Stansell says it is a common practice at Pine Breeze to promise homesick children a visit home and then postpone it indefinitely.

I had another revelation of human perfidy and callousness today. Mrs. S. went again to see Mrs. Guild about recovering her two daughters, and learned that, after promising to telephone at once and let her know as soon as possible, Mrs. Guild had almost immediately gone West. It was a shock to me—I don't know what it was to the poor mother. She does not say much, but seems sick and disheartened.

Unless it is her man's pleasure to help her raise the children, a mother is punished worse than any criminal. If they are illegitimate they are at least her own, but every hand is against her. If legitimate but deserted by her husband, she has them to support but does not have him to contend with. If he simply hangs round he hampers her every move and alienates possible helpers. If she by good luck gets enough law on her side for a divorce, she has herself and the children to support under the world's scorn of a divorced woman. Men are fond of saying that the divorce laws are all on the side of the woman. So they are on the side of the idle, fruitless wives of the rich. The mother, mother of a poor man's family, in the absence of relatives or money to help her, had better kill herself and her children at once.

For every child I have brought into the world I have been worse punished than if I had committed murder. And now I have nothing else but to lie here and remember it all. I cannot endure it. Heaven send the Datura is truly narcotic! I have lost my work, I have lost my life, I have lost even my children; there is nothing else left me.

August 16, 1916

We watched eagerly every car that came up, until mid-afternoon; then we knew that Joe was not coming, and fell into a slough of despond. Frank has let some one else beat him to the Wallace job, as I supposed he would, and is feeling as near desperate as he ever will over the mere matter of support. He said he must make some shift within the next few days.

Well, I thought, you will be relieved of my support and care tonight. For I meant to make the Stramonium ready during the afternoon, and drink it tonight. But he and Mrs. Stansell both stuck to the house like burrs; I could not get five minutes alone in which to prepare the poison.

Then came Mrs. Labar, a Christian Science healer, to see me—a small-featured, pleasant woman with a wealth of beautiful red hair. She wears spectacles and has evidently had a great deal of dental work done, but I was in no mood to be critical or argumentative. To save time I told her at once that I believe the teaching that Spirit is all and nothing else is real, but I don't seem to know how to live my beliefs. I told her plainly that I am not afraid of death, that my trouble is I don't want to live. I don't know that she got my drift or that I got hers; but oh, how beautifully she reads the Bible! She is not highly educated except in knowing how to live. I am educated and cultivated all around her; I can think rings around her; but she made clear to me things I have never realized,—the dangers of self-will, and of wanting what we do not need, and of resentment.

I was deeply interested of course, and could see that Frank was also—for I asked that he be allowed to hear the teaching. She left us a copy of Science & Health, after giving me a short treatment.

I have decided to wait a few days, if only to help Frank get started in the new teaching. They can help him whether I am past help or not.

August 17, 1916

This morning after breakfast I found myself feeling quite comfortable, and remembering the healer's advice to do whatever I felt like doing without uneasiness, I got out of bed and put on my clothes, saying that I would go down hill to the closet and would not be hurt. I did so, and while I was quite tired on my return, a short nap put that all right, and I felt quite well all day. Coughed, but without the usual fatigue—ate heartily and went freely about the house. Found to my delight that I could whistle. Of course it was the Spring Song.

It sounds rather foolish but—One of the distresses I wanted to be delivered from was the everlasting fear of want. Mrs. Labar talked a long time with me about that. Be content with enough for today's need, was one of her counsels, and accept whatever is given in love—because it comes from God.

And today, lo, Mina and Lottie Dewees, and Mary Purvis Andrews, came in and bought three bird pictures, and Mina brought me some fruit and milk, and promised that I should have some out of the store every day!

Wait a few days, says Frank sensibly, and see. I feel that way too. I have been reading Science and Health, and getting a worse and worse opinion of Mrs. Eddy's intelligence and literary ability.[14] But that does not affect the main proposition, of course; much of the Bible is very poor literature, very lamely expressed—although of course some of it is sublime poetry, and the ring of Psalms and Job and Isaiah has haunted me all my life.

I don't know that Mrs. Eddy's story of the father who rendered his baby amphibious (p. 556) is any worse than Jonah swallowing the whale—(or the whale that swallowed Jonah, was it? One is just as credible and valuable a version as the other.)

And probably the original MSS of Scripture contained grammatical errors too, and even such careless expressions as "Matter the antipode of Spirit." (p. 72.) Even if the story be true that Mrs. Eddy did not write the book, that it is the work of Phineas Quimby,[15] that does not affect the power of spirit to heal body and soul. I've made such a hash of my life that I am ready to take advice from any one who has made a success of it.

August 22, 1916

Joe ran away and came to see us. Oh, we were all so happy. He was keen for a little something extra to eat, and I was so glad to receive two nice little baskets of fruit from friends. My self I am not so well—had a fever, and Frank made my bed under the trees. Had a delightful day.

This afternoon Mrs. Labar came, and I was in the midst of her lesson when Edith arrived with the news that a tent has been bought and arrangements made for me to go to Pine Breeze! I supposed that project had fallen through, and was so taken aback that I did not know what to say or think. Frank and I consulted Mrs. Labar when Edith had gone, and she advised us to just follow whatever leading came up and make no plans. She warned me though that if I took any medicine it would at once break off her treatment; this, as secrecy is a necessary feature of the healing, puts me in a quandary. However, she says it will arrange itself—by God's will.

I felt better then, and we ate a happy little supper.

August 27, 1916

Sunday. Mrs. Labar came this afternoon, and again said that she will come to see me at Pine Breeze, if I must go, but that I am not to take any medicine. She told me many helpful things this time: when one has learnt them they seem almost too simple to repeat.

I told her how, although the cough has ceased to hurt me, it still gets no better. That I know it to be a false belief, and keep on saying so, but without apparent result.

"It will leave you; it is not true," she said. And by and by when I coughed she commanded quickly, with a gesture, "Don't do that! It's not real—has no power over you. Don't give in to it."

Frank's ministrations to me sometimes of late remind me of my mother, so tender a solicitude, so luxurious a regard for my comfort do they show. Much of his awkwardness and carelessness has been over come. Surely a special blessing awaits him in God's time for this.

September 1, 1916

I was enjoying a rest on the porch, and rejoicing in returning health and happiness, when word came that Father R. and Edith would come for me at 2:30. Poor Frank was rather disappointed and to tell the truth so was I. But I am sure it is God's way of providing for me, through His good people who do His will, and I know it will be all right.

The ride down, in Father Robertson's auto, did not even tire me; even my heart felt no effect. But when he had blessed the tent and gone, the nurse—Miss Henry, whom I knew at West Ellis—put me to bed.

Joe ran in for a pow wow, fat, noisy and cheerful. Said he was put to bed three days for running away.

The tent is larger and nicer than I expected, well put up—has a fly with porch extension, and is floored and screened to a T. The mosquitoes hang outside near the cot, singing Fe-fi-fo-fum, not six inches from my nose.

The view is heavenly: I shall live upon it. How good and lovely everything and everybody is!

September 3, 1916

Sunday. Such an untoward occurrence this morning—I don't believe I shall ever learn to mind the rules or conciliate Miss Plewes. There was a strong, cool wind in the night, and I had Mrs. S. let down the tent curtains. This made things quite cosy and more private, and we were ever so pleased. After breakfast the patients in the nearest cottage were studying their sunday-school [sic] quarterly and having a dreadful time with Antioch and Iconium, when one came to ask me about it. I thought I saw a chance to start something interesting, so invited the whole bunch inside, saying that I would pronounce the words and help find Paul's travels on the map. We were all enjoying it when one of the nurses came down the walk, looked at us and returned. Almost immediately we heard the sharp tapping of Miss Plewes' heels approaching—a military sort of sound.

"That hateful Miss—! She's told," somebody exclaimed, and several hurried out; the rest stood their ground. I had no idea it was anything serious, till Miss P. began to speak; then I was so taken aback that I didn't know what to say.

Well! In spite of all the C.S. I could summon, I chilled: ran up a fever; forced myself to eat something at dinner, which promptly soured on my stomach and gave me a real old-fashioned colic—upset my splendid digestion!

But Mrs. Labar came as she had promised, and gave me a treatment. I then rested well until Miss P. came bringing some visitors to look at the tent—stupid, kindly people, influential here. They at once began to urge me to keep my tent flaps rolled up. I jumped to the conclusion that she had recounted the occurrence of the morning to them; and was so upset that supper was impossible.

Fortunately Miss Plewes came down again before bedtime, and taking the bull by the horns (heart pounding, and sharp pains flashing through my back at first) I frankly and good-naturedly asked her to be careful what she says about me to outsiders. She got the point at once, but denied having said anything or even having given the impression that I was an unruly patient. "That word unruly," I said, "might be taken to mean something very different from the sense in which you used it, and you know I'm one of these people that folks just like to talk about." I assured her that I wish to keep all the rules, and she graciously allowed that I haven't broken any; so the matter was most amicably adjusted.

September 6, 1916

What good thoughts God puts into the hearts that are willing to do His will. Received a check in the mail from Grace MacGowan, for $25 (which they don't owe me) in payment for Bitter Herbs. Also, from a perfect stranger in Boston, a letter about Christian Science and promise to send me some book—I suppose Science and Health. I shall be so glad to have a copy of my own.

The weather is perfect and birds plentiful. It is very pleasant except for black gnats.

September 8, 1916

Judith and Jean are fourteen today, bless them. I sent Judith a dollar to spend for herself and Kitty, and sent Jean a small box of chocolates, some days since. Weighed in today at 80 ¾ lbs.

September 11, 1916

Oh dreadful—Mrs. Plewes caught Frank in the act of depositing the things in my tent and—subjected him to a sharp public reproof. He merely repeated that he wouldn't do it again.

"Of course you won't do it again," she retorted in her sharpest tones. "One more time and Mrs. Miles is sent off the hill." I should be glad to go, and expected to hear him say so, but lifting his hat to her, and bidding me write to him, he went away.

I expected her to come at once to the tent, but she made the mistake of allowing me time to think, and when she came in the evening I was ready for her. For the first time I refused to be humiliated and cast down. She opened the attack: "What are we going to do about this?" I was about to reply, "Whatever the regulations provide," thus calling the bluff about sending me home; then I thought I had better not force this issue without consulting Edith, and was silent. Then the next question, "Didn't you clearly understand when you came here that Mr. Miles was to come only on visiting days?" gave me the opening I wanted.

"I had also the understanding that I was entitled to Mrs. Stansell's services when you were through with her." This shifted the ground of argument completely and took her aback. I reminded her that she had refused, time after time last week, to allow Mrs. Stansell to go down to the Jew store and buy for me this basket of necessaries.

We finally called it a draw, and she left the tent conceding several minor points and promising Mrs. S. an afternoon off each week.

I got only one degree extra temperature out of it—but I'm not at all sure that this hill is wide enough to hold me and Miss Plewes.

September 15, 1916

Dr. S. came on his round, and we talked whippoorwills—but I did not even ask to get out of bed. Good letters from the twins, but the best of all from my dear man; he is resolved to pass quite over Monday's disturbance and advises me to keep cool too. I am not sure sometimes but his goodness entitles him to be classed as a great man. He is doing something he has long wanted to do, making a wild garden below Grandpap's spring.

There is in truth something militant about unconquerable patience— the meek, which without blood or sweat inherit all.

I have at last finished the flower picture, but badly, on account of having no Cadmiums.

September 19, 1916

My father's wife and the boy came all the way from Graysville— ran away, they said—and their tears and prayers softened the heart of Miss Plewes, although this is not visitors' day. Poor Maggie is in great trouble—wants to bring suit against my father on the grounds of insanity. I understand she doesn't want divorce, but protection. She says he is beating the boy nearly to death. I promised to help her all I can, for my mother went through this same with him and I know something about it.

But such news has run up my pulse and temperature again. I do wish I could keep from getting excited over every little thing. I know it is wrong, and that it tempts the kindliest disposition into unpremeditated cruelties, someway; the best of husbands gets, for such a wife, a feeling such as one has for a kitten that is always being stepped on.

However, I'm well enough to paint a while during the warm part of the afternoon.

September 29, 1916

Much better, as Mrs. Labar promised. But every one on the hill is almost weeping with the cold. No fire is allowed, not even a hot brick. I was too cold to sleep after midnight, but today by dint of piling on all the warm clothes I brought, and staying close in bed, became warm enough to sleep.

A letter from Roy says that his father draws $15 more per month as janitor than he did as teacher—a peculiar feature of American civilization, but a good factor in the situation there I should hope.

Mother's Magazine accepts "A Mess of Greens" and asks for more. Glory! But how do the illustrations in this cold tent?

October 6, 1916

Weighed—gained a pound this week. Beautiful warm weather. There is a Pileated Woodpecker haunting the hill; I have heard, but have not seen it. Rec'd $50 for Mess of Greens.

October 12, 1916

Thursday—visitors. Mrs. Labar gave me a most delightful and helpful talk. Then Edith came with Mrs. Stedman—brought me grapes and N.Y. papers. Then Father Robertson with Mrs. Ellsworth and a young Miss Everett. I was much taken aback when Father R. gave me a number of Episcopalian books and tracts to read, with a view, said he, of preparing me for confirmation! I thought the occasion unsuitable for declaring my stand; will try to explain when I can see him alone. I made up my mind twenty-five years ago to join no churches.

October 25, 1916

Feeling worse all this week; sore inside, ache and feel tired out; high fevers, hard chill yesterday, feel discouraged and exhausted and homesick, but have no home to go to. But it makes me happy to think of my splendid children. Judith is doing well—Jean's letters show a great development. Kitty is as always, a joy to everybody. And today I had occasion to reprove Joe severely for his great fault, talking too much and showing off. He took it so meekly and sweetly that I felt prouder of him than ever; and he did something I never saw a child do before; he took my hand, and held it all the time I was scolding him, his beautiful little face bowed down, flushed and shamed. Then he said "Yes 'm," and that was all. The dear!

October 30, 1916

A flock of small birds feeding on weed seeds and perching in the trees this afternoon. I thought they were Goldfinches, of which there are some about, till I saw their streaked breasts. They are almost certainly Pine Siskins, come south for the winter. Many Myrtle Warblers yesterday.

The mail brings an elaborate drawing from Jean. Her letter says she has "staled on it and don't know what to do," and when I see the work she has put on architectural detail I don't wonder. Thank heaven, she has really worked for once in her life; and at that, she has done surprisingly well. I will help and encourage her with it.

Finished the rough-draft of a little story for Mother's Magazine. It is ridiculous the way things drag; I have been two months on this. Such a heavy weight of laziness holds me most all the time.

All the patients who are able, and some who are really not, slip out covered with sheets and run round the hill this evening—blowing on a piece of rubber tubing for a horn, ringing bells, and cutting shines of all sorts. Finally Miss P. makes the rounds and tried to be very severe. For once nobody is scared or offended.

November 3, 1916

Meadowlarks every morning, whistling about. The big chestnut tree down the hill is a rendezvous for flocks of birds; its dead top is a perch and a lookout to all.

One of the men in the cottage with Joe has a pet flying squirrel. I had no idea these elfin creatures of the night could be tamed, Joe brought it to the tent for me to see. It sat on my hand while I examined all its exquisite details—the bright, full, black eyes, the mouse-like ears, the paws, the long sensitive whiskers, the loose fold of whitish fur, the silky band of the tail—then it suddenly made an investigation of its own, of all my fingers; scuttled down my wrist, hunted out the deepest fold of the blankets for a nest, and curled up to sleep with its tail bushed over its nose.

Mrs. Labar came this afternoon. I told her of my uneasiness about paying her; because Dr. Brooks, Dr. O'Neal and even Dr. Bogart are still unpaid. But she would not hear of it.

This week was the best yet. I gained a pound and three quarters, and feel strong. All the symptoms keep recurring by turns; if the chills disappear I sweat a little for three or four nights; if the sweats cease I have pain and soreness; when that is gone I cough for a day or two; or the fever runs up, and if it goes down my heart goes to jumping and aching. But none of these things frighten me any more; I do not talk of them or think much of them. They are not true: I think of them only as of bad dreams, quickly forgotten.

November 12, 1916

Warm rain, with fog. I expected no one but my man; he came in good health and spirits, and we had a delightful visit together. He says he sleeps well, lying down in a sense of security and confidence, instead of being afraid of his heart as formerly; and he walked up and down the tent, reading aloud the Shepherd Psalm and the 91st Psalm, and then I read some very helpful paragraphs from the C. S. literature, of which Miss Plewes just sent me a bundle; and we were so happy and peaceful, enveloped in the fog. I asked for nothing better, but something better was added. Two visitors—Miss Lucy Montague brought Miss Donnelly [Mossop principal], who is in town on a business trip. Of all dear people! She talked to me of Judith's future. It seems that Mrs. Almond has guaranteed the financial end of her schooling; and Miss D. wishes to try her out as a librarian. This sounds to me just right for my splendid girl; a librarian reaches and helps so many people. And Frank seemed well pleased with it too. I told her I feel sure that whatever she does will be right. She spoke well of Katharine, who is contented and sweet as always. I feel almost as if I had seen both my girls.

November 22, 1916

I am uplifted and rejoiced to find that the cold does not hurt me. Last week I gained two pounds, and with blankets and hot bricks kept comfortable.

But this week I am worse than for a long time. Father Robertson came, very unexpectedly, and Mrs. Claiborne with him. In the gentlest and kindest way he asked me to prepare for my first communion. I was dreadfully alarmed to find what I had let myself in for, and put myself in a false position. I made no objection to Joe's learning the Catechism, knowing that the boy has too much sense to swallow it whole; but in some distress I told the father that I can't possibly join a church. He would not let me explain why, which has left matters rather worse than before, and I have run a tremendous temperature over it—102 3/5 F. I want so much to do just right; I want to know all I can possibly learn of God in his [*sic*] world and of Jesus Christ His Son: but so long as churches teach that the world was made in six days and that God sends sickness, death, and hell fire on all who fail in this short span to measure up to a certain standard, how can I join a church without surrendering my God-given reason? Then, St. Paul and the position of women!

Let the tangle solve itself as God directs. I can think of something else—rejoice in our noble, beautiful children. Jean sends some holly cards, the best she has ever done, which ought to sell easily. My little Skondinoggin, how near and dear to me she is!

November 26, 1916

Frank & I had a good visit alone this P.M. I showed him how I had burned a great hole in my best blankets with the patent foot warmer they sent me—and I read him Fred's verses. They are something like Dunbar's but while very comic, they have no fine poetic feeling. I should be delighted to dig up a new Paul Lawrence [sic] Dunbar,[16] especially just now, when Dixon's moving picture, Birth of a Nation, has inflamed all the passions and prejudices in the South to the danger point.[17]

The Times has a nice notice about my story, A Mess of Greens. I dare say Mrs. Lauderbach put it in.

November 27, 1916

Asked Fred what the negroes think of Dixon. His good-natured face changed; he stood for a moment balancing the nourishment tray before replying. "We don't talk much about him. We don't read his books, nor go to see his plays."

I laughed at his caution. "Not much of that opinion got by the censor, did it?"

"We—we don't think much of him, Mis' Miles."

"Never mind. What I think about Dixon wouldn't be fit to print."

He then suggested writing a New Year's toast "along that line." I said the January magazines are probably made up long since. He thought of the Saturday Eve. Post, being a weekly. I don't know. This chap is full of play as a colt; always laughing, jollying; frolicking with the other orderly, who calls himself Mister Louis and is very dignified and not clever at all.

I can scarcely bear to look at either one of these mulattoes. If the facial angle is too near the perpendicular, the negro does not look like a negro, but like a spoilt white man. It gives me a peculiar vague horror, like looking on a battlefield or any great irrevocable wrong. This feeling is entirely impersonal—one could never be sorry for so jolly a creature as a negro; but it is like regarding something monstrous, unnatural; I turn my eyes away instinctively.

Boston, man-of-all-work and Jack of the electrician's, painter's, plumber's and gardener's trades, is different. I could watch him all day— gigantic limbs in slow, easy action, small twinkling eyes, face sloping back to a very small skull—he looks like a great black cross erected against the tent. He is natural and, in a way, perfect, having his own right place in creation.

December 1, 1916

Yesterday was Thanksgiving and my good man put on a white collar for the first time in ten years or so, and went to the Christian Science service: then spent the afternoon with me. By the time he got here I was very homesick, beginning to cry, and my Thanksgiving dinner was souring on my stomach and giving me a headache. He told me about the meeting, how many people were there whom he knew, and how much at home he felt. I staid in bed, and he read me the C.S. Scripture lesson for the day, and presently my headache was gone. But the high temperature remains and after supper I had another very hard chill, and ran up to 104 2/5 F.

Today felt done up and remained close to bed. The doctor took a look at the chart, and said he would leave me some medicine. But I have had no chill today, and so far have not been confronted with the alternative of taking medicine or declaring for C.S.

Received a lovely long letter from Edith; Frank and I were both afraid that I might have offended her.

Joe has gone, by the doctor's permission, to visit his Aunt Laura's folks for two days.

December 8, 1916

Father R. came up early to administer the communion to Mrs. Allen, and I talked with him a few minutes about Jean. My fear of the Church is somewhat quieted. When I learned that Jean had been approved on the subject of her confirmation, singularly enough I knew exactly the right stand to take, and my confusion vanished. I told her she need not join this church or any church unless from conviction; that I should not oppose the step, nor seek to influence her either way. Then she asked about various doctrines. Perhaps I said the right thing about the Trinity, and the conception of Jesus; these present no difficulties to my mind. But the Real

Presence in the Eucharist! I can't believe that any more than she can, and said so frankly.

Weighed, and have gained 3 pounds! But a most unfortunate occurrence distressed me this afternoon. Dear Frank, who was working at Ellsworth's, received a telephone message that he was wanted at once at Pine Breeze. In anxiety he made the long trip, walking up in the rain, only to find that no such message had been sent. He was not even allowed to see me.

I hope this will be a lesson to us both, that human suffering is due to error, false messages of sense.

December 25, 1916

I must have had more than twenty Xmas gifts—more than I could use, so I gave something to each of the girls in the cottage. The Writers' Club sent me $5 and Mrs. Patten $2 which comes in just right, as somewhat to my surprise Frank has decided to send Joe to St. Andrews' if it can be arranged.

I run such a daily temperature that I did not try to go up to the main building for the morning celebration. The dinner was quite delicious and I ate heartily. Frank spent the afternoon and we had a jolly time. I am now housed in the sleeping porch, and will not try the tent again till warmer weather. Last week it was so cold I begged to go home, and came near leaving.

December 29, 1916

I am proud of my son: he took the "Third degree" most gallantly this morning, and came out with every one's respect. At breakfast, some one at his table printed "DANGER" on a bit of paper, and stuck it in the butter, about which there has been a good deal of complaint. When Miss Plewes saw it she went into one of her unreasonable tempers, and tried to find out who did it. All denied; then all denied any knowledge of the affair except Joe. He admitted that he knew who did it, but refused to give any names. After considerable scolding in the presence of those big, cowardly, guilty men, she brought him before me and explained the situation, apparently thinking I would force the boy to go against his childish principles.

"If he did it, Miss Plewes, he'll tell you," I said at once. But that was not the point.

"He knows who did and I think he ought to consider my position. We can't let this pass."

"Come here, son," I said, "and tell me what you think is the right of it. I want you to do just what's right."

At this he came to the foot of my bed and stood digging one little fist after the other into his eyes, while the big tears rolled. "I know it wasn't right to do it—and I know who did it—but I ain't goin' to tell."

Seeing this was his ultimatum, I explained to Miss P. that there is a very strong feeling here against tale bearers—and told her how poor Mrs. Webb was punished. I could have gone farther and showed how the unfairness and unreasonableness of her punishments breeds such feeling inevitably, but contented myself with pointing out that the one to stand the grilling ought to be at least a possible guilty party, and not the little boy who didn't do it.

Here Joe pulled himself together and gave her a line on the case of suggesting that she question the last one to leave the table, who would certainly have seen the whole thing; and she said she would find out that name from the colored waiter. Joe further suggested a little Sherlocking of the bit of envelope in question.

He was then let go, and later in the day the criminals were apprehended. Concerning their punishment I have heard nothing. But I'm glad Joe stuck to his colors.

January 12, 1917

Is that contentious frame of mind the cause of the fever, or does the high temperature cause the frame of mind? Perhaps a close analysis would discover that the contentious mind is the fever, nothing less.

Worse than ever today; I have not felt so ill for two months. I try my best to treat the chill and fever with Science, declaring the unity of harmony. Last night was very cold, and nearly all the patients suffered. I got through better than most.

Jean writes that she has liverwort, transplanted from the woods, blooming in her room. Few things in life have ever given me such satisfaction as Jean's letters. Her development is just what I could have wished—this turning to nature and to drawing is, at her age, the best thing possible. She says Joe will be allowed to visit her.

Several interesting birds about lately—usually just when I have a hard chill and can't look out. Whitethroat Sparrows under the small pines—a Downy Woodpecker makes a great to-do of chiseling a worm out of an oak bough.

January 13, 1917

Cold rain continuing all day. I broke my thermometer and forthwith recovered from the burning fever. Miss P. remarking that she believed people sometimes have thermometer fevers, proposed to let me go without a thermometer for a time.

Received today a really worth-while appreciation, a letter from one of Mr. Ellsworth's relatives who had just read my little book of poems. It has been a long time since I heard any intelligent comment on those verses that I had lost heart about them too. Here is a reader who understands them for just what they are.

Yet it seems strange to me now that I could ever have written them, or any others. The old interest in beautiful words has gone from me entirely; Swinburne seems not only nonsense, but dangerous and vicious nonsense. Whitman is the only poet I care to read much, though Sidney Lanier's "In the Marshes" seems to me about the finest poem I know of. I could not write so much as a child's jingle now.

January 29, 1917

A spring like day following weeks of rain. Have seen a great flock of Pine Siskins picking over a large pine tree—quite a sight. There must have been a hundred; the tree was alive with them; there was no inch of bark or bough that they did not go over, and every cone had its wee bird standing upside down and working at the seeds.

Joe is with Mrs. Stroop, the school having closed on account of measles. Mrs. Stansell has gone.

I was at a stand, and depressed with loneliness, and prayed for help, and it has come. A new patient, a Miss McRoy, was put into the bed next to mine. I knew at once I was going to take to her; and what was my gratitude for every present help and blessing when she told me she has been studying C.S. for two years! She is very ill, too weak to do her own hair; has most of my symptoms and a digestive trouble besides. We read together, or rather

I read and she listens, and talk a good deal. There is a delightful quiet harmony between us. She is not demonstrative, nor are her attainments at all showy, but exercises at all times a fine, patient consideration.

She has been here about 10 days, and is much improved in some ways. I also have gained greatly in strength and appetite—I am sure because I have her. Her experience has been much like mine—can receive but little help from practitioners and seems at a stand. We must work it out together. And how <u>good</u> that we are placed in adjacent beds! Is it really true, that in divine harmony there is no accident?

February 3, 1917

Coldest wave of the winter; zero weather, the coldest for five years. And I feel well! Of course I feel the cold, but more as a well person feels it,—mere discomfort, without chills. Are the chills and fever finally overcome?

But poor Theodora seems out of courage, and suffers. I do so want to help her.

The doctor brought word this morning that the U.S. has severed diplomatic relations with Germany.

February 8, 1917

The water ran for a few hours this afternoon, raising our hopes—then stopped. No bath this week for anyone, no laundry, no change of clothing.

I feel so cheerful and so well. I told the doctor this morning that I am getting well.

Last evening I tried to sing "Stille Nacht, Heilige Nacht" and my voice came out clear and full, and my breath never once caught. I sit up to my heart's content. In truth I believe I am healed. Certain symptoms remain, as a rattling sound, and some coughing; but I feel that the trouble is really overcome.

A strange piece of understanding has recently come to me as by revelation: I know, at last, the answer to the cruel puzzle that has vexed me for four years. I know why Frank turned against me and abused me so for all the time that we lived on our own home place.

It was because, having put the deed in my name, he saw that he had given me an opportunity for treachery, and feared that I would take from him this, the only property he had.

If he had only said so! how quickly I would have signed the place over to him! But though I begged him he never would tell me, and I could not understand. Some one else put this dark suspicion into his mind I am sure; and having been sown there, I can see now, clear as the sky, how it grew and overshadowed all the good feeling that was in him, utterly absorbed him; how he was racked with suspense, not knowing the day nor the hour on which the shameful blow might fall.

I must talk with him about this. But not to hurt him more than necessary. He has paid full measure for that error.

Poor Theodora! her doubts and fears have resulted in a return of the severe gastric trouble. That questioning, tentative attitude does not bring about the healing. No real, practical faith. It is like Peter's walking on the water—she sinks at the first alarm. I cannot help her just now; she is taking several medicines and crying in her pain for more.

The only thing that really vexes me now is having to live among these petty complaining creatures all the time, day and night. Oh how I long for some big, cheerful human presence—still more for an understanding heart. My one escape is in prayer, on my bed at night.

seven

The Good Gray Mother

As the country was facing World War I, Emma continued her journal. She was still at the Pine Breeze Sanitarium, and dealing with problems related to her tuberculosis. Frank made occasional visits, as did some of her children. In August 1917 she began working on the manuscript of a book she called "The Good Gray Mother." In it she recorded her thoughts on nature and philosophy. In the early spring of 1918 she received a visit from a book editor from Chicago, who made an offer to her for a book on Tennessee birds.

Emma ended her journal on August 19, 1918. She had reached the end of the journal and had no more pages to write on. Frank found work in Chattanooga and rented a house in an area called Hill City, today North Chattanooga. It was not far from the sanitarium. Emma moved into the house in October. She was able to be with her children in the last months of her life, which was slowly ebbing away from the tuberculosis. She was baptized and received her first communion on March 17, 1919. Two days later she died.

March 9, 1917

Warm spring like weather. I begin to eat, and feel better than for weeks. And what! The old responsibility in a new form is coming on me;

I must e'en quiet the noisy, oversee the incompetent, rebuke the froward, calm the hysterical, must I? and generally help to maintain order in the cottage, which is filling up with an irresponsible class of women. For a while they worried me and made me angry. Now I see that they are to be treated like children; and that Miss Plewes expects this of me.

The doctor and all the nurses try their best to help Theodora; but she suffers and is losing ground each day. I wish we had a more responsible nurse on our side of the hill; this Miss Ward is the most thoughtless and incompetent nurse I ever saw in <u>any</u> hospital—and so goodnatured that altogether she reminds me of Frank. I never know what to do with such people.

March 16, 1917

The doctor told me today that I might walk up to the house to supper on warm days—as I am so much better.

Slowly, I am conquering. And I am helping others. I have learned that when people worry me by ill behavior the thing to do is to go up to them and kindly but firmly command them. Before a word of truth, evil gives way like the dark before a candle:—if only one is not afraid or resentful.

Best of all I have induced or rather bulldozed poor Theodora to take her nourishment, cast away many of her can'ts and won'ts, and even to use a bedpan, after all the nurses failed. I have to do her hair and help her with the bedpan. These others are too good for such work, and Miss Ward is no nurse—it took her an hour and a half by the clock to give that weak, nervous sufferer a sponge bath. But I wonder if Theodora is dying. She looks like it.

March 22, 1917

She died at daybreak, glad of the release. She must have really given up weeks ago; and since living was out of the question I am glad I was able to help her die.

April 3, 1917

Jean arrived this afternoon just before suppertime, preceded by a curt postal from Sister H. the principal, saying that she is not to return to St. Mary's. What can it mean? Jean herself could give no explanation. Miss

Plewes kindly allowed us a visit together; and after a considerable talk
I decided that she is simply too unconventional for the Sisters' ideas of
propriety—I remember how often I got severely judged, as a girl, when I
had no idea of doing wrong. Either this or—has she taken something that
does not belong to her? Perhaps we shall never know.

April 5, 1917

Heard the whistles this afternoon declare war.[1]

April 11, 1917

I was awakened early by the first wood thrush, singing quite near the
cottage, joyously, almost hurriedly, as if glad to get back. That wonder-song
of the world—I have heard it again! I have lived to hear it again!

Can I now overcome this strange inability to work which holds me?
I feel able to write or draw every afternoon, but can think of nothing that
seems worth while. Fiction sickens me, and my painting is such poor stuff.
There are several subjects I should like to handle in serious essays, but I
have no idea how to find a publisher for such, unless they should be good
enough for Harper's. Thus I hesitate and dally, though spring has come.

Meantime the cottage has filled with freaks, silly, noisy, ill-mannered,
who take offense if I try to explain to them the motions of the earth or the
war, or advise them about their health; They complain at such a rate that
yesterday I put up several signs—[in a drawn box]:

"DON'T TALK OF YOUR TROUBLES I HAVE SOME OF MY OWN"
which delighted the doctor, but which they have taken in a very personal
sense.

April 23, 1917

Dr. S. examined me with the stethoscope, says that the left lung is
about gone, but after it is destroyed entirely I may get better, able to
paint and get about for years. Well—I'll wait a while and see, but if I am
not much improved by fall I shall not try to make it through another cold
weather; it is not worth while.

The weather is perfect. I am abed now and feel pretty bad, but enjoy
the warmth and comfort.

Miss P. is leaving for a 2 weeks' trip to Philadelphia.

May 16, 1917

At last, after days of misery, comes an afternoon when I can draw a little. The weather has been cold for maybe ten days; there was frost on the mountain. Lenore sent me some new brushes, and Edith bought me some paper, so I began a new series of bird pictures. Edith also brought me a dead Veery to study, a delicate Thrush type. I found a Bewick's wren sitting, under the tent; her nest is all wound up with tangles of wrapping-twine. The male appears to be feeding her.

Little secret things like this—the song of the mocking-bird, the beauty of a single leaf—have made up so much of my life, and help me now through the days. But where it touches people, hard things come up and I do not always know what to do. I have hard work to keep order in the cottage; I had the Brewer woman sent away, but some of the girls are under the influence of an insolent smart-Aleck on the other side, and unmanageable. They have had a great time ridiculing my efforts, till last night. I never lose my temper any more, having nothing to fear from any one. I sat for half an hour, listening to their outrageous screeching; then when I was quite sure, I set in quietly to let them know where they stood. One tried a defiant reply, and before I got through with her she couldn't look up. Mrs. Horton had the grace to be ashamed of her conduct; she did not say so, but has been very friendly and nicely-behaved all day today.

On this porch, however, all is peaceable and almost happy. There is a young girl, worn out early in the hosiery mills, and two married women who have left young children at home.

My own folks—oh dear. If I felt at all responsible for them I should not be able to bear it; but how many times, when I was making my last desperate struggle to ward it off, have I warned them of just what has come! Joe is doing very well; his clothes are not near so good as those I bought to send him to school in, but he can soon clothe himself. He is a caddie on the golf links. Poor Jean is receiving the punishment we all foresaw for her; she has got discontented and fractious in one place after another, and fallen out with everybody, is now reduced to moping around at Larnce's house and sharing a bed with Mamie. Frank says she is unhappy and coughs at night. But she will not come to see me, and he does not want to have Dr. S. examine her. I can do nothing; let God's will lead her.

May 20, 1917

Such a good visit with Frank. He caught a humming bird that drove against the screen and fastened itself by the beak, and nearly caught a little snake in the tent floor. He seems to me to be gaining in courage and initiative: he has repudiated any possible inheritance from his parents, believing that it was not come by fairly. I rejoice in this step: he is free now from those old folks if he will only remain so.

Jean came last Thursday. She is doing nothing now, and discontented as ever. I will let her be till she is really ready to work.

Joe, bless him! brings me chocolate of his own buying; but mercy, how dirty he is!

June 9, 1917

If I could eat I should gain; but I am tired of egg and cereal, bread and meat are not much better, and the price of vegetables is prohibitive. But food is a detail in comparison to peace of mind. I am thankful for every hour of solitude.

Rained most of the day, with a soothing sound on the tent that put me to sleep twice. A cub reporter from the Times came up, but like the others who have come here she could not see Pine Breeze for looking at the view.

Laura writes me concerning what Frank has already spoken of—the danger of Jean's going about with this one-armed school teacher Denton. How do I want to be with my children and mother them! It is mothering they need, no less. And my motherhood has been wasted in drudgery and overstrain. Now I cannot even get a letter from Judith and Kitty—have not even Judith's address.

I am writing Zerelda Rains in the hope that she can arrange for Jean to be sent to Mossop. I wish she were there now; she would be safer and happier. God will surely direct things for the best; it may be that Jean needs a hard lesson before she will learn, and if she must bear it I must too.

As I expected, the clothes and household things are disappearing a little at a time. Frank has hardly a change of underwear left. If I can get hold of the box of books I will present most of them to Pine Breeze, which has already a half wagonload of H. Bell Wright & Gene Stratton Porter [American novelists] and such.

I have begun to write a little on a story, of the blind mare Frank had. If I can do it well it should be an unusual study in animal psychology, and sell even in these troublous times.

June 16, 1917

I was never so close to a living dove as just now; one walked about, feeding for twenty minutes before the tent, not two yards from me.

Poor Judith writes that she does not like the people she is with, that the work is too hard for her. She begs to come home. I don't know how to get her to understand that there is no home to come to. O my girl, my splendid rose! I want to help her, but there is not one thing I can do.

June 17, 1917

Frank has moved into a one room shack and Jean keeps house for him, fairly well he says. If she will only stick at it.

But I can do nothing to help.

And I feel sure that I can never live with Frank again. He thinks it is the hardships I am dreading; but I have not the heart to tell him that it is he,—his callous carelessness, and his unreasoning anger when I try to get him to do better. He believes that he has changed and will henceforth maintain a happy home; but he has thought so again and again and I have trusted his promises only to find them utterly false.

Yet without him and the children I can see nothing in life for me. My appetite for living is gone, like the appetite for food. This is perhaps a clinging to personality, which ought to be overcome. But as it was last year and before, death is ever in the background of my thoughts. God knows!

June 22, 1917

The Doctor is giving me a tonic to make me eat. I laugh at it and take it—the first medicine I have swallowed for nearly a year. He advised me to go away to the mountain for a week, but Miss Plewes is against it. I am not at all enthusiastic about that or anything else.

Judith writes that she is coming home at once. I have urged her to return to Mossop instead; but if those children and their father are determined to stick right among the worse than heathen Mileses, I do not feel that I am any longer responsible. I have done all I could to prevent it.

Light and warmth pour into the tent on this longest day of the year, and make me comfortable. When the sun withdraws, and the misery of steady cold creeps on me, it will be time for me to quit the game. I have thought and thought hard, but have not so far been able to hit on any way of accomplishing this without violence and scandal. Must try to obtain some Datura when the pods form next month.

For years now I have given up all hope of happiness, achievement, or common decency of living for myself, and have hung on solely for the sake of what help I could give the children. Now I can no longer help them in any way. Thus I have nothing left. At times I am seized with a bitter disgust of the man who for fifteen years has taken all I had to give, and now lets me die in a charity hospital. But when I see him I do not feel this, and I am convinced it would do no good to express it.

June 27, 1917

I have fallen away very thin, and am so weak that I spend nearly all day in bed. Dr. Schumacher says my lungs are better. I tried to tell him something of the change that is taking place in me, but since there seems nothing I can say that does not cast a reflection on Frank, I can't explain.

How terribly all gladness, all feeling of any kind, has gone out of me. I used to love the little green weeds that push up through the dust of dooryards; now I hardly love my children. I watched a pink dawn spreading between the earth-mist and the last fading star, while the thrush sang like an angel: but it did not touch me; I only wanted to stop coughing and go to sleep.

But one gleam of feeling—I dreamed I found a pale tall orchid in the woods, and gave it into Mrs. Wheatley's hand. She was walking with me, talking with her old divine sweetness; and for the moment I loved her and was happy. But even happy dreams are rare. There is a fearful blank every way I look.

June 29, 1917

Dr. Schumacher understands perhaps better than anyone else what is killing me. Every one else says it is the heat, which has been severe the past week. This morning he asked if my appetite was coming back, and when I said no, he looked at me with that divinely sympathetic expression that I can hardly believe when I see it on a man's face, and asked: "Is there anything at all you want?"

I said, "No; I wish there was."

"Is there anything I can do, Mrs. Miles?"

I was touched, but answered, "No sir, I wish you could, but people have done too much for me already, I'm afraid." Then I laughed and added, "Yes, there is one thing: you can keep that crazy woman off me!" And I told him enough of my experiences with manuscript fiends to make the tragic moment pass off in a breeze of laughter.

It is a relief to feel that one person knows it is not the hot weather.

July 1, 1917

Sunday. Frank came as usual, bringing me fruit and chocolate which he can ill afford. Every one else has forgotten me, even my children.

Having suffered such distress all week, I was in no mood to make the visit too pleasant. He certainly did his best to help me. He begs me to try to live, if only to help him and the children with counsel and advice; but it was easy to prove to him that neither he nor they have listened to a word from me for a long time. He helps me to see that the girls are very young, and cannot be expected to do better.

A story he told me of Jean is a real comfort. Larnce's tribe has annoyed her by borrowing her out of groceries; also, as usual when I am ill and helpless, they have stolen a good many housekeeping things. Jean tried to recover an aluminum cooker and failed; but afterward she renewed the attack by saying to Mary (who by the way officiated when she and Judith and afterward Joe were born), "You've got our bread-board."

"I ain't neither got your bread board."

"Well, Tiny has; I saw it in her kitchen. I've already been and got our rolling pin from Brick's wife."

"Your daddy give me that there dough board and I give it to Tiny."

"My daddy never done it," said Jean. "I hunted for it all over at Grandma's and he didn't know where it was. I've got to have it."

She went to Tiny's kitchen and presently found the board tucked away behind something.

"Tiny'll be mad," warned Mary as she came forth.

"I'm mad now," says Jean. "I haven't had a board since we moved here." And home she went with it, and Frank says she has been making very creditable biscuits on it.

I am glad that he is a consistent primitive Christian, of course; but I am gladder that Jean is not!

July 6, 1917

The Doctor on his morning visit regarded me with some concern, and proposed changing my medicine again. So I told him plainly that it is of no use,—that it is poor wartime economy to try to keep such a battered wreck afloat. I told him that no doubt I could force myself to eat and improve, but I saw no reason for doing so.

To my surprise he walked over and put his arm round my shoulders, and I just laid my gaunt old head on his shoulder and cried, for the first time in months—foolishly overcome by a little kindness. He told me about a cousin of his wife's who lived to be old with only one lung. I got straightened up a little and tried to say that I am no earthly use or help to any one and no satisfaction to myself. But I could not go on to explain that tuberculosis is the least of my troubles,—that if I were to walk out of here sound and well any day, I should only have to go back to supporting a man and four children who will not try and do not care. I can not find in Christian Science or anywhere else any solution of the problem. I really cannot see any reason for trying to eat. As for these tonics, they might as well be so much rain water.

July 7, 1917

One of the most brilliantly simple ideas I ever thought of came to me before breakfast! I have been noticing for weeks a very common error in quoting "Dixie"—nine out of ten newspapers and even standard periodicals say "Cinnamon seed and sandy bottom." The word is "simmon" seed, that is, persimmon. I have already written the Outlook about this, and had in mind other magazines, but the brilliant idea was to write to Irvin S. Cobb. I feel sure that, though he did misquote the line himself in a story, he will do something to correct this before our liveliest and most popular national air gets into the trenches.

Frank was able on his last visit to give Mrs. Heldermann certain information that may result in a way out of her troubles. She is more hopeful.

Today she lost some things in the laundry, and had others ruined with the poor washing. I was glad to have a very pretty corset cover to give her.

July 13, 1917

On this unlikely day two pleasant visits—the first from a Carolina wren, who slipped in at a corner crevice before I was fairly awake, and made himself at home for some time, peering into chinks, examining everything on the bureau and table, and stopping every now and then to sing, with head up and tail down. Once he ate a bug, and once perched on the cot; once flew close over my face. At last he appeared to feel that it was time to go, and examined the door-crack, and flew about more and more uneasily; but did not go into a panic as most birds do when they find themselves inside. I was interested to note that he seemed to remember having come in at the south corner; he returned to it three times, but could not spy out the chink through which he had come. I got out of bed and opened the door, but he just then found another way of escape. And once out, how he did sing! "Sweetheart! sweetheart! sweetheart! per-cedar, per-cedar, per-cedar, per-cedar! jubilee, jubilee!"

The other visit was an evening call from Roger Droke. He must have got permission for such an infraction of rules. I was very weak, half dressed in my canvas chair, but the conversation was delightful—Mrs. Thorn came with him and Mrs. Heldermann was already here—so we had an unusual evening. He is one of the best young men I ever saw.

July 15, 1917

Sunday. Frank and Jean and Hazel came up in Freudenberg's auto.[2] When the little girls had gone, I determinedly took Frank through a plain talk. For the first time perhaps since Florida, I allowed him no evasions nor myself any impatience—simply held to the point and if he became unreasonable, I refused to talk at all until he would talk sense. At first he jerked all over and I thought he was going to cry; but a little Christian Science does wonders for these occasions. We finally got things considerably straightened out. I told him one thing he surely ought to know,—that any suspicion he may have against me is entirely false. I have dealt fairly with him all these years, though not any too wisely, I admit.

When it was all talked over we felt so much better. I realize now that he has been longing for a right understanding of things for years, but was afraid to face it.

For some time I have been throwing the medicine out at the back of the tent when no one was looking, and now have asked that it be discontinued.

July 29, 1917

A dreadful day. The heat was greater than it has been yet, but I could have got through that. It is Frank's terrible influence over me. I feel so disheartened and degraded by his visits. Is there no escape this side of death, from this frightful bondage! I feel now that the last flicker of love for him is out; yet he will insist on satisfying himself with me. It seems I must tell him not to come any more.

Edith came for a few minutes, late. She must have spent the few dollars held in trust for me, for when I asked for some stamps & envelopes they were furnished by Mrs. Stedman. Well, it doesn't matter.

After supper I tried to get together a Bible class. I'm afraid I did not start it right—did too much talking myself, like a lecture. If I can't do something useful I cannot endure this. And if I cannot be free of Frank Miles I must die.

I am very ill tonight, continually pouring sweat, now flushed and now chilled. Every thing seems wrong. Oh, for a merciful end!

August 12, 1917

Joe came to see me, with a handful of orchids and a piece of chocolate. We had a lovely visit. The boy held forth on Congress and the food bill at length; says Wilson is "bought" and thinks me a mush head, no doubt, for defending him; says we ought to use the English system of food distribution, which he exclaimed in some detail, but comically, because he had forgotten the word "staples." He gave it as his opinion, rather timidly, that wars are due to overpopulation, and that after the war families should be limited by statute to three children! What will this chatterbox be when he grows up? Where does he hear all this?

"This is a dreary old life, mamma," he said. "Seems like the older I get the worse it is. But I don't want to die, though. I want to travel—want to go South."

I don't wonder he finds it dreary. One of his cousins is in jail for stealing a watch. He is underfed, and half cared for. Jean is cross with him. And from what he tells me, Frank has got things balled up in an awful shape. He has not taken a single step toward getting Jean ready for school. "It's no use," says Joe,—an echo this. Now shall I make a trip to town, borrow money for Jean's clothes, and set to work painting & writing to pay it off? Ought I?

Joe is further discouraged at having no money to buy his school books: he has not started to school yet. I have promised him that he shall have his books. Must go to town I think. But Frank and Edith Stroop between them have, I'm afraid, alienated a number of my friends on whom I might have counted for help.

August 16, 1917

Edith brought me a great armload of wild flowers from Lookout this morning. One lovely head of purple flowers I can't place in the botany— seems to belong to the mints. Spurge; phlox—the last; the first goldenrod, asters, and ironweed; brook sunflower; blackeyed susan; hydrangea; lobelia; smooth yellow gerardia; tradescantia; wild carrot; a large-leafed mint and mountain-mint or basis: starry campion; Joe pye; partridge-pea.

She brought my guitar—but she has ruined it! After my careful directions, she has left it strung up in damp weather so that the neck is warped and it cannot be tuned.

And she seems to feel a little uncomfortable about the stamps! I begin to laugh at her.

This afternoon the whole situation brightens. Jean steamed in like a little dreadnought, in a hat she has trimmed over, a skirt she made from one of mine, and a pretty smock for which she first earned the goods and then made herself. She never has the can'ts and the won'ts, the shan'ts and the don'ts: but the clearest, most positive and definite ideas as to what she wants and how to get it. Confound it, they need not bring me any more tales on that girl; she is worth the whole bunch put together. It is not true that she does not want to go away to school. I shall write and complete the arrangement at once.

August 18, 1917

Frank feels much better with his new job, and we had a pleasant visit. He proposes to take me to the mountain this winter, to live in a tent. I don't know what to say.

Mrs. Annis was here later in the evening with another proposition. She means to start a New Thought club this fall, and wishes me to contribute some "philosophy." I fear her idea of Truth is much confused with occultism, spiritualism and the like; I don't want my name identified with such, for I know little of theosophy and care less. Also she asked for a list of names of my friends—wants to beg them to help me somehow I daresay. I want no more of such humiliating schemes. God is my supply.

August 21, 1917

I gain more and more understanding of the meaning of Christ's teaching, but seem to gain slowly, if at all, in real power. I want my health, want to be able to heal as well as to teach. Sometimes a truth long apprehended by the intellect becomes an actual conviction by experience, like a revelation. My understanding of the life and words of Jesus seems to me more real, more vital, than that of any one I know. Then why am I not healed? Why not a healer?

Today I read, "Lord, shew us the Father, and it sufficeth us." It seemed to me the cry not only of my own heart, but of the whole struggling, suffering, degraded world today. I could see Philip leaning forward in the deep earnestness of his plea; I could hear him say just as I would say, "Lord, that's just our difficulty; we believe in the Father but we can't see him as you do. We hear you talk to him,—that is prayer; but we don't know how to pray! He talks to you, alone on the mountain, at the River Jordan, at the graveside—that is your inspiration; but we cannot hear his voice! Unheard, because our ears are dull? Unseen, because our eyes are dim? Shew us the Father—it is all we want! More than any thing else in the world we long to come into that close personal relation with him which we see you have. That's exactly the part of your teaching we can't grasp; we can't get hold of it some way. Shew us the Father, and it sufficeth us!"

Tonight a prayer meeting was held, barely rippling the deadly boredom of the place. I was surprised that twelve attended, taking part in the doleful drawling of "Whaaat a friend we have in Jesus" and generally doing their best. Mr. Stevens, the gardener among the patients, dawned on me as almost a primitive Christian; simple, whole-hearted, joyous, doing each thing as it comes up and putting the whole weight of his manhood behind it, whether it be singing, eating, or hoeing potatoes. He wanted us all to pray for the close of war. I was inclined to laugh at first; then I thought, why shouldn't his word be worth as much as that of His Holiness Benedict, so much discussed now! I like to think of Stevens as typical of the South. An honest piece of Georgia, at least.

Old Mr. Bryant's idea of a prayer meeting is one which sends you home crying over your sins; mine would send you forth to laugh at your troubles and shove them out of your way. But we work together pretty well.

August 25, 1917

Surely this cough can be overcome. Now and again, perhaps two or three times a week, it racks me till I am all sore inside. It is not true and must not be.

Miss Plewes is worse and worse; more rigid in bearing, more notionate, more condescending, more self-centered. The nurses and helpers at the house take turns crying over the harsh things she says. Yesterday she asked Mrs. Heldermand if she had disinfected a certain thermometer. She replied that she had done so, according to directions.

Poor Mrs. Woods is sinking. She had such a bright brave faith, it seemed impossible she could give way, though she was a mere skeleton even on arrival, and her skin transparent as a poppy petal. Her case is similar, physically, to Miss McRoy's. I asked that she be given to me,—that her cot be placed in the tent where I can look after her and help her. I am indebted to the Universal Account for much hospitality, and it seemed this would be a good way to pay some of it back. But they will not consent to this arrangement, and since Mrs. Hennessy and Mrs. Heldermand are out of the cottage most of the time at work now, I fear these careless girls do not look after her comfort.

August 26, 1917

A perfect Sunday, cool and bright. Frank and Joe came. Frank says if I have to leave here I can come straight to him. I think I shall be satisfied to do so if need be. Possibly I could find some way to teach on the mountain; at least, I want very much to take Frank and Joe through the New Testament.

This has been a profitable year of study and meditation—a Sabbath year. I have thoroughly considered the faith and doctrine of the

Episcopalians and the Baptists. Taking these as typical of the Ritualistic and the Evangelistic denominations, I find that the former do not believe what they say they believe, and the latter—the laymen at least—generally do not know what their churches say they believe.

Also I have thoroughly studied Christian Science. Certain aspects of this teaching I can't accept. First, their slipshod habit of thinking which results in inaccurate statements, as the constantly reiterated claims that Mrs. Eddy's writings contain no bad grammar or other errors in English: I find even misquoted texts and mistakes in Bible names & characters in their leading periodicals, while their view of nature is too funny for words. This is to say the least unscientific. There ought to be a great spiritual interpretation of nature in line with this belief: <u>there</u> <u>will</u> <u>be</u>. Henry Drummond's Ascent of Man is a step in that direction. But at present C.S. flouts and condemns all natural sciences, sweepingly,—and then turns round and borrows its most convincing illustrations and parallells [*sic*] from astronomy and biology! I have myself learned too much spiritual law in the study of the natural world, considering the lilies and beholding the fowls of the air, to call my belief Christian Science. Yet if they approached their subject scientifically, that is accurately, and trained themselves to exact thought, it would be the greatest science in the world.

Strangely, the more I study other beliefs, the simpler and surer become my own. I know, I <u>know</u> whom I have believed, whom I have tried and proved. I am like a babe who has learned to stammer a few words, and sees before him the vast possibilities of language. O Father, if I may but learn to speak the Word with power! To heal; to bless, to set free in truth!

But the demonstration is still delayed. At the Bible class tonight I coughed all the way through the lesson, and ran up a temperature. I don't feel the least bit set back or discouraged; shall keep right on trying.

August 29, 1917

Last night I slipped in when no one was in the porch, and gave Mrs. Woods a treatment. This morning Miss Hennessy tells me she had the best night's rest yet—coughing much less.

That vague idea of a spiritual nature, which I have turned over in mind for years, but specially this past year, has suddenly crystallized into the plan of a book. Now I have thought of something worth while to do, I don't care whether I stay here or go. A book in nine chapters, every idea pictured in concrete examples, and set forth in such simple words that it might be used in schools.

This evening I was to lead prayer meeting, but lay down on the cot after supper and forgot all about it until too late! I felt humiliated; but the patients took it very kindly, turning the occasion into a hymn-singing, though there are scarcely half a dozen hymns they can sing.

August 31, 1917

The doctor asked how my book was getting on.[3] I spoke of my need of works of reference & authorities for comparison, and he promptly went the length of advising me to smuggle books from the Carnegie Library if I can, saying there is no real danger of contagion. I know there is not, but was surprised that he and Miss P. should admit it. It dawns on me that most of this talk of germs and infection is bluff, for the purpose of scaring people into sanitation, just as preachers used to frighten sinners with hell-fire. It is precisely on a par with the agitation over eating meat offered to idols, or otherwise unclean, which troubled the early Christians; and Paul's very sensible views are quite as applicable to the present problems of diet, sanitation, etc. That is, I am not a bit afraid of germs myself, but have no right to do anything that will alarm a weaker brother. If he believes that a consumptive's use of the phone is dangerous, why, to his weak conscience it is dangerous—just as Paul says of meats.

How love casteth out fear! The girls in the porch, and old Mrs. Henessy, are so afraid that Mrs. Woods will die among them. I once felt that way myself; but now I have no dread of people, whether dying, getting born, getting married, or even when they ought to get married and don't. I doubt if ghosts could disturb me. As Jean says, if you don't want to see a ghost you can always shut your eyes.

September 13, 1917

Mrs. Woods is dead and the tent disinfected; but I am still too ill to be moved.

Quite the most delightful visit of all today. Zerelda and her sister, Nell Buford, spent the afternoon. They brought flowers, a jar of malted milk, a great stack of magazines. And, oh how we talked. I told her all about my book. She told me of her effort to start a branch art school in Chattanooga, which is meeting with chilling indifference & discourtesy. Oh this old town, how discouraging, how rotten it is! She said the loveliest things about Jean, whom she met but once; and I gave her Jean's letter to read—an optimistic little scrawl to the effect that she likes her new surroundings and hopes to do well.

Oh, what happiness it was to see Zerelda again. My idea of heaven is a place where I shall be around out doors with nice people.

September 26, 1917

If my book does not speak truly and with power, I can never speak at all. It is my Word and my last word! I can not live long in this condition.

September 30, 1917

Such a good visit with Frank & Joe. The boy is healthier and happier since he got started in school. Like myself, he cannot live without something to absorb his mind.

I told Frank something of a plan that has been taking shape in mind for some two months, about Miss Plewes. This abuse of sick people ought not, I think, to go unchecked. At least she ought to be reported. I am preparing a statement of charges against her, and mean to present it to the Board as soon as she returns. Either they will investigate the matter and oblige her to control her temper, or she will send me off the hill: in which case I suppose I shall go back to Frank. He talked more like a man today and seems to be doing right. Though what we should live on is not visible at this writing, since he says it takes just all he makes to feed him & Joe, and I am still flat in bed & can do nothing. He did not think well of my plan except for the possibility of my being expelled from here and having to go home.

October 9, 1917

My spirit is gloriously at peace; I am filled with thankfulness and realize the entire goodness of God.

All I hear from the children contributes to this. They are all doing well, though what little we hear from Judith is discontent. Jean's letters are quite the opposite; she is specially pleased that Miss Rains has arranged for her to have music.

I am still abed, by the doctor's mandate, but feel very well. No chills, even these cool mornings. No fires have been kindled yet, and the patients creep into sunny corners as soon as the morning work is over. Two chapters are rough-drafted. Am trying to smuggle a book from the Carnegie library which would help me in the next subject, the evolution of the nest; but the particular volume I want cannot be found.

October 19, 1917

Old hens should not cackle every time they lay a birthday, yet I did hope that some one would think to write me a birthday letter. The frost has come, and with it the same old chills, harder than ever. Last winter I got through by waiting on myself, going to the stove when I could. Now I am not often able. Writing on my MSS has to be given up, which is the hardest blow of all.

I did however eat my supper by the stove this evening. Miss Plewes kindly sent me a birthday supper with tiny candles, cake and a little fruit, so that we had a pleasant time.

October 25, 1917

No letter from Jean for three weeks. I don't know when I ever heard from the other two. No visitors except Frank and Joe for—since Zerelda was here I believe. I suffer with cold, that is every time I get cold & chill and run a high temperature. What it will be like when really cold weather sets in I dare not think.

Going to live with Frank and Joe is, I now see, out of the question. Frank is already complaining every time he comes, of how hard it is for him to support the one child he has left. He speaks of having stripped himself for his children—referring I suppose to Jean's clothes, which he went in debt for at the last hour after having all summer to prepare in, and to the money for Judith's shoes which he sent this week. I feel utterly discouraged about him; this seems to me one of the yellowest things I ever heard him say. If after a year's study of Christian Science he has not principle enough to want to support his children, I don't think we ought to depend on him at all. If I get a chance I will try to get Joe away from him too, so that he will not have any one to support but himself.

I am of no use or help to any one any more. My heart has given way till I cannot talk well, and it somehow makes me irritable and sulky. This is a good development of the case however; it will not be so tedious dying of heart failure. I may even go in a short time as poor Blanche Fagan did, without having to lie here through the cold weather.

I sent some funny verses to the News, about the car strike. Printed but not acknowledged.

The News sent me a lovely basket of fruit & candy this week, besides two new union suits & a night gown and other things.

November 15, 1917

At the rate Frank's moral disintegration is progressing, it is hardly likely that he will continue to support Joe beyond the coming of winter's hard times. Some provision must be made for him in that case: but I cannot think of trying an Episcopal school a second time. God will not fail to provide a better way than turning his young clean mind from the truth it so loves.

In spite of growing weakness and misery, my book advances a little from week to week. I never had any piece of work so thoroughly laid out, so well in hand; seems to me if I were able to hold a pencil long it would write itself.

If this book is as important as I believe it to be, nothing can interfere with it, and I shall not die before it is finished either. It is now half written. I have begged every one I could get at and made every shift I could think of to get it typed, and failed. But I have not been anxious, for I know that if the book is as good as I think, it cannot fail. So I waited, watching all opportunities with a quiet mind. And now here comes, from a friend in New York whom I never saw, a most kind offer to type it for me! I knew there would be a way.

February 11, 1918

I have not only lived through the worst winter the country has seen for twenty five years, but have gained all the time in hope and faith and bodily health.

About the first of Dec. all the bed patients, whether incurable or not, were moved into the new hospital ward. This I found to be in some ways a great relief, as there is a nurse within call day and night, and hot water almost all the time.

There has been an unprecedented amount of zero weather, with shortage of fuel and the bad roads which in an isolated place like this mean short rations. Worst of all, we were twelve days without water, except what little was hauled in barrels. All the world knows the whole eastern U.S. has suffered this winter. We were uncomfortable for more than two months, but in this building there was little real suffering.

So now with the first pleasant weather I find myself with an excellent appetite for war bread and field peas, sauerkraut and oatmeal; able to go to the bathroom; able to sustain the spirits of some of the other patients; best of all, resuming work on my book!

Death after death has taken place in this ward—each followed by an hysteric wave among the patients. During these periods I have been of some help. For "a thousand shall fall at thy right hand and ten thousand at thy left hand, but it shall not come nigh thee." It is so with me. I have learned to be truly helpful, without being at all what is called sympathetic.

Every Sunday Joe comes,—the soul of loyalty and of truth and of kindness, to look after me the best he can. But yesterday he missed for the first time. Is he ill?

Today Mrs. Milton, my first visitor for weeks, came to help me finish my fifth chapter. Oh! what a delightful day! I am so happy. Ever since the definite break with Frank, my health and spirits have improved.

March 13, 1918

When Miss Hinds told me I was to have a visitor this afternoon, a Mr. Tallant from Chicago, the idea at once popped into my head that he might be a publisher, and that through him I might at least get a line on the book markets. I never dreamed, however, of anything so delightful as really happened.

When he came I noticed that his shirt was crumpled and his collar soiled, and when he tipped his chair back against the radiator and tried to get his heel over the rungs, and began to pull straws out of the seat and break them all over the floor, I though "What kind of a publisher are you—you will be cutting a chew of tobacco next!" But through his quiet manner and rather a few words, it became evident that he knew what he was talking about. I felt as if I had known him for years, and when he found himself unable to think without a pencil in hand, and began to make hieroglyphs on the counterpane and everywhere, I recognized the high sign of brotherhood. I had my own pencil out by that time of course, and we were planning a book on Tennessee birds for school use, with a trade edition somewhat de luxe.

I felt bound to tell him my health is in a very uncertain state, but he takes the risk, and will send the contract soon. This piece of work will certainly keep me alive during the summer, and I may even get able to do a lot of thumb-nail illustrations for the margins. He is willing to accept a pencil Ms. which makes things easier for me.

I feel tremendously set up over this, which looks like a little sure money for the children, and will certainly be a most congenial occupation for me. It seems certain that God works in me to will and to do, because everything pulls together with me and helps me in what I undertake. This being the case I cannot die until the work is done. So why pay any attention to symptoms and ups and downs?

Now wouldn't it be something if I should come back with three or four books to my credit?

March 24, 1918

My dear little son came as usual, bringing me figs and raisins and $3.00 which his father sent me for the girls. He seemed rather downcast and out of heart—homesick I suppose. He put his head down on the bed as if he were going to cry, and said that he had no good times any more,— that moving pictures and everything seemed "hollow." I told him how, at an early age, I learned not to look for happiness in the pleasures of ordinary young folks, but to find a deeper satisfaction in outdoor study and in drawing. I suggested that he would probably find himself in interesting work. He agreed, and brightened; saying that he would rather have a stock farm than anything else.

But the news from across the water today was enough to make the whole nation feel bad. "Oh, I wish I could be over there and help," he said. If only the whole country will feel like that about it! I told him to do his bit for the war by helping Aunt Laura make garden, but he thinks he would rather kill Boches [slang for Germans].

I have finished my book, and mailed the last of the rough MS. to Mrs. Hyman who will typewrite it for me.

March 28, 1918

The bird book starts off so easily that I am wondering how I shall know when to stop. Every page, however, is hampered by a feeling that it is not a necessary piece of work, as there are already too many bird books. I have to keep reminding myself that this is a book of the middle South, and hence unique. I must put in all the local features I can. If I feel able to write a little every afternoon, and if I can smuggle a reference book or two from the library, I should be able to finish the text in six weeks.

For more than two weeks I have been trying to get a package of writing materials brought out from town. It is so difficult to maintain any sort of communication with the outside world. Roger Droke on a visit to Miss Hinds called on me this morning. Oh, poor dear boy, he has had a high temperature again and a hemorrhage; and has his sister to support.

It puzzles me that I have no visitors and receive so few letters. These poor, selfish, empty-headed mill girls have plenty of company, and flowers and candy and fruit. Why can't I get into touch with friends?

It is such a relief to me to be really separated from Frank. I cannot understand how I was deceived by him for so many years. Neither Christian Science nor any other line of thought enables me to see him now as anything but a cowardly slacker and liar. He earns $10 a week and sends me perhaps two, for the childrens' clothes. Now when I was on the News I earned $9 a week and regularly gave him five, besides working at home all day Sunday. And he said it was not enough.

March 31, 1918

Easter. I am not forgotten, I received a present of fruit, jelly, eggs and wine from the ladies of Mission Ridge. Mrs. Sarah Patten sent me a $2 check and very friendly note. Mrs. Hyman sent Joe a present, a crisp new Federal Reserve note for $5. He was delighted, and said at once he would put it in the bank and save up for a bicycle. This is good; a bank account will give him a feeling of stability next to having a home.

Laura writes me such a good letter, quite as if nothing had happened with me and Frank. She is a good friend. She asks Kitty to come and spend the summer with her, but until Joe can find a place to live this cannot be arranged. Joe cannot live in the house with his grandmother.

Laura writes that the old goody has disinherited her, and Frank, and Mary. I have had no confirmation of this.

Cousin May walked in this afternoon, a real good visitor at last. Her hair is nearly white. When she has her teeth fixed she will be handsome. She, like Laura, warns me against letting the twins come down this summer on any terms, while the soldiers are all over town. They are safer at school. But oh, how I want to see them!

April 16, 1918

Wakened before day by a terrific thunderclap, a few minutes afterward heard the first Thrush singing in the rain. A great flock of sparrowy gray birds pecking over the ground during the steady warm rain this morning; some of them seemed to be walking instead of hopping. The morning was too dark to distinguish the markings. There must have been a great migratory wave setting forward, for during the day I heard half a dozen different Warbler notes and many other birds.

I lent Science & Health to the woman in the next bed, who expressed herself as glad to learn something of C.S. Two other patients immediately set in on her with sneers and ridicule. I reminded them that they had not been asked to read it, and one, Bill Head by name, became quite impudent. It is strange how quickly the mere mention of it arouses all the opposition of which these fear-haunted, sin-beset minds are capable.

Frank has sent me three dollars and then three more for the girls.

My book, The Good Gray Mother, is finished; must be copied before going to a manuscript agent. The bird study book is getting on fast—all rough-drafted except the Warblers. I am quite proud of it.

April 19, 1918

Mr. Tallant came again and brought me a package of good writing materials, and a Calla lily plant. He was surprised to find the work of the book so far along, but would not promise any thing in the way of an advance, and I did not urge him. I feel weak and tired the past few days, and have not begun with the illustrations, but we talked the whole thing over and made plans. He even talked of a series of school books, and said if I get better he would send me to Florida next winter to make a study of bird life there. Most likely this is only talk such as people give consumptives—it being supposed to keep their courage up.

He is of a very materialistic viewpoint, earthbound like most men, but evidently very kind. He insisted on sending me a bottle of some kind of sure-cure. I can't make up my mind what stand to take; I don't want medicine. I told him the book is the best medicine. But he was insistent.

Yesterday Mrs. Stedman came to see me, walking up the long hill alone and carrying some nice canned fruit and some tulips to me.

I believe I like the calla better than the Easter lily; its white is richer, its leaves of more grace and dignity: its lines are of a sculpturesque simplicity and purity. O how variously perfect are the souls of plants, and of all living things!

Could I only write a book of insect studies like Lafcadio Hearn's wonderful story of the Japanese singing cricket!—or a book of intimate studies of small backyard creatures of all kinds, with a view to clearing away the superstitious terrors with which ignorance surrounds them! Such a book is truly needed. If children were taught to overcome the horror of unlike forms of animal life, the elimination of race-prejudice would follow quite naturally. First the snake and last the negro would be recognized as a good and wholesome expression of the creative spirit, and wrongs and torturing would cease with the cessation of fear.

This writing of school books appeals to me as being both easier and far more valuable work than the writing of fiction. Maybe it is just what I can do best. I should be glad to write them in memory of my mother, the bravest woman and the best country teacher I ever knew.

Oh, how I wish that I had known her better, that I had loved her more! For in those days, I thought only of self, so that my very love was selfish.

May 5, 1918

Sunday, but Joe did not come. I am not very uneasy about him, for I have a feeling of confidence that he is about his Father's business and cannot get lost or go far astray—that he is being led of the Spirit and can take no hurt. I wish I could feel that way about the girls. Judith has written her father, imperiously demanding money and saying that she can't stay there any longer, must come home as soon as school is out. I am anxious about this display of self-will.

Today I mailed the two MSS—one of the Good Gray Mother, to Zerelda in New York; one of Tennessee birds, to Mr. Tallant in Nashville. I am hoping that one or the other will raise the money for Joe to go to Mossop this winter.

May 9, 1918

Joe came just in time to help the nurse move me into a little room downstairs. We had a lovely visit all to ourselves. He told me all about the hunt, on which they caught no game except one ground hog, and asked permission to go again.

Frank writes me at length about how hard he is trying to be good—about studying the Bible, living the truth, subduing the animal nature, teaching his son, and so on. How straightforward and manly and high minded it did sound to be sure, and how completely I was taken in at first! Then I thought of something, and asked Joe if his father still chews tobacco. Oh, yes; Joe didn't believe he would ever quit as long as he lived in the house with Grandma—and went on reading the Literary Digest. I laughed, as I used to laugh when my old dad lectured on temperance and religion. The whole bubble was punctured at a stroke.

One thing in his letter, though, I do hope and pray is sincere. He says he has come to understand that many times when he thought I was scolding him I was simply telling the truth. If he will only stick to that and get the children to see it. It has been one of the bitterest things I have been called on to hear, that when I tried most earnestly to help him and the children, he has flouted me as an unreasonable and ill-tempered scolding woman, and has caused the children to take the same view. This is why none of them has heeded my advice. Thank God, Joe is coming to understand and listen to me.

May 19, 1918

Sunday. Joe spent the afternoon with me. What a delight, what a joy he is. His health seems excellent; he is growing fast, and is not fat, but solid and brown. Last week he earned two dollars hoeing potatoes, and paid it to his Aunt Laura on his board. He also helped Abb plant corn. He certainly talks like a man. But he is independent even to rudeness. Once I misunderstood something he said, and scolded him so that the tears came in his eyes; I am so sorry about that.

Frank sent me $5 for Judith's railroad fare and expenses. Joe tells
me that he has quarrelled with his mother and is threatening to leave and
board somewhere else, but he will hardly do anything so sensible. She has
most of my housekeeping things, and all of Joe's and Jean's stocking she
could lay hands on, and all their little personal effects; and she certainly
gets most of Frank's wages from week to week. I have made up my mind
that as soon as any money comes in from either of my books I will see if the
law can compel him to support his children. The simplest thing I suppose,
would be to divorce him, then he could not lay hands on any money the
books may bring in.

May 22, 1918

Finished the small illustrations for my book on birds; most of them
very poor stuff I am afraid. I mailed them at once and got the whole affair
off my mind, and began outlining a MS. entitled The Sanitary Mind, which
may or may not grow to the proportions of a book.

Oh, why couldn't I have had consumption before the war knocked
the whole publishing business into a cocked hat—then I should at least
have won some success in a literary way. But I ought not to feel that way
about it, and really I don't. If the books are of any value, that is if they are
necessary to the world, they had better never come to print, for there are
far too many books already.

Received a dear little letter from my dear little maid, with a cunning
childish sketch of a head very erect, with bobbed hair and a ribbon bow,—
such a likeness as hardly needs the label "This is me." She longs to come
"home," but patiently resigns herself with philosophy worthy of a grown
woman. I can but feel it a hard fate that deprives me of the companionship
of this lovely child-soul.

May 23, 1918

Yesterday evening I asked Miss Plewes to stay and talk with me, and
though she had not much time we had a little visit. I now begin to like
her very much. Her ideas are not striking, but her energy is stimulating.
She is really very kind when one considers the ingratitude and treachery
with which these poor sick creatures surround her; her patient combat
with wrong ways of living and thinking, the slow struggle with disease, is a

worth-while work. I have always respected and admired her, and now I feel relieved at finding myself able to like her somewhat.

When the night nurse came on, Velma Horton—or Kitty Malicoat as she is now called, having been granted her maiden name—I was surprised at her asking seriously to be taught Christian Science. I do not take too much credit to myself for this, it is not so much due to the pleasant example of my daily walk and conversation as to the fact that there is an agreeable young man patient here who is also studying C.S. But it is good and sincere for all that. I lent her some books, and recommended her to read the Gospels, which she scarcely knows. Asked me if the life of Jesus was found in the New Testament. I wonder if I could arrange to read a chapter with her every night.

May 25, 1918

This day a strange thing came to me. An old colored woman came in, how she ever found me I don't know, and offered me a letter to read. I saw the name Houston Green and then remembered having seen her before, when she came to ask me not to prosecute her son for throwing me down in the street and taking my pocket book. Four years ago it was, and the negro, still in the pen, asked her in his letter to see me and ask me to write a letter which should free him.

Of course I agreed at once and gladly, for I have always been sorry about that affair. I have said many times that the next negro that steals my pocket book can keep it, for the police are greater thieves than he. As he says, four years is enough. She wanted to pay me back the money, but I would not take it, saying that I only want to have the matter off my mind and be forgiven for my part in it. Then she wanted to "pay me for my trouble" as she put it. She seems a Christian woman in her way, and I hope if Houston gets free he will be a good son to her.

He does not seem very penitent, about the theft itself, neither does she. But considering the character of the police I can't blame them much, in their ignorance and their lack of good influences. They know not what they do—and it's not my business anyway.

I am not at all sure that I can help in this matter, but wrote to Green asking whom I should write to, and hope to be able to accomplish his liberation. The Government needs men very bad now, for laborers and the army; it may be they will be willing to free able-bodied prisoners on a slight excuse.

Now the most curious feature of this curious incident is that I had just been hunting for a text—"But if ye had understood what this meaneth, I will have mercy, and not sacrifice, ye would not have condemned the guiltless"; which is not quite the same as Matthew 9:13. I had not found it, but had the Bible open in search when the old black woman walked in. Houston Green is not guiltless, does not pretend to be; but I hope he will be freed and go into the army. The old mother is guiltless, at least.

May 28, 1918

I have said I hated symbolism; but I have tacked up three little pictures on the white washed wall, and each one is a symbol. The first is a newspaper cut of an etching of the Cincinnati fountain. The second is a photogravure of Rodin's Thinker. The third is a print of a Japanese drawing, of two birds of a species unknown to me, on a pine bough. None except the last presents any beauty to the eye; they are not noticed by chance comers; but Joe and I talk a great deal about them.

The Cincinnati picture, though so small that the bronze figures can hardly be distinguished, has enough of the atmosphere of Fountain Square to recall to me an afternoon of my childhood—a day of awakening. We were visiting the city, and my father and mother, not wishing to tire me out walking the streets, left me to play in Fountain Square. What better can be done to a child than to leave it alone in the presence of a great work of art? I walked round and round the fountain, looking at the figures, for I had never seen sculpture before at nine years old. My mother had just bought two books that were in the teachers' course that year—Ben Hur, and The Marble Faun. From time to time I sat on a bench and read. The books startled and delighted me with a wealth of new ideas; the fountain fed and filled and satisfied me with its beauty. Yet I did not associate the word <u>beautiful</u> with the bronze figures at all; neither was I appalled at their semi-nudity as my mother was; they were too strange to have any associations for me at all. But I shall never think of the Probasco Fountain without feeling again that rapture, of being at once awakened and satisfied.

The second picture is one of the world's great symbols—Thought making its way against all the limitations of material existence. Joe protested, quite naturally, that this small skull and giant muscles cannot befit the thinking type of man—"He doesn't look a bit like a thinker," said the boy. So I told him about it: This is Primitive Man, and he has lost Fire. Through some accident of storm or flood, or somebody's lack of thought, stupidity or carelessness, the tribal hearth is extinguished. All the others are dancing, crying, praying round the cold gray stones of the altar, beseeching the Sungod to return to them in tangible form, with sacrifices and howls; but this man knows that is not the way. He sits alone, filling the hours with thought. His muscles cannot help him now; he must think, not only for himself but for the tribe, and for babes who shall grow to be Man after him. He must think until he is sure that friction produces heat and more friction produces more heat, and so rubbing two sticks together he produces Fire. Then his tribe will make him high priest of the sungod; but it will mean little to the Thinker who found the Way.

The third is one Jean sent me, a pair of Japanese birds, done in the Eastern way which is not a photographic representation of individuals, but a spiritual interpretation of a type. Is not the prime message of Eastern art the same great truth which we Occidentals find so difficult to grasp,—the fundamental proposition of Christian Science also,—that all Being is One?

I want to see Judith, I want to see Judith, I want my rose, my daughter! I have written her to come; we will arrange somehow. This longing is become a tension; I could not have believed it possible that I could so long for any thing in life.

June 1, 1918

Last evening she came, my dark rose, taller than I am and deep-bosomed, superbly beautiful at fifteen years. She has kept her trunk packed for two weeks, and yesterday morning when she received my letter she made ready at once and took the first train. Miss Plewes allowed us to have quite a talk; then at 9 Judith went to bed. I think neither one of us slept much, and my heart feels the strain. If I could only have a whole day, or several days, to talk to Judith in!

Miss P. considerately allowed us quite a space of time through the day together, but the dear girl did quite a lot of work too. Miss P. said this evening it is a pleasure to see how quickly she does her tasks. It is a great pleasure to me to find that she is a good mixer, friendly with everything human. She remarked that it is a fine thing to have a mother whom everybody likes, because everybody is so nice to her. But I know they would be nice to her anyway—the gay, beautiful creature!

June 2, 1918

Sunday. Judith is a peach today in a white middy suit with yellow tie, and her hair in two long curls down her back. I am delighted to see that she has not grown clear out of my reach; she is evidently restless, eager, and hard to control; but she is affectionate and gives me her confidence to an extent I never dreamed of doing with my good mother. Told me about her first proposal.

Joe came in the afternoon, and although he has never admitted that he wanted to see Judith, they fall all over each other—two beautiful, strong, happy young things hungry for life. Joe has the quaintest lover-like ways; he would pretend to quarrel, but would sit holding Judith's hand and patting her affectionately, even while reading "Penrod."

We had a wonderfully happy afternoon. I felt almost too tired to talk, but was all happy to lie still and watch them and hear them laugh and chatter.

Frank writes me protesting that he does not support his mother at all,—which is where the old lady has got him fooled. He wants to come and see me, and of course he will have to come and see Judith.

June 5, 1918

Judith is a joy. Twice she has shed some tears over her very irregular work, but I think she will get on very well. What a relief it is to have the whole family well placed for the summer—if they will only stay put! Joe has even made tentative arrangements for the winter, to stay with an old lady and go to school. I am proud of them all.

He asked on Sunday, "Judith, what are you going to be when you grow up—a married woman?"

"Yes, a married woman," laughed Judith, but they went on to plan for a stock ranch in California where she should keep house for him. It is such a delight to hear their spontaneous ideas about things.

Ah! so then this is how it is. You pass the nine months of secret misery and secret exaltation, you come Heaven knows how through the hours of clamorous anguish, and there is in the world a new creature, terribly sensitive and helpless, a folded bud of life. You are day by day rewarded for service by baby words more poignantly sweet than anything in the world's literature, by the freshness and fragrance of childhood, by play that sends one's heart in deep waves of gladness breaking at the feet of God. Then suddenly the baby is no more, and there stands beside you a daughter comely beyond one's wildest hopes, a sister, a lover, a friend all alive with sympathy and intelligence, with ideas and feelings so unlike your own that you wonder where she came from. That is the way of it, then? And yet there are those who find life empty! Dear God!

She has had nothing but praise. Miss P. usually so cold and rigid, calls her "dear" and says she works rapidly and well. The men patients, I hear, compliment her extravagantly and stare at her; she plays with the little boys, and they write her joint love-letters in red ink. Her bright youth and eager spirits are refreshing beyond words to all these sick, grouchy prisoners. She is a treasure, and will need close guarding.

June 6, 1918

Joe came to see Judith. I never saw a little boy so in love with his sister; he rubs and purrs around her shoulders like a kitten, he kisses her neck, he admires her curls: their soft cheeks are pressed together like two peaches grown on the same bough. All this is so far from what I remember of my childhood that it seems like a miracle of God. There was nothing like it in my youth; I distrusted all the impulses of affection and rigidly repressed them, or if I let myself go in the least it was under such a weight of self-consciousness that the expression was spoilt. I find it difficult to understand my children, who kiss and quarrel and work and play with as buoyant & spontaneous a grace as ever I sang a hymn. They are all fond of clothes, and spend a good deal of care on their appearance. This trait they cannot have gotten from their father or me! But while I can't understand them I find it easy to rejoice in them and to thank God for them.

That bonehead doc, six feet long not counting his nose, stood here this morning and told me that he saw an eclipse of the sun several years ago which lasted nearly all day. I did not ask him why he did not make it all week while he was about it, neither did I tell him what a Joshua he must have been to suspend the laws of nature for that length of time, for I won't argue with a doctor or a preacher. But I was moved to some reflections on the sort of men who are licensed to experiment with the subtle, sensitive intricacies of the human body.

June 16, 1918

Sunday. I have quite recovered from the nervous depression, and am able to watch the interweaving of life in the loom of the woods, and the opening of gigantic blossoms in the gardens of the sky, with gratitude and praise.

Joe's visit was a joy to both me and Judith. Frank sent me $5 and some fruit and new handkerchiefs. Joe brought me maiden hair fern, sourwood bloom and wild hydrangea from the hillside, and a new flower which may be foam-flower or it may be black cohosh.

June 17, 1918

Judith is now working in the cottage, where I can see a good deal of her and hear her singing as she washes the dishes. Thus she is removed from too close association with those tough servant girls and the men patients, who buzz round her like bees. Frank is afraid she may fall in love, but there is safety in numbers; and Miss Plewes is afraid the men may not behave well toward her; but Judith is remarkably level-headed. I am not a bit uneasy. Her work is to bring the food from the kitchen of the main building twice a day, serve it on trays to the 16 patients, wash up afterwards, and keep her floors of the whole building swept and mopped. Also she does many little turns and errands for Miss Ward, the nurse in charge. It is quite a good deal for a young girl to manage. I am very proud of her. She is not temperamental like Jean, but just good and sensible and healthy, and such a beauty!

Now that I have no occupation save to drink quantities of tepid hydrant water and ring for the bed-pan every thirty minutes, I spend a good deal of time in recollections. Whole periods which I have fiercely repudiated and long cast out of mind come back. Thus I find myself still some kin to my father, with the keenest memories of drives and jaunts and boat rides and adventures. He had none of the moral courage that made my mother so fine: but he taught me to enjoy storms and riots; we would go tearing into anything together, in a skiff or on horseback, singing at the top of our voices in perfect unison, utterly reckless, drunk with excitement. He taught me to enjoy being out in any weather and at all hours of the night; to delight in the unusual. We had plenty of accidents, but never quite broke our necks. It is partly this trait which enables me now to look forward to death as the great adventure; and for many other reasons I am now able to bless the old man with all my heart. How I remember his patient persistence in helping me, at twelve years old, to overcome my terror of a gun. He taught me to kill snakes, and not to cry when stung by a hornet, and to go all over the place at night barefooted and in my little nightgown. Thus I had no fear in the woods at their darkest. It was my mother who taught me to look for their poetic mystery and beauty; but she never realized it as I did, because I knew not the meaning of danger. I see now that I owe him a great deal, and I wish I had loved him. But I never did. And now, as he himself declares, he lives in hell.

I have just learned a young girl's definition of home: Home is where you start from when you go to places.

June 23, 1918

Judith had her afternoon off yesterday, so she spent the afternoon in town with Joe and the night with her papa. They are both vigilant chaperones, being jealous of every man she speaks to. They came for a visit this afternoon. I am feeling worse and could not talk well.

I believe Frank is really trying his best now. Most of it is talk as usual; there is something pathetic after all in the way he plasters on the talk, trying to get me to think well of him; but he actually is holding a job and giving most of the money to his children. I shall not drive him away, I shall stick to him for two reasons: first, he is the father of my children; second, the look in his face when he speaks to a small child.

Judith is crying. Why? I suppose she does not like to work hard every day; wants a good time and a pleasant home such as other girls have as a matter of course. She talks very sensibly about it, however I pray that life may have something beautiful in store for her.

To me she is a joy-bringer, a fountain of vitality, a vessel of gladness. I grudge every hour that she is out of my sight.

The parole officer writes me briefly that Green's case cannot be considered before August.

July 7, 1918

Yesterday evening I had one of the most satisfactory battles of all my stormy life. I am a wicked old war-horse to take pleasure in such a thing; but Miss Plewes certainly had it coming to her, and I handed her one jolt after another without the least compunction. I do not think she will subject Judith to any further humiliations. She has the disposition of a sitting hen at all times; as everybody well knows, and for several days she has had a headache and has taken it out on Judith. This morning the elevator broke and hurt Judith's arm, and Miss P., finding breakfast belated, scolded the girl without stopping to make inquiries. Later, being asked to pay her for 5 weeks' work, she made out a check for $6! I told Judith to pack her things and go to her father at once. Which had the effect of bringing Miss P. in a hurry. She intended to plough over me, but it was I who gave her one good going over, and she took the defensive meekly enough. We compromised by letting Judith give her a week's notice. Singularly, I wasn't excited at all; it was no more than taking a sitting hen off her eggs. I intend that she shall pay Judith's wages too.

July 16, 1918

Judith went to her father when her week was out, and yesterday Miss P. sent a check for $8.30 in payment. I asked her if she was satisfied with that and felt that it was just payment for the work Judith did, and she promptly and positively replied in the affirmative. She is now paying a colored girl exactly double what she paid Judith and is getting the poorest service yet. I wish Judith could see these floors and smell that kitchen.

I am humiliated and vexed, and very ill. Cost what it may I am going to leave Pine Breeze. I can't live with my husband I suppose, as I have tried it so many times and found only misery from his neglect. And of course I have no other place to live.

I see now that I have never had any real home but the woods. That is the only place I was ever homesick for; I have gone to the woods at every time of trouble in my life; that is the only place on earth I care to go to now.

Perhaps I shall walk out of the door here some night after every one is asleep and the nurse upstairs, and just keep on walking in the woods till I drop. I can't get far, it will not take long. And then, when I am once out of the flesh, I shall walk on and on: over the waves of the sea, and in palm groves, and through the firs of Norway and the eucalyptus and fern forest of Australia, till I have seen all the woods in the world. It is not travel I want, but acquaintance with all forms of life.

July 18, 1918

Frank came, with Jean and Kitty. Jean it seems is doing well, but Judith has given some trouble and has now run off to her Aunt Laura's.

I told the folks that they may make a place for me, and take me home. If they neglect me, as formerly, very well, I need not live. But I believe that this time, as the girls are older and conditions better, they will make a reasonable effort to take care of me.

The News telephoned that Mr. Milton liked the poem I sent a few weeks ago about the negro situation, and asked me to write one for their next Saturday special. I dashed off some gay verses about my cart and jinny proposition, calling it Gypsy Song.

July 21, 1918

Judith and Joe and Kitty came up with Frank to see me: or rather Judith came to see Postel. I certainly thought she had more sense than to take up with such a low down fellow; he has been to the house to see her, and written asking her to meet him out. I am ashamed before Miss Plewes and every one on the hill.

July 30, 1918

Last night I suddenly lost hold of myself, and cried and cried till I thought I would wake the patients upstairs. At 11 o'clock I rang for the nurse and she gave me something after midnight to make me sleep. This morning had to take another dose for a severe pain in my neck and head.

Frank came up toward noon, but I had no money for him as yet and could tell him nothing. He wanted me to tell him what to do. But I cannot. I feel just as confused and distressed as he.

All along I have been telling them all what they should do, and they would not. Now they are in trouble their first thought is to run to me. But even now if I told them to do something disagreeable they would not do it.

I told Jean before she left Mossop that she must not think of gadding about among her kinfolks, but must stay at home and keep house for her father. Now on her third or fourth trip to the mountain she finds herself sick unto death in a room containing three beds besides being kitchen and dining room, with children running through it and chickens crowing under the floor, and she is not able to be moved. What can I say now?

I told Judith before she left Mossop, and over and over again afterwards, kindly and reasonably, that she must cut down on spending money and new clothes, and must above all things be careful about boys and men at this time. The first thing she did was to spend every cent I had saved; the next was to disgrace herself and me with that dirty Postel. I have just learned from Mrs. Hatch, the nurse, how Judith and Postel hid for more that half an hour in the little nook where they keep the records; and this after the warning of the nightgown episode.

August 3, 1918

Jean is at Erlanger [typhoid fever]. Frank came today, more worried over Judith than Jean. Postel keeps seeing her, hanging around the place, calling her over the neighbors' phones. He will not come where Frank can break his face for him, but is making a perfect nuisance of himself. Frank threatens to have him arrested.

Judith is to go to work on the telephone exchange, and Joe is trying for a job on the iron works. Which suggested to me a poem—Doing His Bit. Today wrote to 4 magazines trying for a market for my outdoor notes.

Judith seems to have come to her senses about Postel, which is a great victory and I bless her for it. She wants to stay and help us this winter instead of going away to school. We will see.

But Frank is just as much of a continual physical trouble and torment as ever. I don't believe I can ever endure close personal association with him again. And how can I be with my children without such intimacy with him? Here is a problem too hard for me to work out. I feel perplexed and distressed about it.

August 7, 1918

Mr. Tallant called this afternoon, and with him Dr. Evans whom I had not seen for years; he says the hot weather makes him ill tempered, but he doesn't seem so overbearing as formerly. Mr. Tallant wished me to make arrangements for the loan of bird pictures to his company for illustrative purposes. Says they are now working on my MS in the Chicago library; checking up its accuracy. I only wish I could be half as sure of the drawings as I am of the MS. He has postponed bringing out the book until next spring, but promises me an advance next month. He asked about a flower book, but would say nothing definite. If I had some such work as that to chew on, I could stand it through the winter. But unless prospects improve, my clock is set for October of this year.

I think the profound consolation I have never failed to gain from the woods is due to a sense of the sustaining forces of the universe,—of foundations beneath foundations. Among the thick trees, one feels the certain recurrence of life's phenomena, each in its due season; the sure progress of nature's processes; the deep strength of the vegetable kingdom; and the breadth of the chemical base it lays for animal conscious life; the infallibility of great, patient, unobtrusive laws; and beneath all the eternal rightness which is Very God of Very God. O fear not in a world like this! says every green leaf, whose grace and health spring from and testify to the innate and imperturbable harmony of things. The mind knows instinctively that such an object as a maidenhair fern could not exist in any but a divinely ordered universe; and no discords of personal experience and no mere logical refutation is able to disturb this conviction.

It is to the wholesomeness and beauty of this natural world that I wish to escape, out of the trap of lies and errors into which I have fallen. Christian Science denies that death is in any sense a liberator—says it takes a man just where it finds him. (If that is the case, how surprised the constituents of the usual old fashioned prayermeeting would be, if their "want to get a home in heaven" were to be suddenly granted! Within a week they would all be knocking on the portals of hell, begging Satan to let them have a chew of tobacco or a dip of snuff, and a chair where they could tip back against the wall and spit on the floor in their wonted sodden idleness.) I expect to be freed of many errors by my escape from the flesh. How glorious not to be bothered with the absurdly complicated business of eating and sleeping, of keeping the body warm, of keeping it clean! Certainly all purely artificial institutions which we recognize as lies will fall away. The slave who dies under the master's whip would, if he believed in slavery as a true principle of conduct, remain a slave after death, and until his false belief changed; but if at the time of death he saw clearly that slavery is an error which has without reason foisted itself on humanity, vicitimizing master and slave alike, he would by the experience of death be set free, as he was already free in spirit and in truth. The fragmentary record we have of Jesus' reappearance after death shows that the experience freed him of persecution by his enemies, and of mortal limitations and disabilities. So I have, I think, good grounds for hoping that after my escape I shall no longer have to work for money which does no one any good, being wasted by self-willed mismanagement; that I shall not be compelled to yield my body to sexual torture; that I shall not be pinched by continual want. These things are lies, as the nails of the cross were lies. I have been forced to submit, as the Son of Man must suffer of them; but my spirit knows these things are not true, and once out of the flesh I shall be free. And I shall not be lonely either; I have long been aware of the infinite reservoirs of intelligence and love; which shall reach me in friendships innumerable, unhindered by the illusions of space and time that prevent them from getting to me here.

. . . Then one will forget one's unhappiness and errors past, and the death-struggle, as a nightmare is forgotten. In the conversation of that company to recall these things is in bad taste, like talk of dreams.

August 12, 1918

Frank came to get my name on a permit for Joe to work. Grandma in a tantrum has ordered them all out of her house—much to my satisfaction. I am getting better and eating well. Wrote another poem, The Novae.

August 18, 1918

I do not understand why defeat and disappointment should always be my portion. Even the children notice. "More bad luck happens to us than to any family I ever saw," said Judith today. She personally is in for worse luck if she does not stop talking with strange men on the street and everywhere. I have told her repeatedly in plain words of the danger. But it seems I am powerless to turn any of the family from the dangers I foresee. It is like a curse—some evil Karma.

Frank has done better than I expected—another raise, $26. per week. Judith is very much pleased with her work on the telephone exchange. Jean, they say, is better, but very thin and weak.

Katharine alone is docile, a perpetual delight. Oh, so short an afternoon with the darlings, so long a week to lie here alone on my back!

The magazines are a solace. I find in an old Hibbert Journal an essay, Life & Consciousness, in which Bergson reaches some of the same conclusions as I in the Good Gray Mother. This is very encouraging, but not so encouraging as an acceptance by MacMillan would have been.

August 19, 1918

Birds go in mixed bands, capriciously. One sees almost nothing of them for a few days; then suddenly the trees are full of their movements, for twenty minutes perhaps—four or five species of sociable inclinations.

Yesterday brought cooling showers, today is cloudy without a breath of wind. The first bird I saw was a black-throat green warbler—tho' these are not supposed to spend the summer so far south. There was no mistake; he came very close to me. About 11:30 occurred one of those mixed companies, a wave of bird life. Mostly red-eyed vireos—are they not getting together for migration? Three came close to my window, and peered at me as curiously as I was peering at them. A Nashville warbler and a black-and-white warbler were among the group, and other warblers farther off among the leaves of which I caught glimpses not sufficient for identification. Downy Woodpecker is rarely absent from these friendly groups—this time I believe there were two of him. The resident female summer tanager was also present but I fear in no neighborly spirit; I saw her descend upon a smaller bird as if resenting the instrusion, the second time with an angry twitter. The ground-loving, closely resident Carolina Wren, excited by visitors as usual, began to scold under the window, and looking out I saw on a dead branch the smallest Flycatcher I have ever seen—Chebec? Three Yellowhammers also appeared, but as they are commonly coming and going, they probably had nothing to do with the others. It was quite a display altogether, and I tired myself out leaning up in the window, trying to see them all and watching them catch insects. All were silent or nearly so, even the vireos.

Many writers have noticed the companionship of Chickadees, titmice, nuthatches, & downy woodpeckers, especially in winter; but I do not remember to have read of these post-nuptial driftings.

epilogue

Emma Bell Miles died seven months to the day after her last journal entry. She left the Pine Breeze Sanitarium in the fall of 1918, and spent her final declining months in North Chattanooga, in a house Frank had rented. Her book *Our Southern Birds* was published just weeks before her death. She was buried close to her mother in Red Bank, at the Memorial Cemetery, near the top of a hill. At the time of her burial, the site probably offered a view of Walden's Ridge, less than five miles away. Today, trees block the view.

notes

Introduction

1. Kay Baker Gaston, *Emma Bell Miles* (Chattanooga: Walden's Ridge Historical Association, 1985), 6.

2. Emma Bell Miles to Anna Ricketson, April 6, 1907, Chattanooga Public Library.

3. Gaston, *Emma Bell Miles*, 11–15.

4. Ibid., 11.

5. Ibid., 13.

6. Emma Bell Miles, "The Difference," *Harper's Monthly* 108, no. 646 (March 1904): 653.

7. Emma Bell Miles, "Homesick," *Harper's Monthly* 108, no. 647 (April 1904): 789.

8. Emma Bell Miles, "Some Real American Music," *Harper's Monthly* 109, no. 649 (June 1904): 118–23.

9. Miles had done some illustrations for their books, and her daughters would later maintain that she actually wrote portions of several of their novels.

10. Grace MacGowan Cooke, *A Gourd Fiddle* (Philadelphia: H. Altemus, 1904). Miles mentions Cooke and MacGowan several times in her journal, but the first entry is not until 1912.

11. Emma Bell Miles to Anna Ricketson, March 9, 1907, and May 16, 1909, Chattanooga Public Library.

12. Kay Baker Gaston, "The MacGowan Girls," *California History* 59, no. 2 (Summer 1980): 116–25.

13. This casting would lead some researchers on Miles to erroneously believe she, too, had been a schoolteacher in a small mountain schoolhouse.

14. Elizabeth S. D. Engelhardt, *The Tangled Roots of Feminism, Environmentalism, and Appalachian Literature* (Athens: Ohio University Press, 2003), 139.

15. Gaston, *Emma Bell Miles,* 20.

16. A search in a national library database shows very few published works dealing with southern Appalachia and its customs prior to the publication of *The Spirit of the Mountains.* Most are excerpts from magazine essays.

17. *Atlantic Monthly* 83, no. 497 (March 1899).

18. Bradford Torrey, *Spring Notes from Tennessee* (Boston: Houghton Mifflin, 1896). In the chapter about Walden's Ridge, Torrey details a conversation with a young girl, who may have been Miles.

19. Horace Kephart, *Our Southern Highlanders: A Narrative of Adventure in the Southern Appalachians and a Study of Life among the Mountaineers* (New York: Outing Publishing Company, 1913); John C. Campbell, *The Southern Highlander and His Homeland* (New York: Russell Sage Foundation, 1921).

20. Mark T. Banker, *Appalachians All: East Tennesseans and the Elusive History of an American Region* (Knoxville: University of Tennessee Press, 2010), 145.

21. David Whisnant, introduction to *The Spirit of the Mountains,* facsimile ed. (Knoxville: University of Tennessee Press, 1975), xvi.

22. Ibid., xvii.

23. *Harper's Monthly:* "The Common Lot," 118 (December 1908); "A Dark Rose," 118 (February 1909); "The Dulcimore," 119 (November 1909); "Flyaway Flittermouse," 121 (July 1910); "Three Roads and a River," 121 (November 1910); *Putnam's Magazine:* "The Broken Urn," 5 (February 1909); "The Homecoming of Evelina," 6 (May 1909); *The Red Book:* "Mallard Plumage," 13 (August 1909), "The Breaks of Caney," 14 (March 1910); *Craftsman:* "Flower of Noon," 21 (January 1912); "Enchanter's Nightshade," 22 (July 1912); *Lippincott's:* "At the Top of Sourwood," 89 (March 1912); "Love O' Man," 93 (March 1914); *The Mother's Magazine:* "The White Marauder," 13 (August 1917). A story titled "Turkey Luck" appeared posthumously in the October 13, 1921, issue of *The Youth's Companion.* Chattanooga publications in which her stories appeared include *The Lookout:* "Thistle Bloom," featured in the October 26 and November 2, 1912, issues; and "A Dream of the Dust," in the December 28, 1912, issue. It is possible other stories appeared in less-known publications, yet undiscovered, since she did not often record in her journal the publication or submission of stories.

24. Shannon Brooks, "Coming Home: Finding My Appalachian Mothers through Emma Bell Miles," *NSWA Journal* 11, no. 3 (1999): 164.

25. Grace Toney Edwards, "Emma Bell Miles, Appalachian Author, Artist, and Interpreter of Folk Culture" (PhD diss., University of Virginia, 1981), 110.

26. Sara L. Zeigler, "Wifely Duties: Marriage, Labor, and the Common Law in Nineteenth-Century America," *Social Science History* 20, no. 1 (1996): 69.

27. In particular, her "Fountain Square Conversations," a column published in the *Chattanooga News* in 1914.

28. Emma Bell Miles, personal journal, Jean Miles Catino Collection, University of Tennessee at Chattanooga, May 11, 1916.

29. For more on this, see chapter 2, "Writing and Self-Culture: The Contest over the Meaning of Literacy," in Jane H. Hunter's *How Young Ladies Became Girls: The Victorian Origins of American Girlhood* (New Haven: Yale University Press, 2002).

30. *Rural Hours*, by Susan Fenimore Cooper (New York: G. P. Putnam, 1850).

31. Miles, journal, July 25, 1914.

32. Zeiglar, "Wifely Duties," 64.

33. Most notable was the biographical article by Adelaide Rowell, "Emma Bell Miles: Artist, Author, and Poet of the Tennessee Mountains," published in the *Tennessee Historical Quarterly* 25 (March 1966), in which Rowell described Frank as "typically shiftless" and claimed he forced Miles in her final days to a "poorly chinked cabin" on Walden's Ridge to tend to him. This article contained other inaccuracies.

34. Miles does note some drinking by Frank in the journal on several occasions, but this does not seem a recurring or consistent problem.

35. Miles, journal, October 1913.

36. "Miami Impressions," *Lookout* 4, no. 19 (March 5, 1910); "A Florida Christmas," *Nautilus* 12 (December 1910).

37. Edwards, "Miles, Appalachian Author," 20.

38. Miles, journal, June 2, 1912.

39. Ibid., January 17, 1914.

40. Ibid., August 10, 1916.

41. Gaston, *Emma Bell Miles*, 24–25.

42. Emma Bell Miles, *Chords from a Dulcimore* (Chattanooga: Self-published, 1912). Miles preferred to use this archaic spelling for the dulcimer.

43. Edwards, "Miles, Appalachian Author," 24.

44. Today the cemetery is still used, even though it is in a remote area on Walden's Ridge. The stones are still there, some with proper markers that were added at some later point. There is no marker for Mirick Miles.

45. Patricia Knight, "Women and Abortion in Victorian and Edwardian England," *History Workshop* 4 (1977): 60.

46. Miles, journal, February 23, 1915.

47. Claudia Thiele, Anton-Rupert Laireiter, and Urs Baumann, "Diaries in Clinical Psychology and Psychotherapy: A Selective Review," *Clinical Psychology and Psychotherapy* 9 (2002): 1.

48. Sharon Hymer, "The Diary as Therapy: The Diary as Adjunct to Therapy," *Psychotherapy in Private Practice* 9, no. 4 (1991): 14.

49. Miles, journal, November 18, 1913.

50. Glenda Riley, *Divorce: An American Tradition* (New York: Oxford University Press, 1991), 130.

51. Miles, journal, September 10, 1916.

52. Ibid., July 24, 1914.

53. Ibid., August 15, 1914.

54. Ibid., February 28, 1915.

55. Ibid., February 6, 1915.

56. Ibid.

57. Rajita R. Bhavaraju and Lee B. Reichman, "Tuberculosis," *Encyclopedia of Public Health,* ed. Lester Breslow (New York: Macmillan, 2002), 1231–33.

58. Thomas Dormandy, *The White Death: A History of Tuberculosis* (New York: New York University Press, 2000), 224.

59. Ibid., 23.

60. Richard P. Mulcahy, "Health" (Introduction), *Encyclopedia of Appalachia,* ed. Rudy Abramson and Jean Haskell (Knoxville: University of Tennessee Press, 2006), 1632.

61. Sharon A. Denham, "Families and Health," *Encyclopedia of Appalachia,* ed. Rudy Abramson and Jean Haskell (Knoxville: University of Tennessee Press, 2006), 1649.

62. Gaston, *Emma Bell Miles,* 220.

63. Miles, journal, June 6, 1917.

64. Ibid., August 11, 1916.

65. Ibid., August 16, 1916.

66. Ibid., August 26, 1917.

67. A search in an international library database reveals just over fifty New Thought periodicals worldwide in print during the early 1900s. By 1910, the *Nautilus* was the most widely read, with over 31,000 subscribers.

68. Miles, journal, August 8, 1918.

69. "Mortality from Tuberculosis in the United States, 1920," *Public Health Reports (1896–1970)* 37, no. 2 (January 13, 1922): 53–54.

70. Emma Bell Miles, *Our Southern Birds* (Chattanooga: National Book Company, 1919).

71. Gaston, *Emma Bell Miles,* 244.

72. Emma Bell Miles, *Strains from a Dulcimore* (Atlanta: E. Hartsock, 1930).

73. Cartter Patten, *Signal Mountain and Walden's Ridge* (Chattanooga: Published by author, 1962).

74. Adelaide Rowell, "Emma Bell Miles: Artist, Author, and Poet of the Tennessee Mountains," *Tennessee Historical Quarterly* 25 (March 1966): 89.

75. In addition to those already cited, others would include *Appalachian Heritage* 33, no. 4 (Fall 2005), which devoted the entire issue to Emma Bell Miles (Berea College, edited by George Brosi, and including several articles or essays on Miles); Engelhardt, *Tangled Roots,* which features a chapter titled "Emma Bell Miles and Grace MacGowan Cooke: Ecological Feminism's Roots"; Katerina Prajznerova, "Emma Bell Miles's Appalachia and Emily Carr's Cascadia: A Comparative Study in Literary Ecology," *49th Parallel* 20 (Winter 2006–7); and the foreword and introduction to the 1975 University of Tennessee Press reissue of *The Spirit of the Mountains,* by Roger Abrahams and David Whisnant, respectively.

76. Jean Miles Catino to Kay Baker Gaston, April 30, 1979, Jean Miles Catino Collection, Special Collections, University of Tennessee at Chattanooga.

77. Robert Sparks Walker to Adelaide Rowell, April 15, 1944, Chattanooga Public Library.

78. Zerelda Rains to Jean Miles Catino, 1952, Jean Miles Catino Collection, Special Collections, University of Tennessee at Chattanooga.

79. Caroline Wood Morrison (?–1918) appears to have published only one book, coauthored with Grace MacGowan Cooke, *William and Bill* (New York: The Century Company, 1914). Morrison did publish several short stories.

80. Miles refers to "Miss Holly" several times in the next four years of journal entries, but the journal provides no more information on her identity, although it sounds as if this friend helped in placing Miles's story manuscripts with publishers or magazines.

81. Miles, journal, April 3, 1912.

82. Ibid., May 11, 1912.

83. Ibid., May 26, 1912.

84. Ibid., September 5, 1912.

85. Ibid., September 2, 1913.

86. Ibid., March 31, 1915.

87. Ibid., September 29, 1916.

88. Ibid., May 25 and September 6, 1916.

89. Emma Bell Miles to Anna Ricketson, February 19, 1908; January 1, 1909; and January 2, 1916, Chattanooga Public Library.

90. Miles, journal, June 6, 1917.

91. Ibid., May 11, 1916.

Chapter 1: Walden's Ridge

1. Summertown was an area along the eastern side of Walden's Ridge where some of the wealthier families from Chattanooga built summer homes, to escape the summer's heat and the yellow fever that had hit Chattanooga in the 1870s. In 1908 the Miles family, although certainly not wealthy, were living in a shack in that area.

2. Laura Miles Hatfield (1878–1921), a sister of Emma's husband, Frank. She was married to Absalom "Ab" Hatfield.

3. The Catlows were a Walden's Ridge family; Grace Catlow (Stroop) was a childhood friend of Emma's.

4. Lassie Hullett, sister of Tina (also referred to as "Tinte" Miles), the wife of Arthur "Dock" Miles, Frank's brother.

5. These are all locations on or around Walden's Ridge, except for Sequatchie, which is the county and area north of Walden's Ridge.

6. Hominy Snow: pellet-like snowflakes, also known as graupel.

7. Miles often referred to Frank as "the man" early on in the journals.

8. Pomace: the remains of a fruit (apple) after it has been mashed to extract the juice.

9. The southernmost tip of Walden's Ridge, looking over the Tennessee River; a site that provides a scenic view of the Tennessee River valley.

10. The *John A. Patten*, built in 1906, burned in Bridgeport, Alabama, in 1910.

11. Raccoon Mountain, which runs alongside the Tennessee River on the west side, across from Walden's Ridge.

12. A reference to Frank Mirick Miles, whom they would call Mark, the last living child Emma would give birth to.

13. A popular bluff overlook high up on Walden's Ridge, with a great view of the Tennessee River.

Chapter 2: Return to Walden's Ridge

1. A brutal Confederate guerrilla during the Civil War.

2. An area on Walden's Ridge where the wealthy citizens of Chattanooga built summer homes.

3. A short story, published in *Lippincott's Magazine* in March 1912.

4. Mr. and Mrs. E. A. Wheatley. Emma had met them in Miami, when they were there in late 1909 and early 1910. They lived in St. Elmo and would take Emma in from time to time, to give her rest, encouragement, and, at times, items to help the family to get by. Mr. Wheatley, an Englishman, worked for the Chattanooga Medicine Company.

5. This house, described by Miles's biographer, Kay Baker Gaston, as a "three-room shack in the woods" was below the Signal Point Road on Walden's Ridge. Frank had traded most of their livestock for the house.

6. Mrs. Barnett was a neighbor who did cleaning for Miles.

7. May Freudenberg, a distant relative of Emma Bell Miles on her mother's side.

8. Probably Sarah Key Patten, wife of prominent Chattanoogan Zeboim Cartter Patten Sr., and daughter of former US Senator and Postmaster David M. Key.

9. Zerelda Rains (1874–1963) and her husband. Miles studied art with Rains, who helped her enroll at the art school in St. Louis in the late 1890s.

10. Frank occasionally worked for a family named Rawlings, which Miles spells as "Rawlins" on several occasions.

11. The *Nautilus* was a New Thought magazine. Miles had published at least one story with them already, an account of their Miami Christmas.

12. Possibly an editor at a magazine.

13. Only two of these stories are known to have been published: "Thistle Bloom" in the *Lookout*, October and November 1912; and "Enchanter's Nightshade," in *Craftsman*, July 1912. The other manuscripts are not accounted for among papers relating to Emma Bell Miles.

14. Apparently never published.

15. Miles would hand-illustrate her book, *The Spirit of the Mountains*, and her booklet of poems, *Chords from a Dulcimore*, for individuals for a small charge.

16. An atmospheric phenomenon in which lights appear around or near the sun.

17. Lines 1–3 of "Attractions," by Émile Verhaeren, from *Poèmes*, in a translation identical to the one that appears in Leo Tolstoy, *What Is Art?*, translated by Aylmer Maude (New York: Thomas Y. Crowell, 1899). 188.

18. A feast with spirits, possibly a tradition dating back to Celtic Europe.

19. "Mystic Words," not known to have been published. "A Dream of the Dust" was published in the *Lookout* 10, no. 10, in December 1912.

20. Grace MacGowan Cooke, a friend and local writer with whom Emma had worked, was a daughter of a local newspaper publisher.

21. It is quite possible that Miles is referring to having had a miscarriage.

22. Joseph Ottakar Cadek, founder of the Cadek Conservatory of Music in Chattanooga in 1904, and Reita Faxon Pryor (1876–1958), music educator in Chattanooga.

23. "Thistle Bloom" was published in the *Lookout* 10, nos. 1–2 (October–November 1912).

24. Whether this is a completed novel is not known, but Emma never published a novel, and a manuscript for a novel has never been located. Her journals contain several references to manuscripts, some book-length, that were never published and have since disappeared.

25. David V. Stroop, an architect, and husband of Emma's friend, Edith Catlow Stroop.

26. This work apparently was never written.

27. A play written in the 1890s by Maurice Maeterlinck.

28. Not known to have been published.

29. Hill City is an area of Chattanooga known today as North Chattanooga.

30. Robert Strauss, a Shakespearean and vaudevillian actor from Chattanooga, who became nationally known on the stage and on radio.

31. This poem appears in a small booklet of poems, *Chords from a Dulcimore*, that Emma self-published in 1912.

32. Grace MacGowan Cooke's novel, *The Joy Bringer*, was published the following year and may have been the novel Miles refers to.

33. Probably an illuminated copy of *Chords from a Dulcimore*.

34. Captain Joseph Chappell Hutcheson (1842–1924), a Virginia native, Confederate veteran, and Texas politician, who had a summer home on Walden's Ridge. Brother-in-law to the mentioned Mrs. Dabney.

35. Benjamin Franklin Bell (1848–1926). Emma was estranged from him during her adult life, as he had forced her and Frank out of the home he owned shortly after they were married.

36. *The Century of the Child*, by Ellen Key (New York: G. P. Putnam's Sons, 1909).

37. Daughter of former Tennessee governor (1903–5) and senator (1905–11) James B. Frazier, from Chattanooga.

38. Not known to have been published.

39. Anne Bachman Hyde, daughter of prominent Chattanooga Presbyterian pastor Jonathan Waverly Bachman; and her sister-in-law, Pearl Duke Bachman, wife of Mrs. Hyde's brother, Senator Nathan Lynn Bachman.

40. Probably personally illustrating a copy of *The Spirit of the Mountains.*

41. Cordelia Reed, who ran an orphanage in Chattanooga from 1886 until 1919.

42. Lone Oak is a small community on Walden's Ridge approximately 5 miles north of the area where the Mileses lived.

43. This is where Miles had her *Chords from a Dulcimore* booklet of poems printed.

44. Sim Perry Long (1879–1944) was a Chattanooga real estate broker. The Read House is a hotel in downtown Chattanooga.

45. Henry Nyberg was a car manufacturer from Chicago, who built cars from 1911 until 1914. There was a plant in Chattanooga from 1911 until 1912.

Chapter 3: *Tragedy and Heartbreak*

1. Tinte was Frank's brother Arthur "Dock" Miles's wife, also known as Tina or Tena.

2. *Chords from a Dulcimore,* her self-published booklet of poems.

3. *Standard History of Chattanooga,* by Charles McGuffey (Knoxville: Crew and Dorey, 1911).

4. Anna Ricketson, of New Bedford, Massachusetts, an admirer of Emma Bell Miles, was especially kind to Emma and her family with gifts and money over the years.

5. Lupton Patten (1907–1958), son of John A. Patten, prominent Chattanoogan.

6. Dr. A. T. Peay (1863–1947), a longtime Chattanooga doctor.

7. A search in the microfilmed copy of the newspaper has failed to locate this poem.

8. The Bonny Oaks School, founded in Hamilton County, Tennessee, in 1896.

9. Balder (or Baldr) the Beautiful was the summer Sun-God, and Odin's son, in Norse mythology.

10. "Chautauqua"—An educational program and school of thought, developed in Chautauqua, New York, in 1874 and which lasted into the twentieth century. Often religious in nature.

11. Elizabeth Towne (1865–1960), founder of the *Nautilus* magazine.

12. Chattanooga was a popular location for Civil War veterans' reunions, for both the North and South.

Chapter 4: *"I Must Be Free!"*

1. *The Wind before the Dawn* (novel), by Dell H. Munger (Garden City, NY: Doubleday, 1912).

2. William F. "Buffalo Bill" Cody (1846–1917). His visit to Chattanooga on June 7, 1913, with his Wild West Show, would be the last of his eight visits to Chattanooga.

3. Either an exaggeration or a false report. Newspaper accounts give Chattanooga's low temperature of June 9 as 59 degrees.

4. Whether this is a poem or a short story is not known, as it does not appear in any of Miles's published work or papers.

5. As Frank had a large extended family of cousins and relatives, "John V." was probably one of them.

6. Friends of the family would eventually arrange and pay for schooling for some of the children, particularly the twins Jean and Judith, at a school in Boaz, Alabama.

7. Nicklin was possibly John Nicklin, a former mayor of Chattanooga.

8. Jonathan Waverly Bachman (1837–1924), former Confederate chaplain and longtime Presbyterian pastor in Chattanooga, known as "the Pastor of Chattanooga."

9. Margaret Severance (1878–1957), actress, poet, and artist, who lived in Chattanooga and befriended Miles.

10. Miles's father, Benjamin Franklin Bell. What Frank meant by uttering this is not entirely clear.

11. Grand Army of the Republic, an organization of Union Civil War veterans, who were having a reunion in Chattanooga.

12. A mother-daughter team in Great Britain who were involved in women's rights.

13. Miles later ripped some pages from her journals to hide some of the more shameful acts from her children, who she knew would read them.

14. A neighborhood about one mile south of downtown Chattanooga.

15. It is believed by many Miles scholars that she resorted to self-aborting several unwanted pregnancies, particularly after Mirick died, and this could be a reference to such actions.

16. J. Fred and J. Herman Ferger, two real estate developers in Chattanooga.

17. While working at the *Chattanooga News*, Miles had a column titled "Fountain Square Conversations."

18. The Frances Willard Home for Women, a housing apartment unit for working women near downtown Chattanooga.

19. During this period, the University of Chattanooga (now University of Tennessee at Chattanooga) had a Professor David R. Lee, a professor of classical literature.

20. Emma's anguish on being pregnant again.

Chapter 5: Pine Breeze Sanitarium

1. A tuberculosis sanitarium in Chattanooga, which had opened in 1913.

2. Wife of Captain Gahagan, an attorney Miles also consulted about getting a divorce. Mrs. Gahagan was the president of the Tuberculosis Association.

3. Miss Natalie Plewes, the first superintendent of the Pine Breeze Sanitarium. Prior to this, Plewes was the assistant superintendent of Erlanger Hospital in Chattanooga.

4. Freudenberg's store, run by a relative of Miles.

5. Clinton Daingerfield may be the writer Clinton Dangerfield, pen name for Ella Howard Bryan (1872–1954), who had lived as a child on nearby Lookout Mountain.

6. From "The Garden of Proserpine," by Algernon Charles Swinburne.

7. A paraphrase of a stanza from "The Ballad of Reading Gaol," by Oscar Wilde.

8. Perhaps a reference to the "Noseless One" of Jack London's 1913 autobiographical book, *John Barleycorn*. In that book, the Noseless One is death, personified by a skull.

9. Perhaps a reference to a line from *The Rubaiyat of Omar Khayyam*.

10. Leo Max Frank, an American Jewish businessman, convicted of murder but whose sentence was commuted; lynched in Marietta, Georgia, on August 17, 1915.

11. The Mossop Memorial School, a boarding school for girls, established in Huntsville, Tennessee, in 1909; moved in 1915 to Harriman, Tennessee.

12. The W is a very crooked, hair-pinned road leading down from Walden's Ridge to Chattanooga, so named due to its W-shaped hairpin curves near the top.

13. By this time, the twins, Judith and Jean, were attending schools elsewhere, supported by friends and admirers of Emma.

14. The Southern Express Company was a delivery service in Chattanooga.

Chapter 6: A Brief Separation

1. A popular early twentieth-century folk song about the murder of William "Billy" Lyons by Stagger Lee Shelton.

2. Before the calendar was moved back eleven days from the Julian calendar to the current Gregorian calendar, Christmas was observed on January 6. Some people in the Appalachian region still observed the original date.

3. Probably a hike from the Signal Mountain Inn to a small waterfall at the foot of Walden's Ridge, running from Rainbow Lake.

4. Apparently never published. The manuscript is unaccounted for in collections relating to Emma Bell Miles.

5. This was never published and the manuscript has never been located.

6. John Alanson Patten (1867–1916), prominent Chattanooga citizen and businessman.

7. The town of Cleveland, Tennessee, is approximately 30 miles north of Chattanooga.

8. Mrs. Cooke was the wife of a prominent Chattanooga attorney.

9. Roy Bell, half-brother to Emma, born around 1906. Her father, Benjamin Franklin Bell, had remarried and in 1916 was living in Graysville, north of Chattanooga.

10. An Episcopalian Church school for girls in Sewanee, Tennessee.

11. The *Chattanooga News* indeed ran three columns, including two of Miles's poems, in an article titled "Emma Bell Miles, Poet of Tennessee Mountains: Broken in Health but Ever Happy."

12. An Episcopalian Church school for boys in Sewanee, Tennessee.

13. From Tennyson's 1849 poem, "In Memoriam, A.H.H."

14. Mary Baker Eddy (1821–1910), founder of the Church of Christ, Scientist (Christian Science).

15. Phineas Quimby (1802–1866), the founder of the New Thought Movement.

16. Paul Laurence Dunbar (1872–1906), an African American poet.

17. The 1915 movie, *Birth of a Nation,* directed by D. W. Griffith, was based on a 1905 Thomas F. Dixon Jr. novel, *The Clansman: An Historical Romance of the Ku Klux Klan.*

Chapter 7: The Good Gray Mother

1. This signaled the beginning of the United States' involvement with the war that would later be called World War I. Miles may have entered the incorrect date in her journal, as the day the United States declared war was April 6.

2. Hazel was the daughter of George and May Freudenberg.

3. Probably "The Good Gray Mother," a book on nature themes. This was never published, and the manuscript has been lost.

index

abortion, xxi, xxxvii, 150, 188, 208, 343n15
Anderson, Lotta, 86, 89
Andrews, Elizabeth Key, 69, 73, 162
Andrews, Garnett, Jr., 162
Andrews, Mary Purvis, 277
Annis, Mrs. (friend), 184, 186, 199, 200, 202, 207, 211, 245, 305
Armstrong, Zella, 73, 83, 95, 104
Atlee, Frank, 111, 158, 159, 165, 169, 180
Atlee, Lenora, 82, 89, 92, 93, 96, 106, 109, 111, 118, 156, 158, 165, 166, 168, 169, 171, 173, 177, 178, 179, 181, 182, 184, 185, 186, 187, 189, 193, 199, 240

Bacher, Mrs. (friend), 208, 216, 225, 227, 245
Bachman, Jonathan Waverly, 159, 342n39, 343n8
Bachman, Martha, 150, 152, 154
Bachman, Pearl Duke, 92, 128, 129, 240, 342n39
Bachman, Nathan Lynn (Judge, Senator), 152, 240, 342n39
Barnett, Mrs. (neighbor), 60, 340n9
Bell, Benjamin Franklin, xxv–xxvii, 88, 260–62, 324–25, 341n35
Bell, Maggie, 260, 282
Bell, Martha Ann Mirick, xxv–xxvi, 316
Bell, Roy, 264, 282
Bird Club, 251, 253, 254, 263
birds, 212, 217, 224, 225, 226, 232, 233, 235, 237–38, 239, 240, 242, 243, 250–52, 253, 254, 255, 256–57, 258, 259, 283, 284, 290, 296, 302, 315, 331
Birth of a Nation, 286, 345n17

Boaz, Alabama, 172, 193
Brown, Mrs. B. J., 100
Brown, Foster V., 238, 272
Bryan, Ella Howard, 344n5
Buffalo Bill. *See* Cody, William F. "Buffalo Bill"

Cadek, Joseph Ottaker, 75, 83, 185, 341n22
Campbell, John C., xxix
Cantrell, Mrs. (friend), 81
Catino, Jean Miles, xvii–xviii, xxi, xlii, xliv, xlv, 10, 47, 50, 53, 54, 59, 60, 62, 70, 71, 82, 90, 91, 94, 101, 102, 105, 110, 111, 119–20, 121, 123, 128, 154, 155, 156, 159, 165, 166, 167, 172–73, 175, 187, 189, 192, 206, 213, 221, 226, 228, 230, 233, 234, 237, 239, 242, 244–45, 246, 249, 250, 253–54, 255, 258, 259, 263, 265, 266, 268, 270, 281, 283, 285–86, 287, 289, 294, 296, 297, 298, 300–301, 302, 304, 309, 310, 321, 327, 328, 330
Catlow, Grace, 339n3
Catlows, the, 17, 339n3
Century, xxx, 189
Century of the Child, The (Key), 89
Chambers, Henry A., 207, 210, 211, 213, 219
Chapin, Mrs. E. Y., 159, 172, 184, 185
Chattanooga News, xxxviii, xl, xlv, 72, 74, 81, 82, 83, 86, 96, 118, 124, 173, 174, 183, 188, 190, 199, 200, 233, 249, 266, 311, 314, 327
Chattanooga Public Library, xvii–xviii, xxxi
Chattanooga Times, xxvii, 190, 286, 297

Christian Science, xlii–xliii, 276, 277–79, 280, 285, 287, 290, 301, 302, 307, 310, 314, 315, 319, 321, 329
Claiborne, Dr., 265, 267–68
Clark, Mr. (*Chattanooga News*), 188
Clark, Mrs. (neighbor), 123, 153, 154, 156, 159, 160
Cody, William F. "Buffalo Bill," 154, 343n2
Confederate veterans' reunion, 129, 153, 342n12
Cooke, Grace MacGowan, xii, xxvii–xxviii, xlvi, 73, 80, 87, 102, 152, 220, 255, 257, 262, 280, 335n10, 341n20, 341n32
Cooke, R. B., Mrs., 258, 344n8
Cooper, Susan Fenimore, xxxii
Craftsman, xxx, 336n23, 340n13
Crutchfield House, 166

Dabney, Mrs. (friend), 83, 87, 159
Daingerfield, Clinton, 212, 344n5
Dangerfield, Clinton. *See* Daingerfield, Clinton
death rituals and observances, 13–16
Designer, The, 120
divorce, xv, xxxvii, xxxix, 130, 170, 187, 204, 206–10, 212, 213, 254, 276, 318, 343n2
Dixon, Thomas, 286
Donnelly, Mary J., 285
dreams, 47–48, 103, 121, 186, 208, 213, 223, 299
Dripping Springs, 168
Droke, Roger, 302, 314
dulcimore (dulcimer), 8, 337n42
dumb-suppers, 71, 72, 341n18

Eddy, Mary Baker, 277–78, 307, 345n14
Edwards, Grace Toney, xviii, xliv
Edwards Point, 24, 34, 340n13
Ellis, Dr., 100–101, 103, 104, 244, 245, 257
Ellsworth, Mr. and Mrs. (friends), 256, 258, 259, 262, 264, 265, 267, 270, 272, 273, 283, 288, 290
Erlanger Hospital, 199, 328

Fairmount, 34, 88, 123, 226, 240
Ferguson, Champ, 51, 340n1
Ford, Judith Miles, xvii, xlii, xliv, 25–26, 48, 52, 54, 62, 82, 87–88, 89, 91, 92, 96, 99, 101, 110, 120, 127, 128, 131–32, 151, 155, 158, 161, 163, 166, 167, 168, 172, 173, 175, 189, 192, 194, 200, 206, 207, 208, 212, 219, 221, 225, 227, 228, 230, 232, 233, 234, 236, 239, 240, 242–43, 246, 256, 262, 263, 265, 266, 281, 283, 297, 298, 309, 316, 318, 321, 322, 323, 324, 325, 326, 328, 330
Fountain Square, 191, 320
Fountain Square Conversations, xxx, xxxviii, 191, 336n27
Foust Mill Branch, 213
Foust Mill Creek, 24
Frances Willard Home for Women, xxxviii, 191, 212, 229, 242, 244, 246, 343n18
Frank, Leo Max, 242, 344n10
Frazier, Annie Keith, 89–90
Frazier, James B., 90, 341n37
Frazier, Louise Keith, 90
Frazier, Sarah, 208
Freudenberg, Emmons, 60, 76, 83
Freudenberg, George, 345n2
Freudenberg, Hazel, 302, 345n2
Freudenberg, May, 60, 69, 76, 82, 86, 87, 88, 100, 172, 201, 210, 212, 315, 340n6, 345n2
Frost, William G., xxix
Fur Top Church, 95

Gahagan, Mrs. A. J., 207, 211, 343n2
Gaston, Kay Baker, xvii, xviii, xxi, xliv
ghost stories, 71, 77
Globe Publishing Company, xlvi
Gourd Fiddle, A (Cooke), xxvii
Green, Houston, 319–20, 325
Gregg sisters, 82, 96, 109, 158
Grindstone Spring, 160

Harper's Monthly, xxvi, xxvii, xxviii, xxx, 58, 189, 295, 335nn6–8, 336n23
Hatfield, Absalom "Ab," 16, 94, 110, 317, 339n2
Hatfield, Grandma, 232, 234
Hatfield, Laura Miles, 13, 51, 54, 74, 91–92, 94, 99, 101, 110, 118, 126, 128, 130–31, 158, 162, 202, 221, 232, 234, 242, 246, 263, 297, 313, 314–15, 317, 327, 339n2
health care, xli
Hearn, Lafcadio, 87, 182, 316
Hemlock School, 249, 250

Hergesheimer, Ella Sophonisba, 104, 122
Herron, Mr. and Mrs., 165, 166, 168, 169, 173, 175, 191
Hill City (Chattanooga), xliii–xliv, 81, 86, 99, 100, 128, 153, 176, 201, 245, 249
Hill City Normal School, 179
Holly, Miss (friend), xlvi, 66, 242, 339n80
Houghton Mifflin Company, 239
Hullet, Ida, 56
Hullett, Lassie, 17, 88, 90, 92, 95, 99, 102, 103, 105, 339n4
Hutcheson, Capt. Joseph Chappell, 87, 88, 194, 341n34
Hyde, Anne Bachman, 92, 342n39

James Pott and Company, xxvii, xxviii
John A. Patten (steamship), 31, 340n10
journal writing (Victorian-era), xxxi, xxxviii
Judith of the Cumberlands (MacGowan), xxvii

Kaufman, Katherine, 69, 73, 76, 77, 78, 80, 81, 82, 86, 94, 153, 156
Kephart, Horace, xxix
Key, Mrs. Albert, 130, 162
Key, Ellen, 90
Key, Mary, 73
Key's Point, 178
Klaus family, 90, 240, 242

Labar, Mrs. (Christian Science witness), xlii, 276, 277, 278, 280, 282, 283, 284
Lane, Mrs. (neighbor), 59, 72, 103, 151, 241
Lanier, Sidney, 290
Lauderbach, Mrs. (friend), 286
Lautermische, Margery, 238, 239
Lautermische, Mr. & Mrs., 238, 242, 286
Levi, George, 16, 105, 274
Levi Falls, 153
Lincoln Memorial University (Harrogate, Tennessee), xxxiv
Lippincott's, xxx, 56, 336n23, 340n3
Long, Sim Perry, 95, 131, 342n44
Long, Mrs. Will, 126, 180
Lookout, The, 83, 95, 340n13, 341n19, 341n23
Lookout Mountain, 24, 37, 74, 75, 100, 184, 186, 199, 250, 263, 304
Lyle, Mrs. (friend), 125, 129
Lyle, Willie, 101, 111, 112, 113, 116, 123, 153, 158, 159, 164, 165

Mabbit Springs, 52
MacGowan, Alice, xxvii–xxviii, xlvii, 255, 257
MacGowan, Grace. *See* Cooke, Grace MacGowan
MacGowan, John Encill, xxvii
Market Street, 81, 82, 90, 173, 244, 247
Marshall Creek, 108
McGuffey, Charles, 105
McRoy, Theodora, 290, 291, 292, 294
Miami, Florida, xxxiv
Miles, Arthur "Dock," 16, 17, 39, 56, 100, 103, 113, 126, 195, 229, 233, 235
Miles, Barney, 17, 106, 220, 222, 229
Miles, Emma Bell: abortions, xxi, xxxvii, 150, 188, 208, 343n15; artwork, xxvii, xxviii–xxix, xlv, 70, 87, 240, 271; attack on, 184–86, 319; death, xliv; divorce considered, xv, xxxvii, xxxix, 130, 170, 187, 204, 206–10, 212, 213, 254, 276, 318; dreams, 47–48, 103, 121, 186, 208, 213, 223, 299; employment, xxxiii, xxxiv–xxxvi, xxxviii, xl, 188; journal writing, xvii, xix–xx, xxi–xxii, xxxi–xxxii, xxxviii–xxxix, xl–xli; lectures, xxxix–xl, 160, 179, 181–82, 202–3, 239, 240, 242, 249, 250, 258; lost works, xlv–xlvii; marital discord, 103–4, 108–12, 124, 129, 154–55, 157, 163–66, 168–72, 174, 176, 181, 193–94, 218, 254, 298; miscarriages, 73, 199; pregnancy, 192, 205, 231; suicide, thoughts of, xxi, xlii, 187, 193, 274–76, 299; untitled manuscript, 80, 239, 298, 310, 313, 341n24; untitled poem, 223–24. *See also* Miles, Emma Bell, works of; Pine Breeze Sanitarium; tuberculosis
Miles, Emma Bell, works of: "The Alchemist," 83; "At the Top of Sourwood," 56, 336n23, 340n3; "Banjo and the Loom," 182; "Bitter Herbs," xlvii, 255, 257, 262, 280, 344n5; "The Breaks of Caney," 336n23; "The Broken Urn," 336n23; "The Candidate at Caney's Cove," 86, 341n31; "The Chemist," 83; *Chords from a Dulcimore*, xxxvi–xxxvii, 70, 98, 103, 337n42, 341n15, 341n31, 341n33, 342n43; "Clay's Marget," xlvi, 66; "Cometh Not in by the Door," xlvi, 66; "The Common Lot," 336n23; "The Cookstove," 81;

Miles, Emma Bell, works of, (*cont.*)
"Cost What It May," xlvi, 66; "Dan
Riley," xlvi, 91, 96, 100; "A Dark Rose,"
336n23; "A Destroying Angel," xlvii;
"The Difference," xxvii; "Doing His
Bit," 328; "A Dream of the Dust," 72,
336n23, 341n19; "The Dulcimore," 98,
124, 336n23; "Enchanter's Nightshade,"
66, 336n23, 340n13; "Falling Weather,"
120; "Flower of Noon," 336n23; "Flyaway
Flittermouse," 336n23; "Fortune's Wheel,"
xlvi; "Fountain Square Conversations,"
xxxviii, 191; *The Good Gray Mother*, xlii,
xlv, xlvi, 293, 315, 317, 331, 345n3;
"The Great World," xlvi, 66; "Gypsy
Song," 327; "The Healers," xlvi, 66;
"The Homecoming of Evelina," 336n23;
"Homesick," xxvii; "If I Were Spring,"
90; "In Quest of the Fountain," 68;
"Introducing Budding Talent," 191; "Love
o' Man," 336n23; "The Magic Casement,"
68; "Mallard Plumage," 336n23; "A
Mess of Greens," xlvii, 252, 282, 283,
286; "Mystic Words," xlvi, 72, 341n19;
"The Nameless," 90; "The Novae," 330;
"The Open Door," 65; *Our Southern Birds*,
xliii, xlv–xlvi, 313, 314, 315, 317, 318,
329; "Poor Tired Mother," 191; "Quest
of the Fountain," 68; "Ragnarok," 124;
"The Sanitary Mind," 318; "Some Real
American Music," xxvii; "A Song of
Shadows," 191; *The Spirit of the Mountains*,
xxvii, xxviii–xxx, xxxv, 341n15; "The
Stack Horse," 182; *Strains from a Dulcimore*,
xliv; "A Sunbonnet at Big Meetin'," 124;
"Thistle Bloom," 66, 76, 336n23, 340n13;
341n23; "Three Roads and a River,"
336n23; "Thrid o' Warp," 157; *A Timber
Redbird*, xlvi, 173, 174, 177; "Turkey
Luck," 242, 336n23; "Warden of the
Southern Gate," 96; "The White Cow,"
xlvii; "The White Marauder," 336n23;
"The Woman Interferes," 80
Miles, Frank, xxxiv, xxviii, 8, 28, 44, 48,
54, 56, 59, 60–61, 62, 65, 66, 67, 68, 70,
72, 73, 80, 83–88 passim, 92, 93, 94, 95,
103, 104, 105, 108, 109–10, 111–12,
113, 114–17, 120, 121, 124, 125–26,
128, 129–30, 131–32, 152–58 passim,
160, 163, 164–65, 166, 168–85 passim,

188, 189, 192, 193–94, 197, 200, 205–29
passim, 231–32, 233, 235, 236, 239, 240,
245, 250–56 passim, 258, 260, 261, 263,
266, 268, 269, 275, 278, 279, 281, 286,
288, 291–92, 297, 298, 300, 301, 302,
304, 306, 309, 310, 311, 314, 315, 318,
324, 325, 327, 328, 330; illness of, 96,
99, 100, 102, 120, 271–72; telling tales,
30, 71, 82; working, 63, 91, 122, 123, 127,
151, 153, 154, 162, 174, 182, 184, 186,
201, 202, 216, 219–20, 240, 255, 258–59,
267, 270, 272, 273, 276, 288, 293
Miles, Frank Mirick "Mark" (son), xxxvii,
32, 36, 39–40, 53, 54, 68, 71, 80, 85–86,
87, 88, 89, 90, 92, 99, 109, 111, 112–19,
121, 127, 155, 162, 166, 186, 187, 205,
207, 209, 223
Miles, Jane Winchester (Grandma), xxviii,
xxxv, 14, 57, 73, 81–82, 83, 99, 100, 101,
102, 103, 151, 158, 199, 221, 223, 226,
231, 235, 237, 272, 317, 330
Miles, Jean (daughter). *See* Catino, Jean
Miles
Miles, Joe (brother of Frank Miles), 170
Miles, Joe "Buzz" (son), xxvi, xliv, 47, 51,
60, 63, 66, 67, 70, 76, 79, 82, 87, 102,
105, 109, 119, 120, 121, 123, 128,
130–31, 156, 157, 159, 163, 174, 175,
176, 177, 180, 182, 192, 198, 206, 211,
239, 240, 241, 243, 244, 246, 250, 262,
263, 267–68, 274, 275, 276, 278, 279,
284, 285, 287, 288–89, 290, 296, 297,
303, 304, 306, 309, 310, 311, 312, 313,
314, 316, 317, 318, 320–21, 322, 323,
326, 327
Miles, Judith (daughter). *See* Ford, Judith
Miles
Miles, Katharine "Kitty" (daughter), xxvi,
38–39, 59–60, 65, 66, 69, 86, 90, 94, 99,
100, 116, 118–19, 123, 128–29, 130–32,
151, 155, 156, 157, 162, 166, 167, 168,
174, 176, 178, 180, 182, 192, 201, 205,
219, 232, 233, 235, 237, 239, 241, 243,
246, 249, 250, 252, 262, 263, 265, 266,
283, 314, 327, 331
Miles, Lawrence "Larnce," 15, 17, 63, 99,
100, 104, 106, 127, 128, 199, 296, 300
Miles, Mary Freudenberg, 15, 106, 119, 131
Miles, Tina "Tinte," 99, 102, 125, 126–27,
162, 235, 339n4, 342n1

Miles, William (Grandpap), 39, 57, 90, 100, 101, 102, 103, 113, 126, 128, 221, 226, 272

Milton, Abbey Crawford, xvii, xliv, xlv, 104, 179, 312

Milton, George Fort, xvii, 124, 187, 327

Miss Holly (friend), xlvi, 66, 242, 339n80

Mission(ary) Ridge, 51, 96, 179, 182, 245, 314

Montague, Lucy, 285

moonshine, 28–29

moonshine stills, 28–29

Morrison, Caroline (Carol) Wood, xlvi, 60, 69, 72, 73, 77, 80, 81, 82, 84–85, 86, 87, 89, 96, 100, 103, 159–60, 167, 208

Morrison Springs, 72

Mossop Memorial School, 242, 264, 266, 285, 297, 298, 317, 327–28, 344n11

Mother's Magazine, xlii, xlvii, 282, 284, 336n23

movies. *See* moving pictures

moving pictures, 60, 81, 86, 172, 180, 183, 286, 313

Mudge, E. Lynn, xxvii

music, 7, 17–18, 195, 226, 229, 233, 235–36, 246

National Book Company, xlv–xlvi

Nautilus, The, xliii, 62, 201, 342n11

Nelson Spring, 48, 57

New Thought Club, 200, 305

New Thought Movement, xv, xlii–xliii, 184, 201, 208, 209, 216

Nixon, Bob, 212

Nixon, Grandsire, 57

Our Southern Highlanders (Kephart), xxix

Outlook, The, 301

painting classes, 150, 158, 159, 166

Palmer, Mrs. (friend), 211, 267

Patten, Cartter, xliv

Patten, John Alanson, 94, 258, 342n5, 344n6

Patten, Lupton, 106, 342n5

Patten, Sarah Key, 60, 74, 82, 87, 94, 95, 100, 104, 114, 118, 119, 120, 160, 166, 256, 288, 314, 340n7

Patten, Zeboim Cartter, 94, 340n7

Pattens, the, 90, 96

Pickett, Allan, 37

Pickett, John, 82, 109–10

Pilgrim's Progress (Bunyan), xxvi

Pine Breeze Sanitarium, xl, xli, xlii, xliii, xliv, 204, 207, 221, 222, 244, 257, 263, 265, 267, 268, 271, 275, 278, 288, 297, 326

Plewes, Natalie, xlii, 208, 211, 220, 279–80, 281, 284, 285, 288, 290, 294, 295, 298, 306, 308, 309, 310, 318, 321, 323, 324, 326, 327, 343n3

Poindexter, Mrs. (friend), 54, 94, 130, 162

poison, 274–75, 299

Prajznerova, Katarina, xviii

Probasco Fountain, 320

Putnam's, xxx, 336n23

Pyott, Mrs. Sam, 102

Pyott, Sam, 118

Quimby, Phineas, 278, 345n15

Rabbit Hash, Kentucky, xxv

Raccoon Mountain, 31, 340n11

Rains, Zerelda, xxvi, xlvi, 60, 160, 182, 234, 235, 236, 242, 297, 308–9, 310, 317, 340n8

Rawlings (Rawlins), Mrs. (friend), 61, 84, 88, 102, 108, 153, 178–79, 232, 235, 340n10

Read House, 73, 95, 104, 342n44

Red Book, xxx, 336n23

Reed, Cordelia, 94, 341n41

Renshaw, Nora, 94, 96

Richmond, Mrs. (friend), 208

Ricketson, Anna, xxvi, xxvii, xxxiii, xxxvi, xlvi, 105, 256, 262, 342n4

Robertson, Father, 265, 279, 283, 285

Rowell, Adelaide, xxxiv, xliv, 337n33

Saturday Evening Post, 286

Sawyer Springs, 42

Schumacher, Dr., 295, 296, 298, 299–300, 301

Scott, Preacher, 8, 9

Scott, Mr. and Mrs. Tom, 125, 127, 160, 166

Severance, Margaret, xvii, xlvi, 160, 166, 167, 168, 169, 172–73, 174, 176, 177, 179, 181, 343n9

Signal Point, 31, 88, 93, 129, 133, 232, 235, 237, 252

Smith, Lewis, 10

Southern Highlander and His Homeland, The (Campbell), xxix, 336n19
South St. Elmo School, 250
Spring Notes from Tennessee (Torrey), xxix, 336n18
springs (water), 55, 161
Stanfield, Mrs. (friend), 188, 192, 206, 212, 232, 233, 234
St. Andrews School, 267–68, 288, 345n12
Standard Designer, 105
Stansell, Mrs. (friend), 261, 265, 266, 267, 270, 271, 274, 275, 276, 281, 282, 290
Starr, Mrs. (Mrs. Wheatley's mother), 73, 75, 76
Stedman, Mr. (neighbor), 160, 182, 215, 219, 225
Stedman, Mrs. (friend), 160, 167, 168, 208–9, 211, 213, 216, 221, 225, 227, 235, 243, 245, 283, 303, 316
St. Elmo, 76, 78, 86, 90, 100, 103
St. Louis School of Art, xxvi
St. Mary's School, 264, 265, 266, 267–68, 270, 294, 345n10
Stooksbury, William, xxix, xxxiv
Stramonium, 274, 276
Strauss, Robert, 83, 341n30
Stroop, David Van, 80, 81
Stroop, Edith Catlow, 45, 87, 108, 111, 120, 187, 205–7, 209–10, 212, 215–16, 217, 219, 221, 227, 250, 252, 253, 254, 256, 261, 263, 265, 266, 268–69, 270–71, 278, 279, 281, 283, 287, 290, 296, 303, 304, 341n25
Suck Creek, 22
Summertown, 5, 54, 94, 162, 242, 339n1

tales, 30, 82, 272
Tallant, George A. (book publisher), 312, 315, 317, 328–29
Tallant, Mamie, 100, 106, 131, 196, 198, 296
Tennessee Historical Quarterly, The, xliv
Thoreau, Henry David, xxvi, xxxvi
Topside, 52, 74, 340n2
Torrey, Bradford, xxix, 336n18
trees, 19–21

tuberculosis, xxi, xl–xli, xliv, 5, 204, 205, 207, 209, 222, 244, 256, 260, 263, 264, 293, 295, 301
Twin Sisters (rock formation), 165

Underwood, Lily, 61, 105, 198

Vandergriff, Mary Miles, 15
Vandergriff, Wash, 10
Van Dusen, Mabel, 60, 70, 81, 82, 102, 104
Van Dusens, the, 177
Vaughn, Mrs. (*Chattanooga News*), 118, 166, 174, 176, 183

W, The (road), 243, 344n12
Walden's Ridge, xvii, xix–xxii, xxv–xxvii, xxviii–xxix, xxxi–xxxii, xxxv, xxxix, xl, xliv, 336n18
Warner, Lon, 118, 167
Wheatley, E. A., 76, 101, 153, 155, 157, 249, 340n4
Wheatley, Mrs. E. A., 60, 69, 73, 74, 75, 76, 77, 80, 81, 82, 83, 86, 89, 94, 100, 101, 104, 115, 119, 153, 154, 155–56, 157, 159, 160, 187, 299, 340n4
Wheatleys, the, xxxvi, 57, 69, 78, 94, 101, 108, 117, 153, 154, 155, 178, 188, 189, 216, 249, 340n4
wildflowers, 11, 192, 235, 254, 263, 304
Willard Home. *See* Frances Willard Home for Women
Wilson, Genevieve, 100
Wilson, Woodrow, 124, 303
Winchester, Joe, 37
Winter's Point, 156
Wiving of Lance Cleaverage, The (MacGowan), xxvii
women's rights, 84
Wood Thrush Hollow, 92, 93, 100
World War I, 199, 291, 295, 313, 318
Wright, Nell, 174
Writer's Club, 288

Youth's Companion, xlvii, 242, 262

Zola, Emile, 225